The Other Glass Teat

FURTHER ESSAYS OF OPINION ON THE SUBJECT OF TELEVISION

BOOKS BY HARLAN ELLISON

NOVELS

The Sound of a Scythe [1960]
Web of the City [1958]
Spider Kiss [1961]

SHORT NOVELS

Doomsman [1967]
Run for the Stars [1991]
All the Lies That Are My Life [1980]
Mefisto in Onyx [1993]

GRAPHIC NOVELS

Demon with a Glass Hand
    (adaptation with Marshall Rogers) [1986]
Night and the Enemy
    (adaptation with Ken Steacy) [1987]
Vic and Blood:
The Chronicles of a Boy and His Dog
    (adaptation with Richard Corben) [1989]
Harlan Ellison's Dream Corridor [1996]
Vic and Blood: The Continuing
Adventures of a Boy and His Dog
    (adaptation with Richard Corben) [2003]
Harlan Ellison's Dream
Corridor Volume Two [2007]

SHORT STORY COLLECTIONS

The Deadly Streets [1958]
Sex Gang (as Paul Merchant) [1959]
A Touch of Infinity [1960]
Children of the Streets [1961]
Gentleman Junkie and Other Stories
of the Hung-Up Generation [1961]
Ellison Wonderland [1962]
Paingod and Other Delusions [1965]
I Have No Mouth & I
Must Scream [1967]
From the Land of Fear [1967]
Love Ain't Nothing But
Sex Misspelled [1968]
The Beast That Shouted Love at
the Heart of the World [1969]
Over the Edge [1970]
De Helden Van De Highway
    (Dutch publication only) [1973]
All the Sounds of Fear
    (British publication only) [1973]
The Time of the Eye
    (British publication only) [1974]
Approaching Oblivion [1974]
Deathbird Stories [1975]
No Doors, No Windows [1975]
Hoe Kan Ik Schreeuwen
Zonder Mond
    (Dutch publication only) [1977]
Strange Wine [1978]
Shatterday [1980]
Stalking the Nightmare [1982]
Angry Candy [1988]
Ensamvärk
    (Swedish publication only) [1992]
Jokes Without Punchlines [1995]
Bce 3bykn Ctpaxa (All
Fearful Sounds)
    (unauthorized Russian publication only) [1997]
The Worlds of Harlan Ellison
    (authorized Russian publication only) [1997]
Slippage [1997]
Koletis, Kes Kuulutas
Armastust Maalima Siidames
    (Estonian publication only) [1999]
La Machine aux Yeux Bleus
    (French publication only) [2001]
Troublemakers [2001]
Ptak Smierci (The Best
of Harlan Ellison)
    (Polish publication only) [2003]

The Other Glass Teat

by Harlan Ellison®

EDGEWORKS
an A B B E Y offering

in association with

E-Reads®

For
WALTER KOENIG
Déjà vu

I have been in this elevator before.

Publisher's Note

It is at the author's request that the words "god" &
"tv" be type-set in lower case unless they appear
in citations or at the beginning of a sentence.

INTRODUCTION

Days of Blood and Sorrow

I'm writing this soon after New Year's Day, 1975. The Port Chalmers Flu has struck me down and I lie here in bed with the typewriter propped on my lap, bottles of expectorants, Actifed, Contac and Empirin all around me, and the little tv on the foot of the bed burbling *Let's Make a Deal*.

I don't know which will kill me first: the flu or Monty Hall.

There is a woman wearing a toilet plunger on her head and her braided hair be-ribboned with asswipe. I can't tell what it is she's won, nor even what Monty is offering her in exchange for it, because I have the sound turned off. I may be down, but I ainout.

From time to time in the writing of this introduction, I will keep you apprised of what daymares flit across my screen; if I have to be miserable, so do you. We can go nutso together.

As you may have gathered, I watch quite a bit of television. Friends (and blind dates who've decided they don't care for the guy their girlfriend fixed them up with and wish they were back home washing their hair) give me a lot of static about how much television I watch. Almost nobody I know will openly cop to sitting in front of the box sucking on that glass teat. They all do it. Most of them would sooner have a haircut from Jack the Ripper than admit when they get home from work they kick off their shoes and watch reruns of *Gilligan's Island*. They'd sooner

share a toothbrush with a leper than admit that given the choice
between a brilliant documentary on the lifestyle of the Jívaros of
Ecuador on the educational channel and an Ann-Margret Special
on NBC they'd pick the latter over the former every time. But
they all do it. So do I. We're a 21" eyeball nation, weaned from
the start by flickering phosphor-dot images.

But there's still that hateful snobbishness about tv. Dips my
age put it down without fail, without redeeming remark, without
a suggestion that the medium has a saving grace. Yet every night,
if one selects one's viewing with anything greater than the
brain power of a maggot, one can find at least an hour or two
of worthwhile programming. It might be Tracy Keenan Wynn's
incredible script for "The Autobiography of Miss Jane Pittman"
or a rerun of those antic spirits John Steed and Mrs. Emma Peel
in The Avengers or Olivia Newton-John on The Midnight Special
or the genuinely bizarre ghouls of M*A*S*H.

For those who tune in to garbage, who have the last act of
Barnaby Jones figured out three minutes into the first act, who
are disappointed that Jack Lord can't act one-millionth as
brilliantly as Al Pacino's left instep, disappointment is a self-
fulfilling prophecy. Or, as a bad movie script once phrased it,
"Lie down with pigs, get up smelling like garbage."

Television is the popular entertainment. It is no better, I
suspect, and no worse, I'm sure, than any of the popular
entertainments were, when they were serving the needs of the
mass. Pulp magazines, "B" movies, vaudeville. They were all the
honorable forefathers of what we get on the tube every day.

(A bald, sallow, snake-eyed hypester is silently trying to sell
me 22,000 acres of California land wrested from the unwilling
hands of Spanish settlers and Amerinds. I don't have to hear
what he's saying, I know this one by heart. He's telling me I can
erect a terrific ticky-tacky cracker box of a vacation home on this
wonderful acreage. He doesn't mention that the nearest water is
eight miles away, nor that they haven't put in any "conveniences"
like electricity or roads. Fuck him. Onward.)

I like to think of Theodore Sturgeon's Law when I hear the
snobs badrapping tv: "90% of everything is crap." That means
90% of everything is mediocre, as I read the Law. And that

goes for books, plays, cars, puddings, people and movies. The percentage is probably higher with politicians.

So if 90% of television is crap, mediocre, banal, yawn-evoking...nobody promised you a rose garden.

There's still that 10% and it's often as good as the best books, movies...well, you know where I'm going.

Add to that simple philosophy that tv is keeping alive old movies and introducing them to a new generation, and the tube doesn't seem as awful as it's slammed to be. Huck Barkin's daughter, Tracy, is fifteen. She would rather pass up a studio screening of something as mindless as "Thunderbolt and Lightfoot" to see Fred and Ginger in "Flying Down to Rio" (1933). When I went to dinner at Huck and Carol's a few weeks ago, I was wearing a T-shirt that said Rick's Café Américain on it. There were four or five people at table when I sat down, and they all looked at it without knowing what it meant. Only fifteen-year-old Tracy, when she came to the table, grinned and recognized the name of Humphrey Bogart's nightclub in Casablanca. At that moment I felt very kindly toward television. In a time when young people seem sadly disinterested in the past—even a past as recent as eight or ten years ago—tv serves a necessary function. It becomes the handservant of Santayana's warning that, "Those who cannot remember the past are condemned to repeat it."

Something that periodically straightens kids' heads about the difference in time-frames between, say, the Early Cretaceous and the U-2 imbroglio of Francis Gary Powers can't be all bad.

(A woman is trying to keep her 1500-lb. mastiff from savaging her hand as she pours kibble into a bowl. I wonder if she knows they've soaked that kibble in lamb's blood and that the poor mastiff hasn't been fed since 1947. Oh well.)

Okay. So that's what's good about tv. But if you've bought this book having read its predecessor, THE GLASS TEAT, you know that as a writer who works in the tv industry—quite apart from my feelings as a viewer—my enchantment with the medium is anything but constant. Without recourse to the remark crude, I have been known to point out that tv sucks.

And so what we have here, in this sequel to THE GLASS TEAT, are fifty more columns of jaundiced and lament-laden (for the most part) diatribe against the corrupt and inept and mediocre bulk of what goes down on that tube.

If you've bought this volume without having read or heard about THE GLASS TEAT, I urge you to go find it and get all the background about how and where these columns were first published. Not to mention the first 52 columns, because the numbering in this book picks up at #53 and that might confuse the hell out of you if you didn't know there was a book that went before this one. Am I getting confusing?

Look: for those who bought this book in good faith and feel that having to go out and buy *another* book to figure out what's going on in this book is a calculated rip-off, I will quickly summarize the plot of the heart-stopping action that went before. Pay attention.

September 1968: Art Kunkin, then publisher of the Los Angeles *Free Press*, asked me to write for the *Freep*. I suggested a tv column. He said fine. First column appeared in the *Freep* on 4 October 68. It went on for two and a half years. I stopped writing it because I figured if a guy couldn't say everything he had to say about tv in two and half years, he shouldn't have started in the first place, because he didn't have anything important to say anyhow. In 1970, the first years' columns (1968–70) were published by Ace Books. Sales started off sensational, book was moving everywhere, hundreds of dynamite reviews, thought we had a paperback bestseller on our hands. Suddenly, the book died. It was being returned by the boxload to Ace. Discovered it hadn't had an incredible 90% sale of the first print run—as we'd been led to believe by early reports—but had sold out on the East and West Coasts and was being shipped back from everywhere else faster than a speeding bullet. August 1970: I signed a contract for a sequel, THE OTHER GLASS TEAT, with Ace. This was when they thought they had a 90% sale. But then the returns started deluging Ace. For no reason anyone could figure out. Then, without warning, Ace jumped out of the contract for the second book. Told me to keep the advance money, just let them out of the contract. Unheard-of for a publisher like Ace, to let me keep the money. Books still thundering in to the Ace return warehouse. Thousands and thousands of copies. THE

GLASS TEAT was being used, by that time, in many colleges and universities, in their media classes; it was being praised by everyone from Cronkite to *The New Republic*; it had become something of an underground rallying-point; orders from lone individuals swamped Ace's offices. But the book had been effectively wiped off the newsstands. Didn't learn till four years later that Spiro T. Agnew himself had taken offense at a line in one of my columns about him (a line that appears in this book, dealing with Spiro's sexual proclivities and *The Reader's Digest*) and his office had passed the word the book was to be, uh, er, how shall we put it...*repressed.* Last February Pyramid took its life in its hands and re-released THE GLASS TEAT. Here it is June, and for the first time in this or any other language, THE OTHER GLASS TEAT is at long last published. Four years after Ace ran scared.

Anyhow, that's the background. It's written in greater detail and (as Kleindienst would phrase it, my fellow Americans) specificity in the new introduction I wrote specially for the Pyramid edition of THE GLASS TEAT, just so you won't think I'm some sort of conspiracy fruitcake.

And just to prove I'm leery of conspiracy bullshit, read the columns in *this* book—particularly the open letter to my mother—and see if I wasn't on to the whole suppression of dissent program of Dick and The Boys. It's all here, two years before you even heard of Watergate. Nyah, nyah, *I told you so!*

(What a terrific thrill, to go back and read those words in 1970–72 and see that I was one of the few clowns who were warning you against Nixon's war on the media. What a thrill to encounter the following quotes in William Safire's book, BEFORE THE FALL: AN INSIDE VIEW OF THE PRE-WATERGATE WHITE HOUSE. Safire was a senior speech writer for Nixon during his first term.

("Was there a conspiracy, as Walter Cronkite of CBS once solemnly charged, on the part of the Nixon administration to discredit and malign the press?

("Was this so-called 'anti-media campaign' encouraged, directed, and urged on by the president himself?

("Did this alleged campaign to defame and intimidate

Nixon-hating newsmen succeed, isolating and weakening them politically? And did it contribute to the us-against-them divisions that then cracked back at Nixon after his election victory?

("The above questions are slanted so as to elicit a ringing response of 'Nonsense!' from people who resist the wave of condemnation washing over everything connected with the Nixon administration. But the answer to all those questions is, sadly, yes....

("I must have heard Richard Nixon say 'the press is the enemy' a dozen times, and there was no doubt that his instincts were to do battle with what he was certain was an ideological bias against nonliberals combined with a personal bias against him.")

But these columns running from early in 1970, well into 1972, are more—to me, at any rate—than a compendium of gardyloos against the Nixon/Agnew axis. There's a lot of that, because that's what was going down at the time, but there's a whole lot of looking-around at the condition of life in these United States, as interpreted by television.

(It's now about 3:15 and I'm watching a bunch of people in loud Hawaiian shirts playing something called *The Diamond Head Game*. I suspect their heads are made of Jell-O and not Diamonds, because they're making asses of themselves. One man is standing in a big plastic tube, with a funny little pouch around his waist, and he's being assaulted by paper money being blown all around him inside this big tube. He's grabbing like a sonofabitch for as much as he can get, thereby epitomizing for me, as I lie here in sight of death through nasal drip strangulation, the core greed and venality of the average American schlepper who allows himself to be demeaned in front of millions of home-trapped housewives and invalid shut-ins like myself. As I watch this jerk, I only have one wish: dear Lord, change all that paper money into silver dollars and brain him to death. Is it any wonder I'm turning into a misanthrope?)

Where was I? Oh, yeah.

The period of time covered by these columns is what I've come to call our days of blood and sorrow. Kent State, Laos, My Lai, Jackson State, the March on Washington, the student riots, the endless busts of dissenters. But things have changed considerably.

The Sentient Sixties are gone and the Sluggish Seventies are with us. All the kids who lost their college careers, their jobs, their security, all those who lost their lives or their citizenship... they're gone now. Gone to middle-class struggles for subsistence living, gone to dull academic jobs, gone to little boxes at big corporations, gone to dust or Canada. And the colleges are loaded with enlightened self-interest now. The generation so many gave their hopes and their lives to set free have enslaved themselves with the vision of Diamond Head blowing thousands of paper dollars around them as they grub in the air for as much as their pudgy little paws can hold. I've talked about this before, don't let it depress you; it's only disillusionment.

Where I'm coming from is that Spiro succeeded. He and the King Thug Nixon managed to clobber the entire dissent movement. The revolution came and went and *plus ça change, plus c'est la même chose, which translates as Hey, Sid, ain't it time to program another doctor series in the nine-to-ten slot?*

But that's your problem, not mine.

In here, we have fifty little time capsules, including a complete television script I wrote for *The Young Lawyers*, a series you may remember from the Season of Relevance. It is the original version, not what was finally aired, and you will find comment before, after and during that will show you how it is to work in television.

In here, we have comment on *Nanny and the Professor* and Standard Oil's big tv campaign for F-310, their anti-pollutant additive, and Baxter Ward, an LA-based newscaster. But things are slightly different now, after all, Richard Long, who played the Professor, is dead; Standard Oil stopped using F-310 when it became obvious to consumers that it was a bullshit ripoff; and Baxter Ward is now on the board of the LA County Supervisors.

In here, we have a couple of years in the life of your humble columnist and his faithful country, Ammurrica.

Like the Early Cretaceous, it's a book of memories, probably no more relevant to college readers than the U-2 flyover or the name Francis Gary Powers. Maybe.

The only trouble is, I keep thinking of Santayana's quotation, and the phrase what goes around, comes around keeps ringing in my head.

(There is a lady with a pained expression on her face who is telling me if I have a ringing in my head I ought to take six of these, or three of these, or one of those.)

Maybe I'll just turn off the set and get some sleep.

—Harlan Ellison
3 JANUARY 75

53: 13 FEBRUARY 70

Shotgun week. Random thoughts on some randy topics.

I always like to know if the men whose criticism I read are beyond corruption, above reproach, out of reach of their own base desires and greeds. I think you'd like to know that about me, as well. So to put your mind at rest, be advised: I can be had. (In fact, I'm such an easy lay, I don't understand why I don't get more dates. But, be that as it may...) How many other critics do you know who'll own up to being corruptible?

I mention this, because I'm going to make some remarks about a new ABC situation comedy, *Nanny and the Professor*, and I want you to know out front that I met and had lunch at 20th with the star, Ms. Juliet Mills, and she is a stunner. She is English, which gives her a runaway head start with me...as friends who know my ladyfriend, Louise, will tell you. But she is also reserved, witty, charming, totally professional, and an Actress with the cap A who speaks about having been on the London stage but doesn't lumber the listener with hideous starlet talk about her agent, her parts, her dressing room, her likes and dislikes in show biz, *ad nauseam*. From all this you may gather that I found Ms. Mills (who is related by birth to John and Hayley and that whole crowd, but who need borrow no credentials from any of them) quite the winner.

And from that you may understand my distress at having to report that *Nanny and the Professor* is about as nitwitty a piece of persiflage as I've been forced to watch in many a season. I think, for dumbness, it even rivals *The Good Guys, Gomer*

Pyle, and *Gilligan's Island*. But it isn't quite as bad as *The Lucy Show*—only because one has Ms. Mills and the other has Lucy.

The situation is a widower, a physics professor, played by Richard Long (whose range of emotions in this show flings itself from boredom to bemusement), with three little moppets, and an English "nanny" with claims to metaphysical/supernatural/ leprechaun-type powers. Mr. Long does what he is required to do, and tries very hard not to look like a man about to get an enema with a thermite bomb. He, like Ms. Mills, is a professional, and we should sometime dwell on the horrors through which we put our competent, craftsmanlike actors. It must be a dreadful life they lead, succored only by the nice green money people give them.

So. Ms. Mills and Mr. Long. They're fine, acting-wise. But those three no-neck monsters, and their moronic dog, are quite another can of worms.

One cannot blame the kids. Several years ago I knew a young married couple who had a sweet child, a blond and blue-eyed moppet in whom they had dumped all their dreams and hopes. This lad had the singular and charming habit of coming downstairs during his parents' frequent parties, standing in the center of the room where he could drink in all the attention, and announcing in a voice frighteningly like that of Walter Brennan, "*I have a pee-pee!*" He would then whip out of his Dr. Denton's a pee-pee-sized penis and piss all over the rug. Well, sir, may I tell you that the first time it happened, I was a bit startled. But, being a true liberal, I shrugged and mumbled something about the kid's doing his thing...or doing it *with* his thing...or something...and went back to whatever conversation it was I'd been having before the interruption. On subsequent occasions, I must say the novelty of the act wore off. It was like your second or third exposure to Jerry Lewis. (I know of few rational people who can report having had a fourth.) But the tot's parents thought it was a wonderful expression of the child's individuality and cleverness and perceptions about his own body and bodily functions. And they applauded wildly every time he did it. Maybe they were right; I don't know. All

I do know is that the first time the kid missed, and scored my pant leg, I stopped accepting invites to their brawls.

Let the little ankle-snapper express his individuality on somebody else's pant leg. Which, of course, is the point about the kids on *Nanny and the Professor*. Let the little darlings express their individuality, their cuddlesomeness, their precociousness on somebody else's television tube. Because, all shilly-shallying aside, they make my gorge become buoyant.

And if you add three lovable urchins to plots devised by a gaggle of waterheads, you have what is unquestionably the lowest point in tv programming this year, and in many years of recent memory.

Please, someone, won't you build a new series around Ms. Mills? She's really lovely, and she can act, and her accent is trilling, and she even ate my avocado so it wouldn't go to waste. Now *that* is a lady.

Onward and downward. George Hamilton. *Paris 7000*. The *Hee Haw* of the dramatic shows. ABC has a positive penchant for masochism.

Of all the things to save from *The Survivors* (and I don't know about you, babies, but I break up and fall down twitching when I think of the irony of that title), why ABC had to save old taciturn George is beyond me. The only difference between his character on the former show and his character on *this* one is that he let his hair grow longer.

If ever there was a no-talent, it is George Hamilton. He walks like a man who has just gotten his peg leg caught in a knothole. His face shows every subterranean bit of dissipation in which he's ever indulged. His sloe-eyed and supposedly sexy glances merely register as heartburn. And if the word "actor" should ever be applied to him by anyone but a studio PR man, the offending semanticist should be taken out, put in the stocks, and flayed alive.

Well, dammit, there goes *another* hour of primetime. But I certainly am getting a lot more books read these days.

Two weeks ago (in THE GLASS TEAT), on the occasion of

the birth of a two-headed calf, I made some passing remarks about war, the love of glory on the battlefield that drenches this country, the way we substitute war games like football for the real thing, and tsk-tsk'd the whole affair.

The other night I saw the film *Patton*, and I recommend it highly to left- and right-wingers alike. It manages to walk a line of ambivalence that should pleasure both extremes, if you can conceive of such a thing. It at one and the same time provides a portrait of General George Patton as a megalomaniacal, psychopathic war-lover whose comment, "Next to war, all other endeavors of man pale into insignificance," sums him up just nicely thank you—and provides superpatriots in the audience with the opportunity to see him as the instrument of a great American Destiny, destroying our enemies and bringing us to the greater heights of nobility through destruction.

That film, and a segment on *First Tuesday* dealing with the basketball mania in Galesburg, Illinois, coupled with a documentary earlier that week called *The Day They Closed Down the Schools*, made a tidy little object-lesson package in my mind about the gullibility of the American People. (You'll forgive me for belaboring the poor American People so regularly, friends, but there just ain't no one else around this country these days.)

I'm reminded of the Romans, in the Gibbonesque days of decline that civilization knew. The people closed their eyes to all manner of really ugly things like slavery, butchery, contamination, violence, and the debasement of the individual, chiefly because they had bread and circuses. You're hip to bread and circuses, of course. Toss a few zealots to the crocs, or let the Nubians battle the Sumatran panthers with toothpicks, and the crowd goes cuddly with joy.

Have you ever thought to compare basketball and football and the antics of Bob Hope to bread and circuses?

Now I dig pro football a lot, and Hope even makes me smile sometimes, but when I think that the schlepps in Galesburg, Illinois, keep putting gold stars up in their windows and can't find anything better to worry about than whether or not they get a season pass to the ball game...well, I begin to think about the last days of the Roman Empire, and I have ghastly visions of Spiro Agnew in the window of the White House, tootling on a harmonica while the land of the free and the home of the brave goes up in a pillar of smoke.

But, then, what more than cynicism can you expect from a dude who hates cute little kids?

54: 20 FEBRUARY 70

Blewp-bleep. Blewp-bleep.

Hello, there, this is your friendly neighborhood astronaut, Scodd Carbindur, coming to you directly (blewp-bleep) from a small corner-set in back of sound stage 17 at Universal City Studios (bleep) with some startling news about the greatest digestive breakthrough since antacid. Now, the Standard Gastric Company of California has pioneered in wind-breakage pollution emission, an amazing additive that virtually removes all odor from fundament leakage.

As you see behind me here, a clear balloon was attached to the exhaust aperture of Sidney J. Partridge, the 345-pound fat man on the dais. Mr. Partridge has been eating baked beans, tuna fish salad and egg salad sandwiches, veal parmigiana, and drinking beer by the pitcher—under controlled research-lab conditions—for over two thousand hours. The balloon, as you can see, has filled with dirty exhaust emissions, causing the hideous green fog that swirls inside the clear container. A graphic example of how backside emissions from clogged systems go into the air, cause unseemly odors, and waste human performance.

But! After dropping only six gutfuls of FAR-10, Standard's new wonder additive, here is Sidney J. Partridge with a similar balloon attached to what we in the emission game call the tuchis. The balloon remains clear! No dirty green smoke. No debilitating odor. Proof positive that Standard gastrics with FAR-10 turn dirty people into good clean producers.

Blewp-bleep. Blewp-beep. Ssssssss...

Mr. Nixon, Mr. Agnew, Mayor Daley, and Judge Julius Hoffman don't understand. They can't figure out why the kids in this country weren't conned by campaign bullshit, by the Big Lie that the cops in the Chicago Riots were not brutal, that the Democratic and Republican conventions were on the up-and-up, that the Conspiracy Trial is a reaffirmation of the validity of Establishment justice. They can't figure out why all the obfuscations and lies they've always used should suddenly fall flat and produce a credibility gap only slightly smaller than the distance from here to Proxima Centauri.

The old men don't really understand what television has done for and to young people in this country for the past eighteen years. They can't grasp the concept that kids have been watching commercials on tv that promise to sweeten this or brighten that or knit up the raveled sleeve of care with such&such. They can't orient themselves to the reality that young people now reach puberty with a built-in avoidance circuit in their logic equipment. The hard sell and the Big Lie don't work on them. They've tried Dial Soap and *still* couldn't get laid, so they know that most presentations intended to hustle them into buying something or believing something are nothing more than dumb show.

And the kids' reaction is interesting.

They don't mind Agnew or Procter & Gamble or Daley or Liggett & Myers *thinking* they're stupid, but they do resent being *talked* to as though they were stupid. Ergo, they simply ain't buying no more bullshit product, whether it be the sanctity of the Silent Majority or hypo-allergenic toilet paper.

Unfortunately, the reaction-formation of avoidance to television commercials becomes a hang-up when we *need* the product. Case in point, Standard Oil Company's new F-310 gas additive that "sharply reduces exhaust emissions from internal combustion engines that cause air pollution."

Blewp-bleep, friends. I find myself in the ominous position of being a huckster for one of the largest oil companies in the world.

But maybe you know me well enough by now, in this the second year of the column, to know I would not willingly shill for one of the Powers, unless it seemed important.

And I'm doing this salesman shtick because it seems to me that the Chevron gas commercials are such a turn-off, with their tame astronaut and his big gas balloon, that too many people are saying screw it and continuing to buy the cheaper gases. Let me give you a f'rinstance.

Friend of mine, helluva writer, guy who is always writing articles in magazines and underground newspapers about the imperiled state of the nation ...this friend of mine, and Ed Bryant, the demon writer from Wheatland, Wyoming; the three of us were sitting around rapping one night a few weeks ago, and I began saying how great it was that one of the oil companies had finally *done* something and how I was using Chevron gas exclusively. I idly asked this friend of mine if he had gotten turned on to the F-310 thing, and he said something to the effect that it was a shuck, he didn't give a damn, and he was saving about six cents a gallon by buying one of the other brands, whichever one was cheapest in the gas war. I confess it turned me off him for a moment.

But then, Ed Bryant said the same thing.

I was amazed. "How can you guys write what you write, spout all those noble thoughts about improving humanity's lot, and when it comes down to something as insignificant as six cents on a gallon, you don't give a damn?"

That was when I got the barrage: (1) It was all a lie. (2) What did it matter if we stopped emission from our cars if the big companies still poured out all that smog? (3) The government should force Standard Oil to give the secret formula to all the refineries. (4) Chevron had raised its price and why should we make Standard rich to do something that was ineffectual anyhow?

The basis for Ed Bryant's avoidance of Chevron gas was the commercials he had seen. They didn't actually come right out and say CHEVRON GAS STOPS POLLUTION. They talked around it, and hyped the sell with how much better your mileage would be. My other friend said the commercials were a cheap come-on and Chevron was no better than any other gas.

I took the position that even if it *did*n't work, even if it was a righteous fraud, on the chance that it *did* work we should support it till we found out it was worthless. I said it was in the nature of personal responsibility for not only ourselves, but others living in the city, this country, and by extension everyone on the planet. They laughed at me.

They rationalized it all away, and said the saving of pennies was more important. These were close friends of mine. Guys I'd heard bemoan all the evils of which I've spoken in this column in THE GLASS TEAT (though my nameless friend averred he didn't care about the ecological problem, that it was a "safe" political toy for Nixon, who was using it to take our minds off more important matters). (I won't deny that, incidentally; I'm sure Nixon is using it for just that purpose, but for once his interests and ours coincide, so it becomes only another rationalization on my friend's part.) And when it came right down to the bottom line, to the place where they could do something, no matter how small and ineffectual, instead of just shooting off their mouths like all parlor liberals, they found a million dumb reasons why it wasn't worth it.

You know: the kind of thinking that always has people who don't care or want to stall integration saying, "Bussing isn't the way." But they have no *other* solution to offer. It's always not good enough, or too complex, or some other exit from the reality of *getting it on*.

The core of the question was: does the gas do what it seems to say it does—that is, sharply reduce the pollutants a car produces?

I got Ed Bryant around to the position where he admitted if I could produce evidence to satisfy him that the gas *did it*, he'd start using it.

So the next day I called W. J. Murphy, public relations counsel for the Western Operations Division of Standard Oil Co. of California. I told him I was going to write this column, one way or the other. If he could convince me it did the job, I'd try and sell his gas for him. But if it was just bullshit advertising again, I'd 'dobe-wall him.

He sent me a press kit with photographs of the research experiments, with facts and figures, with reports from Scott Laboratories, who tested the gasoline for more than 250,000 miles, "using various makes of late model cars and several different grades of fuels and lubricants."

I'm not going to go into the statistics here. If you don't feel like taking my word for it that *the gas works*, you can write to Mr. Murphy at 605 West Olympic Blvd., Los Angeles, and he'll send you what you need to dispel your last rationalizations. But let me go on with what happened…

I got the press kit in the mail, and gave it—unopened—to Ed Bryant. "Here, you read it first," I said. "Then come back and simply give me a yes or a no. If it convinces *you*, I'll speak out for it. If it doesn't, then I put it down."

He went off, read the stuff, and came back. "Okay," he said, "I start using Chevron today."

Hallelujah, brothers! Even the doubting Thomas was lifted up into the kingdom of the Lord.

As for my other friend, he still contends that burning *any* carboniferous fuel to an oxide is going to produce emissions. Agreed. But Chevron has got a way to kill at least three of those pollutants. Now that is by no means cleaning up the streams and rivers, it is not putting the strong arm on the criminal industries who keep slopping up our nest, it isn't even getting people to deposit their Popsicle sticks and old condoms in trash containers.

But it *is* a step. A tiny one, but a step nonetheless. And if you can convince yourself that it does what it's supposed to do, then you are a lousy hypocrite and a hot-air dispenser if you don't use it merely because you can save a couple of bucks a tank when you buy gas.

It comes down to individual responsibility for the welfare of the world. Endless rock lyrics tell us to love one another, to give a damn, to get on the freedom train and save the cities, save the children, save the nation. That's all pretty soft-pink-and-white sentiment, troops, but it's only mouth-to-mouth resuscitation if, when the opportunity arises, you look harder into your pockets than you do at the rotting sky.

Yeah, I think Standard ought to be forced to give the formula to everyone. Yeah, I think Union and Standard and all the rest of them should have the power of their massive Capitol Hill lobbies defanged so they can be forced to stop spreading oil slick in the oceans. Yeah, I think Detroit ought to be made to do away with the infernal-combustion engine. Yeah, I think the airlines should be compelled to find ways to stop the emissions and noise of their jetliners. Yeah, I think all industries that toss foulage into rivers and streams ought to be taxed till they're blind to make them stop.

But that's a bigger job...a job we should all be as heavy behind as we are about getting laid and eating three squares and worrying about our nice sweet selves...but it is a job each individual citizen can't do much about. The gas thing is.

And I would hate to think that all of you out there who go to the rallies and have peace stickers on your bumpers and spout ecological statistics at the drop of a pollution count aren't hip to it. This is the one man/one vote number. It ain't much, but it *counts*.

The time has long since passed when our little fat-ass security is more important than life on this Earth. Because if you don't give a damn, if you count those few pennies as more important, then you are no better than *them*. And we know who Them are, don't we?

Them are the ones who are turning off people to using a gas that can help a little bit, by larding the airwaves with dumb commercials that make people think saving their lives is on a level with cleaning up unsightly acne.

I suggest to Standard that they get it on, and give the secret formula to *anyone* who wants it, and then we'll know the secret is important, because for the first time in a long while one of *Them* will have opted for humanity rather than profit.

Blewp-bleep.

55: 27 FEBRUARY 70

Philosophers are always saying things like *Man is Man, and animals are not Men, chiefly because Man has the power to dream*. Or they make the claim for our nobility because we have the ability to laugh, because we have the opposable thumb, or because we have curiosity. I went searching through a wonderful book called *The Senses of Animals and Men* by Lorus J. and Margery Milne, in an attempt to find out if my own personal we-have-it-and-animals-don't was valid, but there wasn't a word therein, so I'm going to assume I'm right until some naturalist in my readership smacks my pinkies and corrects me.

The reason Men are greater than Animals isn't because we can dream of the stars (as I've said in sf stories from time to time, because it's a nice thought to hold), it's because we have something they haven't. Greed.

I can think of few motivations as strong in the history of our species. Churchmen will no doubt remind me of love of god, and I'd go for it, I suppose, except I keep remembering the Crusades were senseless slaughters fought in the name of the Holy Grail, which in truth were fought merely for the kings of England. Have you any doubt, I recommend the series of novels and histories by Zoë Oldenbourg. And for sheer monstrousness I have never been able to reconcile all that Christian charity bullshit with Torquemada and the Spanish Inquisition, also fielded in the name of god. Mother love is a strong mover, and so is survival, and so is curiosity...but for really getting it on, nothing compares with down-home, earthy greed.

Bringing me perforce to the subject of today's sermon, albeit through the musty pages of history.

Television is about to undergo a tremendous improvement.

Yes, Virginia, the millennium is at hand, through greed, and not nobility.

It's a simple enough conclusion at which to arrive, and I don't take any special credit for having stumbled on it. What amazes me is that the three major networks—with all their trend paraphernalia and pulse takings—didn't get hip to what was happening long ago. (Radio was on to it fifteen years ago.)

The core fact is this: people under the age of thirty-one simply don't watch tv any more.

Oh, sure, under the age of thirteen kids still groove on *The Archies* and *Land of the Giants*, but kids that age have nowhere near the money to spend on gross national product, and the big buying these days is being done by affluent Americans between the ages of fifteen and thirty-five. (And speaking of the national product, it gets pretty gross indeed when discussing *The Archies*. But that is another column, another time.)

All of which sums up to mean that the largest segment of the purchasing public is ignoring the most widespread, most effective, most expensive advertising medium in the world. The *alter kockers* who used to be the big consumers of cars, clothes, condiments, and crap—now they hoard their pennies and wait for better times. So we see automobiles slanted toward the "youth market." We must go—spiked and helmeted—onto streets amuck with Mustangs, Cobras, Barracudas, Cougars, Falcons, Darts, Chargers, Thunderbirds, Road Runners, Gila Monsters, Leviathans, Piranhas, and other symbolically named implements of sudden death and painful disfigurement...all of which are grotesquely over-powered for streets and freeways on which they will never legally be allowed to exercise maximum output.

We see advertisements in which all the actors are youthful, "beautiful" people, selling everything from Love Blush cosmetics to vaginal deodorant (and one can only sit back and smile in wonder at the implications of that one, fellow sex maniacs). Nowhere do we see those crinkled, spasmed senior citizens this country spent so many decades assuring us were the golden fruits of years of honest toil. Silva-Thins being lipped by a Dirty

Old Man? Never! You can take Salems out of the country: shot at Sun City instead of Antibes? Hardly.

The trend has long been up. We are a youth-oriented, adolescence-crazed nation in which it will surely soon be a felony to be old and withered. Growing old gracefully simply ain't good business.

So tv isn't getting the audience with the money—only laundry detergents, seemingly, are holding their own—the unliberated household drudges still flash on the soapers and dutifully buy the sponsor's sheet whiteners, also seemingly, so they can one-up their neighbor lady, who has been crapping cookies because her laundry is only *dazzlingly* white instead of supernova white. And not getting the money makes the sponsors unhappy, which makes them make the networks unhappy, which means pretty jackrabbit quick somebody's going to have to start rethinking the situation.

For a moment: why *aren't* the movers and shakers and buyers watching tv? Certainly it's no worse than in years past—though admittedly that's like saying your cancer hasn't gotten any more terminal—and in terms of public affairs programming and technical quality, it is startlingly impressive. The answer, like the entire concept, is quite simple. TV is no longer relevant for them. They are out moving, shaking, and occasionally buying. But their moving and shaking is in terms of the whole culture, not the mythical little dream worlds proffered on network television. And when they buy, they go to the boutiques—not Sears or Monkey Ward. The *alter kockers* go *there*, and that means that almost 50 per cent of the purchasing public is being bypassed by tv advertising.

So. When Nixon comes out in favor of the eighteen-year-old vote, it means even *that* cinderblockhead has gotten hip to the power of the young, and can the dunces of the major networks be far behind? And the only way they can grab you and me and the kids of all ages who reject the pap sloshed out across the tube, is to make it more relevant. Immediatize the medium, as the boys in the ad agencies would phrase it, clever lads that they are.

Which means, ergo, that very soon we're going to see some

tv fare that will speak to the times, some programming that conceives of young people as something more than receivers for endless pop music and acne commercials.

To bring 50 per cent of the American people back to the glass teat means dispelling the mist images of what network programmers *think* we want to see; it means abandoning the refurbishing of old series ideas with new casts and miniskirts; it means getting *into* things and taking stands and to *hell* with Spiro.

(And so you won't think I've forgotten him, here is the latest. I heard him referred to last week as The Great Kiwani. For those of you who've attended Kiwanis or Elks or American Legion rallies or parades, you know what loveliness *that* accolade contains.)

It won't happen next season, or maybe even the season after that, because the big advertisers aren't hurting that badly yet. But when 10 percent of their buying audience croaks in the next two or three years, they'll begin to understand that young people today have had eighteen years of this drivel and simply ain't going for the okey-doke. *Then* the tremors hit.

Then they start demanding the networks come up with a more immediate product for them to subsidize. *Then*, in the only way it can happen, through the motivation of naked greed, we take over the mass media. *Then* the ground swell trends from the Great American Heartland begin to go in the direction of peace symbols rather than crummy phony American flag decals. *Then* love-it-or-leave-it vanishes and change-it-or-lose-it becomes the *modus operandi*. Then all the good guys who want to get it together will have their chance to put this sinkhole back in functioning order, and guys like me who cry for blood can go back to our pipes and slippers, rocking back and forth on our back porches in the setting sun.

Sure we can.

56: 6 MARCH 70

"Baby, you been took—your idealism slobbered all over your common sense, and you didn't even notice. No wonder you are anti-dope—people who get as high on hope as you do don't need grass."

I got that last week in a letter from Pauline Burton in Long Beach.

"Where do you suppose all the crud from inside those dirty engines goes during the six-tankful treatment with F-310? Into the air, you idiot. I hope you haven't as many readers with as little sense about this as you."

I got that one—sincerely—from Richard K. Koch in Beverly Hills.

Kitty Vallacher from the *Freep* called me the day after the column two weeks ago, the column I wrote on Standard's Chevron F-310 gasoline, and she chewed my ear about how I'd been duped. A man from the People's Lobby called me the day after and sent me reeling with facts, statistics, data, condemnations, and rhetoric. Most of it sounded valid. He said he'd prepare some information to refute the F-310 claims.

A friend told me, "Sure, you did it because you thought you were right, but you were had, friend. You're a good guy, but even good guys can be gullible sometimes."

I spoke at UC Irvine and an audience of three hundred students pinned me to a blackboard with what a tout I'd become for Standard, one of the biggest polluters in Southern California.

Word was passed that the Federal consumer fraud division, the FTC, and the FCC had been turned loose on Standard for their tv commercials and their claims.

Mark Brenizer in Tarzana sent me *The Writer's Cramp*, a newsletter out of Woodland Hills devoted to straightening out our ecology, and its front-page lead story was headlined UNETHICAL AND MISLEADING ADVERTISING BY STANDARD OIL. HOW GOOD IS F-310?

It has been a hellish two weeks for me, readers.

I don't mind Mr. Koch's gratuitous rudeness. That's just his way, I suppose. He has to live with it, not me. I don't even mind the half-dozen unsigned letters I received that insulted me, my beliefs, my genealogy, and my sexual practices. Anyone without the guts to sign his hate mail obviously hasn't the guts to go find out the truth anyway. What I do mind are the letters from people like Michael Boyles and Ms. P.D.W. (who requested I not use her name if I referred to her letter) who obviously like me, like what I write, and think I'm an honest man. They are fans of this column, and they were disappointed in my "having been taken in."

It is very possible I made a stupid mistake. It is also possible I recommended something out of misguided faith and a desire to do "a good thing" that is detrimental to the very cause I was espousing.

I don't know that yet.

I do know, however, that I put my word behind something that *seemed* to be what it said it was, and I've gotten more feedback and static on it than anything I've ever written in these pages. I don't know that I'm wrong...yet. But I'm damn well going to find out. And when I do, I'll let you know.

I urge those of you who have facts, who *know*, for sure, to write me, care of the *Free Press*. Though I try to keep this column tied in with television (however flimsily at times), having put myself on the line on this one, I guess I'll have to follow it through. At this point I need to know, and I need those of you who can help me (and by extension other readers of this column) to send me the various information that can answer the question once and for all. Let's not fuck around with whether or not Chevron used guy wires to hold up that goddamned balloon in their commercials so it could be seen better, or whether they phonied up the plastic bag with the car inside it. Let's deal strictly with the bottom line on this caper: does F-310 help stop pollution or does it do other things that make it a pollutant, or is it a straight fraud?

Because if it does *any* good at *all*, without side effects that are worse than what it's supposed to be cleaning up, then what I said was ethically and morally correct. If it does nothing, or if it increases, say, the nitrogen oxides in the air, then I was stupid and incorrect and I deserve to get my face slapped for commending it to you from a pinnacle of self-righteousness.

This column isn't a forum for debate on the merits of consumer items, but in this case I've maybe stuck my foot in it, so as the next weeks pass I'll be coming back to this, and passing along *everything* I learn. I ask your patience and indulgence and attention till we know.

Additionally, I would appreciate your writing to Mr. William J. Murphy (Public Relations Counsel, Standard Oil Co. of California, 605 West Olympic Blvd., Los Angeles) and suggesting to him, politely if you can manage it, Mr. Koch, that he spend a little time providing this columnist with irrefutable proof that what I was doing for Chevron was helping people breathe cleaner air, and not touting just another boondoggle.

Let us reason together, as another potential jerk once said.

Sunday night I watched *The Ed Sullivan Show* for the first time in maybe five years. I find it the kind of program totally beneath my notice, like the Jackie Gleason hours (which, happily, will no longer consume an hour of Saturday primetime, Mr. Gleason having been put out to pasture, though I find it amusing that, the moment his cancellation was announced, he was phoned up by Nixon, who wanted him to work for the Administration in some nitwit capacity or other). But I watched Sunday because they were doing an hour tribute to The Beatles.

I should have known better.

This seems to be my stage of development wherein I'm easily flummoxed. But then, I believe in the Easter bunny, so what the hell better can you expect?

It was an hour of bastardization of fine music that I suppose delighted the folks in Cedar Rapids and Buffalo. It made me wanna fwow up.

They took the completely original and madly compelling music of four damn-near-nonpareils and turned it into second-rate Muzak. They didn't make love or show affection or decently fuck, they had sexless sex. Faceless fornication. A thoroughly loveless act, because it was performed without soul or gut or understanding.

One can't blame Sullivan. He's an old man who can barely remember his lines, who calls Dionne Warwick Diane Warwick because he just doesn't know; he goes through his paces like a solemn fire horse; I saw him once out near Palm Desert, in killing heat, filming a segment for the show, with his shirt off, and he's more scar tissue than healthy flesh. It's a wonder to me the old guy can still walk, much less do a turn each Sunday. So don't blame him.

In fact, don't blame anyone. But consider this:

Even the music can be corrupted. They can take even something as pure as the sounds and turn them into shit for the monkeymass. And if they can do that, how much easier it must be to take political theory, revolutionary activity, dissent, all of the paraphernalia of the barricades and corrupt them, turn them against their own people, use them to keep us in line.

Watching that Sullivan potpourri—with Eydie Gorme and Steve Lawrence generically, systematically, and artistically incapable of even *approximating* what The Beatles had put down, thereby causing wonder what all the Beatle shouting was about, because there sure as hell wasn't anything happening *there*—I was reminded of the Stones concert at Altamont, in a strange way. Like this:

There is an important new magazine just published, which I recommend to you without reservation (unless my F-310 position has put me in question). It is called *Scanlan's Monthly* and the dude behind it is Warren Hinckle III, formerly of *Ramparts*. It is the complete muckraking journal, and it is so filled with good stuff you'll gladly tote up the buck to buy it. Anyhow, in the first issue, there is a mightily heavy piece on Altamont and the concert, by Sol Stern. In talking about the horrors that went down at that drag-strip purgatory, he spoke of the Hell's Angels and the murder of Meredith Hunter and the music in these terms:

"We hated them, hated them and envied them all at the same time. For all of their brutality and ugliness they had a definition of themselves and their purpose that showed us up. We had all talked about a counter-community for years—and now, with that community massed in one place, we couldn't relate to anything. In their primitive way, and without talking much about it, the Angels were so together that less than 100 of them were able to take over and intimidate a crowd of close to a half-million people. We had talked about solidarity, but they, not us, were willing to go down for each other in a showdown. *We had the music but they had a purpose*, and everyone in that atomized, alienated mass in front of the stage knew it, and that was their incredible power over us."

The italics in that last sentence are mine. One more quote, from Frank Bardacke, one of the Oakland Seven and a leader of the People's Park Struggle, then I'll make my point. "I think the killing of Meredith Hunter was to our community what the Kitty Genovese murder was to the straight community.

"It showed that if you're going to have a new nation in which you make up new rules, then you have to have more than shared needs. You need to have shared values. Out there [at Altamont] we didn't have those shared moral values and so we didn't have the courage to stop the violence that led to the murder of a black man."

Shared needs. The music. A weapon used against us.

Why *didn't* the Woodstock Nation of half a million people rise up against the Visigoths in their midst and stop the Angels? Why did everyone stay on, even after the beating and the stomping grew omnipresent? Answer: to hear the Stones. To get their needs fulfilled by the music.

Easy enough, I guess, to burn down a Bank of America (and while I dig it, I can't really say it was the smartest attack maneuver of the dissent generation), but not so easy in company with multitudes of others to put the arm on just one hundred thugs. What does that say about us?

What does it say about the music being used to lull so many of us, to keep us sated but ineffectual?

I've heard at least half a dozen big rock stars in the past year say they weren't interested in politics, just in the music; that the music would pull us all together. That, obviously now, is bullshit. The music keeps the kids in a state of happy…but sure as hell isn't getting the message of solidarity across. It's one thing to hear some dude singing about loving one another, and really *loving* a strange black man enough to risk your ass by grabbing the pool cue being used to stave in his head.

No, the music isn't enough. It is a tool that can be used to draw us into one nation, but—as the Sullivan show demonstrates—it is a double-edged sword that can be turned to the purpose of anyone smart enough to alter it.

Altamont, the Angels, Meredith Hunter, the Bank of America, the Chicago 7 convictions, repression, solidarity, and Ed Sullivan. Does anyone else out there see the horrifying connections? Or are we so used to holding those little transistor radios up to our ears as we walk the Strip that the noise level has grown too high for us to detect the wail of ourselves, dying along with our dying culture?

57: 13 MARCH 70

VIDEO VOYEURISM: PART ONE

Before your very eyes. Two polarizations:

He's casually slumped in a terrace chair, overlooking what seems to be the Riviera. He's good-looking in that surly *cinéma vérité* attitude, hair longish and eyes smoldering. His clothes are midway between Errol Flynn and Bobby Sherman, shirt open to midchest. A girl who could not *possibly* be filmed in anything but soft focus lounges against the railing of the terrace. Her eyes seem misted with adoration, yet faintly discernible in the lovely contours of her face can be seen the mark of the innocent, the victim. She watches him without speaking. (Has he just come from a sex bout with her, an encounter fraught with mild sadism and screams of passion muffled into a pillow? It seems likely.)

He turns to us languidly. "I know what girls need," he says. "They don't need fake eyelashes and brassieres and all that stuff. What girls need is a little love."

Who could doubt him? Is he not the epitome of caddish self-assurance? Is he not stylish, indolent, surfeited with the unasked-for treasures of the world? Is he not what each of us with our muzzy morning-breath and razor-nicks would wish to be, had we but a genie's boon?

Then—and get this, because it's the key to getting it on with unattainable women—he hauls the girl across the terrace by the waistband of her slacks. She comes, Jack, she just *comes!* She don't linger, she *moves* it!

And he touches her alabaster skin with a gentle/rough finger; a touch of possession, of power and authority over this incredible dream-creature you or I could never even share a dimensional plane with. He touches her face with a holy solution, with a mystic ablutive, with a scented magic, and he says, "Love's a little color...and you can use it to put something on your cheeks, or your chin, or even that little nose of yours. And no one will know you have it on...not even me."

The sun in the background seems to flare more brightly. The nova of passion is approaching. Lord and chattel in the good land. I will go and eat out my heart for that creature of quicksilver movement and holy flesh.

But she's his. Always was, before either of them were born, until the last tick of eternity. His name is engraved in musk and platinum threads on the doe-soft inner thigh of her amazing right leg.

It is wise to know when one cannot compete with gods.

And...

She comes striding out of the darkness. She is Bill Blass-accoutered in free-swinging elegance. Her stride is as the ibex—sure, graceful, drenched and imbued with strengths of femininity and purpose. I hear the voices: "You've come a long way, baby."

She steps into close-up and whirls off her Australian bush

hat with the dia mond pin clasping up one side of the brim. She spins it away and tosses her leonine mass of hair in defiance. She is her own woman. She is the New Woman. She has empathy...but determination. She has gentleness...but cunning. She has love...but on her own terms. She is no man's plaything; she is as far from a Hefnerism folded in three parts and with pubes airbrushed as Mies van der Rohe is from the architect of McDonald's Golden Arches.

She begins to unpeel her cigarettes and she stares at me with an early-warning system of carnality and sensual alertness that dares me to prove I am man enough to compete with her Visigoth lust. She is not to be tampered with. She is the slag bucket ready to catch the white-hot rivet. But only if my aim is precise and proper. She is totally liberated: clothes as *she* wants to wear them, for herself and her comfort and her freedom; makeup or no makeup, whichever suits her purposes; cigarettes slim and potent.

If I think I can whip one of my 1940s male chauvinism numbers on her, I'm wrong. She will toy with me. She will outthink, outconjure, outmaneuver me. Then she will beat me at straight pool, fifty balls at a buck a pocket.

I turn to boysenberry jelly.

What hath god wrought? And where do I go to say thank you?

This will be a study of sex on television. What's that I hear you mumble? There *is* no sex on tv? Situation comedies are as sterile and aseptically asexual as Priapus' birthday in a eunuchs' dormitory? And who'd want to make it with Lucille Ball anyway? Oh, my friends, you have been seeing blindly; you have been led to the land of joy and have wandered witless at the periphery.

For television today is the richest peephole for a voyeur ever conceived. It bubbles, it seethes, it overflows with goodies. Turn on your set, *any*time, and but behold the joys. The most beautiful women history has ever known, filmed in phosphor-dot fantasy with scrims, with gauzes, with gels, with halations and solarizations, ranged and trotted out for the predilection and lust assuaging of the most seasoned connoisseur.

Ignore the soap operas with their psychotic ladies and their endlessly destructive affairs. Ignore the dramatic shows with their surface-skimming attempts to delineate deep emotion and characterization in tissue-paper archetypes. Ignore the comedies that extend misshapen and hideous crones as the *ne plus ultra* of pulchritude.

Flash on the commercials, you nits!

And the late night talk shows!

And for those of you who secretly lust after nubile young wenches, there are the rock dance programs. And for Humbert Humberts in our midst—in the past relegated to lurking in the basements of grade schools or surreptitiously peeking up tots' skirts on subways—try Saturday mornings and the hordes of Mattel and Kenner commercials with their prepubescent Lolitas flaunting their softly rounded bodies beside endless Suzy Homemaker sets.

One has only to open the cover of the current beaver magazine to see to what end all this permissiveness and sexual forthrightness has brought us: scruffy ladies with needle marks tracking their arms and thighs, lying out like slaughtered animals, knees opened and pudenda exposed. Sights of nauseousness more closely resembling massacre photos from My Lai than sexually arousing titillaters. A silken crossed leg is still more pulse-crippling than Gobi Deserts of pimple-studded flesh. We seek not the phony hypocrisies of Victorian prudery or cheap arousal, we merely seek to retain a touch of that mystery that lies between men and women, that indefinable come-on men have employed with after-shave lotions and rugged looks, that women have stated with subtle scents and a certain way of moving their hips when they walk.

Blatancy is to be cast away. Subtlety ennobles.

And what more subtle come-ons have we ever known than those currently on view tube-wise?

Come with me, then, as we run barefoot through contemporary commercials like prep-school boys on a weekend in a harem.

The conscious symbolism, the sexual allegories, the devious but stirring come-ons. For instance:

The flower of Southern womanhood (an idealized image, I

assure you, having spent considerable time below the Mason-Dixon line) in close-up. Curled locks silver and shining. A ripe mouth, petulant and little-girlish. A body lush and fruitful. Like the Life Savers she smiles into being.

And she tells us about the fruit in the basket. The lemons...in which a hole appears. The limes...in which holes appear. The (oh, god!) cherry...in which a hole appears.

And all through the arousing descriptions of ripe fruit and how they are the same tastes one receives from Life Savers...with holes in them...she plays coquette. She turns and smiles over her shoulder; she expands her chest and strains her bosom toward us; she seems gentle and kittenish and altogether available, if only we can grasp the subcutaneous implications of holes in fruit.

Cancel those dates! Forget buying dinner and holding hands in the movie! Pass on picking up girls in rock joints! Get in front of the tv. Sit thyself down and pay attention to the lessons to be learned. Sexuality is rampant in the universe, can you but glean the key messages, can you but recognize the touchstones.

Southern girls sell Life Savers...

What does that say to you?

The synonyms are obvious. The riches incalculable. The mind boggles. The gonads leap.

Watch the screens a new way this week. We'll pick it up from here in the next installment.

58: 20 MARCH 70

I'll bet you thought this week would see part 2 of my exhaustive (and exhausting) analysis of sex on tv, "Video Voyeurism," didn't you? Well, I'd planned it that way, but in the grand old tradition of my wandering mind and more loose ends than the Pentagon's explanations about Laos, something else came up last week that I want to get set down before it becomes outdated, so just kinda stick Part 1 away in your mental pending file—along with that F-310 business, on which I'm still working—and I'll hit it next week. I promise.

Because this week I really have to do a destruct job on the diseased whore of the Fourth Estate, the pimp of the entertainment industry, the bought voice of Clown Town, that estimable rag of endless lies, gossip, and chicanery, the glossy-sided *Hollywood Reporter*. (*Variety* is hardly better, but at least occasionally it makes an *attempt* at honesty and impartiality.)

What I'm about to say is not terribly new or startling. If there is anyone above the age of innocence who actually *believes* the mouth-to-mouth resuscitation the *Reporter* offers as its surrealistic impression of entertainment world news, surely it can only be those beach-bum actors and pudding-minded starlets who confuse shadow with reality. For the *Reporter*, by dint of its reliance on advertising from the very people it reviews, has been a captive sycophant for Hollywood since its inception. When horrendous, gargantuan bombs like *Star!* and *Hello, Dolly!* and *Goodbye, Mr. Chips* and *The Battle of the Bulge* get rave reviews from the genuflecting *Reporter* and its staff of reviewers (all of whom seem to be lineal descendants of Uriah Heep)...all on the theory that big spectacular productions are good for Hollywood because they keep the featherbedding unions at work...ignoring the bald fact that the days of that kind of production are gone and such mammoths have helped kill at least three of the major studios...it becomes awkwardly obvious that the *Reporter* is about as relevant to what is happening in the film world today as a McGuffey's Reader.

That the *Reporter*'s timorous little soul was bought long ago by its patrons—and the specific that forces my lance to tilt against it this week—demonstrates itself in a review by Tony Lawrence on page 16 of the Thursday, March 12, edition of the Reporter. It is a review of yet another in the endless string of moron-movies-for-tv made by Aaron Spelling Productions. A disaster of stupidity and ineptitude, a cataclysm of banality and sterility, a pustule of bad writing and little-theater acting titled *The Love War*. It was aired over ABC on March 10, from 8:30 to 10:00 and in a video universe singularly dedicated to retarding science fiction's acceptance as a legitimate art form (such tools as

Lost in Space, The Invaders, Land of the Giants, Time Tunnel, My Favorite Martian, My Living Doll, and *It's About Time* have dealt it crippling blows in the past) it was a karate chop of no mean strengths. Or weaknesses, depending on how you look at it.

To clobber the *Reporter* properly, I must first describe *The Love War* in all its awfulness. Without comparison, the full dishonesty of the *Reporter* under a headline that reads "'Love War' Has Message, Performances, Good Effects" does not become apparent.

Guerdon Trueblood and David Kidd are the first two culprits in the band of cutthroats who made this stinker.

They wrote it.

They took an idea that story editor Seeleg Lester of the long-dead *Outer Limits* would have rejected in a hot second, and they flaunted their cavalier lack of understanding of the science fiction idiom by turning it, one of the oldest clichés in the pulp bag of outdated sf shticks, into a predictable and insultingly illogical parody of everything valid in speculative fiction. (It always amazes me, the effrontery of writers ignorant of the most basic rules of sf writing, who have no conception of the almost fifty years of writing in the genre, whose temerity permits them to cobble up some pseudo-sf bullshit; they would never try to do a political teleplay without doing the research; they would never do a historical script without checking out the background; why the hell do they think they can attempt sf with the originality and verve of pachyderms trying to be terpsichoreans?)

Two warring planets, Argon and Zinan, have sent battle squads to Earth. (Someone should have advised Messrs. Trueblood and Kidd that argon is not a made-up word intended to sound alien. It is a colorless, odorless, gaseous element found in the air and is used for filling electric light bulbs. Scientific "accuracy" of this sort keynotes my cavils in the paragraph above.)

(Oh, yeah, one more bit of bullshit mumbo jumbo proving plowboys shouldn't try to pull against fast guns: Kyle, an Argonite, played by Lloyd Bridges—about whose performance more in a moment—tries to explain to Angie Dickinson the cosmography of Earth/Argon/Zinan; he puts his hands side by side and says they represent the two alien planets. Then he says they "overlap Earth" and that both planets are trying to take it over. Now, I am by no means Fred Hoyle or even Camille Flammarion, but I am several steps beyond a Cro-Magnon [as I presume are Trueblood and Kidd], and I can look up into the night sky and see that there are *not* two planets "overlapping" the Earth. Now, had the scenarists read even one 1930s issue of *Astounding Science Fiction*, they might have come up with the dodgem explanation that Argon [!] and Zinan "overlapped the Earth in another plane of existence" or used subspace, or another dimension…any one of a hundred writer's tricks sf authors have dreamed up over the years to take care of such problems. But they were rank amateurs playing potsy in a genre where they were illiterates, and so we have someone telling us openly from the screen that there are three planets sharing this Earth space.)

Anyhow. To resolve who will "win" the planet Argon and Zinan have sent three guerrilla fighters each to Earth. Whoever knocks off the other gets to keep Earth. Argon wants to let us go our merry way and eventually let us into the League of Planets, or somesuch. Zinan wants to destroy all intelligent life on Earth and settle it themselves.

If this sounds familiar to you, it is probably because it is a direct steal from such sources as Fredric Brown's classic story "Arena," from the *Outer Limits* segment starring Nick Adams that has been replayed umpteen times on Channel 11's reruns of that series, and from the *Star Trek* segment based on the Brown story. If you get my meaning, I'm saying this was a cornball rehash of a standard idea done to death a thousand times before.

But as if it wasn't bad enough that Aaron Spelling and his production staff (not to mention the authors) didn't know or didn't care that they were using ninth-hand material done better by other people (and I suspect if Fred Brown wanted to sue for plagiarism he'd have a strong case), the stupidities of the plot were compounded with each passing scene.

The aliens were so incredibly inept in their "guerrilla tactics" that they wouldn't have lasted ten minutes with even a semi-competent Green Beret or Viet Cong. They chased each other around, moved from city to ghost town for no apparent reason, blundered constantly, and in the end the good guys lost because the Zinans had sent *four* instead of three. This ending, incidentally, is typical of literary chicanery of the worst sort—wherein the author withholds a salient fact so you can't solve the puzzle—or changes the rules of the story. If they *said* there were three, there should have *been* three. You can't with impunity write a fantasy and adopt as a rule of the game that no one can use his right hand, and then, at a crucial moment, have someone use his right hand to get him out of trouble, without the audience yelling foul.

But that's a minor carp compared to the other foulnesses of this ninety-minute stinker. The acting reeked of bathos: unmotivated, stilted, and illogical. Lloyd Bridges as the Argonite who has been without female companionship for 150 years (for reasons never explained) and his *bête noire* Angie Dickinson, who shows him what love can mean to a man, even if he's an alien, act in a manner even high-school dramatics students would abominate. The only person worth watching in this farrago of senselessness was a girl named Judy Jordan who did a walk-on as a Union Station information desk clerk. When I say walk-on, that is precisely what I mean. Miss Jordan, who in a sexist phrase popular during my youth in Ohio eons ago, is what we used to call back in Ohio stacked like a brick shithouse, came out from behind her desk to show Mr. Bridges where he was going. I'm sure she was brought out from behind the desk to give us a clearer, more complete tallying of her charms, for which bit of intelligent direction (the only one, as far as I could tell) we must thank George McCowan, a director whose work, if we are to judge by this epic, will not soon be clamored for.

When one has to descend to the troglodyte level of a Hefnerism to derive even the smallest scintilla of pleasure from a ninety-minute production, it can easily be ascertained a dereliction of artistry on the part of the producers and creators. Thus we commend *The Love War* and Mr. Spelling's idea of trenchant drayma [sic] to the dustbin.

Which leaves us with the *Hollywood Reporter* and its reaction to this patently flatulent excrescence.

Why not let their own words hang them:

"...solidly believable performances...an attempt at message

and purpose with some interesting visual effects...direction maintained a fairly good balance between science fiction elements and a genuine relationship between two people...Miss Dickinson and Bridges found convincing aspects of their parts and played them out with complementary style..."

Enough!

This they have to say about a supposedly adult drama in which the future of the population of the Earth is at stake, a future decided by (get this) a *High Noon* walk-down and shoot-out in the dusty street of a ghost town. A scene of monumental stupidity and silliness.

The *Hollywood Reporter* has for so long groveled at the trough of show-biz garbage that it can no longer even make a pretense of decent critical judgment.

It is symptomatic of the schizoid nature of the entertainment industry in this town that, even though everyone *knows* the *Reporter* is filled with flack and puff most often existing only in the reality of a PR man's mind, they continue to support it and even believe their own puff. I've known agents who've dreamed up a sheer bit of flummery, sent it in (where everything is accepted without question, thereby pinholing the quality of reportage), and when it appeared two days later, looking at it as though it were real and acted on the humbug.

Mr. Spelling is a mainstay of the *Reporter*. His name turns up in gossip columns therein with stultifying regularity, his every business move is reported with awe and Klaxons, his productions are plumped and ballyhooed as though they genuinely meant something sterling for the industry or the Condition of Art in Our Times. And when his offerings are reviewed, he is applauded. It is a self-fulfilling prophecy.

All this, despite the fact that Mr. Spelling is responsible for the longest unbroken string of rotten productions in the history of television. It is only when other, more tasteful and perceptive men take over the reins of his productions that anything has a chance of emerging with truth or originality.

Yet the *Reporter*, the paid servant of the hypers and shuckers and hustlers of tv land, continues to perpetuate all the myths, all the lies, all the destructive hypocrisy that has brought the

Hollywood Valhalla to a condition of sterility, aridity, and near death. And a few months ago—when the depression hit—the *Reporter* had the audacity to ask for *more* patronage, on the theory that when things are worst is when one should advertise most.

Well, it may be a valid theory in some circles, but I suggest the condemned should not patronize the executioner. One may have to get one's head lopped off, but one doesn't have to aid and abet the axman.

59: 27 MARCH 70

VIDEO VOYEURISM: PART TWO

The sexuality of television commercials has long been of the *double-entendre* variety. That's nothing new. But (as my first two examples indicated, in Part 1 of this dissertation) two important polarizations have come to be the *modus operandi* of almost every sex-oriented commercial going out over the tube these days.

The first posture, what might well be termed a right-wing reactionary stance, is grounded in the archaic concept of male supremacy. As typified by the "Love's a Little Color" commercial (that opened Part 1 of this series), it tenders the image of the modern American woman as a vapid plaything of bright colors and fluffed plumage; a tapioca-brained bastardization of the few remaining feminine traits left to intelligent women who refuse to be typed as militant dyke Liberation haranguers (as corrupt a stereotype as we've had foisted on us recently) or Barbie dolls. It says that women serve their best function—according to these commercials that function is as man-trap—when they remain coy, confused, well-oiled, and transparently ridiculous. In this polarized vision of womanhood, Madison Avenue has marshaled them, ushering them on camera to dupe the little ladies out there in the Great American Heartland who serve as fifth columnists of their own freedom by a mama-instilled belief that they truly are no better than live-in maids with fucking privileges.

At the opposite pole is what one might term the "new left" method of marketing sex in commercials. It plays openly to the liberated woman—the Virginia Slims commercial is the classic of the form—and tells her she can have sex whenever, wherever, and however she wants it, without guilt, without restraints, without even a scintilla of doubt as to retaining her individuality or preeminence over the males of her acquaintance. It very carefully shies away from the lesbian look (in a show of perceptivity that should only hip us more acutely to how into it admen really are). It flashes with color and a touch of sadomasochism, and I know of few men watching these items who don't fall right in line with Woody Allen's old secret dream—"I dreamed it was my birthday and they wheeled in a big cake and a gorgeous girl popped out of it with a whip and long black leather boots...and she dominated me."

Thus, operating from a pinnacle of understanding of these attitudes, we can categorize almost all of the sexually stimulating spots currently on view.

Almost all. There are, of course, those few rare examples that display a shade of cunning, a Machiavellian insight of misdirection, a plethora of unconscious symbols such that our two major categories simply don't hold them.

Let me describe one.

Bread is the *staff* of life. Remember that adage. The operative word is staff.

Scene: Mother is in the kitchen, looking out through the back window into the rear yard. Out there, smiling and doing a buddy-up number are Dad and Sonny. They are attempting to rig up a tent for Sonny. They keep trying to get it raised, but it keeps falling down. They are trying to *get it up*, don't you see? Trying to get an *erection*. They can't get it up. They try and try, but they simply cannot *get it up*. The poles keep falling down.

Mother smiles a knowing smile. *She* knows what to do. So she proceeds to make them sandwiches of Wonder Bread...the *staff* of life. Smug, in control of the situation that has stymied impotent, Bumsteadlike hubby and tied-to-apron-strings Sonny (whose masculinity, I'll take bets, will be in serious question in the near future), she feeds them the necessary sex food, and in the next scene we see Mother standing beside them, beaming with sated satisfaction as Dad and Sonny *get it up*. The tent is erect, rigid.

Let me describe another.

There is a Dial Soap commercial in which a doll of a girl is leading a guided tour. As she walks in and out of rooms and buildings with her charges, we hear a tinklebell of sweetness, and suddenly we have subliminal flashes of this same cupcake in the shower. Nude, of course; commercials deal strictly with reality (and if you thought otherwise, disabuse yourself), and this girl is real if nothing else. She bathes bareass, unlike most of us who wear flight suits and scuba gear in our showers.

She is succulent as hell, rubbing her smooth limbs, and as we shuttle back and forth between her bouncing, assured vivacity and her almost pathological attention to cleanliness, we understand that it is because she is so carnally devoted to keeping her epidermal layers down to the bare minimum that she is so self-possessed. She can be close to all those people for extended periods because she is a water baby. And, of course, all of *that* is bullshit. The implication is that if you swab yourself down with Dial nineteen times a day, bubie, you'll look like that chick. And even that is bullshit, because the sole purpose of the hype is to show us a pretty girl in the buff.

Sex! TV is lovely!

And the loveliest thing about it is that, aside from the two polarizations discussed earlier, and their inherent hypocrisies, and the subliminal symbolism commercials, most of what we're getting these days is just pure enjoyment of the isn't-a-beautiful-woman-nice-to-look-at variety. All the panty hose ads. The feminine hygiene ads. The low-cal and diet drink ads. They all cut to sources. One panty hose advertisement doesn't even bother with the most acceptable extraneousness...all it shows are the legs of a girl as she puts the things on. Now, for leg men in the audience that is Valhalla. For tit men it's murder, but those of us who are leg men always felt tit men were weird anyhow. But that's another story.

I don't want you to think, however, that such surfeits of joy should blind us to the evils of some of the sex commercials. The insidious ugliness of the Tiparillo ad, in which a very groovy, hippy-style chick, in attendance at a straight party, is hustled by a balding square through use of his phallic Tipa rillo. The Swift Butterball Ham commercial, in which the eighth-most-incredible-looking woman in the world moistens her lips and caresses her Butterball the way we might wish she caressed us: a sex substitute if ever I saw one. The ghastly Silva-Thins commercial that tries to tell us women are at their best when they're slim and rich.

These, and others of their sort, are corruptions of the pure sex message being delivered by television today. They are obviously the products of amorously constipated admen and their female counterparts. They are akin to the anti-female designers who feel uplifted only when they have most thoroughly destroyed any resemblance between their mannequins and human beings.

Blessedly for all of us, they are in the minority. Most commercials use sex as it was intended to be used, as a corrupter of morality, as a polluter of our precious bodily fluids, as a leader-astray of the young, and as a balm to our weakened spirits.

Yes, tv has finally come into its own. It has found a job it can do, and do well. It can purvey sex. And it can do it without recourse to any of the shabby trickery of history's previous merchandisers. It never once has to show us the actual act. No offensive rutting and throbbing organs, no smutty language and bad taste.

All it has to do is tease us.

Thereby making sex more undercover and considerably dirtier, despite all the soap ads.

And as I've said repeatedly, all this nonsense about sex being pure and sweet and uplifting is disastrous. If it's clean and frank and open, anyone can do it, and that takes all the fun out of it.

If sex ain't dirty, I don't want any part of it.

So thanks to you, O tv tube, for bringing sex back where it belongs. Into our living rooms.

There's a breakdown in logic there, somewhere, but I'm too horny to think about it right now.

60: 3 APRIL 70

I want to clear up some loose ends this week, and then talk a little about the shows that have been axed...and the new ones coming on to replace them. But, as I say, there are a few straggly ends that need to be tied off.

The first is the F-310 matter. While this is by no means the final word, I wanted you to know the mail has been inundating me, from all over the state, and by way of a progress report, let me say that I think I was, in fact, duped by my own *naïveté* and my need to believe in The Good Fairy. Enough of you have patted me on the head, however, for me to stop pulling this *mea culpa* shit; and as you have suggested in many communiqués, anybody can be had once. It has taught me a much-needed lesson, and in a completely unexpected manner it has shown me that I'm not nearly as cynical a bastard as I'd thought. More to the point, I was *hoping* it was true, and nothing speaks more appropriately to the attitude than a quote from Miguel de Unamuno y Jugo (1864–1936): "In order to attain the impossible one must attempt the absurd."

Expecting Standard Oil to do something for the commonweal—without their megalomaniacal need for usurious profits—was frankly absurd.

Even so, I still have hopes that the worst part of the whole shuck is that the gasoline is no worse than any of the others. It doesn't look that way at the moment, just from preliminary information; it looks as though F-310 does as much harm as good. When I know for certain, I'll either write a straight-news piece for the *Freep*, quite apart from this column (where the space allocated to F-310 is getting to be an oppressive drag), or I'll sum it up as briefly as possible and put it to rest. Till then, my advice is to distrust *everything* you see in tv commercials, including that saintly little old man with the English accent who wants to sell you books of picture stories from the Bible. And don't use your cars at all. Just sit at home and take shallow breaths.

Next on the loose-end agenda is the matter of answering mail. When I started this column, I only received a handful of personal messages, and I religiously answered each one, at least briefly if I was pressed for time. But I suppose it's a mark of the popularity of the column these days (and that cheers me, to be sure) that I get quite a bundle of missives. Where an answer is *really* required, I still try to answer as many as possible. Where it's just a friendly note telling me to keep doing what I've been doing, I consider the appearance of subsequent columns to be response enough. And when it's paranoid horseshit, such as that engendered by Louise Lucks, who is a righteous coo-coo, I dump them and forget them.

But in the main the problem mail is from people with the best of intentions and the warmest of feelings toward this columnist, who require answers to problems I can't (or won't) handle, who want to know where to send scripts, who want me to find agents for them, who want me to critique their scripts or stories or poetry, or who get offended if I advise them I just don't have the time off from my own work to become a pen pal.

So this is by way of explanation and appeal. I genuinely dig hearing from you, particularly—as with the F-310 thing—if I need information and you respond as richly as you have in the past. But I'm up to my ass in nine thousand projects, most of which keep me at this devil typewriter eighteen hours a day as it is, and when I get caught up (as I *haven't* since 1964), I like just to fall down and relax. Sitting down to answer chatty letters, even from nice people, is a busman's holiday of the ugliest sort. And relax time comes seldom to me. So, with very little time for extracurricular correspondence, I have to appeal to those of you who write...don't get pissed off or feel slighted if I don't respond personally. If what you've written is something more than a good luck or well done, if it's a bitch or a subject you want me to cover, keep watching the columns. I'll probably get around to you.

Otherwise I'd never have time to write the stories and

screenplays that earn me my living. And as for people like Ms. Luck...save your postage.

Now, if the nice typesetter has left a one-line space between the last paragraph and this one—to indicate I'm changing the subject—we'll go on to a preliminary look at the terminal cases in primetime, and their replacements for next season.

ABC, apart from alphabetically, deserves to be considered first because—as usual—its death rate is five times higher than either NBC or CBS. Among those slated for the guillotine are *The Flying Nun, Here Come the Brides, It Takes a Thief,* and *Land of the Giants,* all of which had a healthy run for their money and whose loss won't cause much breast-beating among the masses. In the case of *Land of the Giants,* though several of its stars are friends and acquaintances, it is to make happy. The stupidity, vapidity, and eczema-producing banality of this most recent Irwin Allen monstrosity has, for the last two years, brought a wince to the phizzes of anyone even remotely familiar with science fiction. And further joy is ours in the knowledge that Mr. Allen, the Ralph Williams of Television Adventure Series, has no product slated for the new season. But, accepting the theory that bad money drives out good (or that VD can't be stamped out as long as you have one plague carrier running loose), we can expect him to be back in the dismal future.

Somewhat more sad-making is the death of *The Ghost and Mrs. Muir,* which was a nice show when it started, but which, this season, slipped considerably. I personally attribute this slippage to the caliber of scenarists hired to write the segments. When Joe Banaducci moved on, the quality dropped appreciably. Still, it was fun while it lasted.

Vanishing, and with no moans of sadness, for they passed through our culture and prime-time slicker than snot on a doorknob (or doo-doo through a colander, depending how vomitous you'll allow me to get), are such dandies as *Jimmy Durante Presents the Lennon Sisters Hour, The Engelbert Humperdinck Show, Pat Paulsen's Half a Comedy Hour,* and *Paris 7000.* Of this last, the most recent starring vehicle for George

Hamilton, the best that can be said is that Mr. Hamilton should have been under it, rather than in it.

ABC is bringing in a gaggle of gropers, of course, led off by *The Young Lawyers*, starring Lee J. Cobb and a young actor of uncommon brilliance named Zalman King. It deals with Boston law students who staff a legal aid society, and is based on the excellent mini-movie by Mike Zagor. I suspect this will be the show to watch next season. Cobb (replacing Jason Evers, who name-fronted the pilot mini-movie) is always a joy to watch work, and Zal King is the first likely possibility for superstar since Steve McQueen hung up his hawg leg for a Bullitt.

Also arriving come September is *The Young Rebels*. (Do you think ABC has finally gotten hip to the fact that young people aren't watching tv? Do you think the word young in two of their most important series indicates they're on to something? Does a chicken have lips? Does a wild bear shit in the woods? Is Ellsworth Bunker a liar?)

Set in 1777, *The Young Rebels* is about three members of a Yankee guerrilla band aiding General Washington in his struggle against the stamp tax. It will, of course, parallel contemporary problems. And fighting off the British is pretty safe these days. God forbid Cornwallis had a Chinese cook. (I wonder if they'll show the first American to fall in the Revolution...a black dude named Crispus Attucks?)

Vince Edwards lumbers back on camera with *Dial Hot Line*, based on that gawdawful ABC movie of a few weeks back. In the series Edwards heads up a telephone answering service that "deals with troubled teens who have nowhere else to turn." I don't know about you, friends, but if our troubled teens have nowhere else to turn than to Vince Edwards, we are in worse shape than I thought. But...I grow snotty. Onward.

There are a trio of new sitcoms: *The Partridge Family*, about a group of rock singers whose mommy heads up the unit; extrapolating cunningly, I parse this to be a vehicle for The Cowsills. Whoopee! *The Odd Couple* with Tony Randall and Jack Klugman doing the Jack Lemmon and Walter Matthau roles from the Neil Simon film. *Barefoot in the Park*, starring Nipsey Russell and Scoey Mitchell, converts the Doc Simon Broadway hit and film from white to black, which is a rather surprising switch, but which gives us pause to observe that what we may be getting here is more white middle-class bullshit done in black drag. After all, Diahann Carroll is still Doris Day with a suntan, if you know what I mean. I'm waiting for a touching, heartwarming situation comedy about a ghetto dweller, his delinquent kids, his wife who slaves as a housemaid, his amusing trips to the unemployment line, his cute encounters with cockroaches and *Rattus norvegicus*, and his sidesplitting attempts to regain his masculinity in a white world where his only outlet for aggression is kicking the legs off his borax furniture.

Danny Thomas will be back. After his last appearance, on the DANNY THOMAS MELODRAMA CENTURY (or so each hour segment seemed to be), the best we can make thanks for is that it'll only be a half-hour sitcom. They never know when to go to Sun City, do they, troops?

I'll talk more about the sf series, *The Immortal*, after I've seen the new pilot. And the same for *Zig Zag*, which sounds as though it ought to be about a crash pad full of heads but is actually concerned with a trio of master criminologists. (I like my version better.) And the same for something called *The Silent Force*, whatever *that* is. (You don't suppose it's tales of Agnew's Majority, do you…?)

61: 24 APRIL 70

By the time you read this, I'll be back, but as I write it, I'm on the road again. Lectures in Lawrence, Kansas, at the University of Kansas, and at the State University of New York at Buffalo. The other night was the Oscar-cast, Hollywood's annual spasm of chicanery, and I want to get into that, but I'll save it for next week…. Something else is on my mind right now.

And again, dammit, it touches tv only peripherally—in a way I'll describe later. But by this time, those of you who've gritted your teeth and borne it as my mental wanderings (not to mention my corporeal ones) have taken me far afield from the teat will understand that television is frequently only a hook to get to some of the more burning issues of the day...and this week... having encountered something genuinely unsettling during my lecture tour...I frankly state that tv only glancingly involved itself here...and hope you'll forgive me the transgression.

Onward.

(Preamble. My credentials as a vocal foe of repression and conservatism need not be explicated here. I've been doing it, not merely writing about it, for quite some time now. I mention these credentials here, at this time, of course, because of what is to follow, and to assure my readers that my allegiances have not changed.)

I walked onto the campus of the University of Kansas and the first thing I saw was the chalked word STRIKE on the sidewalk outside Strong Hall. I was with James E. Gunn, the science fiction writer, who is in charge of PR at KU, the man who had invited me out to speak to film and writing classes.

I asked Jim Gunn—who is a very good and honest man— what it was all about. He looked troubled. And he explained.

The chancellor of KU had submitted, as a matter of form (as has been the case for decades), the list of faculty promotions in all departments to the KU Board of Regents. It was standard operating procedure for the regents to okay the list *in toto*, as the promotions were always rigorously overseen by the department heads and the KU administration. People on the list were deserving; it was an accepted fact.

Yet last month, when the current promotions came before the regents, two archconservatives on the board decided—for the first time in the history of the school—to defer decision on two names, to temporarily pass over two men.

The two men were Litto and Velvel. What they had done to incur the ill favor of the regents was as follows: Litto, a dramatics professor, was instrumental in assembling a production titled *Kaleidoscope of the American Dream*—part of a project that the State Department has traditionally sent overseas as PR for the United States. Included in this production were snippets of musicals and drama ranging from *Awake and Sing!* to contemporary theater. (Observers of the production report it was not a terribly distinguished production, but then—as Jim Gunn noted—all free speech cases can't be perfectly formed. All obscenity cases, for instance, can't be judgments of Ulysses. Sometimes you have to defend the not so good. But that isn't important here, just a side comment.)

Several of these later scenes caused raised eyebrows. Apparently while they weren't *Oh, Calcutta!* they *were* a bit more earthy than some of the Jayhawkers thought was consistent with decorum. (Though why the theater, any more than any other art form, should give a shit about decorum is beyond me.) Some of the voices in Kansas officialdom began bleating about filth overseas," which is a familiar yahooism. And they blamed Litto.

But compared to the "sins" of Velvel, Litto was the Late George Apley.

Velvel is in the law school at KU. He is a remarkable man. Among his many virtues are the following: his suit against the United States attempting to have the Vietnam war declared unconstitutional went as far as the Supreme Court before it was thrown out; he was brought in as consultant and was instrumental in the success of the Massachusetts bill recently signed into law permitting Massachusetts men to refuse to fight in an undeclared war; he defended the sixty or seventy KU students who were busted last year for interfering with campus ROTC. He is a soft-spoken, rational man whose work in the law school has been above reproach and even, by all reasonable standards, brilliant. He was obviously and certainly deserving of upgrading.

But the regents who singled him out didn't even need his previous liberal activities to skewer him. For during a campus gathering in sympathy with the Chicago 7, Velvel emerged from the law school and said a few words about Judge Julius Hoffman (the Mattel windup jurist...pull his string and watch him enter second childhood). Reports conflict as to precisely *what* Velvel said, but everyone who was uncommitted said it wasn't terribly inflammatory. Yet once again the voice of the Silent Majority was heard, deriding Velvel and saying a man like that shouldn't be permitted to teach law at the university.

So...

Litto and Velvel were to be passed over. But the chancellor, horrified by their intended actions, suggested that the regents were acting on hearsay, and should wait for factual information. The regents reluctantly agreed.

Approbations and verifications of the two professors' worthiness began coming in. The regents were to make their decision at a meeting the third Friday of this month. (Everyone but the regents seems agreed that they really don't have the right to drop names from that list, by the rules of their own formation, stated many years ago. Yet in these perilous, anti-intellectual times, everyone was willing to cool it and hope common sense and the facts would set the gentlemen to rights.)

But the students got wind of the news.

A strike was called.

And lurking in the background is a minor-league Joe McCarthy named Reynolds Schultz, a Senator from the Lawrence district. Mr. Schultz, whose position is somewhat abaft that of Ronald Reagan, our own unbearable cross, is bucking for the governorship of Kansas. (Although it is said he needs another seventy-five grand for campaign expenses and, like most political impotents, he can't get it up.) Schultz, an ex-marine, an ex-farmer, likes to refer to himself as an uneducated but canny man of the people...a self-made man. (Thereby, once again, demonstrating the horrors of unskilled labor.) His appeal is a know-nothing appeal and, as stated above, in these anti-intellectual times just such a clown might well become a governor. We have enough Claude Kirks, Reagans, Maddoxes, and their ilk as it is, without considering another cripple fit to rule.

Schultz, apparently, is slavering for a political plum like a riot on campus to drop into his lap. He's just sitting there praying the kids will strike.

Now don't for a moment even suggest that I'm about to say the kids should have backed off, on the theory that two good men getting zapped is a lesser evil than having a repressive dunderhead in the governor's mansion. The lesser of two evils is a dumb alternative theory.

What I am about to say is that on Tuesday night, Oscar-cast night, it was pretty much common knowledge that the regents were calling an emergency meeting and were going to okay the promotions. Battle won.

Yet on that same Tuesday night, a strike meeting was called— the strike was scheduled for today as I write this, Wednesday the eighth—and when students began asking, "Why are we striking?" none of the militants of SDSers could agree on the reason. The shouting began, and it went on for some time, till someone yelled, "To hell with this—let's STRIKE!" and he got the usual jingo response, "RIGHT ON!"

(A radical student who was in attendance at the meeting, with whom I rapped later that night at a party, sounded like a man who has just found out his puppy dog has rabies. He said the meeting included about fifty out-of-town radicals, all of whom were pounding the floors and climbing the walls for a strike. It is not coincidental, I think, that on that Wednesday Abbie Hoffman was scheduled to speak at the university. "They kept saying, what'll Abbie think of us if we don't strike," the student said, bewildered and frightened. He was getting his first taste of the stupidity and evil that lie not merely at the far right of the activist spectrum, but at the far left as well.)

Did I make the point? The battle had been won, but the hysteria of STRIKE was carrying the entire University of Kansas into the waiting jaws of Reynolds Schultz.

That's Part 1 of this out-of-town journal. Now here's Part 2.

The State University of New York at Buffalo is having a science fiction festival. Lectures and films. Gordon Dickson, Anne McCaffrey, Arthur C. Clarke, me, 2001. They'd been running the film for three or four days when one night last weekend (as I write this), several black female students appeared at the door and sought admittance without tickets. *Everyone* had to have a ticket for the *2001* showings, because there was only limited seating. The young women said they'd left their tickets in the dorm. Bullshit. A dodge. I've done it, you've done it, everyone's done it. But even if it *were* true, so the hell what? Tickets is the name of the game, so either play by the rules or find another game.

The chicks weren't satisfied with that. One of them pushed through past the student at the door, who grabbed her arm. He didn't punch her or kick her or debase her in any way. He merely grabbed a gate-crasher to stop her. The student started screaming. She and her friends went off and hyped a bunch of black students (mostly guys...and we understand what motivates guys, black or white, who leap to the defense of damsels fair...or foul; one of these days we guys will cop to the gonadal urgings that send us off with lance and shield, and all that chivalry bullshit will be revealed for just what it is—the need to look good for the ladies), and they descended on the festival and kidnapped the film.

All of a sudden it wasn't a case of some stupid girl who got stopped trying to pull a hype, it was a deeply significant race relations test of strength, with the honor of black womanhood at stake.

Now understand: the audience was *full* of black and white students. The only difference between them and the gate-crasher is that *they* had tickets, and she didn't. But the BSU Lancelots had swiped the film, all in defense of Bloody Mama. The ransom: a letter of apology, doing a rap on how sorry the festival kids were about having denied a black woman her rights because she was black and accepting a load of ersatz guilt the BSU *unofficially* felt needed to be dumped.

Now the kids putting on the festival were no more bigoted and involved with denial of rights than an elm tree is with urban blight. But they were petrified MGM would sue them for the loss of the film, they were petrified their festival would fall apart, they were petrified they were getting mired in a scam they barely understood and certainly didn't want.

So they wrote the note and got the film back.

The blacks weren't satisfied. The note wasn't "acceptable." So they moved in again, roughed some kids, damaged a speaker, slashed the screen, and copped the film again.

As I write this, the festival is tottering. Films that were scheduled haven't been shown; no one knows which speakers are on, which off. There is an implied position by the BSU that, while they're not in this thing *officially*, if they have to take a public stand, they'll back the blacks...wrong or right.

Now what the fuck is going on around here!?!

This is a war we're fighting, troops. A war against real bigotry and real repression, and what the hell is all this mickeymouse crap in the way of *getting it done?*

There are enough *real* killers out there who are looking for us night and day, waiting for us to open our mouths when we call them by their real names, waiting to run us in front of all the Judge Julius Hoffmans of the world, waiting to use our blood and bones to make their political hay. So why are the personal ax-grinders allowed to throw sludge in the Movement? Why are the idiots and the professional trip-takers and the paranoids and the Molotov psychopaths allowed to fuck it all up for all of us?

There are some very basic core problems involved here, and you know *precisely* what I'm talking about; I don't have to sermonize. There are creeps and pigs who are using the Movement and the fears on both sides of the scene for their own ends. They are the spoilers. And they aren't merely making a buck or getting a little juice for it (though that's bad enough when you're asking people to risk their heads for principles and ethics and morality), they are risking other troops' lives.

In Kansas, Tuesday night the seventh, three people managed to escape apprehension by KU campus cops after they'd set a fire in old Howard Hall, a half-demolished old building in the middle of the campus; on the same night three Molotov cocktails were thrown at an old biology lab building; and the same night a bomb went off, blowing out a window, in the Anchor Savings & Loan (hey, fire bombers, big men, big deals with the revolution in your guts but not your heads, the Anchor isn't the one you wanted...it's the Capitol Federal Savings & Loan that's owned by one of the regents, you assholes!).

Who did it? Certainly not the students of KU who are aware that this particular situation is one in which backing the regents into a hard place where they have to defend their honor and their position won't get the job done. Certainly not the KU faculty or students or chancellor who are all *united* in their stand for free speech...because everyone at KU *knows* that.

Who did it? The coo-coos. The itinerant clowns who see themselves as latter-day Robin Hoods, cavorting around the country screwing up the work being done by the Movement to stop repression, to stop the war on dissent, to stop the stupidities and the brutalities (or at least hold them to a minimum till this country regains its humanity and throws the pigs out on the street). They are the spoilers.

And the worst, the very worst part of it, is that the kids who should have banded together to stop it, to cut away the stupes and get the Movement back on its feet...folded.

In Kansas the kids never tried to stop the out-of-town activists. In Buffalo the film kids bowed to the demands of the black students—who were dead wrong from the start. (Their demands, incidentally, were greater than just a letter of apology. They subsequently demanded that the chick, the liar who started the whole hassle in the first place, be admitted to *all* films free, all year; they demanded the student usher be fired [ironically, the kid was only making a big $1.55 an hour and he didn't *like* being a cop of the aisles]; and, spiraling hysterically into absurdity, they demanded that three blacks be hired to set up a film program relevant to black issues. This last is genuinely ludicrous when one learns that the film society had, all year, been *pleading* with black and Puerto Rican students to come and get into the film operation...and had no takers. Suddenly, with irrelevant and demogogical demands, they turn their own lack of interest into a political and racial question.)

I see in the inability of the KU and Buffalo kids to stop this nonsense the same inactivity and spinelessness of the more than a quarter-million people at Altamont who permitted a handful of Hell's Angel thugs to wreak havoc...and did not move, in love and solidarity, to protect their own.

How does all this relate to tv?

Well, it appeared in a tv column, didn't it?

62: 1 MAY 70

Now, listen, people, this ridiculous paranoia has got to come to an ass-grinding halt! I'm spending more time balming the subterranean fears of you readers than I am causing heartburn among The All-Potent Them.

First was that F-310 thing (the answer to which I now think I have, and in about three weeks I'll do the wrap-up column: I'm waiting for just a few last reports). Then I got a letter from some lady who thought it was evil for the *Freep* to be running advertisements for the record album of Charlie Manson singing his songs, badly. (I wrote her a letter reminding her that Manson might well be guilty but he hadn't even been brought to *trial* yet, and either way the poor bastard was entitled to advertise, which was sorta kinda what free speech was all about.) Now come two communiqués that tie together nicely and lead me to the subject of *verisimilitude* in tv scripts.

Now if you don't know what verisimilitude is, you go right in to your mommy and ask her.

At least I can get back on to tv, thank god.

The first letter is from someone who signs himself or herself "Concerned Viewer." His or her concern is pretty silly, what with all the heavyweight aggravations running amuck, and it all stemmed from my column of two weeks ago in which I was castigating a certain Guerdon Trueblood—a tv scenarist who is coming to represent more and more to me (and to Cleveland Amory, if we are to believe his *TV Guide* column of 28 March) the epitome of no talent in the craft of writing screenplays, the ultimate in hackmanship, the *ne plus ultra* of what Bernard Wolfe calls "creative typing"—and I was castigating him for writing *The Love War*, a half-assed mini-movie that bastardized its science fiction content shamefully. In the column I said: "It always amazes me, the effrontery of writers ignorant of the most basic rules of sf writing, who have no conception of the almost fifty years of writing in the genre, whose temerity permits them to cobble up some pseudo-sf bullshit; *they would never try to do a political teleplay without doing the research; they would never do a historical script without checking out the background...*"

The italics, in red pencil, were Concerned Viewer's. To which statement C.V. responded, somewhat paranoiacally, I feel, "Balls! Harlan baby—the lack of research on *most* tv scripts boggles the mind—and you know it—Where's the old Harlan who said most of his colleagues couldn't write their way out of a pay toilet? Don't sell out. For a small example, most professional 'Western' writers don't know the difference between a Sheriff and a town or Federal Marshal."

Now if any of you except C.V. see a "sellout" in my remarks, I'd appreciate your rationale for same. Let us understand something, troops. The phrase "sellout" is bandied around like a forty-dollar hooker at a fraternity stag party. It's easy to accuse almost *any*body of selling out if they try to see the other guy's side of a problem. So let's define it here and now, for purposes of future accusation in this column: to *sell out* means to desert your ethics or morality or honesty when the pressure is on, when you have something to lose, when the shit comes down; to stick it to your friends or sell out your beliefs for personal gain or aggrandizement; to do or say something opposed to your previous postures or statements because your skin or your rep or your pocketbook is in jeopardy. Now that's what I think of as a sellout. Elia Kazan informing on fellow show-biz folk to HUAC and McCarthy in 1952 so he wouldn't be tagged a Communist and could keep working—at their expense—is a sellout to me. The thirty-six motherfuckers who stood by and watched Kitty Genovese get knifed to death in a New York street without doing anything is by me a sellout. The members of The Lovin' Spoonful who themselves were dopers (and that wasn't *all* of them, remember), who narked on the hangers-on accompanying them on their road trip, to keep themselves from getting busted— that was a sellout. Turncoats and quislings of all stripes (mostly yellow) who desert their buddies when the nightsticks start to fall—those are sellouts.

Now. If you spot even the vaguest hint of a sellout in my remarks about tv writers, fuck you, you're dense.

Which brings me back to C.V.'s hurling of my own words at me. Yes, I once said many of my tv writing colleagues couldn't write their way out of a pay toilet and I don't retract it.... Mr. Trueblood is one such, a man whose abominable scribblings condemn him forever to some isolated potty. But the operative word there is many. I know dozens of extraordinarily talented writers working regularly in the medium—men like Mike Zagor, John Bloch, John D. F. Black, Richard Alan Simmons, Edward Amhalt, Tracy Keenan Wynn, Howard Rodman, Dorothy Fontana, Bob Specht, William Wood, Bobby Kauffman, Lorenzo Semple, and innumerable others—who anguish over their scripts, who take yeoman pride in their craft, who research the ass off their scripts. It is not writers such as these whom C.V. and I revile. It is the hack, the slapdasher, the whore-writer who takes nose from here and foot from there (but somehow always misses adding genitalia) and whomps up a Frankenstein monster of clichés and ridiculosities who gives all tv writers a bad name, and who contributes most of the dreck filling primetime.

(I feel particularly angry about them this week, to be quite frank; for the contract negotiations with the Producers' Guild were presented to a membership vote of the WGAw recently, and once again the hacks and moneygrubbers had their way; rather than leaping on the fortuitousness of this being a "tight money" time to get some artistic control of our work, rather than merely to ask for higher minimum rates on scripts, the venal bastards gave the aye to contract demands that make us more bread but keep us once again in the menial position of hired hands without any say-so about what we can write and how we can write it. This constant reminder that many of my fellow-WGAw members conceive of themselves not as creators or artists but as literary bricklayers or septic tank drainers is a saddening thing, compelling me once again to the pay-toilet conclusion.)

Howsomever, C.V.'s overstatement that *most* tv scripts lack research is simply ignorant of the most obvious facts. Such as:

how much research need one do to write a *Bewitched* segment or *Bonanza* or *The Lucy Show* or *Green Acres* or *Mayberry RFD*? And that's the sort of common-knowledge show that fills up most of the primetime series. So, right off the bat we kill the word most. But further: many shows deal in areas where the form has become so totemized—Westerns and legal-eagle series spring most handily to mind—that the medium has become so much a part of the message it goes unheard. Open on a Dodge City street and without even closing any mental circuits we know approximately the year of the segment, approximately the social and emotional tenor of the people, the level of technology, the limit and range of story plots available to us. The lode has been pretty well mined by this time. So research is ingrained. Only specifics are needed, and *not* knowing the difference between a sheriff and a marshal ain't that debilitating a drawback.

Now let me rush in here with a digression that will become a full examination in a few moments: I'm not defending not knowing the difference between a sheriff and a marshal. What I'm saying is that in this case it isn't pivotally important. Bear the distinction in mind for a second; I'll get back to it. Hopefully.

To tie off the derogatory utterance by C.V. that the "old Harlan Ellison" (a phrase I'll thank you to forget as May 27 and my thirty-sixth birthday lumber toward me) is selling out for some unstated and nefarious reason, is excusing lack of research in some areas while reviling it in others, understand this: frequently a writer may spend *days* getting his facts right, only to have them altered for production or simplification values (?) by the producer, the director, or the network. The writer has to bear the rap for it, though. On *Cimarron Strip* I once saw a segment in which a female character who ran a restaurant served a cowhand "coffee and skittles." I pointed out to the producer that "skittles" is an ancient Welsh bowling game, not a pastry. But they repeated the error in several later segments because someone had gotten it in his head that a skittle was a croissant or something, and it *sounded* correct. Any writer in whose show that error appeared would ever after have to bear the stigma of being a dunderhead. And sometimes, while this is not an excuse but merely an explanation, you simply don't know you've made a mistake, and with the best of intentions, without any conscious attempt to fudge reality, a writer can err. It's only, as they say, human.

Which brings me to the second letter.

Larry D. Farrell, a graduate student in bacteriology at UCLA, who holds "both Bachelor's and Master's degrees in that field and expects to complete [his] Ph.D. in about six months" wrote as follows:

"Recently, I saw the first rerun (and hopefully, it will be the last) of 'The Satan Bug' in NBC's Monday night movie. I counted no less than eighteen technical errors in this pseudo-scientific abortion, ranging from those which would be obvious to the dullest layman to those which would be detected only by someone more knowledgeable. I also vividly remember an episode of the 'Man From U.N.C.L.E.' series in which Percy Rodriguez, playing the role of a 'scientist,' supposedly identified a virus, which had been developed by our old friend Thrush, by a cursory examination of a 'culture' under a light microscope. Bull!!!

"I realize that the studios, for the most part, are not concerned with realism. Okay. But why can't those who strive for realism be certain that their actors correctly pronounce scientific words used in scripts (re: 'Marcus Welby's' pronunciation of titer as t ter rather than t ter). Agreed, these are small points and they affect only a minority of the movie and television audience but they greatly detract from whatever enjoyment one might derive from watching such pseudo-scientific representations. Why don't television and movie studios contact technical advisors before filming such crap?"

While Mr. Farrell's gripes are well founded, in the main they are irrelevant. I'll try to explain why...that is, if you're still bearing in mind *verisimilitude* and what I said about such errors not being pivotally important.

But before I do, he said, throwing in another digression, let me recount a personal experience about how actors fuck up a writer's words, that harks back to Mr. Farrell's complaint about Percy Rodriguez.

I was fairly fresh in town. I got an assignment on the old

Ripcord series, just before it and Ziv Studios went to that Great Trendex Rating in the Sky. I wrote a script about a greater writer, Hemingwayesque by intent, who was dying of cancer and was planning to commit suicide by taking a 'chute drop and not pulling the cord. At one point in the script the writer, Aaron Sparks, is interviewed by a newsman who says to him, "Tell me, Mr. Sparks, how does it feel to be the last of the giants? They're all dead and gone now...Hemingway, Faulkner, Thurber, Camus...you're the last. How does it feel?"

I was whey-faced and innocent. I didn't know what filmed tv was like. The segment was shot and I managed to get invited to see the "dailies" only by chance. But there I sat in a darkened viewing room at Ziv as they ran that scene. To begin with, they'd changed my newsman to a woman (on the theory, I suppose, that there was no sex in the script), and I sat there as she stumbled through her lines like Joe Namath after the KC Chiefs did an adagio on his face. She gibbered through my lines till she got to the part where she said, "They're all dead and gone now... Hemingway, Faulkner, Thurber, CAY-MUSS..." and I came straight up out of that screening-room seat like a man with a Roman candle up his ass.

"No! No no no no, you jerks. It's KAH-MEW not CAY-MUSS! You've got to change that!"

The executive producer, a gentleman named "Babe" Unger, turned around in his seat and demanded to know who the lunatic in the back of the room was, and why he was there, and why he was shouting. The producer, a very good guy named Jon Epstein, sank down in his chair and said it was the writer. "Not *the writer*, I bellowed, "I'm T*H*E W*R*I*T*E*R!" (In those days, before lumps, I was surfeited with the belief that the creator of the story was more than a piece of shit to be flushed away after the words FADE-OUT were written. I've since learned better, but I still bellow for the cap letters and the little gold stars.)

"Toss him out," Unger mumbled.

Jon Epstein promised they would loop out the offensive word because god knows it might cost them a couple of big nickels to have the actress come in to dub that line, but either he forgot or he couldn't, because every time they rerun that idiot show,

some friend calls me from N'walens or N'Yawk and laughs at
my stupidity…don't you know how to pronounce Camus's name,
Ellison, you morphodite?

So don't talk to me about boob actors, Mr. Farrell. I've suffered
far greater indignities at their mouths than you.

But again, it plays right back to *verisimilitude* and the validity
of being minuscule-point accurate. What does it matter to the
great mass of viewers whether titer or Camus is pronounced
correctly, as long as the show makes its point and hits them
where they live?

For you or me, a great deal of difference. For them, none
whatsoever.

Which is why *most* directors and actors (on whom falls
responsibility for accuracy of dialogue and pronunciation) are
little better than illiterates on any subject's minutiae save that
of directing or acting. They can rap for endless boring centuries
about motivation and sense of space and relationship and all that
other semi-psychiatric bullshit, but they haven't the faintest
idea how to pronounce Goethe or of the difference between an
EKG and an EEG. Since no one *really* gives a shit, no one insists
they go to school and learn what it's all about. Again, I said *most*
directors and actors, not *all*. Bob Culp and Leonard Nimoy and
Lee Pogostin and Jim Poe are typical of the exceptions: brilliant,
educated, literate.

And thus, through C.V., Farrell, digressions, and other
sidetrackers, we come to the central thesis of this piece (which,
because I've gone on at such length, will probably have to be
condensed).

It doesn't matter what the truth is, as long as it looks real.

That may seem heresy coming from a dude who keeps
bleating constantly about TRUTH THIS and TRUTH THAT, but
both C.V. and Farrell pick nits from privileged viewpoints. To a
physiologist, the giantism of *Land of the Giants* is laughable. It
ignores the inverse cube law. It can't be. It never could be. But
kids all over this country dig the show, and after a while you
are willing to suspend disbelief to groove with the story. That
is, you *would* be willing to do so were not the plots so fucking
stupid and boring.

What I'm saying is that in many areas of human knowledge as they apply to tv scripts, it isn't necessary to the *enjoyment* of a certain show that every little nut and bolt be screwed down tightly. Mr. Farrell even contradicts himself in one sentence, the second from the end, when he says that (a) these small points affect only a *minority* of the audience but (b) *greatly* detract from their enjoyment. Well, you can't have it both ways, Mr. Farrell. If you're hip enough to realize that there may be only .006 percent of the total viewing audience who can spot such an error as a "culture under a light microscope," then that means 99.994 percent of the audience doesn't know they've been messed over and they don't care. And if they dug the show, and it made its point and it entertained them, then, for all rational purposes, it doesn't matter.

It's a matter of education, on the big end of the funnel. At one end we have the actors, directors, writers—the creative folk. On the other end we have the Silent Majority. If you get all the creators educated, it still doesn't mean anything because the Mass doesn't know.

Where it matters, and this is the ultimate answer, I think, is in expanding the parameters of *general* knowledge of the Mass. For the last thirty years no one but a righteous hermit would have written a Western with the posse riding giraffes, because everybody knows they used horses in the American West of the 1800s. The courtroom farces of the twenties and thirties can't play today because we've had eighteen years of *Perry Mason* and *The Defenders* and *The Law* and *Mr. Jones*, et al. People now know the feel of a court of law (which is why the Chicago Conspiracy guerrilla theater trial is such a shocker). Similarly, even hack writers no longer write sf screenplays in which meteors *whistle* as they zoom past a spaceship. Everyone *knows* there is no sound in a vacuum, and they know space is a near vacuum, so there ain't no way a meteor can whistle. Their knowledge, because of exposure to more facts, has grown.

It seems to me that up to a certain point (and that point is gross, glaring inaccuracy that invalidates an entire story) the only thing that counts is verisimilitude. It should *seem* right. It should *feel* right. It should at least give the *appearance* of truth and accuracy, because the essential point is that tv is *not* reality.

Who really believes there are witches like Samantha? Who really believes people can be as idiotic as those on *The Beverly Hillbillies* or *The Brady Bunch?* By the very act of *watching* such shows, we *accept* the illogic, impossibility, and irrationality of what they're doing. We accept the hype in exchange for some few moments of cheap pleasure.

I quite agree that on serious dramatic shows absolute accuracy should be the goal, but I hardly think we can take too much affront at scientific bungling on *U.N.C.L.E.* or *The Satan Bug.* They are fantasies, friends. They can no more be accurate than relevant.

If you want truth and reality and decimal points in the right places, watch *The 21st Century* or *First Tuesday. Don't look for truth on The High Chaparral or Face the Nation.*

63: 8 MAY 70

In an attempt to keep my house from getting ripped off while I'm out of town, I didn't bother mentioning two weeks ago that, as soon as I returned from my lecture gig, I was going out on the road for eight days, touring with Three Dog Night. But I did, and I'm back, and aside from being an unshakable believer in the grandeur and nobility of that particular rock outfit (and don't none of you effete underground snobs give me no shit; just go and hear them play this week in San Berdoo and you'll be where I am, proselytizing-wise), I have come back with material for a lead article in *Show* magazine that will put you *all* away. Humbly, I urge you to keep watch, maybe three issues from now, for "Dogging It in the Great American Heartland."

All of which brings me to my ramble for the week: the singular place of television in the lives of rock musicians on tour.

I picked up the group in New Orleans. They'd already done

Monroe, Shreveport, and Baton Rouge. I stayed with them through New Orleans, Houston, Austin, Lubbock, Fort Worth, and Dallas. Then I came home and collapsed. Those guys earn every dime they get paid.

In New Orleans, we were billeted at a two-hundred-year-old hostelry called the Bourbon Orleans. Refurbished, classy, big suites with the bedrooms up a winding staircase above the sitting rooms. And the first room I wandered into was Chuck Negron's. The tv was going. Chuck wasn't there. He was out sunning himself beside the pool and his room had been commandeered by a clutch of groupies who work at the Warehouse (New Orleans' answer to the old Fillmore), who needed a place to hang out till the concert. Negron, one of Three Dog Night's lead singers, was *not there.* I mention it again, and I underline it, because you see— *the television set was on.*

I heard that. So what? The little girls were probably watching it? Forget it. The chicks were so spaced, all they were watching was the granulated interior of their own skulls. No, Negron had turned the set on, had left it on when he went out, and it was my first encounter with the syndrome known as Acceptance on a Lower Level.

I got rid of my bags, washed up, and went looking for skinny Danny Hutton. He was in his room, rapping with the roadie (road manager to you), Gary McPike, and the assistant promoter for Concerts West (who'd set up the tour), Joe Gregg. They were talking earnestly about the forthcoming heat problem in the Warehouse, they were listening to the new Van Morrison album...and the tv set was on behind them.

No one was watching it.

Mindlessly, *The Edge of Night* was talking to itself.

We exchanged hellos, dropped a few zingers into each other's libidos, and I went off to meet the other members of the group I hadn't met in Los Angeles.

Floyd Sneed was selecting a crushed-velvet, tie-dye jacket for the gig. And the tv set was going. He wasn't watching it.

Joe Schermie was spraying his room with strawberry sachet to get rid of the scent of incense to get rid of the scent of... anyway, the tv was going and he wasn't watching it.

Cory Wells was answering fan mail. His back was turned to the tv set, and it was going, and he wasn't watching it. Are you beginning to get the idea?

During the eight days of the tour, living in and out of hotels and those ghastly Holiday Inn coffins, the tv sets in *all* the rooms (even mine, after a while) were going *all* the time. Even after the late late news, and the last Brian Donlevy flick, the farm parity reports, and the sermonette, even after the test pattern...the sets still buzzed on mindlessly. Through the night, and all through the day. Usually it was nothing but snow.

For members of my parents' generation, that will seem like a blasphemous act. Those of you too young to recall the Depression, when Mom and Dad went around the house turning off lights behind themselves, moving constantly in shadow, saving on the electric bill, will not understand how uptighting it can be for older folks to walk into a room to find a tv set going. Think of the electricity! But for rock musicians on a hideous hegira from here to there, living in Saran-Wrapped rooms, eating hamburger and whipped potato meals that look like dirty Brillo pads with a side order of soggy tennis ball, it is a necessity.

I'll try and explain. And thereby make a new comment on the uses to which tv can be put.

Road touring is a singularly dehumanizing activity. The days seem to be only six hours long. You get up, in a room that looks precisely like the room in which you woke up yesterday, and the day before. You panic for a moment; where am I? What town is this? Then you call the desk and ask. You have only time to shower, shave, and pack to make the limousine for the airport. Then the flight. Into a new city, into another horrendous Holiday Inn. Same room, different city. Time to kill. Two hours, three hours, four hours. But dead hours. So you go shopping. (The average rock musician's wardrobe expands greatly on tour.) Then a fast meal. Then the concert. Then back to the motel for whatever. We can't talk about that here. Libel, busts, aggravation. You know. Then, finally, you crash. To awaken the next morning and do it all over again.

What kind of man can stand this sort of alienating, brutalizing routine? No man ever born of man and woman. He must become little better than an automaton, a zombie, a myth creature whose existence need only be supported for the hour and twenty minutes during which he is onstage. After that, his bodily functions are slowed, his breathing becomes shallower, his eyes glaze, and he manages to slouch through the time till the next appearance onstage.

It is like being a ghost.

There is no individual reality. A rock musician on tour is like the sudden genie-from-a-jug materialization of acetate sounds pressed on a twelve-inch disc. He appears, full-blown, like Athena from the forehead of Zeus, for six thousand hyped-up aficionados. He does his turn, and leaves the stage to his afterimage, still burning in the minds and pudendas of his audience. But he is still just a human being. And on tour, that isn't nearly enough.

So everyone he meets relates to him as a shadow. To his fellow group members, he is just another unit of a whole in which they, themselves, are units. Relating to them is like relating to one's large colon or big toe. To the roadie or the promoters or the managers, he is a commodity that must be both humored and pampered, yet must be kept in line like an irresponsible child. To the fans he is either something to ogle or something to fuck. They want a piece of him.

Genuinely touching anyone, reaching anyone on a human level, is impossible for a superstar rock musician. They are all treated as totems, and no one really wants to know that god has graveyard mouth in the morning.

So there is loneliness.

So there is boredom.

So there is a heaviness of spirit that leads a man into sublimating his natural tendencies toward gentleness and cleaving to those around him. He uses, and is, in turn, used. For Three Dog Night it takes different forms in each of the members of the group.

Jimmy Greenspoon, the brilliant organist, vanishes behind a veil of existentialist poetry and Delphic utterances. Trivia and compulsive wisecracks save him from having to examine the ugly territory around him.

Michael Allsup, the little guitarist, has gone deep into god. He buys health foods and fresh fruits in markets and contemplates the pure life. It is a strikingly removed existence from that through which he moves.

Joe Schermie spends time with his Fender bass and his music and his brad-studded wristband, grooving on the life of a matinee idol, remembering his youth in the streets, trying to reconcile himself as a whole entity, and caught between laughter and mock violence.

Cory Wells, the second of the three lead singers, literally becomes faceless to the observing mass between performances. He holes up in his suite, he writes to the people who write him, he reaches out from within walls of his own making for a touch of gentleness.

Floyd Sneed, the drummer, vibrates silently to the emanations from the town around him, picking up the feel of prejudice or picking up the feel of wholesomeness, and waits for the nighttime, in which he can flex his muscles and dominate through his music an audience that was single souls to begin with, that is now a unified entity. He trips on power, the power to meld an auditorium into one mass mind.

Chuck Negron exists from moment to moment, living out the time till he can go home to his new bride. He can eat filet or Jack in the Box, because neither is real. It is all dream fantasy, extending back into a childhood past when he sang on the stage of the Apollo in New York, extending on into the future to the time he will no longer be singing. And trapped between the two, like the chambered nautilus—a snail that carries its many-roomed shell on its back—he moves through the days of a tour like a doomed prisoner serving his time.

Danny Hutton, the third of the three lead singers, celebrates his existence by savoring everything around him. The most dreary little Texas town is seen in multifaceted images, never as the reality. Condemned to the ninth circle of Dante's Inferno, Hutton would work behind the varying colors of crimson. His is perhaps the perception most removed from truth, yet closest to maintaining sanity.

And all of them use the tv set.

They turn it on when they enter the motel room, and they

frequently leave it going as they pack their bags out the door on departure. It is sound, it is movement, it is life-of-a-sort. It is companionship, demanding nothing, saying nothing, really. Unlike the vampire hordes of groupies and fans, the tv gives and expects nothing in return, not even attention.

It is acceptance on the lowest possible level.

It is having life going on, during the death hours of inactivity and banal conversations with stoned strangers. It is a piece of moving art, sitting there. It is no more significant than a lava lamp or a landscape painting in a strange house. But it serves a purpose no one who ever helped develop television could have guessed. It soothes and accompanies and staves off loneliness.

Television, the great enervator of the American people, has come full circle. It is now—in the most precise sense of the McLuhanesque idiom—merely a medium. A moving, talking, nonreacting adjunct to the life going on in the room where it stands. No one watches, no one hears, yet it plays on. Phosphor-dot paladin guarding against the shadows of loneliness.

The only question that must be asked is this:

If the music is so ennobling, if the enrichment of the "love-peace-music" trinity is so messianic, why do the very creators of that holiness need the debased and mindless movement on a tv screen to help them support their lives?

Perhaps the answer, cryptically, lies in the fact that the favorite tv show of Three Dog Night is...*Sesame Street*.

64: 15 MAY 70

Dear Mom:

How are things in Miami Beach? The weather here has been balmy and pleasant. The news has been dark and destructive. But then, I guess you get the same news in Florida that we get here.

You know, it occurred to me the other day, Mom, that you

have always been very groovy about my writing for the *Free Press*. Since my background—Midwest Ohio, middle class, et cetera—is the same as yours, I *know* you have got to have some trepidations about this column and where it appears, yet you've never said a word. I send you the paper each week and you sometimes mention it, but you never really venture an opinion. Perhaps it's because we got it understood between us many years ago that I'd live my life my way and you'd live yours your way, and we don't bug each other about what each of us does, but I sorta *know* that your finding my words every week, sandwiched in between ads to immortalize the penis and Mao Tse-tung posters for sale, has got to give you pause.

So I thought, this week, I'd just drop you a note to explain why it is that I write a television column for such an unsettling (from your position) newspaper.

First of all, I suggest you read *all* of last week's *Freep*. Not just my words, but all of it. The Kent State slaughter, the Ohio State debacle, the draft board illegality item, all of it. You won't find much of that stuff in your Miami Beach newspapers, Mom, and I know sure as hell you won't find it in the *Los Angeles Times*. And where you get most of your information, from the 6:00 news, you'll find only vibrations of what is *going down*. Uh... going down, Mom, means *happening*.

Vibrations that are as untrustworthy as the refracted pain just before a coronary. It tells you there is trouble in the system, but not precisely where, nor just how bad.

So let me hip you, Momma, that the trouble is bad. Very bad. Worse than the alienating aspects of the 6:00 news and its Spiro-inspired insistence on impartiality can possibly tell you. I watched the news clips from Kent State and I saw the kids fleeing in horror from the guns of kids no older than themselves. It was a terrible personification of the two sides of *today's* American morality, Mom. Kids killing kids. But the ones who pulled the triggers—with what I suspect is the same emotional fracture to be found in the Jack Armstrongs who slaughtered at My Lai— were puppet-mastered by fat old men who lived elsewhere. I saw an interview soon after the murder of those four students, with the brigadier general who had ramrodded the National Guard outfit that went into Kent. He was a liar, Mother. It didn't take any particular political position to see that the man was a weak, frightened buck passer, petrified that he was going to be brought up on charges of incompetence and dereliction of duty. He lied, Mom; he sat there and his chin quivered and he evaded and he mumbled phrases to offscreen voices. "Snipers on the rooftops," he mumbled. But the highway patrol reports that have been published since the tragedy—which have not been exploited on tv for some obscure reason—insist that the cops on the rooftops who had a full view of the scene saw no snipers. "My boys may have acted hastily" was the nearest thing to an admission of wrongdoing the good general mumbled, Ma. Then he went into a long mumble about how they were only boys, were scared, weren't trained in combat tactics. He did go on, Mom. And no one seems to be horrified that they're offering as an excuse for the murder of four innocent kids and the wounding of god knows how many others, that untrained, trigger-happy, inept kids were sent in to a *college campus* (not Cambodia, not Vietnam, not Laos, not West Berlin, a *college campus* that belongs, at least in large part, to the students who were butchered) with *loaded* weapons.

Even Spiro did a tv interview with David Frost, in which he excused it all with that rationale.

So if you wonder why I write for the *Free Press*, Mom, it is because I know that the tv you are watching every night allows these obfuscations to obtain some weight. It allows the clouding of horribly simple incidents, and it permits you and the other members of the Silent Majority to dodge the responsibilities of joining with youth to end this madness before the country kills itself.

You see, Mom, I write the column because the cop-out that is built into the apathetic life for you and all the other good, uncommitted folks out there is one that wears ever thinner by the day. The explanations grow less reasonable, the smiles grow more strained, the faces of Mitchell and Nixon and Spiro and that general tell us they are lying, even as you try to believe them. Because if you can believe them, Mom, it will mean you won't have to face the fact that time has caught up with us. That

America today is being intravenously fed on the blood of its own children. I write the column so your generation will just *once* simply ask the question: who is the enemy?

Because it seems inconceivable to me, knowing what a loving, reasonable person you are—as must be all those others out there—that you could come up with the answer: *the children*.

They're killing our kids, Mom.

They're slaughtering them at home and abroad. No longer can long hair or liberal lifestyle be offered up as reasons for this kind of charnel-house behavior. No longer can the fat old men in their eyries far away be permitted to send kids to kill kids, with moron alibis as shabby afterthoughts, and tv announcements that support of Nixon's war policies are running two to one against.

Because you see, Mom, for all the wonder tv offers, it cannot catch the tenor of the times. For all the computer analyses of the way voting will go in an election, television cannot sniff out and predict the winds of change that sweep across our land.

Walter Cronkite and Howard K. Smith won't tell you this, Mom, but the country is finally getting unified. It's tragic that it took the deaths of those four kids to do it, but it's happening.

So I'm writing this column every week to tell you that truth, Mother. To tell you that I received sixty letters last week from all over the country, saying the column helps, that lone people pretending to be scuttlefish are actually in accord with the hopes and dreams of the kids at Kent, that those people need to look somewhere for words of hope that will lift them out of their doomsday depressions.

Because you see, after the Kent State horror, and the four-hundred-some colleges that went on strike, and the complete victory that got that scumbag Fascist egg-sucker Reagan to shut down the schools in California (and even his cue card that said: NOW WEEP, RONNIE didn't fool any of us), people wandered around simply wanting to hide. Simply wanting to turn off. Simply wanting to throw in the towel. Simply wanting to cry and say fuck them, fuck them all, let them die, every last sonofabitch of them! And that's so wrong, Mom, so terribly wrong, that I have to write to you and tell you that it's finally happening... that the country is pulling together.

Not the way Nixon wanted it. Not the way Spiro keeps demanding it— behind our Leaders. But in the right way, the best way, the way born out of troubles so great and evils so omnipresent that room for political positions no longer exists.

In New York, Mom, people are standing on street corners and arguing, trying to reason it out. In Austin, the demonstrators are putting the girls three-deep in the front ranks, hoping the National Guard won't willingly shoot down females. In Ohio, four thousand people turned out for the funeral of one of those Kent kids. And they're massing in Washington today. With Senators and Congressmen beside the longhaired kids. And there will be more marches and more demonstrations, and more action.

Because Nixon went too far this time, Mom. He defied not just the "vocal minority," but *all* the people. Drunk with his importance he said to hell with the whims of the people, and he acted like a petty tyrant. And the kids felt the tremors first, and they acted. And already frightened, the Establishment acted, and killed. And those four didn't die in vain, Mom, because for each one of them that sank beneath a bullet, ten thousand uncommitted swelled the ranks of the people who speak for humanity, not property rights.

Had tv the guts, Mom...did it but acknowledge its obligation... it would tell you that. It would tell you that the time is now for all of you who have sat back and hoped the storm would pass to join us. To come with us into danger and possible death...to bring this country back to a position of sanity.

But tv won't, so I do. I tell you of the letters and the phone calls, and the frustration of the people, and the need for unity. I tell you we can no longer call each other rotten names, and click our tongues with disapproval. We have to cling together, Mom, or Nixon and his death legions will kill us all, working from the left straight across.

That's why I write this column, Mom.

So take care of yourself, and a happy Mother's Day.

Your loving son,

Harlan.

65: 22 MAY 70

In the week following the most divisive horrors in recent American history—Kent State murders, Cambodian quagmiring, New York construction workers amucking, Georgia blacks slaughtered—*TV Guide* comes forth with the most consummately hateful cover imaginable. As though intent on taunting the tenor of the now vocal majority, that singularly Establishment-oriented handbook proffers the Right-Wing Dart Board: a painting of Spiro Agnew by Norman Rockwell.

It is impossible to talk about the many things on the agenda—the wrap-up of the F-310 business (use Texaco Lead-Free), the *60 Minutes* segment on the Bill of Rights, a Susskind spectacular featuring a dozen ex-GIs who opted for sanity over lunacy by exiling themselves to Canada, the truth about how our boys in Vietnam booed Bob Hope when he toured espousing his rally 'round the flag shtick—because the eyes cannot leave the news shows, the mind cannot escape the volcanic temblors threatening to split this country, the emotions cannot wrench free of the overriding misery and sadness of hopeless frustration to which we have been consigned.

How can I dote on some silly situation comedy and its banality when my mail brings me letters like these?

"Dear Mr. Ellison:

"I have never before felt the urge to write my thanks to an author but your book, 'The Glass Teat,' deserves thanks not only from me, a thirty-five-year-old establishment cat, but from the whole range of American conditions …I believe that in the quiet, alone hours, even those people who are embarrassed by the smell of their own bowel movements know that what you say is true. Reality, like douche powder, must be sold…As shitty as it makes my mouth feel, I must say, 'You're a good man…'"

Signed, Harold Conrad, Portsmouth, Virginia.

And, from the other side, this one:

(Included with this letter is a news story datelined Kent, Ohio, from *The New York Times* Service, bearing the headline: Should Have Kept Agitators Out of Kent, Residents Say. Just a few excerpts from the article, which my correspondent has pencil-annotated as "The Common Man: Part III."

("It's a shame it had to take killing to do it, but all those kids were someplace they shouldn't have been," said Dick Richards, a florist lunching at the weekly meeting of the Lions Club...there is little disagreement among the townsfolk of Kent. It's too bad, they say, but the National Guardsmen were right—the students shouldn't have been there. There's a minority that cause trouble, and outside agitators that shouldn't be let in. And the troublemakers have long hair, use bad language, go barefoot, and even destroy property, and they had to be stopped.

("I make my living in Kent," said Don Ruble, who operates laundry machines in dormitories. "But I wouldn't send another son there." The teachers fill them full of wrong ideas, he said, and they come home rejecting the adults and their values. His eldest son went to Kent and now teaches retarded children in Cleveland. "I respect him for that," but the two have grown so apart in thinking that "I don't even want to see him."

("My own gas station man said they should have shot 100 of them," said Tom Bohlander, who sells Fiat cars and Honda bikes near the campus.... "They've got to keep order some way. One thing they ought to do is chase them all out if they don't get their hair cut and cleaned up," said Harry Miller, a 58-year-old house painter. At Water and Main Streets, the center of Kent, five men talked about the shooting. "If I would have been shooting, I'd be shooting more than they did," one said.

("If I would have had townspeople with guns out and on their roofs to protect their property, you would have had a lot more than four dead kids," Mr. Richards said at the Lions Club meeting.

("The people I talk to say it's a terrible, terrible shame they had to be killed, but how long are we going to put up with these punk kids?" said Dale Miller, who works at a bank.)

"Dear Harlan:

"Quite literally, these quotes scare the shit out of me. The rage, the fear, the willingness of people to kill merely because someone rejects their values; one sits stunned and says, 'How? How could people *be* like that?' And the sad part of a...book like 'The Glass Teat' is that the people quoted here, the people who really *need* to read it will never see it. You may not convert any of the Silent Majority of Common Men but I'd like you to know that at a time when events were conspiring to make some of us feel that there was just no hope, no use in going on in a nation where Cambodia and Kent and New York construction workers can occur, that your book was dug, that it gave at least a ray of hope that we *do* have a spokesman who may be heard and that as long as one voice remains unsilenced there is a chance. So tonight we'll go on the demonstration no matter how futile it may seem and at the very least we'll have the satisfaction of knowing that our countries did not go to Hell unlamented. Thanks for your book, Harlan. We needed it."

Signed, Mike Glicksohn, Ottawa, Ontario.

And, oh god, the other letters. The one from the sixty-year-old man in Moline: terrified, concerned, lost, asking for personal words beyond the book or the column, suggesting what he can do. The letter from the GI in Vietnam that ended with inarticulate grief for not only any strangers he may have killed while firing into a village, but for those four kids at Kent State. A letter of shame and remorse and hopelessness at his own inability to flee the battlefield and suffer the prison to which they would certainly send him. The letters, the many letters, so many voices from both sides...

And *TV Guide* gives us Spiro, by Norman. God, how can such blindness, such terrible cruelty exist?

Mr. Conrad says I am a good man, and Mike Glicksohn says I am a spokesman for him and the others who demonstrated. No. No!

I can't be trusted, either. None of us can. Over thirty isn't the gauge. Pollution of the morals is. Don't trust me...trust only yourselves. I didn't die at Kent State...you did. Your brothers and your sisters. Shot down by the editors of *TV Guide* and the prime rib and pork diners at the Lions Club, and Spiro, of course, and all of us who got past your age and learned nothing. Our morals and our ethics have been hopelessly polluted by decades of killing and lying and rationalizing and seeking vindication in the wholly untrustworthy approbation of that killer animal, "the majority."

How can people be like that, Mike Glicksohn? I'll tell you. McLuhan was right. We've watched the deaths of thousands on the glass teat for almost twenty years, and now we are systemically ready to witness the deaths of tens of thousands, of millions, if necessary. They are no longer human beings going to meet their various Makers with blind eyes staring at dreams that will never be. They are statistics.

"280 Viet Cong were killed in the human wave at Bunker City, Cambodia. One American dead."

Bullshit! Do you believe that!?! Every day the tv news dons its Howard K. Smith serious face and tells us nine million VC were planted, and three Americans stubbed their toes. Yet at week's end, the legitimate (?) totals are released, and last week, a week in which the daily newsvideo reports totaled 13 American deaths, the final tally was 168, highest in four months. They are lying to us. Even as I lie to you. I lie, and they lie, because we are weak, and we have been lying so long we don't know what it means to be honest and upfront.

So don't trust us, any of us. None of us who live good and dine at the Lions Club and say tsk-tsk what a terrible shame, and stuff more prime rib in our mouths.

Trust only yourselves.

Work to change it, if you can. But it may even be too late by years for that.

If we were truly to work for something, we should work to have all guns banned in this country. Take the guns and the gas from the cops. Turn them out on foot with batons if necessary, but let them work in the community the way London bobbies work, sans firearms. *Then* they would have to deal with the kids vis-à-vis, face to face, and maybe, just maybe, they would have to start acting like human beings, not killing automatons.

Talk about tv? Maybe next week. But this week my thoughts—and yours, for god's sake—are on the other choices.

Choices like the bomb, like the fire, like the swift knife in the dark.

They are terrible choices, because they are no choices at all. They are hideous extremities to which we are being pushed.

TV this week? No...my thoughts are somewhere else. They are with small groups of guerrilla fighters in Ohio and Kansas and Georgia, ex-students who have renounced their names, their homes, all ties. Who, packing *plastique* in haversacks, roam the countryside blowing up the Lions clubs, shooting down Ohioans like Dick Richards and Don Ruble and Tom Bohlander and Harry Miller and Dale Miller where they stand on the corner of Water and Main, discussing how they will protect their fucking property. My thoughts are of an America seeded with killer-skirmishers who have been driven mad as mudflies by the death clutch on outdated values and phony patriotism of their parents, the government, and vested interests.

Four died in Kent and the world mourned. That is because we have been so morally polluted by McLuhanesque imagery that it takes a new *kind* of death to move us. Six blacks were gunned down in the streets of Augusta, Georgia, just a few days later, and no one mourns. But we mourn those four white middle-class kids. That is the final extreme to which we have been brought by lies and unilateral brutality and the holy informant, God-Mother tv. We have become a nation melded into one Roman arena surfeiting on various kinds of murder. Kill blacks and we yawn...we've seen that...lions and Christians are old stuff...but move on to a fresh thrill...kill the white middle class ...and we sparkle.

How can people be like that, Mike? If a man sits and sips his beer placidly at the sight of thousands writhing in the love grip of jellied gasoline, how can he be terribly concerned about four more?

And you expect truth from them? You expect to be able to reach them? Dear god, I hope so. I hope all of you who have cut your hair and are moving through the communities speaking softly, all of you know what you're up against. And from even those of us who lie and know we lie, there is a desperate hope that you can penetrate to us; because if you don't, the next time we'll see you, you'll be part of some smash&grab kill force moving through the Great American Heartland, and you'll have been reduced to the level of bestiality on which the Lions Club diners exist.

Television comment? Not hardly. These are days of blood and sorrow. If only there were some light.

66: 29 MAY 70

Repression, like politics, makes strange bedfellows. Consider CBS. A monolith whose sins against public sensibilities crawl the trough from silencing the Smothers Brothers to hiring Edward "Ned" Hamlin as News Coordinator of Broadcast Research "in a position in which he will have ready access to the CBS News film library, including outtakes." (Mr. Hamlin was, until recently, an employee of the CIA since 1965, climbing high enough in the ranks to direct research projects on Latin America, and—for the last year—was on assignment from the CIA's Office of National Estimates to the National Security Council. No conclusions are to be drawn from this tiny item secreted at the bottom of a column in *Variety*, of course. The inferences, however, are painfully, ominously obvious.)

How strange it is, then, to find ourselves allied with CBS in the battle of the mouth gag. For since Spiro the Mad began his rabid frothings against anti-Administration comment on the networks, the only one of the three major nets to not only refuse to bow in the direction of the White Pentagon, but also to *step up* its criticism of Nixon and his saber-rattlers, has been CBS.

And this past week Americans were treated to a display of battling-back-at-the-bully that leads me to some effusive praise of an otherwise chicken-shit organization. Last week, CBS defied the Pentagon. And they won. And it was a nice thing to see.

For those of you who may have missed the brouhaha, I'll fill in the details.

On November 3, 1969, CBS News aired a film clip narrated by correspondent Don Webster, in which a South Vietnamese soldier brutally stabbed a wounded, captured Viet Cong prisoner. It didn't make much of a splash, Silent Majority-wise...just one more fish-eyed gook type sliced open...fuck'm. But the Pentagon went straight up the wall, did a fingernail hang and promptly fielded an accusing finger: CBS was guilty of falsifying the film.

Spiro-primed, the Pentagon (drunk with a seemingly unstoppable inertia which, had it a voice, would say if you can't store nerve gas in Oregon, send it to Alaska...tell the American people the Minutemen missiles won't be fielded till late in July, and plant them in April...and break your ass to get that damnable Cooper-Church bill subverted and weakened and defanged and clobbered and killed) leaked to such soul-purchased columnists as Jack Anderson and Richard Wilson that the CBS news department had (a) faked horror scenes from Vietnam on at least three occasions, (b) planned a "staged invasion" of Haiti so they could film it as a special, (c) "staged incidents of police brutality" during the 1968 Democratic Convention, and (d) arranged to film an illegal pot party in Chicago. But more than these charges, the White House and the Pentagon were pissed off at CBS because, unlike ABC and NBC, they have refused to cooperate with witch-hunting, whitewashing Army investigators in revealing their news sources. The White House doesn't like that. It smacks of freedom of the press; and as one of those "secret" White House memos (that *always* seem to get leaked, in the style of hypocrisy pioneered by American Presidents as far back as Rutherford B. Hayes, but brought to its fullest flower by LBJ and Nixuleh... mickeymouse politics, cynicism-weaned younger folk call it) puts it: CBS shouldn't be allowed to use "freedom of the press" to get away with "fraud by the press."

Well, hell, friends. On Thursday night, May 21, on *The CBS Evening News with Walter Cronkite*, the youth protest and antiwar and up-against-the-wall-with-Spiro factions all climbed into the same big king-size bed with CBS for a mutual gang bang using the Pentagon as trollop. Whooooopee!

The Pentagon charged the film shown was not of American helicopters, they were Australian. Or if they were Yankee, they were Medevacs. They charged the film was not of a fire fight, it was a South Vietnamese grenade practice maneuver. And they charged the VC was already dead. (And since we saw that South Vietnamese soldier pull out the knife and jam it in again, this must mean mutilation of bodies is okay. But then, after all, those Orientals "think differently" and who are we to condemn their inscrutable manner? We are only to intrude in their inscrutable wars, apparently.)

CBS refuted every point. Handily. The choppers were quite clearly attached to the 187th Assault Helicopter Squadron based out of Tay Ninh. They proved it wasn't a training maneuver by pinpointing the date and location of the filming—October 1969, near the village of Bau Me, four miles north of the district town of Trang Bang in Hau Nguia Province. And CBS fielded the accusation that there were no American advisers standing by and watching the atrocity by rerunning the film clip, stop-action, see that man there? Well, he's wearing a patch on his right shoulder of the U.S. First Air Cavalry Division.

And when it got right down to the core of the presentation, CBS flipped the Pentagon its own screaming bird by not only naming the soldier, but his rank, serial number, and…an on-the-spot interview with the slob in which he admitted having done it. He spoke with some pride.

His name is Nguyen Van Mot, a sergeant first class, HQ Company, Group 21, South Vietnamese Regional Forces, serial number 178-704. As CBS put it, through the mouth of the much-maligned Webster, who was narrating: "Not only is Sergeant Mot still on duty, but he was named soldier of the year for 1969 for all regional forces in three corps."

It figures.

And when Webster questioned a first lieutenant who has been with Mot's unit since February, CBS viewers were treated to the following delicious interchange:

WEBSTER: What kind of a soldier is Sergeant Mot?

FIRST LIEUTENANT RICHARD SHOWALTER: Sergeant Mot typifies, I think, the hard-nosed, hard-core…what you might say, Vietnamese soldier. If I had a company of Sergeant Mots, I think everybody could go home over here in...within the next year...without a doubt.

WEBSTER: Among his own troops he has a reputation of being very tough...a killer. Is he really tough?

SHOWALTER: Ah, definitely so. Ah, if he finds a prisoner or anything in a bunker or anything...ah, if we can get some firsthand information from him, Sergeant Mot's the man to find him and the man to get the information.

WEBSTER: What does Sergeant Mot do when you do take a prisoner?

SHOWALTER: Well, Sergeant Mot, as you know, is a short, kind of a husky character in comparison to his Vietnamese counterparts and ah, he is forceful to a degree, but this is necessary since the information we can gain out here firsthand is most important to us, and ah...he...ah...can definitely get his point across to the prisoner.

Tasty, eh? To be sure, Sergeant Mot can get his point across; but it's doubtful how much information he can get from prisoners (unless he receives spirit messages), because CBS then ran a bit of the film they'd excerpted...the prisoner shortly after Sergeant Mot had left the scene: the poor sonof abitch had been sliced open and gutted, from neck to sternum.

Well, why go on. The Pentagon got caught with its mouth gag showing. It tried to intimidate one of the three largest disseminators of mass information in America, and it didn't pull off the job. CBS fought back and whipped the piss out of the Secret Masters of the Universe.

All of which goes to make two very obvious points.

The first is that for anyone who cares to examine what is coming down *de facto*, it is apparent that all of Spiro's protestations notwithstanding, the Administration is trying (and probably succeeding more often than we know) to regulate the news, exercise police state repression, and keep the mindless mass convinced everyone is lying save them.

The second, and more encompassing, is that the forces being brought to bear on us to keep us in line will not stop with far lefters, with militants, with Black Panthers, with hippies, with dissidents, or even liberals. Those forces will continue sweeping straight across the boundaries and begin trying to silence the moderates, the middle-of-the-roaders, the conservatives, and finally be left with none but the most slavishly devoted of the right-wing lunatics.

This kind of hammering of our rights into a shape more acceptable to a President who throws a fit of pique when someone catches him with his paws in the cookie jar...this kind of censorship and flummery...this kind of brutalizing intimidation cannot be allowed to continue. It is to be hoped that CBS's example will serve to toughen the moral fiber of its two rivals, and the battle won will be taken as a signal to the more humane elements in our government that now, *right now,* this moment, is the time to bring to an ass-grinding halt the onrush of totalitarianism being used to steamroller freedom in this country. Greased by the military-industrial whatever, this forward plunge of lunacy and intimidation can end only with all power in the hands of a cabal whose members will all wear the faces of Spiro Nixon and sport screaming eagles on their epaulets.

Well done, CBS, you otherwise crummy bastards.

67: 19 JUNE 70

The letters to remember are *V* and *S, T* and *V.* The last two you may recognize; they stand for Terrible Viewing. To change their meaning, we must add the first two letters, whose meaning is Viewer Sponsored. Put them all together they spell VSTV, which is hardly mother, but then it isn't garbage television either. But before we get to the good guys, there are villains to make their appearance. Here comes the first one.

How's this for a smash evening lineup on a Los Angeles channel:

6:00 - Monday night—Parent Education, Preschool

7:00 - Monday night—Careers in city and state government
7:30 - Monday night—Opportunities in the military service
8:00 - Wednesday night—Adult Education, Gerontology
8:30 - Wednesday night—Showcase Theater (Student
　　productions from local colleges and universities)

(And *here's* a heavyweight guaranteed to keep you rooted in front of your set):

7:00 Friday night—What's new at the Public Library?

But don't think these are only the high points of the schedule. There are others, equally as mind-boggling and scintillant. And lest you think I'm making this up, this brilliant viewing fare (perhaps as an ideal week's tv for inmates of a Beverly Boulevard convalescent home), let me hip you that what I've noted above is the parital content of a proposed weekly schedule of programs for Channel 58...should the Los Angeles Unified School District be awarded the license to operate 58...*the last unused channel in a major American city.*

That ghastly feeling you have in the pit of your stomach is nausea. You may recall it from the most recent Spiro Agnew film clip.

Yes, there is one remaining license to be granted for a television outlet in Los Angeles. Fifty-eight is up for grabs, and one of the three contenders for ownership is the Board of Education. The chains you hear rattling in the background are a ghoulie named Reagan and a ghostie named Rafferty.

But don't panic, the B of E isn't the only outfit making a bid for that license. There are two alternate choices.

The first is the cadre at KCET, Channel 28, the ones who employ the good offices of National Educational Television, that NET all you wondrous highbrows are constantly writing me to promote. Well, they're good folks at 28 (hell, I went and auctioned for them last week, didn't I?), but I fear they have trouble even keeping KCET on the air. And I don't see much sense in giving *two* television outlets in the same city to a group whose thirty-five-member board of directors represent the moneyed classes heavily but which do not represent Blacks, Chicanos, Orientals: in short, any ethnic or racial minorities or groups of low socioeconomic standing. (To be specific, a study of KCET's board membership, by Professor Harry M. Scoble of UCLA, turned up a number of interesting aspects of interlocking proprietorship, not the least of which is that something over 53 per cent of the board membership is made up of bankers, business corporation executives and directors, members of the commercial media, and dudes involved inextricably with real estate, advertising, investments, and random CPAing. "Furthermore," as Professor Scoble summarizes one section of the survey, "there is *no* known producer of documentaries, *no* producer, *no* director, *no* critic [academic or otherwise], and *no* academic who...has concentrated upon the socializing effects of the mass media.")

None of the above, of course, is intended to imply that the ladies and gentlemen who make up KCET's board of directors are anything but good guys. What it *does* speak to, however, is a statistic that showed up in a fairly recent survey done by the University of North Carolina (July 1969) titled *Three California Television Stations: A Survey of Public Affairs and Entertainment Content*. The survey included programming on KCET and two commercial channels and provides us with a startling, rather dismaying fact about 28's output. That fact—which ties in with the makeup of KCET's board of directors, I feel—is that existing educational television facilities provide approximately the same volume of "controversial public affairs programming" during prime- time as is provided by those venal rascals on the commercial channels. About 1 percent of its schedule. (Maybe it's up to 5 percent since 1969. Big deal.)

It isn't NET that's bidding for 58, it's KCET. And while they are good guys and do the best they can, they simply don't strike me as potent enough to fill the abyss created by the lack of controversial programming in Los Angeles. We have this peachykeen situation here in L.A. All the right-wing-oriented stations with their Tom Reddins and George Putnams—bush-league Agnews so blind to the realities of changing times that they persist in inflaming the kickers and hardhats with paranoid nightmares—and KCET, doing as well as it can and occasionally delighting us with goodies like *The Andersonville Trial*, Johnny Cash's *Trail of Tears, Hospital, The Forsyte Saga*, and *Sesame Street*, but having a hard time keeping people awake the rest of the time, and still not reaching the scuttlefish who opt for *The Brady Bunch* or *Nanny and the Professor*. And none of the channels presenting really unpopular or controversial viewpoints.

And here we are with the last chance up for grabs. Fifty-eight will be awarded to one of three bidders at FCC hearings beginning very soon (maybe as early as mid-July). The choices are slim. First, the Board of Education. As dull a buncha stiffs as ever scraped chalk down a blackboard. Second, KCET, well-intentioned but timid about sticking out its neck in a witch-hunt time when Agnew is just *looking* for scapegoats, and unable to handle its own channel without recourse to an annual auction of motel art and Beverly Hills gold-leaf dreck.

And third…

VSTV.

(I thought he'd *never* get around to it!)

It was necessary to file my objections to the two most apparent contenders, to validate my reasons for urging you to support VSTV, the Viewer Sponsored Television Foundation; because while VSTV isn't the second coming *either*, it is quite clearly the best choice of the three, maybe the best bet we've had in some time for creative, *relevant* social programming, and (as usual, dammit) the underdog.

VSTV is the brainchild of Clayton Stouffer, whose life since 1967, when he formed VSTV as a nonprofit corporation whose intent it is to operate UHF Channel 58, has been something less than fraught with riches. Stouffer's handout on the intents of VSTV reads, in part, as follows: "The Foundation proposes to operate a UHF television station that: (i) presents primarily in-depth public affairs programming that goes beyond 'safe' and popular points of view and (ii) emphasizes close cooperation between socially concerned media professionals, community activists and the viewing public."

I think that says it.

There is much more to be said about VSTV, of course, and if

you need to know such salient facts (such as, for instance, that a VSTV requirement for its own board of directors is that at least two-thirds of its members be of the type Professor Scoble said were missing from KCET's board, paragraph 14, above), drop a line to Viewer Sponsored Television, 1539 Westwood Boulevard, Los Angeles 90024, and they'll send you a little brochure that gives you all the hype you'll need to reassure yourself that we are not slipping into power an alternative batch of scoundrels.

But right now, what they need is something more vital than merely good wishes and fine words. First, they need office help desperately. The FCC hearings are coming up shortly and VSTV has to raise three hundred and fifty-one thousand dollars—that's $351,000—almost immediately, so they need people who can type and file and follow up phone solicitations, and help with the mailings...stamping, sticking, stuffing, and sorting. They also need on-campus types to help with leafleting. If VSTV can get students to sign pledges of $12 or more, it will stand in good stead with the FCC. They won't need the actual bread at sign-up time, just verification that the money is *there*.

They also need money, naturally.

VSTV (in an amazing display of playing the Establishment's game better than was intended for underdogs) managed to float a Public Loan (Debenture Sales) deal, and with $100 bonds subscribed by viewers, the money can be amassed in a relatively short time, if response is good.

Pledges, as noted above, also swing. For residents of the barrio and ghetto, pledges are $2.50. For students and the elderly, $12. And for the rest of us well-to-do white motherfuckers it's $25.

This is literally "People's Capitalism," because it means there will be no funding from uptight or special-interest foundations or groups. No pressures from the forces that castrate all *other* tv channel programming. It means we will for the first time control one of the outlets of the mass media.

It has got to be one of the nobler endeavors offered us recently.

So: money, first. And office help. (Some of you lovely ladies who answered my secretarial ad a couple of weeks ago, if you're still unattached, why not devote an hour or two a week to helping them out at the office?)

This is a crusade we can win. KCET more than likely won't get
the nod from the FCC. It, too, is leery about giving two outlets
in the same city to one corporation. But the Board of Education
has that money to back up its bid, and if you don't want to spend
Friday nights finding out what's new at the public library, or
Monday nights being informed of the dandy opportunities in
the military, I strongly urge you to get off your rusty bottoms
and help poor old Clayton Stouffer get the job done.

After all, *anything* is a viable alternative to the *Lawrence Welk
Show*.

68: 26 JUNE 70

This week I would talk of bacon.
The pigs.
The poe-lease.
D'fuzz, dat is.
Now when I was a lad in Painesville, Ohio, many moons ago,
before the white man came to my land and sprayed it evenly
with a film of bowling alleys, motels, used-car lots, Tastee-Freez
huts, cost-plus Nipponese import shops, and Stuckey Pecan
Praline Emporiums, I believed policemen were my friends. I
read *Dick Tracy* and clipped his Crimestopper Clues and pasted
them in a scrapbook. I listened to *The FBI in Peace and War*
and was even able to sing many stanzas of the L-A-V-A theme
song. "Crime does not pay!" I could be heard muttering at odd
moments when I wasn't muttering, "The weed of crime bears
bitter fruit." I was a law-abiding, violence-eschewing child of
six or seven, and I remember a cop once let me wear his cap and
gave me a raspberry sherbet cone. (He also had his hand on my
thigh, but I tend to put *that* kind of thought out of my mind.)

The first worm-nibble I remember at the bright apple of my
trust in law officers was when I was eight years old. I had this
thing for the comic character pins to be found in boxes of Kellogg's

Pep and, getting hip rather quickly that, with duplications and all, one could wind up resembling Kate Smith if one was to eat all the Pep it took to collect a full set of eighty-six pins (the incidence of duplicates of Felix the Cat was disheartening), I took to the unlawful pursuit of ripping up the boxes in the A & P and ripping off the comic character contents. It was my first encounter with the specifics of trashing; it was also my first encounter with the criminal life.

Such depredations against what Tom Reddin calls *lawn-order* could not long go unpunished.

I was busted and taken to the Painesville pokey, where (with flawless Spockian logic) the cossack-in-charge ran me through a chamber of horrors guaranteed to traumatize a septuagenarian, much less an eight-year-old: I was hustled through the drunk tank and the corridors of cells, staring at local thugs and unfortunates who had been caged up for unnameable offenses, who leered and jeered and beckoned and puked in my direction. Well, sir, may I tell your face that when I got out of there I was a candidate for a nursery school run by Rimbaud and de Sade. And though I am now aware of the misguided philosophy behind the cop's actions—scare the little snotnose and he'll be a law-abiding citizen from this point on—it was my very first understanding of the limited humanity of many minions of the law.

I say *many*, rather than *all*, because I've known a few very decent peace officers whose intent and activities were based on respect of the people they served and a sense of themselves as human beings. Steve McQueen, who has had many contretemps with cops, told me once that it was very easy to be anti-cop, and it took a special concentration to view them as merely servants of the society. Well, I wouldn't quibble with that. As I've noted in columns previously, a cop is merely a postman or a dogcatcher, a guy in uniform who exists out on the skin edge of the culture, reflecting physically what the emotional needs of his employers (the people) seem to be. If cops are brutal and unfeeling and panicky and trigger-happy, it's because the hardhats and scuttlefish are the same, but don't have the guts or badges to whip some kid's head with a baton. None of which, naturally, excuses the *individual* cop when he dances a storm trooper pavane.

And, all Agnewesque obfuscations aside, it becomes more apparent with every passing day that the very model of a good cop is cast in harsher and harsher tones of cruelty, stupidity, harassment, provincialism, paranoia, self-justification, and fear.

Put it out of your mind that there is any strength to the backlash effort on the part of the pigs to convince the country that swine is spelled P-ride/I-ntegrity/G-uts. A pig is a pig is a pig. If it oinks, it's a cop.

(Ed Bryant, a clever young writer from Wyoming, came up with a dandy alternative to pig, however. He found that the Spanish translation of the word *aardvark* is "earth pig," and we have taken to calling the boys in black leather boots 'varks. They know they're being insulted, but they don't understand the philological origin, so they can't use the baton...unless they're so far gone already that calling them *patriots* would cause that reflexive chop across the neck. As a science fiction writer the appellation delights me, even as does the word hardhat, for its explicates out of cultural origins and current events a kind of slang that speaks to the moment. I commend the term 'vark to you. Use it in good health.)

Yet those seedy little pig tie-tacks that so pitifully express the 'varks need to convince themselves they are good guys, members of an elite cadre, beloved by all but Commies and longhair radicals, are but one more weather vane whirling in the wind of public opinion. And it is in the area of public opinion—as viewed through the beady little eyes of a beat cop—that my television note for the week deals:

•Middle Americans who deplored and reviled the radicals who burned the Bank of America in Isla Vista in the past few weeks of riots have come to understand, at last, what it means to have berserk 'varks amucking through locked doors pursuing a scorched-earth policy. They have become anti-porker and in many cases radicalized.

•"Tommy the Traveler," an undercover 'vark working for the Ontario County (N.Y.) sheriff's office, had his covers pulled on Cronkite's CBS *Evening News*, revealing him as something a bit more active than merely an observer. He was, quite plainly, an *agent provocateur* who, when he could not egg on students at Hobart College to civil disobedience, ran a few such numbers on his own. His instigations very probably caused the fire bombing of the Hobart ROTC building for which students Tommy had hemlocked have been indicted. Most militants involved in the Movement now understand that Tommy has many brothers-under-the-covers, narks and finks and snitches who have been directed to stir up trouble in an all-out effort to discredit dissenters and radicals.

•Gwen Bagni (half of the excellent tv writing team of Bagni and Dubov), an elegant woman of midyears, mentioned recently that she finally understood at a gut level why her kids hated cops. During the bomb scare that cleared the Writers Guild meeting at the Beverly-Wilshire Hotel last Monday night, a 'vark, ostensibly "serving the people" by trying to clear the Grand Trianon room, gave her one helluva good shove and looked as though he wanted to club her for not moving fast enough. Gwen contends the cop was suffering from riot-training shock and was unable to react to masses of people in any other way. Another moderate who now gets the message somehow other than intellectually.

•A sociologist named Vermeer from one of the Ivy League colleges recently published a study that shows the ghetto-originated attitude of "tell the cops nothing" has spread to over 65 percent of the population. People would rather fail to report rapes, robberies, riots, or random rottenness than have to deal with the servants of the people.

If we are to take all of these isolated items as indications of the lousy public relations image of the 'vark as a member of our society, one would assume the badge bearers would either try to clean their houses or at least mount a PR campaign to bring back the image of the policeman as a good guy who crosses old ladies at the intersection and offers little lost kids raspberry sherbet cones.

But they don't do either. (And, frankly, why should they, when they have the illiterate support of hardhats and scuttlefish? Old men at Naval ROTC ceremonies who beat up pacifistic antiwar demonstrators and misguided football players who won't let flags be lowered in memory of murdered college students are their accomplices in all the horrors and indignities with which 'varks get away.)

Instead, they bring to bear the lobby influence and fear motivation for which they have earned the term pig. And it manifests itself on tv as follows: You know the Dodge commercials in which the fat-gutted redneck peckerwood Suth'rin sheriff appears? The ones in which that beer-belly, Stetson-accoutered, speed-trap devil begins harassing a passing motorist or a Dodge salesman? Well, there has been outcry against this "inaccurate, insulting, cartoonish" representation of the rural peace officer. Several peace officer organizations have complained loudly and demanded something be done. (In trying to track the specific information from the LAPD and the Sheriff's Department, I got a clutch of different answers to the question *what organization was it that objected?* I was variously informed it was the Sheriff's Association of Indiana, the National Sheriff's Association, the Ohio Highway Patrol, the International Association of Police Chiefs and "some sheriffs'" group down South." One can only conclude from this that *all* 'varks get uptight at the representation of themselves as two-bit highway hustlers. One also notes that the pigs have more associations than might be considered normal for any single group. Paranoia, it would seem, huddles these lads together for mutual approbation and succor.)

So the upshot is that the sheriff in those commercials—who has been selling Dodges like crazy, apparently—will be toned down, made sweet and compliant and lovable. The pressure group has won. The potency of the cop lobby in this low-level tv censorship should not be underestimated. It is a very real example of the gap between what cops want us to *believe* they are (as represented by Jack Webb's *Dragnet* and *Adam-12*) and what they *really* are.

I got a letter from a kid in San Luis Obispo who asked me to warn my long-haired readers if they were heading toward San Luis O. to keep right on driving; the cops up there are raising mayhem with freaks and "hippies."

It's only one more in a seemingly endless stream of warnings from stringers and readers and correspondents all over the country, warning those of us who don't wear our hair cut up to the occipital ridge that the cops have declared war on anyone out of the ordinary.

So we know the truth in the streets. Anyone who has ever faced a 'vark across his visor or been formally introduced to the hard-rubber batons that bust you up inside but leave no marks on the outside *knows* that that Dodge sheriff is closer to reality than Marty Milner of *Adam-12*.

Ever been stopped in a speed trap in the South, friend?

Sure they're lovable.

And so was Gaiseric, king of all the Vandals.

But tv knuckles under. (Well, what the hell. What can you expect from an advertising agency that sells cars that soup up for highway patrols and sheriffs' departments all over the country? Expect nobility from pimps, go ahead, dream your dreams, Ellison.) And so we have more representations every year of the 'varks as the guys in the white hats. We have *Dragnet* and *Adam-12* and *The FBI* and *The Mod Squad*, and those of you (of us) who've seen the psychotic glaze in the eyes of a 'vark just trembling to pepperfog us, we wonder how many Isla Vista deputy district attorneys arrested it will take, how many Middle American scuttlefish falsely busted it will take, how many innocent students cut down it will take, before the Good Folk will realize that their simplistic image of the cop as a benevolent Sergeant Friday is as out of date and incorrect as believing Mussolini was a good man because he made the trains run on time.

The time has come, and long gone, to accept the truth that the 'varks no longer serve and protect. They work their will in fear and Fascism, reflecting the paranoia of our society, reflecting the fear-baiting of monsters like Agnew, reflecting their own individual needs for power and sadism. And the ultimate horror of it is...we pay them to do it to us.

69: 3 JULY 70

There's a lot to clear up this week, just a gang of potpourri, so hold tight because I'm going to whip through it fast: after last week's column I expect momentarily to hear the thud of a beheaded chicken hitting my front door, and my time may be growing short. Remember, friends, I want my body donated to medical science.

First on the agenda is the final word on F-310. Those of you who refuse to listen to me when I tell you not to tell me how honest and trustworthy I am should take this column as proof that I'm as fucked as the rest of you.

F-310, from all the evidence I've now amassed, is a hype. It is virtually worthless. Stop using it, if you were going on my recommendation.

I'm sorry. My unquenchable naïveté got in the way of my constantly resurgent cynicism. I forgot just how corrupt the Big Corporations can be. I stupidly decided that even though the government had indicted Standard Oil on something like seven hundred charges of polluting the Gulf Stream with oil blowout, they had a worthwhile product in F-310—and we shouldn't cut off our noses to spite our respiration. Proof positive your columnist is a boob. Of *course* it was a hype. Mrs. William Hughes of *Write for Your Life* told me it was a shuck, and Sandy Cartt ran her own tests and came up with the same conclusion, and at the end of April the California State Air Resources Board released its much-delayed report on F-310 affirming the same conclusion. And Ed Koupal of the People's Lobby spent hours beating me over the head telling me I was being had. You were right, Ed. Even Bill Murphy of Standard Oil, who tried to walk that fine line between keeping his boss happy by supplying me with the latest refutations of F-310 put-downs, and telling me the truth, could do nothing but sadly comment that "Chevron was not entirely happy with the Air Resources Board report." He is a good man who does his job well, but even he could not drum up a PR rationale for all the evidence that has piled up against F-310. Jerome Kirk of Laguna Beach wrote me and said, "You've gone crazy again. I'll be damned if I'm going to pay a nickel/gallon tithe to the consumer shuck of one of the two companies which refuses to participate in the drilling moratorium off Santa Barbara." He was right. He was smarter than I.

And so, I don't know what to tell you by way of an alternative. I've tried the Texaco Lead-Free gasoline and it fucks up my car so badly I sound like a funnycar blowing off when I cut the ignition. So I switched over to the Union 76 Low-Lead product, and the car runs, but not well. What they tell me now is that I'll have to buy a 1971 model that's equipped to handle these low-lead fuels. All of which smells unpleasantly like a locked-hands policy between the oil companies and those swine who make the tin cans we drive. I swear, if they allowed horses in the city of Los Angeles, I'd go and buy a hay-burner to trot down the bloody freeways. But they don't, and I'm stymied as, I suspect, most of you are. If *anyone* out there has an answer, please dear god send it in! *We need to know!*

But one way or the other, boycott Chevron!

Second item: somehow I gave you the wrong phone number for Viewer Sponsored Television Foundation, two weeks ago. A good many of you tried to call it, to pledge money or offer yourself as office help, and you got some poor dude who was crying with desperation he'd never even *heard* of VSTV. So the number you want is 478-0589. (The explanation for that allegedly incorrect 272-1072 number is that it is the number telephone information gives you if you ask for VSTV. Clayton Stouffer, head of VSTV, swears he doesn't know what that number is, but I suggest he contact one of his friendly phone reps and ask her why they give it out. And he might clarify the discrepancy between 478-0580, which appears in the VSTV brochure, and 478-0589, which the telephone operator will grudgingly dredge up if you tell her 272-1072 doesn't sound right. It's all very confusing, and all I can tell you for certain is that VSTV needs your help desperately, and it's a worthy cause. Try smoke signals.)

Third item: yesterday, as you read this, Channel 13 started reruns of *Burke's Law*, every night at 10:00. For those of you who wonder what I write like when I'm writing tv fare, I commend to your attention the following "Who Killed—" segments: Purity Mather, Andy Zygmunt, one-half of Glory Lee and Alex Debbs. They are four shows I rather pride myself on having written, although it was a few years ago. They help sustain me in moments when the knowledge that I wrote *The Oscar* gets too much for me.

Or if you don't want Ellisonian reruns, I do not think you will revile me too much if I recommend the Friday night CBS reruns of *He & She*, a superlative adult sitcom of several seasons ago, starring Paula Prentiss and Dick Benjamin and Jack Cassidy and Hamilton Camp and Kenneth Mars, five of the surest comedic talents spawned by the sixties. The shows are *always* intelligent— never gibber down at you—and *always* funny. Frequently they are brilliant and unforgettable. Note, particularly, Cassidy, who is rapidly emerging as one of the finest actors in America.

Fourth item: KCET (Channel 28) is starting a sort of visual *Credibility Gap* with Lew Irwin and Len Chandler, who created that ill-fated satire news format for a rock radio station that will henceforth be nameless and consigned to Coventry. The shows on the education network begin July 8, at 9:30 p.m., and will run for thirteen weeks. The series is called *The Newsical Muse*, and I'll be doing a full-length takeout on it as soon as it debuts. But I didn't want you to miss their opening night. It promises to be a gut wrencher, and as an answer to Spiro it may be just what we've been waiting for.

Fifth item: Chuck Barris Productions (they who bring us such charmers as *The Dating Game*, *The Newlywed Game*, and other airwave-polluting innovations in modern American viewing) have sent me a press release about a one-hour rock musical special titled *Do It Now!* Their puff says, in part, it "will be a nonprofit venture and all parties concerned with the project are donating their services or working for the minimum union fees...As in the Do It Now Foundation's 'First Vibration' LP the emphasis of the television special will be a low-key drug pitch, stressing the fact that hard drugs can hurt. Participation of an entertainer will indicate endorsement of an anti-hard-drug stand. Pot and psychedelics will be regarded as a controversy and will not be put down or advocated in the content of the show or in the follow up. Among the heavies who donated their talents for the 'First Vibration' LP and public service radio tapes are The Beatles, Donovan, Hendrix, The Jefferson Airplane, Canned Heat, Buffalo Springfield, Eric Burdon, Frank Zappa...many of these artists will also participate in this unique television special, plus the good possibility of performers such as Joe Cocker, Leon Russell, John Sebastian, Cass Elliot, Crosby/Stills/Nash & Young, Sly & The Family Stone, Sha Na Na, Dion and others."

Now, aside from the hypocrisy of some of the doper-performers listed above "indicating endorsement of an anti-hard-drug stand" by their inclusion (one of whom may still be the biggest pusher of hard stuff on this coast), it sounds like a good effort, and I'll keep you apprised of its progress as Chuck Barris Productions proceeds. (And someday remind me to tell you about the time I was asked on *The Dating Game* and they wound up burning the tape.)

Sixth item: we've seen a great many manifestations recently on the part of the Middle Americans of a longing for the good old days of yore, before hippies and dissent and revolution...a yearning for a return to the periods of American history during which values like patriotism, civil obedience, cleanliness, Protestant morality, and hard work were constants. Essentially, the fear of the hardhats and Good Folk is based on a lack of understanding of the breakdown of these "trusted eternals." I attribute the lashing out of the scuttlefish at protesters to this fear and this yearning. And last week one of the networks went considerably further than *Hee Haw* toward succoring that yearning. A week ago today, CBS premiered one of the scariest shows I've ever watched. Eight o'clock every Thursday you can watch *Happy Days* and get the ass scared off you.

Even for someone (like me) who digs nostalgia, *Happy Days* is a frightener. And it is hardly the entertainment content of the show that so terrifies, because having Bob and Ray, Helen O'Connell, Louis Nye, and a pair of brilliant madmen like Jack

Burns and Chuck McCann at their best can hardly be called ugly. Yet there is a creeping fear as one watches the music and comedy of the thirties and forties re-created on this show. A strange miasma of the past, of an unsealed grave. One senses it as one watches the elderly, balding, paunchy couples dance the jitterbug (note one token black couple in the crowd—they're re-creating the period 100 percent). One senses it as one listens to the prerecorded voice of Bob Eberle straining in vain to reach the notes of "Tangerine" that once belonged to him alone, and one senses it in the sad shoe-polish blacking of Eberle's hair. One senses it in the grotesque imitations of W. C. Fields and Laurel & Hardy. One begins to realize that our national middleclass hunger to return to two decades of Depression, world war, Prohibition, Racism Unadmitted, Covert Fascination with Sex, Deadly Innocence, Isolationism, Provincialism, and Deprivation Remembered as Good Old Days has become a cultural sickness.

The past has always been a rich source for fun and profit. Nostalgia is a good thing. It keeps us from forgetting our roots. Readers of this column know I trip down Memory Lane myself frequently. But it is clearly evident that when an entire nation refuses to accept the responsibilities of its own future, when it seeks release in a morbid fascination with its past, and when it elevates the dusty dead days of the past to a pinnacle position of Olympian grandeur...we are in serious trouble.

It is not merely that our over-thirty and over-forty citizens want to recapture the *Happy Days* of their youth (no matter how wretched they actually were in reality), it is an attempt, stemming from fear and paranoia, to hold back change, to harness the future to the decaying corpse of the past. We see it all around us every day, and it evinces itself in *Happy Days*. If you cannot cope with today, ignore tomorrow and revel in yesterday.

It is a saddening thing to see. Particularly when it has to leach all the joy out of the past for the rest of us who need to know whence we came.

It is a dead end. As you will understand, with a chill, when, in the episode's Tag, they reprise that flashy Aragon-style ballroom in which the *Happy Days* acts perform, featuring

Louis Nye. Spangled and scintillant throughout the one hour of nostalgia, at the end Nye (as emcee) stands in the ballroom festooned with cobwebs, rotted and falling around him. He slowly shambles through the debris, sad and lonely, and goes out through the darkness, closing the door, leaving the past in dust and emptiness.

It is an eloquent message.

70: 10 JULY 70

It has nothing to do with anything directly, but it makes a strong parallel, so I'll lay it on you. I've got this sister, see, her name is Beverly. She is eight years older than me, and a dreadful person. I don't hate her, I despise her. There's a big difference. Hate means you have affection somewhere in you; despising someone means they are so contemptible they are beneath rational notice.

The historical antecedents for my feelings about Beverly have their roots in my youth, and I won't bore you with them; it's only the recent past that matters, as a parallel to my coming— these past two months—to despise my fellow members in the Writers Guild of America, west.

I didn't even speak to my sister for almost five years. Oh, occasionally, when my mother had a heart attack, for instance, I was thrown into contact with her, and we barely managed to exchange a few words. But it was as strangers. She doesn't understand the way I live my life, and I understand the way she lives hers too well.

But about three months ago, she and her husband Jerry, who is a very good man indeed, much too good for her, I suspect, came out to California for a visit. During that visit I learned... *relearned*, for I'd known those core truths intuitively for many years...that my sister was not only prejudiced and a bigot, but she is essentially a *stupid* person. It is not an easy thing to accept:

blood of your blood is bone, stick, stone stupid. And a bone, a stick, or a stone could serve as well. But it became painfully, irrevocably clear to me, in such harsh terms that never again will the absence of years soften my memory so I delude myself into thinking there is warmth or saving grace there.

She is alien to me in her thinking, in her references to blacks as "those people," in her lack of understanding of why students go to the barricades in an effort to save a country they love in a much deeper way than those who fly their flags on the Fourth or festoon their cars with jingoistic bumper stickers love it, in her callousness about the conditions of life that make us ripe for police stateism. She is alien to me, not only because she lacks soul in the most basic ways, but because she is typical of the majority of people in our country who worry about #1 and give not a damn for the commonweal.

Were I a more devout Jew, I would sit shiva for my sister; for me, she is dead.

And for precisely these same reasons, I have come to despise the larger part of the membership of WGAw. I do not despise Carey Wilbur, nor Danny Arnold, nor Gene Coon, nor Chris Knopf, nor George Clayton Johnson, nor Paul Dubov, nor any of the other minority members of the guild who tried, vainly, helplessly, outnumbered and doomed from the outset to failure, who tried to swerve the guild earlier this week from accepting a new contract proposed by the Producers' Guild that is a cowardly, shabby, simply bad contract. But I do despise the men and women who put the fears of losing their plush homes and cushy sinecures before their obligations to their fellow members, to their guild, to the mediums of film and tv, and to the country and world as a whole.

These may be grandiose accusations, but I think they obtain, and I take this opportunity to explain why, for I waited many weeks, as the WGAw negotiating committee worked to extract a decent contract from the Producers' Guild of America and its affiliates, before I sat down to write these words. My fellow guild members will find this difficult to believe, but I am a guild man all the way; I commend my union for all the good things it does; but I would be a cop-out were I not to suggest that they are something less than godlike for their actions this past week. That I *did* put in abeyance this column till the contract had been settled, one way or the other, is my small demonstration of allegiance. But now that allegiance is superseded by my obligation to greater causes.

A momentary digression, before outlining chapter and worse: to explain why accepting a shitty and demeaning contract helps push the world's head underwater for the third time.

The two-thousand-odd members of the WGAw are the most powerful group of communicators the world has ever known. In an age when the mass media literally control the thought processes of the world's population, can sway their attitudes and directions virtually unassisted, the writers stand directly in the eye of the hurricane. They are able to reach more people more effectively than Shakespeare, Dickens, Harriet Beecher Stowe, Funk & Wagnalls, and Mickey Spillane jammed together.

Had they the slightest, smallest vestige of control over the material they contribute to television, the members of the WGAw could conceivably arrest the trends in this land toward repression, violence, mass ignorance, and the death slide down the trough to ecological and sociological ruin.

But writers in this industry have allowed themselves to be brainwashed into believing they are no better than bricklayers, crop-dusters, sewer maintenance men. They are creative typists. They fill the somnolent hours of vapid primetime with stock characters, reinforcing the massmind in its preconceptions and clichés about women, youth, minorities, social conduct, political issues, and most tragically of all, a way of life that has not worked adequately in this country since the early thirties. Instead of demanding the right to speak of the world as it is, of the world as they would wish to see it, they succumb to mingy blandishments of money and comfort, living in a show-biz world of Los Angeles pseudograndeur. They fiddle as the world burns. They ignore their responsibilities. This time, they had a chance to alter that condition. Perhaps not in a massive way, but it was a potential foot in the door.

This time, a vocal coterie of younger WGAw members tried to make a heavy issue of censorship, in an attempt to gain some

small measure of control over the material they contribute
to television. To have some minor-key say in matters usually
decided by old men on faraway mountaintops: advertising men,
network executives, studio heads, pollsters, test firms, continuity
acceptance officials, FCC nabobs.

In a forty-two-demand contract, censorship was the forty-
second item. It followed concerns about new minimum wage
scales, about representation of writer-producer hyphenates,
cable and cassette usage of material written by WGAw members,
and a host of other workaday problems with which writers are
concerned.

The first offers from the producers were so outrageously
demeaning, the guild saw dollars being taken from pockets, and
they turned them down. But it was no show of solidarity. It was
fear of rollback, to levels that were lower than our last contract.

Those of us who have virtually cut ourselves off from writing
episodic tv because we cannot stand the unartistic hassles of
seeing our work butchered, continued to insist that money was
not the important issue: control of our work was. And when we
were presented with a workable system for preventing some of
the censorship—what is called "The English System" because
it has worked so well on the BBC—we felt the last argument
against a strong stand on that issue had been answered. We
made our wishes known to the negotiators who were, admittedly,
concerned with the welfare of *all* WGAw members and special-
interest groups.

Well, we had a feeling—born out of experience and, sadly,
cynicism—that if push came to shove, if it became a matter of
money against control, that the censorship issue would be soft-
pedaled and sacrificed. We felt this was a hideous alternative.
The issues are too large, the times too deadly to allow expediency
to dictate our actions.

The negotiators did a splendid job. Every man, from Ranald
MacDougall and John Furia, Jr., on down, did yeoman work. But
the contract was not a good one. It was a sop to each group in the
guild. The money was inconsistent with the cost-of-living index
rise, the cassette issue was postponed, control of our writer
hyphenates was sidestepped, and the censorship issue wound up

being under-the-rug material. Oh, they agreed that complaints of censorship would be referred to a committee of ten men each from WGAw and the PGA (with network people sitting in at their discretion), but we all know how ineffectual *that* sort of mickeymouse is.

The contract was presented to the membership, and it was explicitly stated that this was the final dollar we could get from the producers; if we rejected the deal, it meant a strike. That was last Thursday night.

Now, let us understand something. It is not the strength of the negotiating committee that forces employers to accede to demands. It is the implicit strength of the union's membership. The negotiators had done the best they could; they had wrung the last drop of honey from the producers. Unfortunately, it wasn't enough. At that point it was time for the *members* to show their strength, to firm up their resolve, to display some spine, and put *themselves* on the line. To risk *losing* something. To stop the mouth to mouth resuscitation of parlor liberals and actually go to the barricades. No one wanted a strike (particularly not me; had we struck, it would have meant killing an impending feature film deal, negotiations for which were going on *at that time*). But everyone was unhappy with the contract.

Particularly those of us who saw our chance to have a say in the future of tv slipping away.

Many people got up and spoke against the contract. But I looked at the faces of the members. They were bored. They were frightened. They didn't want to hear that they might have to strike for sixteen weeks to get a decent contract. They were willing to accept the word of the negotiators that this was the limit we could get. They had been more than willing to let Furia & Co. go and do their damnedest, but now it was up to them. Now the words and the threats had to end and the militancy show itself. All the bullshit rhetoric about "We are a strong guild!" had to cease, and some muscle show itself.

They accepted the contract.

They chickened. They could not go that last step to danger. They didn't care enough about making it better for themselves and their brothers in the everyday hour-to-hour Perdition of television. They didn't care that the world is falling to pieces around their ears. All they cared about was they'd made a dollar or two, and if we struck it would be painful.

Several meetings ago, Nate Monaster—a past president of WGAw—got up and brought to the attention of the membership that moneys set aside for us in the WGAw Pension Plan were being invested in war stocks. Nate fielded the outrages of many (again, in the main, younger) members who wanted this heinous practice ended. He proposed a motion that the Executive Board of WGAw *find* a way to have our money transferred to nonwar stocks (we had been advised that since the plan was governed by law by trustees, our hands were tied)…even if it meant we lost money in the sale and transferral. It was a nice gesture, and one many of us hoped would get some action. It hasn't, of course, but that's beside the point. The thing about that motion and about that meeting that impressed me most was the moment one of our esteemed members (I forget which one now) took the microphone and could not *believe* Nate and the rest of us were sincere. Could not believe we would actually *lose* money rather than be involved with Dow and other firms of its ilk. He was not abusive, he was not angry, he was flatly flabbergasted. He was all at sea. Could not *believe* we would find the idea of our money being used to produce war matériel so abhorrent that we wanted out no matter *what* the consequences.

He was a nice man, probably a good man, surely a man who would not condone burning babies, but he was one with the massmind. He was the Silent Majority speaking out in confusion at this demonstration of ethic and morality at the expense of dollars.

It was not a nice thing to find out that my fellow practitioners of the noblest craft in the world were Spiro's people. It was not nice to find out my sister Beverly was a bigot. It is not a nice feeling, despising men I've honored.

But they turned their faces away from the world last Thursday night, and they thrust their hands into their wallets for succor. And for that, I despise them. They are cowards. So I ask, a bit sadly, when the noblest among us cop out…what hope have we?

Mel Shavelson, president of the guild, do you have an answer for us?

71: 17 JULY 70

I watched television last Wednesday night, the eighth, and it occurs to me that the March of Dimes never *intended* to put itself out of business. What I mean, the March of Dimes was out to get infantile paralysis; for *years* they sent me these dumb stickers—kind of a moral blackmail number through the mails—and for years I sent them some bread. The guilt was *adult* paralysis: I was such a sucker for their poster kids, I would have felt like Adolf Eichmann if I hadn't slipped a tenner into an envelope. Never even *used* the goddamn stickers. But the thing that always got to me was their insistence that they were in business to put themselves *out* of business: that when they got infantile paralysis cleaned up, they'd throw a big bash and smoothly dissolve their organization. So they did away with infantile paralysis, then went and got themselves into the birth defect market, just so they could keep hustling me every Christmas with those tacky little stickers.

Which is not to say they don't do a good job for a good cause. It's just I hate their hypocrisy. Those clowns wound up thirty years later with such a heavy organization they weren't *about* to end it all and go out looking for new jobs.

The same might be said for the social protesters in the entertainment media. I mean, one would get the impression that they'd like nothing better than to clean up violence and misery and poverty and pollution and prejudice and Spiro, and then quietly go on to some other line of work, maybe crop-dusting or antimacassar tatting.

But it's obvious there is considerable bread in dissent, even as there is considerable profit in pollution....

(Digression. Texaco is advertising its lead-free gasoline. It is vastly overpriced. Lead is an additive. They charge us to put it in. Now they charge us again to take it out. Women's Liberation, as the hippopotamus, currently suffers the services of the vanga-shrike of advertising: Virginia Slims, Feminique, and other useless artifacts insist in their commercials that the only way to be "free" is to use what they purvey, thereby not only demonstrating how shamelessly they will try and exploit the most noble endeavors, but also proving once and for all that they have no understanding whatsoever of what the Movement is about. The spoilers have never been more cunning...they can make a buck off death, or life, or clean air or dirty air or freedom or slavery. It makes one pause for a moment to consider the massed benefits of Capitalism, but since Howard K. Smith assures us America is not Imperialistic, I guess we needn't dwell too long on it.)

And in *safe* dissent there is a fortune.

Safe dissent, as opposed to dangerous dissent, is identifiable in a number of ways, which specifics I offer here as a public service. If it is heard or read in a medium where no one will take notice of it—such as "little" magazines, science fiction periodicals, the back pages of underground newspapers, or at liberal cocktail parties—it is safe dissent.

What we might call, to coin a phrase, *defanged dissent*.

Further identifying keys: if it is dissent on a subject already socially acceptable—abortion, pollution, anti-Semitism, sit-ins at lunch counters—it is defanged; if it's couched in phraseology so complex you have to have a double-crostic dictionary to unravel it, if it starts with phrases like "I think the kids today have the right idea..." and then uses the words *but, however, even so*, or some other grammatical linkage that leads into phrases like "we still have laws in this country," it is defanged; if Tom Reddin or George Putnam could say it and appear to be making a fair statement of both sides of the issue being presented, it is defanged; if *Life or Time* does a cover story on it, it's defanged; and if it appears in primetime, it is definitely defanged.

Which is to say, I watched tv Wednesday night the eighth, and I saw just a lot of defanged dissent. It showed up on the first half hour of *Johnny Cash Presents The Everly Brothers*; it put in an appearance on the debut of Channel 28's *Newsical Muse*, to which I switched, midway in the Everlys; and it was rampant on the return of the Smothers Brothers, on ABC. It was all pointed and clever, and it didn't mean a damned thing, because it was safe and decidedly defanged and if you saw it you just knew no secret police would come beating on any doors to roust the subversives and you knew you wouldn't read in the *Times* the next day about the mysterious suicide/accident/death of any of the video dissenters. It was all so clean and safe even Mrs. Mitchell might have watched it and chuckled mommily and murmured, "Oh, they're such *chil*dren!"

I suppose Don and Phil Everly thought they were being terribly dangerous and right on with Johnny Cash singing "The Lonely Voice of Youth Asks What Is Truth." I suppose they thought they were taking a healthy swing for youth and truth against the Forces of Evil when they brought on Joe Higgins, that fat little guy who plays the Southern highway patrolman on the Dodge commercials (see this column for 26 June) as a Fascistic ABC security guard. I suppose that's what they thought, I suppose.

And I suppose the endless references by the Smothers to their expulsion from CBS, their singing of "Okie from Muskogee," the brief shtick with the bird that says, "I'm high," and the dummy with the hardhat were considered pretty daring dissent, too. Yeah, I guess.

Actually, it was about as dangerous as a routine by Flip Wilson, whose most recent video forays in support of his people have manifested themselves as advertisements for suntan lotion and recruitment for the National Guard.

Only on *The Newsical Muse* did we get anything even remotely approaching serious comment on the current scene. Lew Irwin and folk singer Len Chandler, who talked and sang themselves out of jobs on KRLA's *Credibility Gap* by being too on target, did a half hour of creditable gadflying, and I commend their Wednesday night stints to you with *hardly* any reservations. I say hardly, because I think they will have to add some visual shticks to the fare before it will entertain as well as the *Gap* did; but with Chandler's acidic and heartfelt lyrics, with Irwin's editorializing tone of Administration disapproval, they are the only ones currently working who come near to the core of anguish in all of us these days, Left *or* Right.

But, again, it is defanged dissent.

Because it is sung.

I hardly intend to put down Chandler. His work is well into the neighborhood of brilliant. But the past fifteen years have been surfeited with folk songs bemoaning everything from the "company store" to the paving of Paradise in order to "put up a parking lot." Songs don't get it. Songs are too easy to ignore. Songs—particularly for the young, whom I regularly bless in these columns—appeal more strongly on the levels of syncopation and rhythm than lyrically. And even more noticeably these days, with the Sound trending more toward Joe Cocker than Julius La Rosa, it is virtually impossible to understand the words until you've heard the song a dozen times or caught the artist on a tv variety show lip-synching it. (And usually, when you do, you get the bullshit lyrics of The First Edition's "Tell It All, Brother" or the Vegas-lounge shuck of Bobby Stevens and his Checkmates singing "I Have a Dream," vibrating there in his tuxedo, telling us how he's gonna go back t'Jawjuh to straighten things out. Sure he is.) So the social protest of the songs only occasionally endears itself, as in "Blowin' in the Wind." Essentially, what it is, is defanged dissent that sounds nice.

Politicians don't take songs seriously. I can't think of one demagogue, from Bilbo to Reagan and including McCarthy, who was ever unseated or mobbed because of a song.

Which brings me back to my original point—excluding Cash, Chandler, Irwin, and Tommy Smothers whom I believe seriously *care*—that dissent is good business. As witness Flip Wilson or Bobby Stevens, not every black man gives enough of a damn about blackness beyond his own career to take the kind of positions or speak out as forcefully as Dick Gregory. They've seen that Greg doesn't work too much on tv no more. But a few socially oriented zingers in any act make for spice, give intimations of guts, and so they toss them in.

The same for paddys, of course. We're hip-deep in white entertainers who do such a great job of lip-serving freedom and equality that one really has to check the record to see how far, if at all, they've gone beyond making the sounds of genuine action.

TV˙ is rife with defanged dissent, and it is this virtually harmless protest that gets the Orange County Birchers up in arms. Hell, they sometimes think Robert K. Dornan is a Communist and he's little better than a hyperthyroid Joe Pyne. What television, Los Angeles, and the country need right now is a bold, muckraking series of shows that do what *Ramparts, Scanlan's Monthly, Esquire*, the *Free Press*, and occasionally even *Look* do: exposés.

Using staffs of investigators, any one (or all) of the three major networks could field a weekly program that could amass evidence that could be presented to the proper authorities for action. Scripts based on accumulated evidence proving which legislators are on the take, which industries continue to pollute the environment, which city and state projects using tax dollars are merely boondoggles, which restaurants are substandard according to health department regs, what the incidence of random phone-tapping is and who's doing it...a host of subjects that need a crusading, muckraking attack. And documentaries on subjects studiously avoided in the past: what it's like for a white hooker in black neighborhoods; the revelation that Reagan is using the Rand-style think tanks to create a police state; the proportion of wealthy liberal Jews who own and operate tenements and schlock stores in ghetto areas; how many undercover 'varks actually provoke violence to enable their badge-bearing buddies to bust a parade or meeting; how effective the FBI *really* is, after all the director's publicity bullshit is swept aside; how Isla Vista got radicalized.

That would be a dangerous series of shows to watch. Not safe and tidy like the excellent *National Geographic* specials, or defanged like Mark Lane hurling statistics while Dick Cavett mugs.

Tommy Smothers is a good man, but he's been pretty effectively neutralized as a dissenter. It has to happen, and it's a tribute to his past effectiveness. Because when the spokesmen get effective, they are put out of business, at least in terms of credibility to the massmind, which is the enemy that has to be convinced. It happened to Tommy, it happened to Benjamin Spock, it happened to Joan Baez, it happened to Dick Gregory and Malcolm X and Eldridge Cleaver and Ramsey Clark, and it will happen to anyone else who speaks out. But new spokesmen must be brought up to the barricades. For every Stan Bohrman or Les Crane who gets deactivated, we must find two others, who will keep the rascals honest, or point out how they have their knives in our backs.

Steve Wilson and Lorelei Kilbourne of Big Town's *Illustrated Press* used to handle that kind of muckraking job on radio and early tv, but when Britt Reed and The Green Hornet went over to the side of the 'varks, the dissent movement lost much of its effective news-handling. What we need now is the emergence of an honest, ballsy, crusading tv editor who will take on some of these onerous tasks, and get some things said.

What we need is some dangerous dissent, some heavy talk, and some unassailable facts that will make it uncomfortable for the forces of evil in our times.

Songs about loving one another and mild comedy by the darlings of *TV Guide* is nice to have, also, but let's not delude ourselves that the insipid little snipes we hear in primetime are causing the Monster Men any sleepless nights.

It ain't that easy, friends.

72: 24 JULY 70

Well, it's kind of a dumb story, but since you asked, I'll tell you.

About a month ago, I mentioned somewhat casually that I'd once been a contestant on *The Dating Game*, and in my usual offhand fashion, being cute and not thinking you'd really take me up on it, I mumbled, "I'll tell you about it sometime." Some cute. I got a dozen letters demanding the story. Y'know, *you* people have positively a *lust* for the ugly.

But, as Art Baker used to say before Jack Smith replaced him with that big jar of Skippy Peanut Butter, this is for you, Mrs. Aline Tegler of Playa Del Rey...

You Asked for It!

Hardly a soul left alive today remembers the event, for it transpired *before* that now-infamous ABC monstrousness went on the air for its first season. That would have to be five or six years ago.

Well, what happened was this: some young women I'd been dating at the time, quite apart from one another, were asked to try out for the show prior to its first few tapings. Part of the routine through which they were put was filling out an office form on which they were to note the names and phone numbers of other lovely girls and eligible bachelors who might make personable contestants. So three of these nice ladies—none of whom knew the others—quite independently wrote down my name. At the time I was an eligible bachelor. (I'm *still* an eligible bachelor, but now I'm an *older* eligible bachelor. Which probably says something ominous about me as marital timber, but that's another story, for another time. *Don't write letters!*)

So one morning when I was still living in a tree house in Beverly Glen, I got this call from a silken-voiced houri representing someone I'd never heard of, Chuck Barris and his Productions. This siren urged me to haul my fair young body down to an office building near Hollywood and Vine (if memory serves) where the joys of the world would be revealed to me. Promises of mounds of pliant female flesh were openly made. It was like recruitment for a Marrakesh harem. Well, sir, being a healthy young lad, I got into my best threads (which at that point of poverty were no great shakes, let me tell you) and hied my ass thence.

Once into the reception room of Chuck Barris Productions, I saw half a dozen great-looking girls, three great-looking secretaries, a great-looking receptionist, and about a dozen schlumpy-looking guys, some of whom had terminal acne.

Thinking I'd been singled out in some special manner, because of the lofty tone of the siren's phone call, I went up to the receptionist and said, "My name is Harlan Ellison. I was asked to come down to see so-and-so." She didn't even bat an eyelash. (With phonies *that* length, she was lucky to've been able to *open* them.) "Take a seat with the other supplicants," she said.

Crestfallen, amazed that my charisma had not whelmed, if not *over*whelmed her, I went and sat down next to a guy in a shapeless wine-colored corduroy sport jacket whose hairy white ankles were showing above his white sweat socks. He was busy gnawing on a hangnail. Things weren't quite as glamorous as I'd expected.

Finally, we were called by name, taken to a ready room (separating men from women, naturally), and there we filled out nineteen different kinds of forms. After which we were divided up into smaller groups, and in company with four other guys I was hustled into a tiny room where a girl sat behind a small table covered with note pads and suchlike paraphernalia. Behind a screen—but still visible—was a rather plain but happy-looking young girl who was reading a mimeographed sheet.

Now bear in mind, this was all *before The Dating Game* aired, so I didn't know what the hell was going on. All I knew for sure was that there was a good chance to meet some heavy females and, all shuck aside, friends, I had not at that stage of existence achieved the satori of truth and beauty and wisdom I display so casually today. But, onward...

The interviewer behind the table briefed us on the format: scripted "questions" to be asked by the girl behind the screen, and a "choice" made by her from the men's answers, as to which of us she would want to take her on a date. This was a village idiot format that seemed a trifle brutalizing, but, well, not blasphemically so. At that point.

So the questions were asked of the five of us, and they were mildly amusing questions to which I gave mildly amusing answers. Now understand that at no time during this preliminary "weeding out" run-through was I anywhere near scintillant in my humor. I was just being Paul Pleasant, and Charles Charming and Sidney Sex-Starved. But compared to the dullards with whom I'd been grouped, my responses were positively Benchleyesque.

Upshot: the girl picked me.

Hurray! I was through the prelims and was asked to appear on such-and-such a date for an actual taping as one of the three male contestants. I was told the girl behind the screen had not made it, and that I'd be vying for the attentions of another, much more memorable young lady.

So, came the day of the taping, late in the afternoon, and I went down to the ABC studios. Here the story thickens.

The cavalier treatment that had been mild and barely acceptable in Barris' offices, was magnified a thousandfold. We were treated like cheap foreign labor turned out to repair ten miles of bad road. Pushed here, ordered there, chivied and demeaned from the moment I (and the other two guys who were to appear with me) entered the studio.

And they made a small error. Probably because it was one of their first tapings and they hadn't gotten the system down pat yet. I saw, actually *saw* the girl I was to try and coerce into going out with me.

Oh, Jesus!

Bear in mind, friends, that at that time in my life, I was a shallow, superficial, callow youth who judged women not by the enlightened standards of integrity, intelligence, and humanity inculcated in me by Mary Reinholz and Anne De Wolfe and other females of the Women's Liberation Movement, but by wholly shameful considerations of physical beauty. Turn of ankle, height of bust, fairness of face, luster of hair, absence of moustache...*these* (oh, shame, shame) were my yardsticks. And by such judgments, in those days I would have decided the girl was considerably less than desirable.

Today, I'd simply call her a waste of time.

Anyhow, we were being hectored from one small waiting room to another, and we passed this peach of perfection in the corridor. My eyes widened in horror as might those of a Transylvanian peasant meeting Lawrence Talbot, The Wolf Man, in a foggy forest.

We were quickly hurtled from sight of her. But my knees had begun to shake.

Finally, we were brought out onstage, seated on high stools, and—the warm-up having been done—the show got under way.

I'll cut to the payoff.

Here we are, these two other guys and myself, behind a modernistic backset, with pseudo-Herb Alpert music rattling, and they introduced the charmer I'd seen in the hall.

She sits down and asks the first question: "Number One, describe the worst of your bad habits." So Number One, who looked like an out-of-work Via Veneto pimp, replied, "I snore. But you won't have to worry about that because I know I'll stay awake with you." He thought that was really dynamite repartee. Then Number Two—a collegiate football hero if ever there lived one—denigrated himself with his bad habit of drinking beer and watching sports on tv every Saturday and Sunday. But he assured her that in the light of her wonderfulness, Kareem Abdul-Jabbar was nowhere. Then she got to me, Number Three. "Number Three," she said, "do you have any bad habits?"

"Well, frankly, no," I said, smiling a Huckleberry Finn smile she was the poorer for not being able to see. "My friends say I'm without flaw, if you ignore the fact that I'm an ax murderer and rapist.

"But everybody has a few minor character flaws," I added.

There was a hushed silence from the other side of the set. Then she recovered and went on to her second question.

"Number One, describe what we'd do if you took me out, what kind of an evening you'd consider a big date."

The Via Veneto pimp did a fast ramadoola about how she was the kind of girl who should be treated to a fancy dinner, the theater, and dancing thereafter. One could almost mentally envision this lad squiring the lady to a series of (what he thought were) high-class places like Frascatti's, the Victory Drive-In and the then-extant Cinnamon Cinder.

Number Two opined the lady was a "down-to-earth kinda girl who's more interested in simple things," and he conjured up a dream date consisting of hamburgers at McDonald's, bowling, and making out in his car at Malibu.

It wasn't hard to beat *those* two efforts.

"Well," I said, adopting a Ronald Colman voice, "for you I would plan a formal evening with you in Pucci gown and me in tuxedo. I would have the chef at Scandia prepare for us a picnic dinner of breast of guinea hen under glass and jeroboams of champagne—Taittinger's Blanc de Blanc '45 possibly—and then I would have us, with our dinner, chauffeured out to the city dump where, with ivory-handled .45s, we would sip bubbly and amuse ourselves by shooting rats."

"*Shooting rats?!?!*" The shriek from the muffin on the other side of the set was a ghastly thing to hear.

Again, silence.

The recovery was much longer this time.

But recover she did. And proceeded through the rest of the questions concentrating on #'s 1 and 2. Number Three was conspicuous by his silence and his satisfied smirk.

As you may have gathered, by this time I was thoroughly nauseated by the whole thing. It was demeaning, it was vapid, it was like a hiring hall for dock wallopers. It removed from male and female alike any pride in self, any sense of self as worthy, any depth or loveliness. I wanted out of there.

Finally, because it became apparent that she was ignoring me, I suppose, my potential ladylove decided to include me in a final question. It was a beauty.

"Tell me, Number One," she began, "how you would go about convincing me I should go out with you."

I could not believe my ears. She didn't *really* ask that, did she?

But she had, and he did, and I wanted to puke. Number One did a seedy Continental number unctuous with double-entendre. Then Number Two all but fell to his baggy knees pleading with this brainless excuse for a woman to go out with him. Then she got to Number Three: "Con*vince* me, Number Three," she said.

"Convince you, you idiot!" I snarled. "I wouldn't go out with a nit like you if they offered me the governorship of Hawaii as inducement. You, and this whole dumb show can go take a sunbath in a cyclotron!"

And I got up and walked off.

There were screams from the stage. The director and the tape editor and the cameramen and the producer and the emcee and the advertising men and the grips and maybe even that nifty little guy, Chuck Barris, started screaming. "Burn that goddamn tape!" I heard someone shriek from back out there.

"Cut! Cut! Cut!" the floor director was shouting. It was bedlam. People were running everywhichway. I couldn't see her, but the female contestant was hawking in a dry-heave sort of way over her chest mike. The other two guys were still sitting on their stools, dumbfounded.

I saw a horde of people advancing on me from backstage, and I ran like a thief. Got away with barely my skin intact.

The show was never aired, of course. And I got word through friends (and a secretary at Barris Productions I dated occasionally) that my name was high on the list of war criminals, on a par with nonbiodegradables, lung cancer, Minnie Pearl chicken, and Hermann Goering.

Every once in a while, even today, some new recruiter for the show, not knowing my past history with the show, will turn up my name, or see me on a talk show, or read some article I've written, and call me, asking if I want to go on the program. I always, very conscientiously, explain to her what happened, and then suggest she go and ask the producer of the show specifically, then get back to me if they want me on again.

To date, those calls have never been returned.

73: 31 JULY 70

You're not going to believe this, but after having spent three full weeks out in the Great American Heartland, spreading the warmth and loving-kindness of my own true self at Clarion College in Pennsylvania, in the darker corners of Pittsburgh, and in the literary jungle of New York City (you'll be overjoyed, I know, to learn there'll be a second volume of *The Glass Teat* early next year; Ace Books is contracting for same; seems they are selling the dumb book like mad; a clear case of hyping sandboxes to bedouins), and after writing this column for several weeks in advance, just so none of you would retch yourselves into withdrawal, when I sit down and sweat my ass off writing

this week's installment, a column of such incredible scintillance
the mind cannot contain the wonder of it, and it comes out at
3300 words of tightly constructed prose, and I bring it in and
lay it on Brian Kirby and his troll staff, they have the temerity,
the audacity to tell me I'm only five days past my deadline
and I can take my column, roll it into a tight little funnel, and
insert it carefully in a place that was never intended by god or
proctologists as a repository for verbiage; and *such* a column, as
my tanta Bernice would say; such a thing about Vincent Edwards
and Universal's new *Matt Lincoln* series from the ABC movie *Dial
Hot Line*; such a column fraught with significance that they're
gonna run it next week and here I have to sit down in the dumb
offices of the *Freep* and tap out 19½ inches of a new column as
filler and I'm so pissed off at the vagaries of newspaper deadlines
that I've decided to write this replacement shtick as one long
sentence and if you can follow the convoluted and prolix track
of this, my literary revenge, you will see a feat of superhuman
stupidity...but anyhow, the only thing I have to write about
at such abbreviated length is the Channel 11 *Creature Feature*
horror flicks they've been running Sunday nights over KTTV,
which come to notice only because I received a letter from a
two-man group calling itself "Quasimodo" (thereby once again
proving what flippos old horror movie buffs are, you'll pardon
my sacrilegiousness) which is actually two dudes named Reaves
and Bertges from San Bernardino who complain—quite rightly,
may I add—that the licensed taxidermists at KTTV, inured to
the values of artistic truth and the eternal verities inherent in all
great creations from the Pietà to the manhole cover, have been
using pinking shears on the great horror classics of the Thirties
in order to run two features in a two-hour time slot (thereby
leaving Dracula with only one fang, what a stupid thing, a one-
hole neck puncture) instead of letting the films run their natural
(or unnatural, depending on how you feel about guys who turn
into wolves and other hippie pastimes) courses which, because
of the six-thumbed ineptitude of the KTTV butchers, reduces
Frankenstein and his monster to something resembling Frick &
Frack in the Transylvanian Highlands and the famous Karloff
opus, *The Black Cat*, to babbling incoherency; well, sir, they are

rightly pissed off, and in an effort to function as the Avenging
Sword of all just causes (can you dig how lightweight this column
must be, when I don't rant about EVIL and REPRESSION and
WAR and allathat good stuff, and I have to put significance on
a bunch of guys who can't find anything more constructive to
do with their Sunday nights than watching old creepies when
they should be out trashing the nearest VFW hall or sending
in bogus solicitations of George Murphy's name to the Famous
Tracheotomists School) I checked over the Xerox of the letter
they'd received in answer to their beef to KTTV, and I got on
the horn and called the executive producer of *Creature Features*
(knowing in front the guy has got to be a bitter sonofabitch: I
mean, a grown man, and the best job he can get is executive
producer for a bunch of things that slither and go boomp on the
tube) and he turns out to be Jon Ross, with whom I played the
Synanon game in the halcyon days when I was in need of tender
psyches against which to vent my groupistically therapeutic rage,
and here he is, good old Jawn, giggling and simpering until I tell
him to shut up and explain why it is he's doing these wretched
shitty things to perfectly good fillums, and Jon stammers a little
bit, because he knows if he doesn't give me a straight answer
I'll spill in this column all the ugly, twisted, demented, and
perverted things about him I learned in those Synanon snake
pit sessions; so he comes clean that there've been nine hundred
thousand catcalls and complaints on the emasculation process
where these old horror flicks are concerned, and he says he
doesn't know what to do about it, and I decide in the name of
Quasimodo and all those other unfortunate loons who'll suck
their thumbs if I don't get them their monster movies to direct
and advise poor befuddled Jon Ross, so I says to him, I says,
"Jon, buhbie sweetie chickie pal, what I want you should do is
stop ripping out whole sections of *Dracula* just so you can show
an hour of *Soul of a Monster*, which is a piece of unmitigated
shit anyhow, and let the films run full length. Otherwise, Jon..."
and I leave it like a lynched longhair in La Habra, hanging there
with its eyes bugged and its tongue lolling, and he gets the ugly
tone of my message at once and he begins to whimper, "But we
have it all scheduled out through the month of August, and uh,

er, eh, we, uh…" so I take pity on the poor sot, and I tell him I'll let him continue his rotten and rapacious methods for the month of August, but that by September, by jiminy, he'd better run only one feature, uncut, and he practically slobbers his thanks and gratitude…so that's why, Quasimodo, and all you other flips, you can count on a complete change of face by KTTV and its band of Quantrill Scissors Wielders a month from now, so don't say there isn't a god, or even a Zorro, because I always wanted to be a force for good in my time, and here I've actually gone and done it, and just because Kirby that egg-sucker stuck his head in the door and said he found another two inches of dead space and I should write to fill, I've had *my* fill of this sentence, and this column, as have you, probably, and so I'll tag out by reminding you that Ace Books has published a full year of my demented ravings; and if your local newsie doesn't have it and won't order it, pour salt on his fields, rape his oxen, badmouth his wife, give his kids the crabs, and getahold of a copy for the betterment and upliftment of your mingy souls, which brings this sentence, this column, and, hopefully, Brian Kirby to a blessful end. Blues.

74: 7 AUGUST 70

If there's anything I hate, it's a veiled threat. ("Blackmail is an ugly word, Fawkes.") So I'll just rip off the veil. Matt Lincoln, we got our eyes on you, baby!

If you detect a strong resemblance between Matt Lincoln, M.D., community psychiatrist, hot-line director, surly problem-solver and all-around, granite-hewed hero and Ben Casey, M.D., brain surgeon, head resident, surly problem-solver and all-around what I said before…the resemblance is more than superficial. A rose is a rose is a rose is a Matt Lincoln is a Ben Casey is a Vince Edwards. And we have been called upon, gentle readers, once again to police the channel waves.

How it goes is this: Universal made a two-hour film for

television called *Dial Hot Line* with Vincent Edwards as the
Mr.—*not* Dr., as he continually pointed out—whose uncommon
rudeness somewhichway magically bound together a group of
concerned lay-social-worker types into a gestalt that tended a
hot-line switchboard, bringing succor and straight talk to the
troubled masses.

After the show was run on ABC, it was announced that
(surprise!) this sterling 120 minutes of taut, contemporary
drayma would be the pilot for a new series debuting this fall
on ABC, a series that would utilize the hot-line concept as a
jumping-off springboard for stories of raw emotional content and
searching, probing honesty about the frustrations and terrors of
the young and old in our tottering society. In the pilot, Edwards
was known as David Leopold, a name that rings with reality;
in the series, he will be called *Matt Lincoln*. There is a clue to
something in the change of name, something that smacks of
alteration of persona, but I can't quite put my finger on it. Maybe
by the end of the column I'll have worked it out. (Inquiring of
the Matt Lincoln series' producer, Mr. Irving Elman [whose
screen credits include the script of *The Challenge*, the excellent
Darren McGavin vehicle in which America and an unnamed
Oriental power solve a confrontation with personal combat, each
pitting its top dirty guerrilla fighter against his opposite number
on a nomansland Pacific island], as to why the name change, I
was informed there had been a number of jokes about the name
Leopold at Universal. Leopold and Loeb seem to have been the
peculiar nomenclatural hookup that prompted the dropping of
a real name for a patently phony one. Fearing, apparently, that
if there were jokes about Leopold and Loeb around Universal—
thereby accurately pinning the level of humor one finds at that
singularly humorless studio—the jokes might occur nationwide.
Putting aside the sheer bullshit reasoning of this, it indicates
once again the lack of perceptivity of tv programmers about the
condition of the country today. A few weeks ago I had a date
with a fairly literate college lady, who was born in 1951, and
when I mentioned, at different times in the evening, Kiska and
Attu, Wendell Willkie, friend and companion Margo Lane—the
only one who knows to whom the voice of the invisible Shadow

belongs—and G. David Schine, I was greeted with a size-seven blank stare. Now I am by no means denigrating the intelligence of America's Burgeoning Young Folk, but it is patently obvious to all but dunderheads that kids today have eschewed roots and historical antecedents in favor of a zippier "now'" orientation, which only time will advise us is a good or bad thing. What I'm trying to point out—in a painfully complex digression—is that if we are to take Mr. Elman's explanation of the name change at face value, if he wasn't putting me on—which is not difficult to do—then we have another example of arteriosclerotic thinking. If kids today consider anything prior to Buddy Holly and the Crickets as prehistory, then they sure as hell aren't going to make any mental linkup between the name David Leopold and that of one of the kidnap/killers of Bobby Franks in 1924. Which allows the question to ask itself unbidden: with all this talk about "youthizing" the network schedules to hook the 18–36-year-old audience that does most of the consumer product purchasing, aren't the tv moguls masturbating when they ask the same old men to think fresh and young?)

All that, just from the name change.

Can you imagine what is to follow?!

Lincoln, indeed. What a phony. Who ever heard of anybody with a name like Lincoln!

Anyhow, soon after the *Dial Hot Line* film was aired, I received a rather impassioned letter from Ms. Martha Rosen of the Youth Emergency Service, a hot line in Minneapolis. She was terribly upset by what she had seen in the two-hour version, and she wrote enlisting our aid *ante bellum, ante omnia,* in retaliation—before the fact—against the horrors she saw forthcoming on the weekly series. I'll quote Ms. Rosen at some length, to give you her thoughts.

"The organization for which I work, YES, is a telephone-counseling-and-referral service for young people, what is commonly called a hotline. There are between 150 and 200 hotlines and switchboards (the difference, at its simplest, is that switchboards include walk-in facilities) in this country as well as several in Canada. There are quite a number in the Los Angeles area; you can find ads for several in the *Freep.*

"Phone services are mainly volunteer organizations. All kinds of people are involved: college students, drop-outs, ministers, teachers, entire communes, social workers, hippies...anything you can name, although very few (if any) are staffed by policemen. They work on the theory that young people can benefit by free anonymous help. Services offered by most include general counseling, legal and medical referrals and general information. Also, a lot of drug counseling and/or advice, including bad-trip help, is done. Some services have housing, bail funds and mail drops also. YES is receiving 90 calls a day. The need is really there for these services.

"*Matt Lincoln*, presuming it follows the outline of the movie, purports to be about a hotline in Los Angeles. The title character, played by Vince Edwards, is Ben-Casey-as-social-worker: a hairy-chested, impatient, downright nasty (but 'hip') psychiatrist running a 'hotline.' (The character makes me think of your essay in 'The Glass Teat' about tv 'heroes.' He is not a true representative of either social workers or the sort of people—by and large—who are involved with hotlines. Hollywood has failed to learn the lesson of *East Side, West Side*.)

"To give you an example of the sort of 'hotline' Matt Lincoln ·runs (totalitarianly): a young man calls who has just been arrested for failure to report for induction. (It is significant to note that he is not resisting out of principle; he says something like, 'I just flipped out.') So who do they turn him over to for advice? The AFSC? A draft counseling service? A lawyer? Wrong! They turn him over to a *cop*, who is, god save us, one of the volunteers.

"Further evidence against this mess: Matt Lincoln at one point delivers a monologue explaining what he sees as his service's purpose (this is not a word-for-word quote, but I believe it is an accurate paraphrase): 'I don't want people on this phone who have never taken drugs or had abortions; I want people who have had abortions and can tell other people why they are wrong.' (In one week last month, YES referred 9 girls to Planned Parenthood for pills, 16 to an abortion information service and 36 for pregnancy tests.)

"I really believe that this show, if it continues as it has started, could do terrible things. It could ruin the credibility phone services like ours have built up with young people. It could make parents and other Establishment members expect the wrong things of us. It could turn the kids off phone services so they would never seek our help.

"A national conference of hotlines held in Los Angeles last April condemned the show. I realize this is not on the same level of importance as the War, CBW warfare, or racism. But too often, we are the only friends some of these kids have. I don't want Hollywood's idea of reality to screw that up."

Well, that is pretty cogent, and pretty direct. So I watched the rerun of *Dial Hot Line*, and though the script was tense and well written—and the direction needlessly artsy-craftsy in the Richard Lester vein—what Ms. Rosen said was quite true. There *was* a young cop on the service; in fact, Vince Edwards spent a considerable portion of his time trying to get the cop to come back to work on the hot line after an unfortunate (and methodologically imbecilic) suicide which the cop's ineptitude precipitated. There were more crises per intracommercial segment than a daytime soap opera, Vince Edwards was several megawatts crankier than his most unpleasant Ben Casey incarnation ever permitted, and the telephone answerers seemed to me as muddled and maladroit a crew as could have been assembled this side of the Menninger Clinic. Yet I would forgive all of these gaffes (excluding the cop, which seems to me a needless concession to middleclass thinking and an error in judgment which, if it occurred in real life, would make the concept of hot-line "privileged communication" highly suspect to any aware kid) in the name of interior dramatic tension were the consequences of such blatancy of error not so serious.

Ms. Rosen is precisely on target when she speaks of the thin tie that binds the callers to the called. Credibility. It is so rare these days, so easily ripped apart, one fucks with it at one's own risk. And were it only for ourselves, it wouldn't be so bad. But a *Matt Lincoln*, done wrong, can tear it for hundreds, perhaps thousands of young people whose only help might come from that last important phone call to a hot line. (Hell, a reader named Neil Greenberg in Philadelphia lost his credibility in me because of my July 17 column about "safe dissent" on tv; apparently I wasn't radical enough for him. And that, after I bust my ass to get all the facts, deal fairly with as many sides of the problems as I can locate, and set it all down straight. Is there no god?! Is there no justice?! Ah, well: as Vonnegut says, "And so it goes.")

In an effort to allay Ms. Rosen's fears about the series' impending debut, I contacted Irving Elman and quoted some of the letter you've just read. Mr. Elman was polite, if a trifle cool, and I have at hand his response to my hectoring. Equal time, as the FCC demands:

"Dear Harlan:

"As I told you on the phone this morning I won't attempt to defend the 'Dial Hot Line' pilot against the charge of inaccuracies as all of us here are now aware of them and hope not to repeat them in the series."

Ellison again. It should be pointed out that Mr. Elman had nothing to do with the two-hour pilot. Onward.

"As I also pointed out, there has been a change of direction since the pilot, which is the reason for the change of title from Dial Hot Line to *Matt Lincoln*. The hot line is now only a fractional element in the series which will be focused mainly on the person and professional activities of Matt Lincoln, community psychiatrist. The hot line is only one of the many projects with which Dr. Lincoln is involved. He also directs a psychiatric walk-in clinic at the hospital, teaches at the medical school, and under the aegis of the 'Community Mental Health Center' serves as consultant to many public agencies: educational, child welfare, legal aid, police, and so on.

"I am attaching herewith a brief description entitled, 'What is a Matt Lincoln?' which should give you some idea of the man and how he operates.

"D. F. Muhich, M.D., who is himself a community psychiatrist, is now our technical advisor and should be able to help us avoid any future errors.

"I hope this will help clarify some of the confusion and concern as to what we are about.

"Sincerely, Irving Elman."

That, in its entirety, was Mr. Elman's response. As to confusion, I think there is none. As to concern, I don't think the letter will serve overmuch. The series précis, "What is a Matt Lincoln?" I will not quote in full; there isn't space. But I'll chomp out a few phrases that will, I hope, serve fairly to convey the tone of said document:

"Matt Lincoln, M.D., is a community psychiatrist. That says, almost, everything about him. He is of the new breed, oriented to serving the many, rather than the few...He is principally concerned with 'crisis intervention.'...Accordingly, most of his activities are channeled into crisis-handling agencies. The first of these is the hotline, which he directs.... The second is the Walk-In Clinic, which he also heads. Here, for those who need it, and who can't afford private therapy or counseling, is the professional help of a psychiatrist—Matt Lincoln—and whatever others of the hospital staff who may be required...A third area of operations is his private practice, which he limits to 10 hours a week—just enough, he says, to supply the bread he needs to live on, since the rest of his activities pay little or nothing. He is also called on, from time to time, to serve as court psychiatrist by a judge or lawyer, either to testify as witness, or make a psychiatric investigation of someone in custody. He is also a member of the hospital's teaching staff. Spread too thin? Not at all. He is only typical of the way this new breed operates. (Our technical advisor is a prime example and in fact our model!) His personal style in dress and manner is relaxed to the point of complete informality...For transportation he drives a Mustang... For living—and fun—he has an apartment at the Marina, where he keeps a small sailboat..."

I can go no further.

Shunting aside, for the moment, that this sort of prospectus is calculated bullshit, handed out to writers bellying up to write segments of the series, I find in that welter of stock clichés reason for more of the concern felt by Ms. Rosen. First, I find it inconceivable that Vincent Edwards, with a career built on thespic surliness, could be "relaxed to the point of informality," whether he was dressed in sports clothes or mukluks, a caftan and scuba gear. His character's list of accomplishments and interests may well be logical—I don't know Dr. Muhich or how accelerated is his nervous system—but if Matt Lincoln is, indeed, based on this living model, I submit we have in our midst either a man who has discovered the 37-hour day or who moves only slightly slower than The Flash. On the other hand, maybe he just does all of those jobs badly. At least sloppily.

The giveaway, I think—and this goes back to the name change from Leopold to Lincoln—is the dichotomy between Matt Lincoln's professional pursuits, dealing with the broken, the twisted, the poor, and the deprived, and his status symbols of the Establishment. Mustang, indeed! Marina apartment, my ass! Sailboat, are you *kid*ding!

The same essential flaw that presented itself in the two-hour film—old people trying to think like young people—is present in the projected series. Matt Lincoln is a ridiculous samaritan festooned with physical possessions and dabbling in good works for god only knows what sick needs. He is that moronic figment, that artificial construct of bad television, the all-purpose hero. He is doctor, wizard, guru, playboy, adventurer, idiot savant, and figurehead of a breed that is hardly new or daring. He is merely Paladin in sports clothes. It does not bode well for the series, in terms of the fears Ms. Rosen expresses. It merely widens the scope so that now Matt Lincoln can cast his shadow on walk-in clinics, community social workers, legal aid, child-care centers and—hot lines, as before.

When I spoke to Mr. Elman, I asked him if it might be possible to preview a couple of segments of the show to present more accurately the "new direction" of the series, the film version having aroused such disquiet. I was informed, most politely, that ABC would not allow such a thing. I don't understand that. Perhaps you do.

In any case, this column has presented the concern, the replies, the prospectuses, and some obviously slanted conclusions on my part (albeit culled entirely from what Universal threw up on the tube and what the producer sent me, hardly from whole cloth). At this point, my gentle readers, you have all the facts to date.

Mr. Elman noted that the film of *Dial Hot Line* was researched with psychiatrists, doctors, and Los Angeles-based hot lines before its production. If this was the case, and the final product became something Mr. Elman will not even defend, then I wonder just how much hope we can hold out for a weekly dose of Vince

Edwards as Super Shrink, with only the superfast assistance of
D. F. Muhich, M.D.

But we'll be watching, won't we, gang? We'll be right there
on debut night, in September, Thursday, ABC, and we'll let you
know as soon as we can, Mr. Elman, and Vince *tatelah*, whether
Martha Rosen was wrong in her fears, or whether she had you
prognosticated accurately, and that you have messed with the
minds and the trust of those who have too few ways to turn.

Let's hope you-all consider your responsibilities as carefully
as we-all consider the hideous consequences if you dial a wrong
number.

75: 14 AUGUST 70

THE DAY OF THE YAHOO: PART ONE

It is the last day of July 1970 as I write this, and I am sitting
here, and it is nine minutes after midnight (which I guess makes
it Saturday, August 1, technically) and I want to capture the
date and moment exactly because so help me god I have just
witnessed the lowest possible point of bad taste possible to the
species Homo Sapiens.

I am watching the *Merv Griffin Show* on CBS and Jacqueline
Susann has just finished talking about her reaction to the death
of her dog, Josephine (the one about which she wrote her first
book, before she discovered that sex and drugs and gossip sold
better than stories about canines), and she has compared the
way she took the dog's death to the way Ethel Kennedy and the
other Jackie reacted to the death of John F. Kennedy.

Let me make this perfectly clear: Jacqueline Susann, the
authoress of *Valley of the Dolls* and *The Love Machine*, has just
compared the death of her dog with the death of JFK.

Were Merv Griffin something nobler than a simpering,
posturing nitwit, more intent on hyping his round-the-corner-

from-the-theater pub, Pip's (named after Arthur Treacher, the usually potted truckler whose effete presence, gray eminence at best, can be found lounging beside Griffin every show), than in promulgating a little sanity on the enormous amount of air time given to him, he would have shied back, appalled, poked her in her snout, and hurled her tackily dressed body off the stage for grossness above and beyond the buoyancy of gorges.

(Perhaps I'm being unfair about Treacher. He's a thundering bore, to be sure, but at least he's more urbane than the *lumpen* Ed McMahon, toady to Carson, or any of the other superbland second bananas that have festooned talk-show emcees since Morey Amsterdam or Jerry Lester of the old 1950s *Broadway Open House*. They serve, it seems to me, the purpose of producing in video terms the familial equivalent of the boring, but occasionally ridiculously amusing idiot uncle who comes to visit in August. Once a year, for ten days, it can be stomached; but every night year in and year out is considerably more than a bit much.)

Understand something: Mrs. Irving Mansfield was quite serious. It was not a put-on. She actually and literally equated the death of a pet with the death of a man who, for all his flaws, has become as close to a myth figure as anything we've had in this country in many decades. It never occurred to her that she was in monstrous bad taste, gauche to the point of the bizarre. Nor, apparently, did it strike Griffin that way.

I can understand *her* not recognizing the nadir of misshapen values to which she had descended: her books are indicative of the unbeautiful way her mind works and the level of grossness on which she operates. (I find it troubling to speak so of a lady who has commended my work: I was the first writer employed to bring that most illiterate of best sellers, *Valley of the Dolls*, to the screen, and though my work was passed over for that of subsequent scenarists, Ms. Susann confided to friends that, had my screen treatment been used, the film would not have been the horrendous disaster so well-remembered and easily forgotten. Nonetheless, my pride as a writer compels me to point out that it is this selfsame "writer" who, when being queried on the *David Frost Show*, when asked if she thought she was

writing great literature, replied, "Do you consider the work of
Irving Wallace or Leon Uris or Harold Robbins great? I write
with the same sort of greatness." And since I consider that trio
of slovenly hacks outright disgraces to the auctorial art, it tells
me not only where Ms. Susann keeps *her* head, but to what
degree her personal debasement may be gauged. My heart dies
in me a little bit every time I see some slack-jawed straphanger,
or salesgirl, or cement worker, on a public conveyance, pawing
a well-thumbed copy of some entry in the Susann canon. They
dull their senses of what is graceful and meaningful by dumping
the swill of brutalized fiction in their intellectual brainstreams,
but if one has read Ms. Susann, one can well understand that
her comparison of the death of Josephine with that of Kennedy
is in keeping. And so, it is not surprising that she was unaware
of her grossness.)

Nor is it out of line to expect Griffin to be insensitive to the
horror. Dealing as he does, for endless hours, with flash and
filigree (as Terry Southern would term it), he encounters so
much of the corrupt spirit that his sensitivities must be as well-
honed as a stone ax.

What *does* surprise me is that apparently (from the sound,
or lack of it) the audience found it quite in keeping. They
listened with awe and delight to Ms. Susann, Mrs. Mansfield,
the personification of success in our times, the glamorous and
glorious jetsetting manifestation of everything to which they
aspire: wealth, position, acclaim, prestige. They paid dutiful,
respectful attention to her mewling and distasteful parallel. It is
surely destiny that ordained that the basest utterance of modern
man should emerge from Jacqueline Susann.

Which brings me to the Winston cigarette commercials
and what they, along with Ms. Susann's pronouncement, add
up to in these declining days of the American Empire. The
deification of the yahoo. The ennobling of anti-intellectualism.
The aggrandizement of the gauche and the idolatry of ignorance.

There's a linkup, yes there is.

Surely it hasn't escaped you?

*Hee Haw, Nashville Music, Petticoat Junction, The Beverly
Hillbillies, Mayberry RFD, Where's Huddles?, Happy Days,* of

course, George Putnam and his interpretation of the news...but most flagrantly, the Winston cigarette commercials, all of them personify a frightening trend toward anti-intellectualism that goes far beyond the rube, hick, yahoo fear of erudition that has haunted this country since its earliest days.

In his sheet, on his horse once more, the Common Man rides again!

As this is another of those nebulous yet very real trends—like McCarthyism or Reagan's police stateism—it'll take two columns really to get into it, so for this week's tag I'll just remind you of the Winston commercials, refresh your memories, let you dwell on what they portend on this subject, start the fear tremors, and go away.

A young, longhaired, obviously snotnosed punk driving a sports car he can't afford (his daddy prob'ly bought it for him; you can tell that little bastard never did an honest day's labor with his hands) pulls up in front of a country store. Rocking back and forth, whittling on a stick, sits a front-porcher of venerable years, looking insular, looking canny, looking down his nose at the city kid. The little prick gets out of his car and points to a cigarette billboard declaring WINSTON TASTES GOOD LIKE A CIGARETTE SHOULD. "Hey, Pops," the kid says, in early *Blackboard Jungle* jargon, "don't you know that's bad grammar? It oughta be, 'Winston tastes good as a cigarette should.'" At which point, from the woodwork possibly, leap half a dozen rural toughs, who bound about in a highly threatening manner, bleating the accusation, "Whuuuuuduya *want*? Good grammar or good taste?" (As though the two had anything to do with one another or were incompatible.)

They chivy and harass this model of what all rural folk despise and fear in urban life, and quickly show the upstart what they think of his highfalutin' ways. They dump his ass in a watering trough. He pops up after a minute, in a vain attempt to stave off lynching (which surely takes place as the commercial fades out), and recants, averring that, "Winston tastes good *like* a cigarette should!"

Again. A tall, thin, pince-nez'd gentleman, very likely a professor of linguistics or philology, finds his way to a truck in a loading dock. There's that Winston sign, omnipresent on the side of the van. He says to the foreman in charge, in a snooty, nasal, smart-alecky way, "Bed gremmeh, don'ch'know? That ought to be *as*, not *like*." And sure as hell, here come a horde of muscular troglodytes from the warehouse, and they threaten the bejeezus out of this old guy, and like the kid, he pulls a Galileo and renounces correct grammar to save his hide.

One more. An emaciated, birdlike dude with glasses wanders into a secretarial pool and pulls the same dumb number. Bad grammar. So the chicks attack him, slam his skinny tail into a typing chair and run him around the pool till he begs off and joins the illiterates. (Well, no great loss; it's obvious from the stereotype that the guy couldn't fuck worth a damn anyhow, so why should all those leggy, made-up, sexy chicks treat him like a human being? He's an intellectual pisshead, we all know that, and we also know that that kind of creep never gets all those great, brainless mannequins hipped on Gregg and suchlike to fall down and Do It.)

Are we getting the message, friends?

The Visigoths are with us. They are telling us that it's hardhat time, that Adlai Stevenson was a fag and Albert Einstein needed a haircut and if you want to read a book, try Jacqueline Susann.

And if you want to survive the pogrom, bookworms, go yahoo.

But whatever you do, don't come back here next week for the second and final, smashing concluding installment of *William Faulkner Meets Jerk Man*. You might learn something, and god knows these days that's a ticket to destruction.

76: 21 AUGUST 70

THE DAY OF THE YAHOO: PART TWO

My secretary, Hallie a.k.a. Susan, points out to me that the anti-intellectual trend in America is even evident to those of you not concerned with the Glass Teat. She notes, for instance, that newspaper crossword puzzles now have the solutions published the same day, not the next or a week later. She'd offer me instances off the tube, but she doesn't have a television set. (She contends it's bad for the complexion and gives her "female troubles" three times a month. I thought I was in bad shape when Crazy June went on to other pastures. I didn't know when I was well off.)

Well, she doesn't need to bring such video vacuities to my attention. I see them all. Such as the raising-to-god status of *Lumpenproletariat* like the football player-cum-college student who stood guard over the flagpole soon after the Kent State massacre, who refused to allow his fellow students to lower the flag to half-mast in memory. It's okay to half-mast Old Glory for Ev Dirksen, one of the more corrupt public officials to go to his much-deserved judgment, but it's a patriotic no-no to weep for kids senselessly slain by golem in Reserve uniforms. That silly git, that muscle-brained pigskin patriot, has received thousands of letters from similarly minded humanitarians, commending him for his defense of a scrap of cloth. It is a manifestation of the anti-intellectual attitude that property rights far outweigh human rights.

And, of course, Winston Cigarettes (emphysema in a cylinder), not to be outdone, has its rousing huzzah in favor of the proletariat in its never-ending struggle with the aristocracy: a commercial break, friends.

This old lady with the lace collar and the lorgnette makes the error of correcting one of her servants that Winston tastes good as, rather than *like*, a cigarette should. The minor altercation takes place in the old lady's stately rococo mansion, and *noblesse oblige* being what it is, not to mention *mon dieu et mon droit*, one would expect the scullery maid to fall to her knees and beg the grande dame not to buggy-whip her. But in appealing to the boob mentality, it is a foregone conclusion that the Common Man is better than the aristocracy, simply because he has good down-to-earth common sense and none of that high-falutin' manner. (Images of the duke and his men, riding their horses through the peasant's potato patch...images of Madame Defarge rocking and knitting as Marie Antoinette gets the original skinhead haircut...

images of Jim Fisk and other robber barons grinding the faces of the poor with their gold bootheels...images of the stalwart country lads at Lexington, freezing their asses off...lotta images reinforcing that arid Leninist doctrine that all workers are saints, all bosses are bastards.)

So instead of groveling—as a proper servant should—the arrogant serving wench has the audacity to point her (remarkably well-manicured for a servant) finger at the old woman, and out of the walls emerge other servants—butler, footman, cook, upstairs maid—and they begin to chivy and hector the old lady till it seems certain she'll have an occlusion right there before our horrified eyes. "Whuuuuuuduya want, good grammar or good taste?" the staunch defenders of illiteracy demand. The old woman is shocked; the *servants* are revolting!

(Revolting, hell: they're downright disgusting!)

They drive her before them like the last remnants of the royal family, and finally pen her up in a sliding panel behind a bookcase, and take over the house, cavorting and rampaging like groundlings in a castle. Finally, the panel slides back and the old woman, having learned her lesson (presumably, not to mess around with John L. Lewis or the Wobblies), mumbles in a cowed voice, "Winston tastes good *like* a cigarette should!"

End commercial.

Just what have we seen, gentle readers? What do the Winston commercials with their browbeaten and physically threatened college professors, ped ants, city slickers, emasculated Ichabod Cranes and aristocratic septaugeneric shrikes say to us? They say, the day of the yahoo is on us. They say, the time of the booboisie is here. They say, the Common Man knows best. They say, there is only equality in nonintellectual views of the universe.

A statement echoed in the speeches of Spiro T. Aggrandizement when he attacks the Hatfield-McGovern antiwar bill on grounds Nixon knows best and no one should argue with The Man.

Well, what *of* all this equality business? Take the ten-second pro/anti-intellectualism test: would you rather everyone was free or equal? One or the other. None of the above is not a responsive answer. Okay, made your decision? Then consider this quote from Will and Ariel Durant's *The Lessons of History:*

"...freedom and equality are sworn and everlasting enemies, and when one prevails the other dies. Leave men free, and their natural inequalities will multiply almost geometrically... To check the growth of inequality, liberty must be sacrificed... Even when repressed, inequality grows; only the man who is below the average in economic ability desires equality; *those who are conscious of superior ability desire freedom; and in the end superior ability has its way.*" The italics are mine.

The point being, of course, we must have equal opportunity for freedom. When every man is given free access to the reins of self-realization and power, we allow each man to do the best he can. *De facto* imprisonment by caste or economic ghettoization (which is what we now have) is a hype. It is lip service to liberty. But actual, real unfettering of the total population being the answer, give me freedom over equality every time.

It is only Spiro and Winston who want everyone equal.

(It reminds me of the Johnny Hart B.C. strip that had a bitter bite for male chauvinists. One of the cavemen was making fun of a prehistoric Women's Lib type. He gibes at her, as she walks past, "Hey, I hear you want to be my equal." She takes a long, pointed look at him, continues walking, and tosses over her shoulder, "Frankly, I had something a little loftier in mind.")

Which is the inherent horror of anti-intellectualism. It postulates that anyone who seeks to be *better* must be evil, must be—by inference—putting down the poor commoner. Well, that's *malarkey*. (You remember malarkey: a common word of the thirties and forties.) Smarter and quicker and more inventive is *better*, dammit, and we're wallowing through a world where slower and dumber and more compliant is dangerous. I did all this on the Common Man in my columns of 17 and 25 October, last year. You can find them in my book, if you need reinforcement of what's coming down, as explicated last week and this week.

By serving to gap us once again, this time by IQ and intellectual pursuit, "they" reinforce their hold over the mass of us. Young against old, liberal against conservative, white against black, Jew against Arab, "they" will use any difference to keep us apart. One of these days we'll run a list of names, telling exactly who "they" are, so you can fit titles to your paranoias, but for the nonce it serves us here to name them as the Winston people and their amoral advertising agency who dreamed up the vicious eyesore commercials that pour hardener into the prejudices of the scuttlefish out there in the Great American Heartland who fear civil disobedience, student unrest, dissidence, change... intellectualism.

You see, it's like this. The times are perilous. The government feels the tremors. There are too many people asking questions, too many people using their heads for the first time. Too many people suddenly saying, "Hold it a minute. I didn't know *that!* Is that what it's all about?" And when that happens, Spiro love, it means you get a plague of Hatfields and McGoverns. And neither you nor Baby Dickie can handle it. You can drive people like Angela Davis and Abbie Hoffman mad as mudflies, so they do something brutal and stupid and self-destructive, but you can't cope with all the Hatfields and McGoverns who operate on your level and won't bully under to that venomous bullshit of character assassination and slanted reportage.

The only way they can keep us quiescent, the only way they can make every man look askance at his fellows, is by keeping us dumb. And anti-intellectual pogroms are a strong weapon in the armory.

It's all around us. And the Common Man will go for it every time. History says so. The beware signs are up.

The question thus becomes: are we smart enough to drag the dummies up to a thinking level, to get them cerebrating...or do we allow ourselves to be slaughtered or driven off?

Think about it. Yeah, think.

PUBLIC CORRECTION: Several weeks ago, doing a number on the upcoming *Matt Lincoln* series, I made the unforgivable error of attributing to one man the writings of another. I said *The Challenge*, an excellent script for an ABC Movie of the Week, was written by Irving Elman, producer of *Matt Lincoln*. It was a strong point in his favor, I thought. Where I got the information that Mr. Elman had scripted that particular piece of joy, I don't know. But I was woefully inaccurate. The scenarist who wrote *The Challenge* was Marc Norman. Let me say that again, in caps (because corrections and retractions usually appear on back pages, in unreadable type): MARC NORMAN WROTE *THE CHALLENGE* AND IT WAS A HELLUVA FINE SCRIPT.

The correction came to my attention through several sources, not the least of which was Mr. Elman, whose response to my column may interest you. I print it herewith, in its entirety.

"Dear Harlan:

"You goofed. I did not write 'The Challenge,' starring Darren McGavin, etc. Any more than I wrote 'The Oscar.' You threw your tomato at the wrong target.

"But then your column was full of misdirected tomatoes.

"When I made the Leopold-Loeb crack, if I thought you'd take it as a straight line, I would have spelled it out as the j-o-k-e it was intended to be. I had assumed that from the context of our conversation you'd understand that since everything else about the character had changed, it would have made no sense to call him by the same name. So we threw a bunch of names into a hat and came up with *'Matt Lincoln.'* Sorry you don't care for it, but at least it wasn't 'Harlan Ellison' or 'Irving Elman.'

"As for your reviewing a *series*, the first picture of which has yet to be finished, let alone seen by anyone, and judging it lousy, I consider that a miracle of critical prescience. How are you at reading tea leaves?

"Anyway, I don't mean to carp, because I did enjoy your column. It was a lot of laughs.

"Peace, Irving Elman."

Well. How about that? And after I went so far out of my way to be fair and upfront about Matt Lincoln. It just goes to prove you shouldn't play j-o-k-e-s on dumb, humorless bastards like tv columnists, doesn't it? Because I assumed that you were telling me the serious, straight truth, Mr. Elman. I mean, now you say the Lincoln name came out of a hat. That makes three different versions of how Leopold was changed to Lincoln, all from your mouth, sir. (I commend those of you who need back information to the column of two weeks ago.) Which are we to believe? If you say a hat, sir, then I guess we're lucky his name wasn't Matt Stetson 8½. But I'd even have settled for "Irving Elman" as a realistic alternative. "Harlan Ellison" sounds phony and made up. You're wise not to have used it. And just politely to refresh your memory, I didn't review the series, I reviewed the *pilot film,* and made some comments about what I hoped not to see in the series, based on fears of my correspondents. But then, you know that, Mr. Elman. You didn't *really* think I was reviewing a series I hadn't yet seen, did you? Huh, did you?

My tea leaf ability is almost as bad as my *Oscar* scripting, but it's nowhere near as good as my evaluations of people who play mickeymouse with me when I ask them if I can see a segment of two of a series and they tell me no, they can't show them to me...*not* "the films aren't yet finished," but *no,* you can't see them. If they weren't done, why not just say that instead of giving me a blanket lockout? As Marc Norman will attest, I can make mistakes, Mr. Elman, but at least my books are open for examination at all times. How's *that* for laughs, sir?

77: 4 SEPTEMBER 70

The Catholic Church is, I believe, generally credited with immortalizing the directive, "Give me your children till they are six—and they are mine forever." That's pretty heady stuff, when you stop to think how many *kinder* there are growing up in the shadow of the Holy Trinity. But it is nothing compared to the scale on which American Society debases its female population when it says, "Give me your girl-children till they are old enough to enter the World's 'Our Little Miss' Variety Pageant—and they'll be doomed forever to be either hookers or consumers, or both."

How it came to pass that I was provided with the knowledge that informs this week's installment is a small trip, so I'll take you on it, as I was taken. It was a week ago Wednesday, August 19. About eight o'clock. I was getting ready to go out to a screening, when the phone rang, and a voice said, "You don't know me, man, and it isn't important, but you ought to turn on Channel 11 right now. You are not going to be*lieve* what's going on, on that channel!" I asked what it was, and the guy on the other end just repeated, "Turn it on for one second. If ever there was a column, that's it, man."

So he hung up after I'd thanked him, and out of wild curiosity I turned it on, and there—about three-quarters over—was something called the WORLD'S "OUR LITTLE MISS" VARIETY PAGEANT. I was only able to watch five minutes of it, and then had to split, but I was so intrigued and horrified that when Mary Reinholz called me the next morning—to inform me this week's *Freep* would be a Women's Lib edition, staffed and prepared by the ladies—to ask me if I'd slant my column toward Women's Lib, I was able to tell her, "Dear heart, I was gonna do it anyhow. I've got myself a doozy this week." (Just so you don't think I'm pandering.)

And I called KTTV and asked them if they'd screen me a tape of the live telecast of the pageant, and they said yes, and so it was that last Monday I went down to the KTTV studios and sat for ninety minutes as the Universal Broadcasting Company (of Baton Rouge, Louisiana) piped a replay through its Dallas affiliate to a color tv at Channel 11. Ninety minutes of unrelenting bad taste, petty hokum, deadly degradation of innocent children. Nincty teeth-clenching, stomach-bubbling minutes of ghastliness as a clique of dirty old men and their exploiting associates debased and corrupted a dozen little girls between the ages of three and twelve.

Thereby keynoting, most appropriately for this edition dedicated to the ennoblement of the female image, one of the most insidious maneuvers utilized by our snake-twisted society to fuck up the minds of its female population.

Uh, Hef, that's about 50 percent of the crowd. Which, in case you hadn't noticed, makes the Catholic Church look like really inept small potatoes.

The "Our Little Miss" Pageant (we are told by a publicity release) is more than a beauty pageant! It is a youth development program designed to give young ladies early goals in good grooming, social graces, talent training, and scholarship! It is the only outlet of this kind for deserving youngsters!

The brochure goes on to tell us that OLM (as I'll refer to it hereafter) has 1200 local preliminaries sponsored by civic and service organizations throughout the nation (as opposed to a mere 54 local pageants for Miss Teenage America). Are you hanging in there?

There are over 100,000 local contestants (second only to the Miss America Pageant, whoop whoop!). There are 32 state pageants. And in 1969 there were 177 international contestants. And there is even a motto: THERE IS NOTHING SWEETER THAN A LITTLE GIRL!

That all of this bullshit serves the major purpose of hyping children's clothes and toys and (god save us) cosmetics, is something that seems to escape the attention of all save the venal swine who cobble up this monstrosity from, well, from whole cloth. ("The La Petite winner will appear on one million Martha's Miniature Dress hangtags during 1970.")

But, why linger any longer on the background? Why not come with me now to the Great Hall of the Dallas Apparel Mart ("The fact that the Pageant is emanating from the Dallas Apparel Mart gives it a fashion connotation...a world-wide glimpse into the children's sphere of fashion.") for the 1970 World's "Our Little Miss" Variety Pageant.

There's no business like snow business...!

Frankie Avalon and Shari Lewis were the guest stars, and the show opened with Frankie singing (naturally) "Thank Heaven for Little Girls," a song which has abominable lyrics and is difficult to sing by anyone but Maurice Chevalier, and even *he* looks a trifle embarrassed. As for Frankie, I've known him slightly better than casually for many years, and while he is a lovely guy and I don't want he should take offense, he *still* only has one note in his repertoire. It was not an auspicious opening. Followed by Shari Lewis and her sex-crazed hand-puppet, Lambchop.

Announcer: "Live! From the Great Hall in Dallas, Texas [home of hyperthyroid provincialism], the 1970 World's 'Our Little Miss' Variety Pageant...hosts Frankie Avalon and Shari Lewis... featuring 250 of the cutest, most talented little girls in the world! Brought to us by Royalty Toys!" And they run a commercial for this blatant tie-in, the "Our Little Miss Toy Doll," a strangely

grotesque little blank-eyed mannequin wearing a princess tiara
and a cape with a train.

Commercial over, the announcer informs us there are two
divisions: 7–12 years old, the Our Little Miss finalists; ages 3–6,
the La Petite finalists. They will compete in sportwear, party
dresses, and talent.

Frankie and Shari came down, then, to be introduced, and
they virtually had to sprint the 146 miles across the polo-field-
sized stage to the cameras. And oddly, there was no audience.
Just a bleacher section set up with hundreds of little girls ranked
one after the other.

They were introduced by two superannuated elves named
Bob Something and Chuck Something, who sat in a kind of
sportscasters' box and spouted treacly aphorisms at one another:
"Isn't this a marvelous pageant, Chuck?" Chuck bobbled his
head like a puppet minus its puppet master. "Well, it certainly
is, Bob!" "And aren't these little girls just marvelous, Chuck?"
"They really are fantastic, Bob!" It went on that way for minutes,
entire minutes.

Then came someone named Mr. Lynn, a gentleman of
questionable demeanor (I'm avoiding lawsuits in my phraseology,
friends), who is variously referred to in the publicity brochure
as "the 'Bert Parks' of the OLM pageant," "nationally famous
personality," Charming of the Children's Pageant World," "In
the words of Mister Lynn, the international master of ceremonies,
'When Little Miss hits national television it will steal the
hearts of all America,'" "a kaleidoscope personality," and in an
advertisement he obviously took for himself in the brochure
(check the spelling of this international personality), "One of
America's foremost authorities of femenine [sic] beauty."

Mister Lynn, who looked to my jaundiced eye like the sort of
failed hairdresser who lures little children into the basements of
churches with M & Ms, simpered his way through a saccharine
introduction in praise of Shari and Frankie. At this point I called
for a shot of insulin. One could get diabetes just *watching* this
abomination.

But this was all preamble to the very genuine horrors about
to be unveiled. In party dresses, out came the six finalists in

the OLM division. They marched out as a cadre and all stood there with right foot extended and twisted in that improbable model's stance seen *ad nauseam* at fashion shows and being held by women at parties, the kind of women who feel uncomfortable at parties. And art gallery openings. All six had ghastly Miss America smiles on their little faces. That wholly unearthly rictus that denotes neither joy nor warmth. All teeth and cheeks stretched back like papyrus; smiles as if painted on, or as though Mister Lynn and his fashion thugs had held by the head each of the children just prior to emergence onstage, and attached clothespins at the back of the neck, under the hairline, to stretch the faces into that monstrous *sardonicus*. I had visions of the ballet *The Red Shoes*, of the ballerina dancing till she danced all time away and finally died. I had a vision of these unfortunate little moppets smiling like that through all the days of their lives, till they were put in the final box, smile still strictured.

Then they brought out the half-dozen La Petite division children. Ages three to six. Tiny. My god, small. Innocent. And...oh, Jesus Jesus...they had *blue eyeliner* and lipstick and that awful model's pose...three to six years old...Oh, Christ! They look twenty-five!

How can they do it? How can they turn kids under six into jaded strumpets of twenty-five? Mother of god, they all look like *hookers!*

It's been years since I've felt the need to cry.

My lady, Cindy, watching the pageant with me, said in a stunned voice, "The producers of this thing must be ex-convicts who've served time for child molestation!"

On it went, without respite. The 1969 OLM winner, Miss Lauri Lynn Huffaker of Dallas, Texas, came on with "the world famous Riley dance troupe" (?) and did a cheap-jack production number cavorting to "March of the Wooden Soldiers." Meaning no disrespect, but for a big-time national winner of a big-time national talent pageant like this, Miss Huffaker struck me as a rather ungainly little girl with no visible talent.

Into another commercial, surfeited with sloppy sweet sentimentality about little girls, pushing that goddamn OLM doll that "comes complete with crown, robes, and beautiful clothes."

It bulks obvious: beautiful clothes are one of the cornerstones
of this entire vomitous operation. Not only is it bad enough to
portray little girls as vapid creatures fit only to sit around and
play momma to their dolls—an image our society reinforces
from cradle to dishpan, thereby assuring itself of generation
after generation of unpaid, highly skilled day-care and kitchen
help—but in preparing these prepubescent Lolitas to be good
consumers, devourers of the Grossest National Product, in
preparing them to be mindless automatons who will buy every
midi-length superfluosity economists and *Women's Wear Daily*
feel are necessities to save a sagging economy, they are infected
by cynical and demented hypes like the OLM pageant with
the virus of believing if one does not have good grooming and
the latest clothes, one simply is out of it, unfit not merely to be
Our Little Miss, but disallowed from having any feelings of ego
strength, any intrinsic worth, any right to the bounties of life. It
is, quite literally, the corruption of the young.

And for all his lisping sentimentality about the wonders of
little girls, they held the camera just a few beats too long on
the Prince Charming of the Children's Pageant World and Mister
Lynn, with a monstrously sinister smile carved on his face,
exposed his inner nature with one look. It was like looking out
of the mad eyes of Vincent van Gogh at *The Starry Night*. It was
one of those inexplicable, unpredicted moments when one sees
straight to the core of another human being, and in that glance
was all the cynical exploitive rapacity of a man in no way above
using children to further his own sick needs. The man caught
unaware in that camera glare was not a man I would leave to
baby-sit with *my* children.

Frankie was cut in quickly on camera, sitting with the La
Petite finalists, reading from some loathsome Edgar Guestian
rodomontade about "What Is a Little Girl?" I reproduce just a
snippet here. More would be to dare safety:

"God borrows from many creatures to make a little girl: he
uses the song of the bird, the squeal of the pig, the stubbornness
of a mule, the antics of a monkey, the spryness of a grasshopper,
the curiosity of a cat.... The little girl likes: new shoes and party
dresses, small animals, first grade, noisemakers, the girl next

door, dolls, make believe, dancing lessons, ice cream, kitchens, coloring books, make-up..."

It went on for some time, painting a pastel picture of prewomanhood consigned to its place: in the boutiques and the kitchen. The little girls sat there and arranged their skirts about them, ensuring the exquisiteness of their appearance every moment, all of them terribly involved with themselves, already poisoned by their parents into thinking superficial attractiveness, the right image, the way they look to the rest of the world...are the only matters of consequence a properly brought-up young lady should worry about.

Then the OLM finalists came out, one by one, in their sports clothes and Mister Lynn quavered minute descriptions of their ensembles. The children pirouetted and did that models' slouch, and when they finally stood all in a row, it was terribly sad-making to realize that, for all but one of them, from this moment on, everything in their lives would be downhill. In the bleachers, the little girls who had already been weeded out clapped on cue. They all wore little white gloves, and when they applauded it looked like a pigeon freakout in a dirndl shoppe.

Commercial: "Little child, with your eyes shining and dimpled cheeks, you will lead us along the pathway to the more abundant life. We blundering grown-ups need in our lives the virtue that you have in yours. The joys and enthusiasm of looking forward to a routine day, with glorious expectation of wonderful things to come. The vision that sees the world as a splendid place ...Challenge that forgets differences as quickly as your childish quarrels are done, and holds no grudges, that hates pretense and empty show. That loves people for what they are; the genuineness of being oneself; to be simple, natural, and sincere. Oh, little child, may we become more like you. And now, from Royalty Toys, the Little Miss Doll: the doll that epitomizes the beautiful, talented, and poised little girls of the world. Little girls: curious, inventive, playing pageant with *their* Little Miss Dolls. Little girls who, in these times of stark reality, can escape into a world of gumdrops and lollipops. There is nothing sweeter than a little girl, and no finer playmate than a Little Miss Doll.

The Little Miss Doll, coming soon to leading toy and department stores. By Royalty, of course."

The Little Miss Doll, symbol of white America. Tell the ghetto kid playing among the stripped-down shells of discarded cars in an empty lot that there is no better playmate than a Little Miss Doll. Tell the little black girl raped first at ten and pregnant by gang bang at thirteen that she needs poise so she can escape into a world of gumdrops and lollipops. White little doll, blonde little doll, sweet little doll. In these times of stark reality we know you are the answer.

Pure cornball, but corrupt cornball. Straight out of the antediluvian forties. Dallas, Texas, for god and home and country and escapism. With kids in high schools, grade schools radicalizing themselves, with kids in colleges getting their brains blown out, it defies belief to sit and watch this sort of madness and know that there are people who really believe it matters, that it has some relevance to what our world is really like. This exploitation of the young, this brainwashing of the female, it is part and parcel of the conceptual inability of most of our society to realize that all the senseless persiflage over which they've cooed for fifty years is invalid, harmful, criminal.

Invalid? You tell me: the reigning OLM came out with an introduction from Mister Lynn (now wearing a sequined jacket and looking exactly like an overaged Jim Nabors with that incredible Alfred E. Neuman "What, Me Worry?" grin) and did her pouter-pigeon walk before the throng. All she did was walk across the stage, and the look the poor child sported was one of expectation, of waiting for the applause, merely because *she was there*, as though her mere appearance should spark ovations. Invalid? You tell me how relevant to an ennobling lifestyle can be an orientation that says because you are lovely, you deserve approbation and riches.

But even this congeries of evils did not plumb the bottom. Yet to come was the talent division and the final selections of winners.

The first little girl in the talent division of the OLM came out and sang "I Believe." You know—I believe for every drop of rain that falls, a flower grows ...you know the one. The poor little thing trembled and shook so badly her voice had a ghastly tremolo. She was petrified out of her mind. Her parents and the pageant coordinators, putting so much emphasis on what is little better than an inadequate version of the *Original Amateur Hour*, had invested success, in this child's mind, with such portents, that she flubbed and twitched terribly. The torment of the young; dance for our guests, honey. Sing your song. Say da-da.

As Cindy commented, the really sick ones are the parents. Feeding their own failed dreams on the flesh of their children. How much money, how many grueling hours of training go into battering a child to perform like a monkey? How much surrogate pleasure do the manipulators vampirically enjoy molding a child to dance and spin and raise her hands to god in song, so she can tremble like a pneumonia victim for an audience of clothing merchants? And oh, goddamn goddamn the shadow of Shirley Temple still sprawled across those children. Jennifer Childers, eight years old, from Satellite Beach, Florida, singing and dancing to the old-time Temple favorite, "Animal Crackers in My Soup." One more little girl in the image of cute Shirley... long blonde locks, crackly voice, ineffable coyness, old before her years. I would send their mothers and fathers through meat grinders with their shoes on.

What have these children by way of natural resources? At that age, plastic, still opening, they have only innocence that they can perfect. And that being stolen from them in the Dallas Apparel Mart—they have nothing, they are perverted at the touch.

Mae Rusan, from Fort Worth, belting like Sophie Tucker, rolling her hips, gutter-voicing her "Happiness Medley." So anti-child, so anti-innocence, I had to turn away. Ninety minutes of primetime on Channel 11 while the universe burns.

There was more, much much more. But why belabor it? Women wonder why men wage war, why they think of women as empty-headed totems to accouter their evenings out, why gold star mothers take pride in the corpses of their sons blasted to bits in the Nam. Why wonder?

Why try to find complex reasons? They are all there, in

ninety minutes of prurience and debasement, as the bastion of Democracy works its way on its young.

Channel 11 has asked me to point out that it did not originate this show, that it merely carried it through the facilities of the Universal Television Network, that it is responsible for such excellent shows as 1985 and the upcoming special, *I'm 17, Pregnant and Frightened*. That it will be broadcasting in stereo *Midsummer Rock* on Wednesday, September 2, at 7:00 p.m.

Okay, I've mentioned it, and I spread praise to them for their good works. Now tell the ladies how good you are, KTTV; I can dig it, but what about "Our Little Miss"?

Did someone mention pornography?

78: 11 SEPTEMBER 70

In a week when my eyes have seen yet another Los Angeles riot; the bizarre death of another good man, KMEX news director Ruben Salazar; the Middle East about to explode; Nixon ignoring his responsibilities at home in favor of "saving the world" while his own country tumbles to dust; American Legionnaires loudly protesting their patriotism while the antique ethics they espouse wither and atrophy; high schools and colleges postponing their openings because other patriots won't support them; taxes raised again despite Yorty/Reagan promises to the contrary; in a week such as this, I choose to look away and try to support my life minus the pain, absenting the anguish …just for a little while.

The good thing about indulging myself with this column is that I can escape when the need arises. I can turn from the rivers of lava that flow through the streets and talk about friendship and good acting and retying old bonds. It's nowhere near as important as the pivotal issues of our day, but, Jesus, friendship is one of the few things to which each of us can still cling, and few things are as necessary for maintaining one's sanity.

So this week I'll talk about Zalman King.

I'm back writing television. The last foray was early in 1969. *The Name of the Game*, remember? It came to naught, and naughting was good enough for me.

But Mike Zagor, one fine writer, and the guy who created the Writers Guild Open Door program that instructs minority talents in writing teleplays, called me many months ago, and said he'd created a series called *The Young Lawyers*. And would I come down and look at the pilot? Yeah, sure I would. Mike is a fine, committed writer.

So I went down to Paramount and saw it—and so did you, on the *ABC Movie of the Week* twice last season—and it was quite good. Mostly because it starred a kid named Zalman King. I'll repeat the name: Zalman King. Remember it. If he isn't the hottest thing on the tube by this time next year, I'll eat this entire edition of the *Freep*, second section, freak sex ads and all, covered with peach butter.

Well, one thing and another, and the story I wanted to try for *The Young Lawyers* got turned down and I went my way. But about three weeks ago the producer of the series, Matt Rapf, got in touch with me and said let's try it again. So I did, and they dug my treatment, and thus far they've let me do the story the way I want to write it, and who knows—in a month or two you may see a script of mine (currently) titled "The Whimper of Whipped Dogs" on *The Young Lawyers*. I'm into the first draft of the script now, and in a later column I'll do a rundown on the interesting sidelights accompanying the writing of it for a production schedule that has to take into consideration only twenty shooting days for Lee J. Cobb, who also stars in the series.

But this week I want to talk about Zal, and about friendship, and about what a gigantic talent he is. Not only because it's nice to once in a while stop crying doom and look on the happy side, but because I think it's as much my responsibility to draw your attention to the heavyweight joys in this life—in this case, Zalman King—as it is to tell you the world is coming to an end.

And because my weary soul needs the respite.

How I met Zal was like this:

I was one year into Hollywood. What a nightmare. Got here from the other side of the land with a dime in my pocket and the pieces of a marriage that had to be set to rights in two separate lives where there'd been one before. Broke; Jesus, broke. Nothing to eat the last five hundred miles but a box of Stuckey's pecan pralines. But I had an agent—through a lucky break, a fluke, a chance, I had an agent. And the agent got me television assignments, and I danced my elfin troll rigadoon for story editors and producers and they gave me assignments. And I blew every one of them. No one'd bothered to show me how to write a script. So I blew them. But there'd been enough money from the story treatments—before I was "cut off"—to keep going. Rice Krispies and spaghetti five nights a week, but it was still going.

The only deal I didn't blow was an adaptation of my book *Memos from Purgatory* for Joan Harrison who was then producing *The Alfred Hitchcock Hour*. I wrote the script, and about a year later rewrote it, and finally they went to shoot it. At Universal.

It was my first big show. I'd done a half-hour segment of *Ripcord* previously, but they wouldn't let me on the set, so *Memos* was the first time I was to see my words turned into people moving. I was scared and arrogant and puffed up with pride and uncertain and worried and that whole dumb crowd. But what it *felt* like! Like Otis Redding sweating "Shake" at the Monterey Pop Festival.

I went out the first day of shooting, early in the evening. It was a back-lot shooting, on a mock-up New York street. The book was based on some time I did with kid gangs in Red Hook, in Brooklyn, and there was James Caan playing me, Harlan Ellison; and Lynn Loring; and a bunch of young guys hired on as members of the Barons.

The first shot was of a semi coming down the street, and Caan/Ellison escaping a horde of kids trying to stomp him by rolling under it, and escaping into a shoe repair shop across the street.

The director was Joe Pevney. The clackboard man got ready, the sound man yelled, "Speed!" and the assistant director yelled, "Quiet onna set!" and the clackboard man stepped in front of the camera and said, "Scene twenty-six, take one," clacked his board, and Pevney said, "Roll 'em!" and there went Caan across the street into the path of the big truck, hit it at a dead run, jumped up into the link between cab and trailer, boiled through and jumped off the other side, across the sidewalk, and into that shoe repair shop. Everyone applauded. "That's a take!" Pevney yelled.

I turned around and was looking at Zalman King.

I know women who think Zalman King is beautiful. His wife, Pat Knop (one of the most remarkable sculptresses I've ever met, whose statues are as breathtaking as Zal's acting is muscular), certainly thinks so. But encountering Zalman King eight years ago, fresh out of New York and on his first acting assignment in Hollywood, many words came to mind but none of them was beautiful.

Zal King has a "beautiful" face the way Charles Bronson has a "beautiful" face. Craggy is the exact word. Hewn from heavy substances describes it. Smoldering, intense, underlit with humor but informed by obvious intelligence. He looks Jewish, with all of the physical strength that connotes, and none of the weaknesses. When he wants to look mean, it is a subtle shifting of musculature, and it chills.

He was playing a killer delinquent in my show, and he wanted to look mean. I turned around and was chilled.

To another person on the set whom I knew casually, I said, "Who the fuck is *that*?" And was told Zalman King.

I shivered.

(Judging books by their covers is a stupid habit, and one hard to break. Had you, for instance, never met Robert Bloch, who wrote *Psycho* and other chilling novels, you would assume he was a deranged madman. In truth, Bob Bloch is the sweetest, kindest, gentlest man in the world, with an unbelievable sense of humor. As he is fond of saying, he has the heart of a child. He adds, "I keep it in a jar on my bookcase." The same holds true for Zal King.)

The next day I went down to Universal for some indoor sequences and was dumbfounded at the level of intensity he brought to any scene in which he played a part. He literally "upped" the other actors. (And I watched him work with Walter Koenig, most recently of *Star Trek*, who was at that time fresh to tv also. Walter was the other sensational actor in the show.

Together they worked as professionally and as *heavily* as any two actors I've ever seen. And not coincidentally, I became friends with Walter, too.)

After the shooting, we rapped, and subsequently met on a social level. We became casual friends. Not close, but with considerable respect for each other's work. For Zal King is a *serious* actor, with none of the sententious and asinine connotations that phrase usually contains. He works on a vibratory level that virtually gathers all light to itself when he's into a role.

Time passed and Zal went back to New York and married Pat and did a horde of underground films and a television special I missed (but heard raves about for the next two years) about some gang kids who rape a woman on a subway.

And then I went to see *The Young Lawyers* pilot. And there was Zalman King, playing Aaron Silverman, one of the law students working for Boston's Neighborhood Law Office. He was better than ever. Time had put even more incalculable character into his face, and experience had sharpened his technique so he was able to play the most emotional scenes with a soft voice.

When I was finally asked to write for the series, I said, "I'll write for that guy." And they showed me a segment of the series slated for September. Yoked with Lee J. Cobb it is a remarkable visual experience to see Zal King at work. Cobb and King call back memories of Cobb and Cameron Mitchell in the original stage version of Miller's *Death of a Salesman*. The same levels of emotion, the same electricity, the same respect of one fine actor for another. God, they are good on screen. "Yeah," I said again, "I'll write for those guys."

Then I went down on the set and watched Cobb and Zal work under the eye of the camera. Jud Taylor was directing them. A scene in Cobb's office at the NLO.

There is a feeling one gets on a set before a show has premiered. If you've ever felt it, you know what I mean. It is expectancy. It takes two forms. If the show is a bomb, if the stars are pains in the ass, if the directing is sluggish and the writing spotty, the crew radiates a miasmic aura of depression. They perform skillfully (at the rates they get, they'd damned well better!), but the heart isn't in it. The other form is like getting an enema with a Playtex glove studded with cactus needles. It's painfully buoyant. Everyone moves swiftly, there are no tanglefeet tripping over cables, the takes go smoothly and quickly, the director can joke with his people, visitors come away nodding and smiling. Everyone feels a success. *The Courtship of Eddie's Father* had that feel, before it aired, and so did the Cosby show; so did *The Fugitive* and *Batman* and *Run For Your Life*.

The Young Lawyers has that feel.

It comes from the leads, of course. Without the stars really giving, it is all by rote. But when Lee J. Cobb and Zalman King have at one another, everyone on the set knows what is going down is something close to art.

When they broke, Zal came out from under the lights and squinted in my direction. It'd been seven years. No reason to expect him to remember. He came through the set and over the cables and past the makeup table and stuck out a hand the size of a badminton racquet. "Hey, Harlan," he said.

Friendship is a nice thing. It helps mortar up the chinks in one's wearying soul.

I'm writing for tv again, troops. Writing for Lee J. (if my mother could see me now) Cobb and Zalman King.

And if you miss *The Young Lawyers*, if you miss Zalman King, you will be the poorer for it.

79: 18 SEPTEMBER 70

This coming Sunday, September 20, I think you'll want to forgo watching the first half of *The World of Disney* or *Hogan's Heroes* or even the debut of the new ABC series, The Young Rebels (don't fret; I'll watch it and tell you what you missed), because at 7:30 on Channel 11, Metromedia will be airing a one-hour "documentary drama" of some significance. It's titled *I'm 17, I'm Pregnant…And I Don't Know What to Do*.

KT screened it for a group of radio people the other day, and they asked me to take a look, and I must tell you as anthracite-hearted as I am, when it ended, I sat with tears in my eyes. It is quite a piece of film, friends.

The Children's Home Society of California (under a grant from the James Irvine Foundation) produced it with Lee Mendelson Films, and quite apart from its instructional importance, it is an artful dramatization of a subtle and heartbreaking social problem: what do pregnant girls without husbands *do* with their babies, if they don't miscarry or have an abortion? What do they *do* if they decide to have the children? In simple, graceful, and unpretentious fashion, this most exemplary hour gives one answer.

Through the story of Pam (played with understated brilliance by San Francisco State theater arts major Denise Larson) and her agonizing decision to carry her child to term, the merits of the adoptive family program are outlined. It is such a familiar story, so terribly commonplace, that it immediately ties in to our emotions, and as we hear Pam's boyfriend express his feelings about the pregnancy, as we study the tormented faces of Pam's parents, as we see Pam appeal for help from the Children's Home Society and finally engage in group confrontations with other unwed mothers, we are carried without effort to the heart of what must surely be one of the most awful situations in which a young woman can find herself. Through gentle hints and careful suggestions, the characters and attitudes of potential foster parents, social workers, pregnant girls, and teenaged friends are limned, all of it done with a sureness of craft and an ambiance of *humanity*. And when, *in extremis*, Pam must give up her (now) fourteen-month-old little boy, we have seen what both sides of the decision are like. We understand that choosing to keep a child may be as wrong for the child as choosing to give him up.

This is an area of information that needs cogent and kindly exploration. We all know a girl can have an abortion, we all know she can take steps to prevent pregnancy in the first place, and we know she can give up the child for permanent adoption. But the Children's Home Society of California is another alternative. It provides *temporary* foster parents until the natural mother can get her head together and make a decision either to raise the infant herself, or give it up forever.

And I think it is all to the credit of the producers of the film that they do not include such facts as:

One out of every eleven births in the United States is illegitimate, an all-time high. Twenty-five thousand of these children are in foster homes in California, and, in the Los Angeles area alone, eleven thousand children reside in a kind of limbo where the odds against them are such that if a child remains in a temporary foster home for over a year, chances are that he will be part of the 25 percent that will never, *never* have a reunion with the natural mother. The darkness into which such children are cast is a lonely and chilling thing to consider.

I think it is to the producers' credit that none of the above is explicitly stated in the film, for cold statistics would only serve to raise in us a guilt reaction to the problem, when the film itself steadfastly deals with the human beings involved, and pierces unerringly to the core of human sorrow.

In these days of planned parenthood, of appeals to help defuse The Population Bomb, of contraceptive measures that steadily gain acceptance despite the criminal dogma of such as the Vatican, we fail to realize that not all young people are ultrahip, not all teenaged girls know where and how to go and get the ring fitted, not all high schoolers coming to sex far earlier than their parents can summon up the chutzpah to go and have an examination before getting The Pill. There are uncounted thousands of young women who simply do not know. We are still merely an emerging nation in terms of sexual enlightenment; the Judeo-Christian ethos still holds sway throughout most of this country. Parents still fight sex-education classes in schools. Do-gooder organizations, motivated for the most part by their own Puritanical constipations, continue to stymie free and open dissemination of sex information. Exploiters and pariahs (such as some of those who advertise in the *Free Press*) continue to make of sex a seamy and corrupt activity. Otherwise *au courant* mothers and fathers still choose to turn away from the reality that their sons and daughters are having sex, and continue to shroud it in secrecy, giving it a clandestine and unsavory appeal.

Perhaps the greatest benefit for men and women alike from the Women's Liberation Movement will be to unfetter our thinking in this area.

For if one sees this hour of superlative documentary-drama, one will realize that the important part of freeing us from our sexual ghetto is not that anyone can Do It when he or she desires, but that hopeless traps such as the one into which Pam is locked need never be again. I venture to say no one who sees this memorable hour of television will come away from it thinking unwanted pregnancy is just a matter of poor planning. The effects on people, on naïve girls and young men who never intended to be calloused rakes, on bewildered parents and helpless infants who must grow up in orphanages, are too brutalizing, too terrible to be allowed to go on. Toward a clearer understanding of the frail human condition, and as an hour of utterly worthwhile and memorable viewing, I urge you to do Sunday the twentieth at 7:30 with Channel 11.

Then I won't feel so silly about having sat there close to tears.

Correspondent Herbert Bernard adds this interesting footnote to the "World's 'Our Little Miss' Variety Pageant" column:

"Did you happen to observe that when Frankie Avalon read his touching poem on 'What Is a Little Girl?' the lines included something to the effect

'...Little girls come in all colors,
white, red, yellow, black, etc....'

and though I watched carefully, I detected nothing but pretty little white faces in the large audience of tots."

I have been watching the KCET coverage of the hearing into the death of Mexican-American newsman Ruben Salazar. I watched it late into last night. I saw a blue-ribbon panel of delegates to that hearing from the Chicano community storm out in protest, and I had the eerie and chilling feeling that this was very much what it must have been like at the Chicago Conspiracy Trial. And I went a little colder realizing the game of justice in our courtroom arena is not necessarily the Game of Truth. The system is so complex, the machinery so ponderous, and the technicians keeping the system's machinery functioning are so locked into "accepted concepts of the natural order," that Pontius Pilate by comparison seems a paragon of impartiality and ethical purity.

80: 25 SEPTEMBER 70

THE NEW SEASON: PART ONE

Last year at this time, I did minute capsule reviews; it sufficed. Almost all of last year's product was wretched, and it didn't deserve more than a passing note. Blissfully, almost all of the stinkers died and so they will not be with us this year. (Unfortunately, *Bracken's World* was not among the deceased, and I now realize that though I promised you a full-length takeout on the series, I never got around to it. There seemed to be too many other things of importance happening to bother with anything as trivial as *Bracken's World*. But with the addition of Leslie Nielsen as studio head John Bracken this season, I watched the series opener last Friday and I solemnly promise sometime within the next five or six weeks I'll do a full column on that particular running sore of a series.)

The shows *this* year, however, are something else again. They are so full of commentable material it may take me three or four weeks to sort it all out, and it will provide substance for months to come. Because...

Time magazine called me the other day. Apparently one of the entertainment editors in New York reads this column, and knowing that each year I manage to find a common thread that defines the tone of the season, I was asked what label I would arbitrarily paste on the 1970–71 viewing scene. The 1968–69 season (if you tonstant weaders recall) was the Year of the Widows; 1969–70 was the Year of the Plastic People. And this year, certainly, the content and formats of what I've seen in just the first week mark this as the Year TV Exploited Social Consciousness and Youth.

(I should interject right here that I seldom preview the series' offerings. What I report is what I've actually seen. I realize in this way you don't get the word beforehand, as you do with *Time* or *TV Guide*, but since this column is for readers and not network executives, it seems to me I serve the commonweal more effectively by keeping myself as divorced from the PR aspects of the industry as possible. I see the new shows at the same time you do, and in this way we can compare ruminations. And I don't have to feel guilty about lambasting some show written or produced by a friend of mine. Distance, in this case, breeds honesty.)

THE YEAR TV EXPLOITED SOCIAL CONSCIOUSNESS AND YOUTH. Yes. That's the tag. And, brother, it is rampant.

No more perfect example offers itself than the debut of the new Andy Griffith show, called *Headmaster* (Friday, CBS, 8:30 p.m.).

Griffith's new incarnation is that of the headmaster of a private coed high school, with Jerry Van Dyke as the football coach, and Parker Fennelly (octogenarians may remember him as Titus Moody on the Fred Allen radio show) as the custodian. First of all, we have a private high school. In this time of turmoil over school integration and bussing, of bigoted and frightened parents rushing their tender little urchins into private schools before they can learn black is as good as white, a *private* high school assumes special meaning—particularly when the pigmentation of the students in Griffith's school is overwhelmingly Caucasoid.

But I may be stretching the point. I'm sure CBS would deny any appeal to beleaguered middle-class Americans forced to bus their kids a mile or two, all in the name of destroying racial prejudice. It just *happens* to be a private high school.

And it just *happens* the opening segment of the series dealt with dope. Even as it just *happens* that *The Name of the Game* dealt with kids who dope, that same evening. But it just *happens* that the manner in *which* it dealt with the topic highlights and keynotes the ludicrousness of tv's blatant attempt to cash in on the 18–35-year-old market by exploiting youth and the concerns of youth today.

The plot was simple (it's a half-hour show). Young teens at a party in the home of a kid whose parents are always conveniently away. (Incorrect Assumption About Youth #1: parents who don't oversee their kids' habits are inviting trouble, ergo, the parents are at fault.) Host comes up with a box filled with reds, yellows, whites, uppers, downers, sidewayers. Everybody starts dropping the caps, except one kid, Ritchie. He's afraid.

So everybody starts to chill him. (Incorrect Assumption About Youth #2: since it was always the case for past generations that if you didn't follow fashion or the group you were an outcast, old-timers writing these scripts believe it is still the case today. But there are so *many* different lifestyles for kids today, and for the most part all but the most loutish prize their individuality, so they wouldn't be as ripped up as this show indicates, if one of their number chose not to indulge. It's true, dopers—like drinkers—try to get everybody at a party involved—on the theory that anyone who doesn't drink or turn on is a "downer"— but if you say no, and mean it, and aren't disapproving of what others are doing, nobody puts you down for it. Scriptwriters and producers continue to use the idiot argot "doing his thing," but they don't seem to understand what it means, in just such cases as this.)

So *Headmaster* Andy gives them a lecture on dope. And he uses all the cornball, square, cliché remarks to make his case. The kids don't listen. They think Andy is square. They're right: he is. His manner, his holier- than-thou, sanctimonious, doom-crying manner, is square and hideously counterproductive.

Upshot is that Ritchie doesn't want to be an outsider, so instead of swinging with Andy's admonitions to stay away from pills, he goes to a party, turns on, and gets an overdose. He's in the hospital, and Andy lectures the class again...something maudlin about we have to live together on this planet and we can't do it by dumping alien substances into our bloodstreams, et cetera.

The credits hadn't even rolled before reader Ed Granzow called from downstate, to say the show was stupid and I should put it down in this column. Well, I'll put it down, but for artlessness and stupidity, not for its position on drugs.

As readers of my words know, I am far from a praiser of the drug culture. I've lost too damned many friends—o.d.'d in bathtubs, the hair streaming out like seaweed; locked away in violent wards in three states; dead in public toilets, the spike still hanging out of the big artery—to say anything other than that those who drop or do or turn on are assholes. But I also say everyone is entitled to go to hell in his own way. Better they should commit violence on their own bodies and minds than that the systematized and legalized violence of the Establishment screw them into early graves. But that's another story.

I know Ritchie's plight. I don't get invited to as many parties as I used to. Not because I'm not liked (in point of fact, I've become a lovelier human being than I ever was) but because my friends know I don't turn on, and they choose to spare themselves and me the awkwardness of being at a bash where everyone is using and I'm still straight. That doesn't bother me... even as I know it would not bother a real-life Ritchie. When my friends want to see me, they get together with me, and we all know the ground rules. I don't do their thing, but I don't pin them for it. The reverse is true for them, of me.

And so, knowing the attitudes of those who use drugs, I know that Headmaster (ironic title in the context of this commentary) was written by an older man, speaking to older men. It was certainly not addressed to kids, who need most to hear it. Because it was square. It reinforced all the dumb arguments against dope that kids have heard spouted by hypocritical politicians and ignorant parents since the evil was corn silk smoked behind the barn. Kids see their parents poisoning not only the world, the atmosphere, and the environment, but also their own systems with nicotine and alcohol; and the maudlin arguments an Andy Griffith spouts are one with these. Kids laugh at that kind of bullshit...if they even watch it. It is a manifestation of the lip service adults and tv as their voice pay to the problems of our society. Look, they say, we are talking about the drug problem!

But to illustrate just how far off the target such attacks must be, consider this, from the current, October 1970, issue of *Psychology Today* (page 12):

"To be able to treat the country's growing 'drug problem,' you first have to admit that most young people don't think drugs are a problem, say the directors of Number Nine, a multi-purpose help house at 649 State Street, New Haven, Connecticut. Among the first 3000 youths who asked Number Nine for help after it opened a year ago, 85% had used drugs, but only a handful identified drugs as their problem. 'They see drugs as a solution to a given set of variables,' says Ted Clark, one of the center's three young nonprofessional directors, 'and if you treat the solution as a problem or as a symptom, you won't get anywhere.'"

More clearly than anything I've heard or read on the subject, that brief comment sums it up. We've brought into being a couple of generations of Americans who believe there is a chemical answer to everything, from acne to cancer. So how dare we pillory kids for thinking pills and acid and smack are chemical answers to the worries and pressures that assail them? You can't stock drugstore after drugstore with pharmaceutical goodies guaranteed to ease tension, straighten heads, and improve one's complexion, without suckering kids into believing they're entitled to the same benefits by the use of Mother's Little Helpers.

And to attempt answering this lie with *more* lies, with hypocritical, uninformed, sanctimonious finger-wagglings by the likes of Andy Griffith, is compounding the felony.

Headmaster tried to say something heavy about drugs. But if it had any weight, the force was applied to already-panicking adults. The kids—like Ed Granzow—laugh at it. The horror of it was that that show *might* have had significant impact, had it been thought out and written by someone who *knew*.

That Friday night, September 18, the kids would have been

receptive. It was the night we all heard Jimi Hendrix had died from an overdose, before he'd reached the age of thirty.

CBS, Andy Griffith, and the Adult Establishment had chosen, however, to exploit the young, had chosen to pay parlor-liberal lip service to its social conscience...and so, once again, no one heard what was blowin' on the wind.

THE SENATOR segment of *The Bold Ones*
(NBC, Sunday, 10:00 p.m.)

This one had good vibes going for it as early as the pilot, last season, played as an NBC movie-for-tv—*A Clear and Present Danger*. It had Hal Holbrook (best known for his incredibly adroit "evenings" as Mark Twain) in a masterfully underplayed re-creation of his sensational role in Robert Thom's/Barry Shear's film, *Wild in the Streets*. The promise was kept with the opening installment of this new addition to The Bold Ones' rotation plan. (Hari Rhodes and Leslie Nielsen as *The Protectors* are gone; *The Doctors* and *The Advocates* remain.)

The script was heaven: intelligent, informed, *au courant* without recourse to jargon, simplification, or sensationalism, unencumbered by trivial formula accouterments, and best of all it spoke to an audience I thought Universal and television in general would never acknowledge: the thoughtful viewer.

Without even a tinge of the yellowleg cheap-jack writing that characterizes so much current video fare, "The Senator" told the story of an assassination threat on Senator Hays Stowe, and his determination (for ethical and sensible reasons) to speak at a college despite the warning. Holbrook portrayed Stowe with such devotion and care that I found myself wishing nature would once again imitate art and *all* our legislators would take him as their model. In supporting roles Michael Tolan, Sharon Acker, and Cindy Eilbacher were so good they elevated the word *competent* to the Olympian level of craft perfection.

A noteworthy element of the show—and one I sincerely trust will obtain in every segment—were the serendipitous discussions of current social and constitutional concerns. In this script, for instance, we were treated to an honest (if inconclusive) scene between Senator Stowe and a cop (outstandingly rendered with shades of perception by Gerald S. O'Loughlin in one of his several memorable appearances on various shows this week) anent the relative merits of the no-knock provision of the criminal control bill.

If all television was this thoroughly decent and rewarding, it would put critics like me out of business and I would rejoice at the loss of employment. I cannot recommend Holbrook and his show highly enough. They are a wonder and a joy.

THE NEW RED SKELTON SHOW
(Monday, NBC, 7:30 p.m.)

CBS, heeding demographic studies in praise of the 18–35-year-old purchasing dollar (and the consumer-viewers in whose pink little fists said Yankee dollahz are clutchened), dumped Red Skelton. NBC, believing (quite rightly) that older members of the audience also deserve to be able to see their favorites, picked up the aging gentleman. I will not comment on the enormity of ego that convinces a 57-year-old man that The Show (meaning him) *Must* Go On! I won't comment, because it's the same insanity that motivates me. This similarity notwithstanding, I have never been a Skelton fan. His humor is a trifle too coarse for my taste— David Steinberg sits somewhat better, gourmetically speaking. But I watched Mr. Skelton in hopes that twenty seasons on tv and all those high-paid comedy writers he uses would have led him to realize his humor has become distinctly mildewed. Hope rises eternal as (apparently) does Red. And his gags.

Old, old, incredibly old. Pratfalls, the perennial sea-gull jokes, that moronic Silent Spot, his unfailing phony laughter at his own jokes, and in case no stone of low comedy was left unturned, the abominable Jerry Lewis (fresh from new horrors on his telethon) added a maudlin show-biz note of cheap sentimental homage à la Danny Thomas.

It was a half hour appropriately introduced by Spiro—like Skelton, one of the great clowns of our time—at least that's what they keep telling us—for it demonstrated more of that middle-class, middle-brow anti-intellectualism about which I ranted several columns ago, to wit, portraying scientists as loonies (a stereotype that went out with "Miss Jones, with your glasses off you're *beau*tiful!" and all Jews have big noses and all blacks salivate for fried chicken and Latins are lousy lovers; that whole crowd of nitwit clichés from the Keith Circuit) and telling a dumb lab assistant, "Keep that up and you'll be back at Berkeley next year."

There was also an embarrassingly bad female singer named Robin Something, who ought to learn to at least lip-synch properly before she tries network tv again.

I'd give the same advice to Red, but what the hell does a young punk like me know about the living legends of entertainment? Hell, I even thought the Ed Sullivan AGVA show was a monumental pain in the ass.

THE STOREFRONT LAWYERS
(Wednesday, CBS, 7:30 p.m.)

Despite the flagrancy of the exploitive uses to which the liver-spotted moguls of videoland are putting youthful passion this season, it cannot be denied: dealing with contemporary problems, no matter how simplistically or slickly, has improved the caliber of scriptwriting. Denied the easy avenues of raw violence and pulp-fiction plotting that held sway for so many years in the idiom, scenarists are now finding they must get to the heart of characterization (well, into the neighborhood of the spleen at any rate, if not actually all the way to the pulmonary artery), and they must substitute genuine plot for mindless chases only a notch above Tom and Jerry (a comparison unfortunately invidious to those noble cartoon creatures). So *The Storefront Lawyers* reap this benefit. Which is to say that, aside from a marvelous A-B-C revelation of how interlocking corporations fleece innocent consumers, the opening segment of this series didn't show much more than a standard *Perry Mason* episode. The lawyers are younger, the courtroom theatrics a bit more current and flashy, but essentially it's another of those series so dear to the bar associations. It makes attorneys look like Mr. Clean, like nobility incarnate.

Fierce, committed (gawd, that *word*, that weary, overworked, invalidated, and corrupted *word*: again again again and again), incorruptible—they work within the Establishment to bring justice to the poor, the lost, the underdogged. Nothing wrong with that, and nothing really wrong with the series opener...just that it seemed to lack...well, for want of a better word...*soul*. I suppose that's praising with faint damns, and I don't mean it to do that, but the three whey-faced attorneys (played by Robert Foxworth—dominating the show with little more than one change of expression—and Sheila Larken—who is marvelously lovely but didn't have much of a part to work with—and David Arkin—whose talents were wasted entirely with chiming in straight lines for Foxworth) seemed so humorless, so rigidly devoted to inscrutable ethic, that I kept wishing someone would rerun one of those Peter Falk *Trials of O'Brien* shows of several years ago, just to show them that attorneys are human, too. As Barry Bernstein continues to tell me.

McCLOUD segment of *Four-In-One*
(Wednesday, NBC, 10:00 p.m.)

Every critic in the country will be saying this is Dennis Weaver without the limp, with the dusty drawl less nasal, so I won't. What I will say is that this one is a clear winner. After years playing second banana to the Colossus of Rhodes and a dopey bear, Weaver has found his forte. Sam McCloud, deputy marshal from Taos, New Mexico, on detached duty to the NYPD, is a boot in the butt. It is a joy to watch Weaver work. The rolling gait is just right for a man wearing goat-roper boots on those Manhattan sidewalks. The funky Stetson is a signifying fraud, but such a delightfully irreverent put-on that it is wholly in tune and acceptable. With his shirt off, Weaver is a little soft in the gut and *that's* real. And though they're cautious about showing it on camera, he is a whorer, a rakehell, and a flouter of authority. It's merely *Coogan's Bluff* (the Clint Eastwood starrer of last year, also from Universal) with a different leading man, but it is so *correct*, so damnably entertaining, and the scripting is so *tight* only a wimp would find fault. (Except, would someone point out to the producer that once the killer had McCloud at gunpoint in the barren wastes of Long Island at five in the morning, he wouldn't do that "put your hands up, turn around, you drive the car" routine that only works in bad men's magazine fiction... he would simply s-h-o-o-t him on the spot. Said the wimp.)

It's a shame we'll only be getting six weeks of Weaver as McCloud before they rotate to the second of the Four-in-One programs. I'd like to see *lots* more of Diana Muldaur, who acts as memorably as she looks, of J. D. Cannon as the irascible chief of detectives, and they might even give Terry Carter a little more script to play with. But Universal being the catbird it is, I suspect they'll be hip to what they've got going soon enough, and McCloud may turn into a weekly. It can't be soon enough for me.

THE FLIP WILSON SHOW
(Thursday, NBC, 7:30 p.m.)

I'm reminded of the few times Lenny Bruce was allowed to work network tv and how even *his* irreverent, armor-piercing humor was softened, downgraded, cleaned up if you will. And Lenny was a comedic genius. If it could happen to the likes of Lenny, what right do I have to hector Flip Wilson, who is simply blah? As tonstant weaders of this column may recall, I am hardly a fan of Mr. Wilson and his humor. He seems to me terribly white in what he does, but again—as I've been reminded by my betters—I have no right to put the man down for not doing a black thing onstage. Maybe they're right. It just seems a shame with so few black comedians making it, that one of them should opt for all the mannerisms of a hundred other paler jokers.

All I can say for sure is that when he was aping the material of Vegas shtickmeisters like Jack Carter and Shecky Greene, he was a drag. He was no better than any of the other downer comedians tv has persistently thrust at us these past ten years, a put-down than which is no greater. The only times the show came to life were when Sunday's Child, a trio of young and very swinging black foxes, came on (and even *they* were treated with super-whitening enzymes...they sang Glen Campbell's hit, "Wichita Lineman," rather than something soul-oriented...and there is nothing whiter than Glen Campbell, god knows, unless it's Pat Boone; even so, they managed to juice up the song in a way that made their stint so impressive, it made James Brown's embarrassing by comparison), and the other instance was Wilson's portrayal of Reverend Leroy, a storefront minister of the larcenous old shout-'n'-stomp school. Utilizing the incredibly rich materials of black humor, Wilson made this an individual few moments of special ethnic hilarity.

But to be honest, if I get home late on Thursday nights, and miss Wilson, I won't go searching for razor blades to slash my wrists. I'm probably being unfair, but fuck it, who cares?

———————————

THE BROTHERHOOD OF THE BELL on the CBS *Thursday Night Movie* (9:00 p.m.)

They opened the new season with a Cinema Center fillum made specially for the tube. I guess they thought this was their heaviest-weight item, a real grabber, based on a so-so 1952 novel (*The Brotherhood of Velvet*) by David Karp, who produced and scripted the film. It starred Glenn Ford, who looked very, very tired and looked as though he needed the job.

It was about this secret cabal of powerful men who...but you know the story. Paranoia based on our contemporary fetish for conspiracy. It went on and on and on, and only Will Geer (delightfully omnipresent all this week, no matter what channel you tuned) made it worthy watching at all. Most of it was cheap, illogical, patently ridiculous, and if this is what CBS thought was their hottest available item, it bodes ill for the new season of tailored-for-tv flicks on this channel. In summation, friends, in the words of William Conrad, who played a fat Joe Pyne in this script...dingdong.

THE INTERNS
(Friday, CBS, 7:30 p.m.)

There is very little they can show us inside a soundstage hospital that we have not already seen a thousand times on *Dr. Kildare, The Doctors, The Doctors & The Nurses, The Bold Ones, Ben Casey, Marcus Welby, M.D., General Hospital, Medic,* and the other, even lesser Hippocratically oriented series with which tv has healed itself. We are an eighteen-year-old, tv-weaned generation, and we know all about EEGs as opposed to EKGs, we know hospitals don't allow longhaired and bearded hippie freak orderlies in the drug room, and we are weary of stupid network idea men thinking they can pawn off old movies as fresh series ideas with the addition of some "sparkling young talents." *The Interns* and *The New Interns* were a pair of moronic feature films over eight years ago (distinguished, in the eyes of exploiters, chiefly by a "wild" party sequence, reverberations of which tremble on, even into the opening segment of the series). Converted into choppy, triple-plot-thread segments weekly, they are no big deal.

The first show was a systole/diastole of boredom, filled with mawkish bathos, superficial characterization about as penetrating as a carny crystal-baller's palm analysis, with wretchedly familiar sets and actors who chose templates rather than performances, and with a flagrant waste of whatever talents Broderick Crawford has left in him. This is a sad, pitiable dud. Or, as we say, here in surgery, the prognosis looks shitty. Probably terminal.

THE MARY TYLER MOORE SHOW
(Saturday, CBS, 9:30 p.m.)

I would tell you right out straight. This is a funny show. You
know how it is I know a funny show from a not-funny show? A
funny show, I sit and laugh. A not-funny show, I sit and pick my
nose and scan the new *Scanlan's* and begin putting my hands up
Cindy's skirt and cutting Danish Nibbling Cheese and scratching
Ahbhu's stomach and whistling the theme from the old *Topper*
series and wondering whatever happened to Anne Helm who
was beautiful and who hasn't done much acting lately and I wish
I was in my office working at something I like and talking on
the phone to Norman Spinrad and reading part of a new (old)
Doc Savage novel and just a gang of other stuff. But funny, I sit
and laugh. So you wanna know, I laughed like my godson Eric
Coltrane Kirby when I quack like a demented Donald Duck for
him.

Edward Asner is interviewing Mary Tyler Moore for a job, see,
and she gets upset because he's been asking her these personal
questions, see, and she snaps at him and Asner says, "Y'know…
you got *spunk!*" and everybody laughs as Mary preens, and
Asner says, "And I hate spunk!"

That is *funny.*

And Lisa Gerritsen from *My World—And Welcome to It* is
there, and so is Cloris Leachman, and so is Gavin MacLeod, and
most of all there is Mary Tyler Moore and Asner—both of whom
are outright, unmitigatedly, without reservation *brilliant*—and
damn it that is a funny show. Hello! Stick around a few seasons.
We need you to help offset *Hee Haw.*

THE YOUNG REBELS
(Sunday, ABC, 7:00 p.m.)

If you watched the special on Channel 11 I recommended last

week, you missed the opener of this series and, as I promised, I watched it for you, and here's my report:

Seventeen seventy-seven, and three twenty-year-olds from Chester, Pennsylvania (which is an awful town today—I don't know how it was in 1777—I was once married in Chester and it was a real pesthole), decide to slow General Howe's march on Philadelphia through the daring use of some Leyden jars, some guerrilla tactics, and a lot of Yankee Doodle spunk. And in the words of Edward Asner, "I *hate* spunk!"

It was more of the bullshit video heroics so familiar to students of the glass teat. That infantile fantasy view of war and violence imparting nobility without once touching reality. In this show, cannon blast troops with grapeshot and men do somersaults. In reality, grapeshot whistled through lines of troops like red-hot shrapnel, tearing off arms and ripping holes in men's faces. In this show, that fabled "Yankee ingenuity" rescues the situation at the last moment as mere youths defeat trained troops that outnumber them a hundred to one. Now I'm not saying it can't be done—nor that it *wasn't* done in the days of muskets and horse soldiers—but I say that implying this romanticized view of revolution against King George has any parallel with revolution today is imbecilic. And misleading.

By showing a twenty-year-old Major General Lafayette, and by hitting over and over again at the youth of these rebels, the producers undoubtedly think they are making a point the scuttlefish will recognize as relevant to student dissenters and campus revolutionaries. Hogwash! They've phonied up this show with so much bogus patriotism and superman heroics, all it does is make peace protesters with stones and placards look like cowards. If the Movement were ever to take steps such as these Yankee Doodles employ, in pursuit of a goal of freedom easily as noble as the original, martial law would be declared in every American city and every radical would be in a prison camp by week's end. Hell, the bombings have already set Congress and Mr. Mitchell to work drafting new repressive measures, and the death toll on Panthers mounts geometrically week by week.

No, there is no comparison between revolution then and

revolution now. To suggest otherwise, as this series does, is to lie to both sides.

As entertainment, I suppose the series does all right. It has color and pace and action, and if that's all you want, that's all you'll get. But to this critic, *The Young Rebels* (produced, appropriately enough, by the people who gave you *The Mod Squad*—and how about drawing some parallels *there*) is a deceitful, time-wasting exercise in chicanery and false allegory.

THE TIM CONWAY COMEDY HOUR
(Sunday, CBS, 10:00 p.m.)

Had some lively moments, such as a spoof of Christmas shows, a Japanese pilot trying to convince his fellow airmen they must become kamikazes, and a hilarious portrayal by Conway of a lushed private eye named Danny Draft. C+ rating.

All of which brings us to the concluding review for this week's special section, the closing bracket of an analysis of the exploitation of social consciousness. The opening bracket was Andy Griffith's old-man lecture on dope, and the closer is—

ARNIE
(Saturday, CBS, 9:00 p.m.)

When Arnie Nuvo, loading-dock foreman at the Consolidated Flange Corporation, leans across the breakfast table and says to his son—who is about as shaggy as, say, David Eisenhower—"Get your hair cut," and the son asks why, and Arnie says, "Because you're starting to look like your mother when I proposed to her seventeen years ago," I get a trifle chilled.

Why? Because I've seen the movie, *Joe.* Because I've been razzed by hardhats constructing office buildings on Ventura Boulevard. Because I've seen that giant crane out in the Simi Valley that has an American flag flying from its platform after hours. Because I've seen newsreels of the New York "patriots" beating up peace protesters. Because the week the construction workers pounded kids to jelly in the streets, Nixon had their leaders to lunch and praised them for their fervor. Because I remember that fine middle-class scuttlefish who started the riot at the UCLA Naval ROTC graduation ceremonies; a riot started by *them*—the Arnies of the world—that resulted in peaceful protesters being beaten and then jailed. That's why!

And as the half-hour situation comedy progresses, and as I see uptight Arnie being squeezed by taxes and future shock and an archetypal Simon Legree boss and orthodontists who want $250 for his daughter's corrective braces, and as I hear him say to character actor Tom Pedi, "A man can't live this way; there's always an emergency; there's never any money; is this any way for a man to exist?..." I grow even colder.

Because I realize that the "social relevance" that has hit this season's tv fare with a vengeance has even reached the usually mindless little sitcoms. And I wonder if it is the Utopia for which I've hoped.

Or, as Gulley Jimson said, "It's not the vision I had."

If Arnie *is* Everyman 1970, it is an alarming conceit. Reluctantly, I must agree: Arnie is the Human Condition in this country in the last third of the twentieth century. And he's *right*...it *ain't* no way to live! The local, state, and Federal governments are draining our blood to an extent that makes it impossible to live comfortably, secure in the knowledge that we've got a few bucks laid aside for an emergency or for a getaway week or two when pressures compel.

No wonder this country is divided, with the middle class taking up the cudgel and the blunderbuss to maim and kill dissenters. They are being squeezed to death and the pressures are turning them into amuck monsters. And the men responsible, the deluded, nest-feathering military and administrative Draculas who see life as an endless series of conspiracies against which *any* amount of tax-levying and brutalizing procedures toward its people are in the name of some nebulous Higher Good, have thrown the hardhats a flock of scapegoats rather than admit their own culpability. Thrown to the slavering, demented hordes of homeowners and lathe workers are longhaired hippies, rabid black militants, freeloading welfare cases, cowardly draft dodgers, bomb-hurling campus radicals, marijuana-puffing maniacs, and intellectuals.

So when Arnie Everyman says to his son, "Get your hair cut," my blood runs cold.

We are seeing the elevation of "Joe" (the one in the film) to the level of cultural totem.

And as we have seen the exploitation of the young at one end of this season's programming, here at the far right end we see the exploitation of the fears of the older generations.

They don't know what's happening. They work their asses off and still never get ahead, and the city council ups the rates another 6 percent. It is enough to drive them to mass lynchings, and the monsters who did this to them need never worry, for with all the scapegoats listed above, the middle class need never seek out the real culprits: the power-mad Pentagon hardware buyers; the dissembling politicians with their hands in the lobbyists' pockets and their conceptions of the state of things frozen at 1927; the corporate heads who warp-and-woof with one another to take over what should be a country run by people, not computers; the gimme-gimme unionists who demand higher and higher wages for shoddier and shoddier workmanship; the liars, the cheaters, the carpetbaggers who rape and run. The Silent Majority is being told in every way, through every day, that it's the small band of dissenters who are turning their world and their lives into hell and desperation.

And in *Arnie* we see the personification of the condition.

As art, the show is interesting. Herschel Bernardi, in the title role, is perfect. But then, Bernardi is perfect. He is one of the genuinely great character actors of our time, and it is a blessing to have him back in a regular series appearance (his last was as Lieutenant Jacoby in *Peter Gunn*, and you know how long ago *that* was), even if he is cast as an analogue of the struggle of Common Man to remain human under the brutalizing and crushing pressures of Corporate-owned America Today.

This, more than almost any other I've seen so far, will be a series to watch carefully. Not only for Bernardi's brilliant acting, but for the undertones of what it will say about the condition of life in our country today. I'm sure I'll have more to say about this in later columns.

This has been a special triple-length special column. The next two or three installments will deal with the remainder of the series debuts as they are aired. Try to stick around; things look interesting this year.

81: 9 OCTOBER 70

THE NEW SEASON: PART TWO

There is a story told in the Industry about the weird and dramatic circumstances that led to the firing of a certain network head about five years ago. The way the story goes— and it's strictly gossip, he said innocently, his forked tail lashing impishlyparticular dude had an eye for the ladies, as do so many of us. (In fact, his eye was so good, he managed to get for a mistress one of the outstandingly gorgeous actresses of the past decade. And to keep her on the hook, he set her up in a classically moronic situation fantasy/comedy, which happily only lasted one season. Or was it *half* a season? My memory is sometimes weak on minutiae.)

Anyhow, one ethereally beautiful creature wasn't enough for our protagonist, the network head, and he used to play pretty heavily in the Courts of Eros. The only trouble was, he played a little too rough. He was a puncher. Used to like to knock his playmates around. Gave him a heavy jelly to bat women about. Charming dude.

One weekend in Vegas, the network head was playing heavily, and he got eyes for an attractive, dark-haired young girl at the tables in the casino of the hotel where he had a suite. So he hyped her, and she came up to his rooms, and what with one thing and another he not only knew her in the Biblical sense (as we of pure thought and action put it), but he beat the shit out of her. For no particular good reason.

When she managed to escape the dubious joys of our boy's love nest, she went straight to her father and made some complaints... through bloody lips. Which wouldn't have been so bad for the network head except that the girl was the beautiful daughter of a well-known Mafia don. So he instantly put out a contract on the stupid bastard. Which was no more than he deserved.

In a justifiable panic, the network head appealed for help from a buddy of long standing, an ex-actor who was a godson of an even more powerful Cosa Nostra boss. The ex-actor, a bright kid who had fallen on hard times career-wise, saw it as a once-in-a-lifetime opportunity to recoup his fortunes, and he agreed to ask his godfather to intercede...for certain considerations.

The considerations were that the ex-actor would get his own show—a summer replacement song-and-dance hour—and that the network head would form a production company with him that would produce shows to be included on the prexy's fall schedule.

Well, to make a sordid story as squamous as possible, the network head bought, for his schedule, a handful of shows produced by the ex-actor (whose own show rated so low in just the few weeks it was aired that it *had* to be yanked before suspicion grew rife). Except the deal was so ugly the shows were bought *before* any pilots were made. And so the network was stuck with a couple of comedies and a couple of dramatic hours that were so awful the bloodhounds got on the scent. No one could figure out how a man with the successful track record of the network head could buy such a crummy product. And every one of the shows plonked to the bottom of the ratings, and the president of the network started investigating, and when he found the shows were all owned by the ex-actor in partnership with his own network head, he fired the larcenous bastard outright.

Time has passed and the ex-actor wrote a book about the Industry, and after a few years on the outside looking in, the ex-network head is back in the Industry, in a powerful (but different) position. Thereby proving something or other about the nature of an Industry so corrupt that it continues to rehire members of its cadre it *knows* to be thieves and degenerates. But that's just an aside.

What this story is in aid of is the manner in which a network—ostensibly in business to serve the public welfare and make a good buck on the side—gets itself in hock to a producer of video product, and how these sweetheart deals invariably result in debased and incredibly rank series that eat up endless hours of prime time.

Let me make the point that not *all* long-term deals with producers come up with garbage. There *are* honest men in the Industry, and they care deeply about the product they purvey. Quinn Martin is one (though, for the most part, I don't care for the kinds of shows he chooses to produce), and even if he does get fifty grand above budget to produce a segment of *Dan August* (thereby making it look sensational production-wise on the screen, and ensuring it'll be a hit) for ABC, it is money well spent. Though the producers of other ABC shows stuck with budgets of $182,000 ought to be just a trifle pissed off that they have to struggle along with such pittances. (It seems incredible that a decent segment of any given series can't be made for that sum of money, particularly when one realizes that the core of the show, the script, only costs $4500—less than 2½ percent of the total budget for the most important element necessary to bringing forth something worthwhile—to be precise, it's 2.47 percent—but when you stop to consider that 40 percent comes off the top for studio overhead before they even *start* production of a given segment, you begin to understand the evil nature of the money-grab in Hollywood.)

Back to the point: Norman Felton is an honest man who makes solid series. He had a term deal with NBC. David Dortort has done well by NBC with *Bonanza* and *The High Chaparral* on a similar deal. Sheldon Leonard's contract with NBC produced *I Spy*, among others. And Lenny Freeman gives solid work for the dollar on his CBS pact. But ABC, locked in as they are with Aaron Spelling and his three and a half hours of primetime product, have made a wretched deal. But, like the network with the sadistic thief they finally canned, ABC has a sweetheart deal with Spelling, and what we, the viewing public, get from this unholy alliance is an endless gag fest (gag, as in retch and vomit) of half-witted, worn-out hack series, one more imbecilic than the last.

Among the Spelling-originated offerings littering Channel 7 this year we have *The Mod Squad* returning in all its loathsomeness and success, adding to its list of crimes wasting the talent of producer-writer Harve Bennett; we have *The Most Deadly Game* which debuts next Saturday and which I'll review in next week's column; we have something like a dozen ninety-minute *ABC Movie of the Week* abominations (you may remember my column on *The Love War*, a Spelling-fostered *Movie of the Week* that holds, in the pantheon of tv films, the position of The Oscar in theatrical films); and—through fables and circumlocutions to The New Season, Part Two—we have:

THE SILENT FORCE
(Monday, ABC, 8:30 p.m.)

Never let it be said Mr. Spelling is one to let a tried-and-true cliché founder. He has taken *The Mod Squad* concept—the undercover fink as a symbol of righteous endeavor—aged the male principals by ten or fifteen years (for Michael Cole we have Ed Nelson; for Clarence Williams III, we have Percy Rodrigues), retained the young, sexy *look* for the female member of the law-enforcement trio (Lynda Day is so sensational just to look at that it only dawns later that she is a better actress than Peggy Lipton in a similar part)...and sent them out to "lop off the tentacles of the octopus of organized crime." Or something.

It was an idea that worked for *The Untouchables*, that flopped horribly as *Cain's Hundred*, that made Mr. Spelling's current fortunes soar with *The Mod Squad*, but which is so redolent of 1930s gangster films in its present incarnation, one can only assume ABC bought it because they were umbilically joined to the Spelling operation and, like paperback distributors who force newsstands to take fifty titles they don't want and can't sell in order to get their doles of *The Love Machine* and *The Godfather*, if they wanted those important (?) movies, they had to buy this unquestionably doggy item.

To begin with, ennobling Mr. Mitchell's or Mr. Hoover's subterranean sneakos (who spend most of their time tracking longhaired student militants and teenagers smoking grass while the Mob chews ever more ravenously at the core of the American Economy) is to hype the scuttlefish into believing some genuine progress is being made against organized crime. Which is patently ridiculous.

Further, it helps foster the know-nothing attitude of many Americans that the government knows best: that a no-knock law and wiretapping and entrapment and false arrest provisos and hideous conspiracy laws such as the one on which the Chicago Eight were indicted are in the public interest. It promulgates the impression that these incursions into civil liberties are all in the name of slaying the squid of big business crime. Which is bullshit. Extralegal outfits like the Silent Force (and the *Mission: Impossible* crew, while we're about it, though the latter somehow escape censure because of the unreality of what they get into weekly) are certainly as great a threat to our freedoms as the gutter rats of the Syndicate, if for no other reason than that they constitute a secret police—and we've seen what such constituted "authorities" can do to *anyone* who does or says anything they consider not in the interest of the state. To glorify such insects is to dupe the uninformed and to validate any expediency they choose to get the job done. It is justifying the means because of the supposedly glorious ends. And *that* is bullshit, too. Ask Adolf Eichmann.

On an entertainment level, the show is humiliatingly offensive. It is badly acted, moronically plotted, cheaply produced, illogical, and so hack familiar one need only watch the teaser to know the denouement. And worse, it is a bore. The time is past when any but the dullest of us believe in such derring-do by cadres of "specialists."

But the most irritating thing about the series—aside from the fact that it eats up valuable viewing time in the first place—is that it proffers more of the same old crap Mr. Spelling has been dispensing for years.

Its only saving grace is that it's a half hour long, rather than an hour. It can only be improved by making it an irregularly scheduled 0.6 of a second subliminal flash, shown after random deodorant commercials.

MAKE ROOM FOR GRANDDADDY
(Wednesday, ABC, 8:00 p.m.)

Angela Cartwright has grown up to be a lovely looking young woman, and there ceases any praise of any sort for this mothball special. I have no idea who the producers think the audience might be for such drivel. Young people will sneer at the cynical attempts at "social relevance." Old viewers will find it all terribly familiar and inapplicable to the condition of their lives in these times of tax-bludgeoning, verbal assaults from left and right, and the terrors of a changing social order. And all but the kind of phonies who used to hang out at Sunset Strip discothèques will find Danny Thomas' treacly sentimentality and showbiz humbleness too much for their digestive tracts. Mr. Thomas has not been watching the newspapers. He apparently still thinks it's 1944, when that "we humble showfolk only live to entertain you good people" nonsense seemed apropos, coming from nightclub stages. It only plays in Vegas and at Friars Club dinners now. Mr. Thomas is one of a dying breed, and even though this last gasp of the species has national exposure (thereby making it the best-attended death rattle in the history of genocide), one can only suggest that he take his vast fortune, his admirable charities, his transparently phony self-effacement, his dialogue straight out of twenty-year-old segments of *I Married Joan*, his

studio sets that look like paupers' homes (because they've been
used so long), and retire to whatever elegant Xanadu is reserved
for outdated comedians, where he can smoke his cigars in peace
and say what he really *thinks* about those goddamned Israelis,
without worrying about the opinions of "dear Jewish friends"
like Aaron Spelling. Maybe Angela Cartwright can get some
worthwhile gig.

MATT LINCOLN
(Thursday, ABC, 7:30 p.m.)

After the full-length column I did before the fact on this
series, I was afraid I was going to find it so evil and hurtful that
it might take another full column to deal with it.

Happily, such was not the case.

Matt Lincoln is so dull, so uninspired, I suspect its initial
audience will melt away within the first thirteen weeks, and we
won't have to worry about it again.

And so saying, he passed on to other topics.

BAREFOOT IN THE PARK
(Thursday, ABC, 9:00 p.m.)

This is easily the most offensive show of the year. Turning
Neil Simon's thin and inoffensive little comedy into an all-black
vehicle was perhaps a good idea...in concept. But the execution
is as distasteful as it is witless.

The inherent flaw is in trying to transpose white for black,
item for item. Blacks and whites do not live, look, act, or think
alike. We've spent three hundred years in this country making
sure of that. And trying to pretend such is the case is dishonesty
and stupidity of a rare high order. As the token black in an
all-white legal firm, the hero of the series goes through all the
life-style movements of a mingy little middle-class white-collar

worker who has all the verve and imagination of a ribbon clerk. His aspirations and interests are those of the dullest suburban homeowner, even though he lives in a ratty under-the-eaves apartment. It is virtually *The Brady Bunch* sans moppets.

The lie of all this is one blacks have been trying heroically to dispel since the first civil rights sit-ins: that blacks want to be just like whites, with cars and washing machines and all the other garbage accouterments that have turned *white* living in America into a materialistic search for status and creature comfort.

By denying the black heritage, and the wealth of black humor that has enriched it, the series literally lies to black and white alike. It pretends to a view of "negritude" that is virtually Caucasoid with Man-Tan slathered on. It is a latter-day analogue of "passing." It is Tom to a fare-thee-well. And it stinks to high heaven.

I understand Scoey Mitchell, who plays the lead in the series, was such a troublesome lad—whose capers and time-wasting (i.e., money-wasting) finally culminated in his punching the nose of a Paramount VP—he's been fired off the show; and they are currently casting around for a replacement. And the odd thing about it, from what I hear in the trade, is that Mitchell wanted to play it more white. So perhaps the series will take a turn for the better, later in the year…sure it will. Yeah, sure.

My doubts are based on the character interrelationship between Corie, the hero's wife (played with all the ghetto soul of a DAR delegate by Tracy Reed, who is to the image of the modern black woman what Little Annie Fanny is to the image of the white woman), and a neighborhood hipster named Honey Robinson, played by Nipsey Russell, in whose few moments of street humor we have the closest approaches to black truth of which this series apparently is capable.

Honey comes up to Paul and Corie's apartment at regular intervals when Paul is away; he mooches around the city with Corie; at one point Paul comes to Honey's poolroom and finds Corie with the other man instead of being at home making his dinner. Now what's wrong with that, you may ask…if you're white? Until last year, I would have made the same query. But one of my black students in the Open Door program of the Writers

Guild drew my honky attention to the difference in black and white thinking in such matters.

I had written a scene at a black party, in which a black man arrived with his woman, who saw an old boyfriend and dashed across the room to kiss him. It seemed right to me and it played well. Wrong, said Denny Pryor, my student. It wouldn't be. Why? I asked.

Because for so many years the black man has had the balls cut off him culturally by a society that lets his women work as maids and housekeepers and domestics of all sorts, while he went jobless, and he was forced into the image (if not the actuality) of an out-of-work bum. Because now black men are fighting to amass the pride they've always had, that has lain dormant because of the pressures on them, and their women recognize the nature of the struggle. Because when a black man enters a party, his woman is with *him*; she supports *him*; she can be friendly with other men but there must be no scintilla of doubt that she is his woman and they are strong together. In private it's another matter, but in public—particularly at a party—her man's appearance in the eyes of others is of paramount importance. The mickeymouse behavior of white women with other men at parties—hugging, kissing, fawning, flirting—would be anathema and deadly at a black party. *That* is a difference in white and black thinking and social conduct.

Similarly, the way Corie hangs out with Honey, the way she belittles her husband in the eyes of others, would be grounds aplenty for a beating or a shoot-out. No black woman hip to her responsibilities with her man would *do* this kind of white bullshit, and no black man with an ounce of pride or dignity or muscle would *allow* it to go on past the first time. Whites put up with this kind of emasculating monstrousness week in and week out, which is why we have swap parties, plenty of divorces, and a nation of gutless men who "don't want to get involved."

It is one of the things no white man can know. And for you and me, I suppose it doesn't much matter if we aren't hip to it. But the producers and stars of a show like *Barefoot in the Park* should know it, and act on it, if the series is intended to be anything but a token gesture aimed at placating the FCC's integration edicts.

And since everything I've seen so far on this series indicates that it is *precisely* such a gesture, I suggest the fraudulence of the concept will turn off black and white alike. Despite this, because of the hypocrisy that informs such gestures, even if *Barefoot in the Park* is a rating disaster, the network will keep it on. Out of a deranged and uninformed feeling that the black community or the FCC will pillory them for dropping it.

When I suspect, in fact, that the black community despises a series in the initial segment of which a lawyer is asked to serve as a waiter for an all-white party. And the producers and network think that's a *funny* situation. If that's funny, next season we can expect the appearance of *The Stepin Fetchit Natural Rhythm Shuffle Hour*, brought to you by Kentucky Colonel Fried Chicken and Chiquita Watermelons.

THE ODD COUPLE
(Thursday, ABC, 9:30 p.m.)

is a delight. Neil Simon's Broadway comedy translates exquisitely on the tiny screen. Jack Klugman as the slob, Oscar, is a rare delight, poetry and music in every word and motion. Tony Randall as the anal retentive Felix is brilliant. And the two of them together make this a half hour of joy and luminous comedy. If there are carps, they are minor...Oscar seems a little too clean and neat to be the slob we expect him to be...Felix frequently seems more petulant than prissy...we don't see enough of the wonderful Pigeon Sisters. But these are cavils that really don't count. And it's sad-making in this not-best-of-all-possible worlds that there is much more to say about stinkers like *Barefoot in the Park* than winners like *The Odd Couple*, but in the final analysis, what more is there a conscientious critic can say after he's said watch this show, you will like it enormously?

THE IMMORTAL
(Thursday, ABC, 10:00 p.m.)

I waited two weeks before reviewing this series. I wanted to be ultra-fair, for any number of reasons, not the least of which were that I *wanted* to like it and that the series is based on a science fiction novel by a good friend of mine. But two weeks' airing forces the conclusion that *The Immortal* is a nitwit's delight.

Totally devoid of any reality or purpose, it is an endless video version of a Pavlovian rat-response, with the negative charisma of the hunted Christopher George serving to cast a downer pall over the labyrinthine scurryings of stalked prey through blah settings. More than half of each show I saw was devoted to mindless chase-sequences. It is *The Fugitive* stripped of sanity.

On the second week's episode even Ross Martin—whose ability to elevate the most moronic part to at least the level of craft expertise is legend after years of wallowing through *The Wild, Wild West*—even Ross was hopelessly bogged in the clichés and caricatures of an archetypal rural boob. Of plot there was little: just more of the first week's vapid scampering hither and thither, with George at one end of the line, and faceless, dialogueless baddies in their Continentals at the other.

It is so patently conceived by and for pinheads, that it must surely be a hit. But the lunacy of postulating a series based on a science fictional theme (a man whose blood produces antibodies that virtually guarantee immortality and freedom from the aging process) and then *ignoring* the fantasy elements, out of fear the "audience won't accept it," when it was *precisely* that acceptance that generated interest in the series to begin with, defies belief, rationality, or discussion.

Yet, perversely, a hit it will surely be. For it offers nothing *but* movement and action; and in a time when young people turn off the sound to allow the screen's multicolored images to function as moving artwork on a wall...what more could one ask than video in its purest form, stripped of impediments like plot, purpose, or preachments? For those who are catatonic, strobismic, spaced, or senile—it is a surrogate for thought or involvement.

And if (as our sociologists ever more frequently advise us) we are a nation desperately trying to avoid involvement with life, *The Immortal* could easily become our New Testament.

Subtitled, Where Are You Tonight, Catherine Genovese?

THE PARTRIDGE FAMILY
(Friday, ABC, 8:30 p.m.)

Mother of god!

82: 30 OCTOBER 70

If Jean-Jacques Rousseau can make a living from his confessions, I see no reason why I can't do the same. I will confess: I have been a bad boy. I missed my deadline last week and those of you who've dropped me notes cursing my name because you laid out a quarter for the *Freep* and found no infuriating Ellisonian bullshit are well within your rights at being angry. What happened was that instead of hunkering in front of the juju box all last week, catching up with the few remaining new series unreviewed in this space—*The Most Deadly Game, The Don Knotts Show, Nancy, Dan August, The Men from Shiloh*—I spent my time trying to beat the recession by writing a script for Zalman King, Lee J. Cobb, and *The Young Lawyers*. Which is why I haven't reviewed *that* one either. (I may not review the series et al. at all. Having written for it, and being a friend of Zal King, I suspect my judgment will be highly impaired; and while I can state with certainty that watching Zalman work is a delight sufficient to make the show a hit, I am by no means blind to the weak scripts that have been aired thus far. So to keep my hands relatively clean, I've pleaded *nolo contendere*—writing a legal show can do that to you—and you can make your own decisions on this one. Jesus, do I have to tell you *every*thing!?!)

Soon enough, old dears, I'll get around to those final five. I don't think you'll suffer too much withdrawal if I postpone judgments on Nancy and Knotts and suchlike.

Upcoming in this column, just to whet your appetites, are two columns on the treatment of the image of the American Indian on television (with research provided by a genuine Kiowa medicine man), the long-promised evisceration of *Bracken's World*, a piece on Baxter Ward and his stand in re the Salazar inquest travesty, a compilation of recent letters from outraged correspondents about such epics as *The Interns*, a lightweight frippery about watching tv while doing Dirty Things on a water bed; and I feel I should share with you some scrutinizations of the network censors at play (those wonderful "continuity" folks, the ones who brought you deballing). (Some rather interesting information has fallen into my hands on this subject, and while I am fully cognizant of how they can railroad one for publishing "stolen information" that is free and open to the public, I feel it is within the scope of my duties as your juju columnist to share with you the contents of some confidential continuity memos from the three major networks...not to mention a delicious sprinkling of the recent crop of censorship-on-tv stories currently in vogue among the members of my Industry.)

However, this week, and for the next three weeks, that ole debbil serendipity will provide you with something rather unusual, in response to a number of requests from curious and venal readers of this column.

Each week I receive at least a couple of letters from aspiring television writers, wanting to know how to write a script. Sometimes these lovelies even honor me with scripts they've already written, asking with chutzpah unparalleled in the Western world, nay *demanding*, that I read and critique (and sometimes even agent) the work for them. In order to retain my sanity, to put an end to such unconscionable hectoring (which only draws rude responses from me, gentle soul though I be), to answer all appeals for the look and style of a script, and to show you what I've been doing for the last two months, "The Glass Teat" (through the good offices of producer Matthew Rapf, his story editor Jim McAdams, and those swell guys at Paramount and ABC) will publish—uncut in its first-draft version, unexpurgated and in its entirety—the full script of my upcoming segment of *The Young Lawyers*.

That's funny. I was certain there'd be huzzahs and handclapping. Well, anyway...

The script runs to seventy-five pages, so that means you'll get one act a week, for four weeks. The first installment will include the "teaser" and the last installment will include the "tag."

I commend these four columns to your attention not only so you can savor of the luxuriance of my prose and pithy dialogue, but so you can see the differences between what a writer writes (as well as *how* it's written for the visual media) and what winds up on the screen. By saving all four installments and comparing the word with the action, we can all be enlightened. Hopefully.

I do this not only because I'd like you all to see my show, but also because I am secure in the translucent beauty of the story I've told. As it is based on an actual incident that happened to me last year, a situation in which I was aided gloriously by the very editor of this newspaper, the stalwart Brian Kirby, it assumes new relevance for all of you out there panting for the inside info about life and working conditions in videoland.

And so, without further ado, I lay my innermost creative self before you. Just remember, in years to come when you talk of this—and you will—be kind.

When it's all over, we can critique it. That'll be fun.

Author's Note: In 1974 I won a Mystery Writers of America Edgar Allan Poe Award for the "best mystery story" of the year. Its title was *The Whimper of Whipped Dogs*. It bears no relation of any kind to this script or its plot. I grew so enamoured of the title while writing this show that, when no segment titles were used onscreen during airing, nor were any used in the main tv information outlets such as *TV Guide*, I felt I should save the title for a short story. Now that the script is published and the short story has achieved a degree of prominence, I felt this footnote necessary to avoid confusion among those who follow such minutiae in bibliographies. —he

THE YOUNG LAWYERS
"THE WHIMPER OF WHIPPED DOGS"

Part One

<u>TEASER</u>

FADE IN:

1   INT. AARON'S APARTMENT — FULL SHOT CLOSE
ON MIRROR — AARON'S FACE — NIGHT

Devoid of expression. Aaron looking at
himself in the mirror, which FILLS THE
SHOT. HOLD two beats.

MATCH CUT TO:

2   MEMORY SHOT — SOLARIZATION OR SIMILAR
ETHEREAL EFFECT

MATCH-SHOT OF SNOWMAN'S FACE (SLOW THE
MOTION IN THESE MEMORY SHOTS — NOT FULL
SLOW — MERELY TO A STATELY PACE) FILLS
THE SHOT as Aaron's face filled it a
moment before.

CAMERA PULLS BACK as Aaron's face pops
up from behind the snowman. As he
appears, a snowball plonks him full in
the snoot.

CUT TO:

3   MEMORY SHOT — SAME EFFECT AS ABOVE
    — EXT. COUNTRYSIDE — ON HALLIE BENDA
    (PROCESS)

who has obviously thrown the snowball.
Bundled prettily, wearing winter clothes,
a scarf, pink cheeks, an extraordinarily
lovely girl in a delicate Dresden Doll
sort of way. Rebecca of Sunnybrook Farm
with an impish sensuality. She's laughing
at Aaron; she's blonde and fine.

                              CUT BACK TO:

4   INT. AARON'S APARTMENT — FULL SHOT CLOSE
    ON MIRROR AARON'S FACE — NIGHT

CAMERA PULLS BACK to show Aaron tying
his tie in the mirror. Behind him,
slouching in a chair, sidewise, her
long legs dangling attractively, CLAIRE
ZELAZNY watches him with a bemused
expression. She is as dark and buxom as
Hallie was slim and blonde. They must
be instantly identifiable as two different
girls.

                    CLAIRE
          Have you ever been on time,
          even once...your whole life?

                    AARON
          I couldn't help it. Serving
          humanity knows no hours.

                              (CONTINUED)

4   CONTINUED:

                    CLAIRE
              (mock exasperation
         Please. You don't even <u>look</u>
         like Albert Schweitzer.

                    AARON
         Mr. Barrett'll understand.

                    CLAIRE
         He might: I don't.

Aaron turns and gives her a winsome
smile.

                    AARON
         But just think: by meeting me
         here instead of me having to
         go pick you up, we save time.

                    CLAIRE
              (looking around)
         Also, thereby, compromising my
         reputation. Secret trysts in
         men's apartments!

He goes back to tying the tie.

                    AARON
         To you, I'm just another pretty
         face.

                    CLAIRE
              (to the sky)
         Why me? What did I do wrong?

                                        CUT TO:

5   MEMORY SHOT — SAME EFFECT AS 2 — AARON'S
    APARTMENT — NIGHT

But things are arranged differently.
Another time, long ago. Aaron reading to
Hallie from a book as she sits by his
feet. Very intense, both of them.

                              CUT BACK TO:

6   ANOTHER ANGLE — THE APARTMENT

as Aaron finishes, turns, grins. Spreads
his hands.

                    AARON
          Dinner is served.

Claire gets up, shaking her head at him,
and he helps her into her coat, shrugs
into his own. He goes around the room
shutting off lights as Claire opens the
door to leave.

                    AARON
          I pay the electricity.

                    CLAIRE
               (in doorway)
          Someday I'll meet a wealthy
          man with charge accounts,
          lots of credit cards.

Aaron comes to her and they step through
as he delivers line:

                              (CONTINUED)

6   CONTINUED:

> AARON
> You're a product of a corrupt
> environment.

He shuts off the light, and closes the
door. A beat. The phone RINGS. Another
beat. PHONE RINGS AGAIN. The door opens
after lock fumbling, and in the light
spilling through from the hallway, Aaron
dashes to phone in f.g. Picks it up.

> CUT TO:

7   MEMORY SHOT — SAME EFFECT AS BEFORE —
EXT. CITY — WINTER — DAY

Aaron, standing on the top step of a
municipal building, hands cupped to
mouth, calling down to the far bottom
step, where Hallie stands. Then he flails
his arms, as though declaiming a great
address to multitudes. Hallie laughing,
throwing him kisses.

> CUT BACK TO:

8   CLOSE ON AARON ON PHONE — DOORWAY IN B.G.

> AARON
> Hello?
> (no answer)
> Hello?

> CUT TO:

9   MEMORY SHOT — SAME SOLARIZED EFFECT —
    HALLIE BENDA'S FACE

moving into CLOSEUP. A measured
scrutinization of her loveliness, her
openness, her gentleness.

                              CUT BACK TO:

10 AARON IN CLOSEUP

as Claire comes back into the doorway
behind him, watches him.

                    AARON
                  (annoyed)
            You wimp!

He starts to hang up. Phone three inches
from his ear on the way down — a VOICE
crackles out at him.

                    HALLIE
                  (filter)
            Aaron…

He stops. The phone stays in mid-
movement. He doesn't move. Beat. Beat.
Again, the voice:

                    HALLIE
                  (filter)
            Aaron…it's Hallie…I need help…

                              (CONTINUED)

10 CONTINUED:

He wants to hang it up, he righteously
wants to slam it down. His hand trembles
as CAMERA CLOSES on the hand, the phone,
his face half-in-shadow. But slowly he
puts it to his ear.

                    AARON
            (with difficulty)
            Hallie?

                                        CUT TO:

11 MEMORY SHOT — SAME EFFECT — HALF SLOW
    MOTION — AARON, HALLIE IN CLOSEUP

She is kissing his eyes.

                                    CUT BACK TO:

12 AARON IN CLOSE

                    HALLIE
            (filter)
            I didn't want to call you…but
            they gave me only one phone
            call…Aaron…

                    AARON
            (softly)
            Where are you?

                    HALLIE
            (filter)
            I'm at the Charles Street
            Station.

12 CONTINUED:

                    AARON
               (two beats)
          For what?

                    HALLIE
               (filter)
          Using a stolen credit card.
               (beat)
          Aaron, I didn't know it was
          stolen...my girlfriend gave it to
          me...I didn't want to call you, I
          didn't want you to know...there
          isn't anyone else I can ask...

Aaron is terribly tense. CAMERA FOCUSES
on Claire in doorway behind him, worried
about him and the call that is obviously
upsetting him, then CAMERA FOCUSES on
Aaron again.

                    AARON
          I'll get a bail bondsman. Just
          take it easy; I'll have you out
          of there as soon as I can.

                    HALLIE
               (filter)
          Aaron...?

He waits silently.

                                        CUT TO:

13 MEMORY SHOT — SOLARIZATION EFFECT

Hallie and Aaron, on a slight hill,
rolling down and down, locked in each
other's arms TO CAMERA where their faces
come into CLOSEUP and they kiss deeply.

                                    CUT BACK TO:

14 AARON IN CLOSE

                    HALLIE
                (filter)
        I love you…

Aaron finds difficulty speaking. He can't
respond as he wants to respond. His reply
seems gruff, but the rough tone tells us
he is trying to cope with his feelings.

                    AARON
        Yeah.
                (beat)
        Take it easy. I'll have you out
        real quick.

He slowly hangs up. CAMERA PULLS BACK
TO FOCUS Aaron and Claire, still in the
lighted doorway.

                    CLAIRE
        Aaron?

                    AARON
        Let's go. We'll be late for
        dinner.

                                    (CONTINUED)

14 CONTINUED:

                    CLAIRE
          Trouble?

                    AARON
                (carefully)
          No…just someone I once knew.

He walks to her at the door, steps
through and door closes. HOLD two beats
on the dark apartment and then the ROOM
SOLARIZES AS IT WAS IN THE MEMORY SHOTS.

                              FADE OUT.

          END TEASER

ACT ONE

FADE IN:

15 INT. BARRETT'S TOWN HOUSE — CLOSE ON TV
   SET — NIGHT

as CAMERA PULLS BACK RAPIDLY to show
Barrett's living room. The sound is off,
but the picture running is KING KONG. In
the f.g. DAVID BARRETT is mixing a drink
for JUDGE KATE KNIGHT — a tall, elegant,
very feminine jurist whose distinguished
career has in no way impaired her good
looks or her femininity. Claire sits
on the sofa, dividing her attention
rather markedly between the fascinating
conversation of Barrett and the Judge…
and Aaron who, in the b.g., is talking in
low tones on the telephone.

                    KATE
         My contention is still that
         King Kong can be taken as an
         unconscious symbol of male
         supremacy.

Barrett hands her the drink as Kong
lumbers about with Fay Wray wrapped in
his hairy paw.

                    BARRETT
         Ridiculous! Next you'll
                    (MORE)

                              (CONTINUED)

15 CONTINUED:

> BARRETT (CONT'D)
> be saying Fay Wray was
> representative of Women's
> Liberation because she didn't
> wear a bra.

> KATE
> Forgetting for the moment
> that your strongest argument
> is the smell of that chicken
> paprikash coming from the
> kitchen, Counselor, in my
> capacity as the only Circuit
> Court Judge in this room, I
> overrule that remark as
> extremely snotty.

> BARRETT
> I suppose Kong is a male
> chauvinist because he's brutal,
> rapacious and has bad breath…
> Your Honor.

> KATE
> No, because he manhandles
> women.

> BARRETT
> (corrects her)
> Monkeyhandles.

> KATE
> (sips)
> Sustained.

(CONTINUED)

15 CONTINUED:

> BARRETT
> In point of fact, I submit that
> poor simian is a symbol of
> man's never-ending search for a
> little true love, a good woman…
> and a thirty-foot banana…

They are about to go on, but Barrett has
been eyeing Claire and Aaron, and now
he turns his attention to the young girl,
who is openly watching Aaron talk on the
phone.

> BARRETT
> Miss Zelazny…
>   (she doesn't respond)
> Claire…
>   (she turns)
> What is Aaron doing?

> CLAIRE
> Talking to someone named
> Yoakum.

> KATE
> Bernie Yoakum? The bail
> bondsman?

They all three stare at Aaron.

16 CLOSE ON AARON AT PHONE

> AARON
> Thanks, Bernie.
>   (MORE)

(CONTINUED)

16 CONTINUED:

> AARON (CONT'D)
> When you find out how much
> they'll fix bail, call me here.
> The number is 542–2575.
> (beat)
> Okay. Okay. G'bye.

He hangs up and CAMERA PULLS BACK to
include group as Aaron comes to them.

> AARON
> Sorry, Mr. Barrett, Judge
> Knight.

> CLAIRE
> (concerned)
> Is it all right?

Aaron shakes his head. He doesn't want
to talk about it. Barrett instantly
gauges the tone of Aaron's worry. The
Judge is waiting for developments.

> BARRETT
> Aaron?

> AARON
> I'd just as soon not talk about
> it, sir.

> BARRETT
> (pauses, decides)
> That would be fine, Aaron, if
> you hadn't come three-quarters
> (MORE)

(CONTINUED)

16 CONTINUED:

> BARRETT (CONT'D)
> of an hour late so the
> paprikash lost its juice,
> if you hadn't spent the last
> twenty minutes on the phone
> to a bondsman, and if I wasn't
> sure this was N.L.O. business.

Aaron starts to sit down, wearily, beside
Claire. He halts in mid-sit.

> AARON
> Shouldn't we start eating? I
> don't want to hold it up any
> more...

> KATE
> It'll wait, Aaron.

He nods, sits down, starts to tell it.

> AARON
> My first year in school, I was
> pretty much involved with this
> girl...for a while we got it on
> okay...

                                    CUT TO:

17 INTERCUT — MEMORY SHOT — SOLARIZED

Aaron and Hallie, playing Monopoly.
Hallie puts a house on one of her
properties. Aaron puts three. Hallie
puts six. Aaron puts ten.

                              (CONTINUED)

17 CONTINUED:

Then they're jamming all the houses and
hotels on two blocks, one on another,
till they're clutching each other
laughing.

CUT BACK TO:

18 SAME AS 16

> AARON
> Hallie Benda. Lasted a while,
> then we just sort of …it went
> away…No fights, nothing like
> that, we were still friends…
> it just wasn't us together any
> more. She called tonight, just
> before we came over. She's in
> jail and she called for me to
> get her out.

> BARRETT
> What are the formal charges?

> AARON
> I'm waiting for Yoakum to call
> me back to find out. Something
> to do with a stolen credit
> card her girlfriend gave her.

Barrett nods. Then he makes a decision.

> BARRETT
> Come on, let's eat. We can talk
> over food.

(CONTINUED)

18 CONTINUED:

They rise and start into the other room
as we

                                    DISSOLVE TO:

19 MEMORY SHOT — SOLARIZED — AARON'S VOICE
OVER THROUGHOUT

Character studies of Hallie and Aaron,
in soft focus with Hallie looking young
and vibrant, a flower just opening. Aaron
deeply in love with her. And there can
be intimations that it is sexual as
well as esthetic, if we are to retain a
semblance of reality.

                    AARON
          Her mother is dead, her
          sister's some kind of a
          prostitute, I guess: Hallie
          didn't like to talk about
          it too much, but that's the
          feeling I got. There wasn't
          anybody else. She wanted
          better things for herself.
          Music, books, we learned a lot
          from each other.
               (beat)
          Then I didn't see her any more.
               (beat)
          That was all. It just stopped.
          Till tonight.

                                DISSOLVE BACK TO:

20 THE LIVING ROOM — LATER

Everyone sipping coffee, to indicate the
dinner has been eaten and it is later.
The PHONE RINGS. Aaron gets up.

                    AARON
                 (to Barrett)
           Maybe it's Yoakum.

Barrett indicates it's all right for
Aaron to answer his phone. Aaron goes.
Barrett and Kate exchange glances.

21 CLOSE ON AARON AT PHONE — INTERCUT WITH
    CLOSE ON YOAKUM ON PHONE

(Alternate filter where necessary.)
YOAKUM is a character. Bernie Yoakum is
about forty, balding, wearing jeans and
a T-shirt that bulges over his belt. But
he is canny, compassionate, efficient and
very very upfront with information.

                    AARON
           Barrett residence.

                    YOAKUM
           Aaron Silverman, please.

                    AARON
           It's me, Bernie. What've you
           got?

                    YOAKUM
           You sure you want to do this,
           babe?

                              (CONTINUED)

21 CONTINUED:

                    AARON
     Come on, Bernie — what is it?

                    YOAKUM
     They caught her trying to use
     a stolen credit card to rent
     a car. They've got her and a
     girlfriend in the lockup.

                    AARON
     Will they release her?

                    YOAKUM
     They don't want to.

                    AARON
     Why? That isn't that heavy a
     charge.

                    YOAKUM
     There's more. She's got a
     record, Aaron. A nasty one.

                    AARON
     Hallie?

                    YOAKUM
     About three weeks ago she was
     pulled in. Neighbors heard
     her baby crying like she was
     beating it. Cops got there and
     she was gone. Baby deserted.
                    (MORE)

                              (CONTINUED)

21 CONTINUED:

> YOAKUM (CONT'D)
> They took it to the County
> Home, and a couple of days
> later she came home, neighbors
> called the cops again and they
> pulled her in.

> AARON
> (stunned)
> I don't believe it.

> YOAKUM
> It's on paper, Aaron.

> AARON
> But she isn't even married!

> YOAKUM
> When was the last time you saw
> her?

Yoakum's remark stops Aaron. He tangles
with it for a moment.

> AARON
> (finally)
> Okay, I want her out of there.
> Won't they fix bail?

> YOAKUM
> You haven't heard it all.
> (beat)
> She's got a hundred and thirty
> dollars in outstanding traffic
> tickets.

(CONTINUED)

21 CONTINUED:

Aaron lowers the phone. He can't cope
with all of this. Barrett suddenly comes
INTO THE FRAME. He reaches for the phone.

>   BARRETT
>   (gently)
>   May I?
>   (Aaron gives him the phone)
>   Bernie? David Barrett. What
>   have we got down there?

22 FULL SHOT — FAVORING AARON

as he walks away from the phone. Barrett
is talking in the b.g. Aaron walks back
to Claire and Kate.

>   KATE
>   Is there anything I can do,
>   Aaron?

He doesn't seem to hear. Then he lets it
penetrate.

>   AARON
>   Huh? Oh, thank you, Judge. No,
>   I don't think —

He stops.

>   AARON
>   The police won't fix bail on
>   Hallie.
>   (MORE)

22 CONTINUED:

>   AARON (CONT'D)
>   It's Friday night...I can't let
>   her sit in there till Monday
>   morning. She was crying when
>   she talked to me.
>   (beat)
>   I know her, I know this is all
>   wrong. Judge, would you sign an
>   order setting bail for release?

23 REVERSE ANGLE — FAVORING JUDGE KATE
KNIGHT

She looks uncertain. She's watching
Barrett talking.

>   KATE
>   Are you sure that's what you
>   want, Aaron? There seems to
>   be some trouble if the Desk
>   Sergeant won't fix bail.

>   AARON
>   Judge, I know this girl. She
>   can't be mixed up in all this.
>   It's a mistake...she's a fine
>   person; I can't let her stay in
>   a cell all weekend...

>   KATE
>   All right, Aaron.

Aaron smiles with deep gratitude.

                                    (CONTINUED)

23 CONTINUED:

> AARON
> I'll have Bernie Yoakum bring
> the papers.

> KATE
> I'll set a high bail, Aaron.

> AARON
> (pauses, then gratefully)
> I understand. Thank you.

He goes to the phone as Barrett finishes,
and takes the receiver. Barrett stays
and listens.

> AARON
> (to Yoakum)
> Bernie, Aaron. Judge Knight
> of the Circuit Court is here.
> She's prepared to sign an order
> setting bail and permitting
> release. Can you bring the
> papers here for her signature?

He listens. Barrett has heard all this,
and is terribly upset. He turns and
stares across the room at Kate.

> AARON
> (to Kate)
> Judge, Bernie'd like to speak
> to you for a moment.

Kate rises and comes to the phone. Aaron
hands it to her.

(CONTINUED)

23 CONTINUED:

                    KATE
          Mr. Yoakum, Judge Knight.
          Can you tell me the charges,
          please?

She listens for a while, hmmms and nods.

                    KATE
          Fine. If you'll bring the
          papers here, Mr. Barrett will
          give you the address.

She hands the phone to Barrett, who
looks at her for a long moment, then
turns away and speaks to Yoakum as Kate
and Aaron return to the sofa and Claire.

                    KATE
          Aaron, I'm setting bail at
          fifteen hundred dollars. Mr.
          Yoakum will probably ask two
          hundred dollars for the bond;
          and you'll need one hundred
          and thirty dollars in cash
          for the traffic fines, otherwise
          they won't release her.

                    AARON
          Three hundred and thirty
          dollars.

Barrett hangs up and comes to them. He
is quite angry.

                                    (CONTINUED)

23 CONTINUED:

> AARON
> Sir, can I get three hundred
> and thirty dollars from the
> N.L.O.? From the bail fund.

> BARRETT
>   (hard)
> No.

> AARON
> It's to get this girl out of —

> BARRETT
> I know what it's for, Aaron.
> I'm afraid not.
>   (to Kate)
> And I think you're making a
> serious mistake, Kate.

> AARON
>   (bewildered)
> Why are you doing this?

> BARRETT
> Because you're making a fool of
> yourself.

By Aaron's reaction, and Kate's stiffened
spine, and by the sound of his own words,
Barrett instantly recognizes his error.
He's used the wrong tone, the wrong
words, the wrong approach entirely. He's
angry, and it's made him miscalculate.

(CONTINUED)

23 CONTINUED:

> BARRETT
> (continuing)
> I'm sorry, Aaron. I didn't mean
> that the way it sounded.
> (beat)
> This girl is in deep trouble,
> and you're going out on a limb
> without considering carefully.

> AARON
> I've considered. I want her out.

> BARRETT
> That's fine, but perhaps she
> should be in.

> AARON
> I thought there was only one
> judge in the room.

> CLAIRE
> Aaron!

> BARRETT
> That's all right, I deserved
> it. But it doesn't negate my
> opinion. Abandonment, possible
> child cruelty, grand larceny
> and possible fraud. Not to
> mention traffic citations worthy
> of a renegade motorcycle pack.

> AARON
> She didn't know the card
> (MORE)

(CONTINUED)

23 CONTINUED:

> AARON (CONT'D)
> was stolen…there must be an
> explanation for the child — I
> don't even think it's her —
> Hallie isn't <u>married</u>!

> BARRETT
> Aaron! You're an attorney, not
> a social worker.

> AARON
> I <u>know</u> her!

> BARRETT
> You haven't <u>seen</u> her in three
> years. You <u>don't</u> know her!
> You only have feelings, Aaron
> — feelings and memories. An
> attorney can't work that way.
>   (beat)
> It's as reliable as getting
> spirit messages!

> AARON
>   (to Kate)
> Judge, I don't want to cause
> any trouble. If you want to
> reconsider…

> KATE
> David may be right, Aaron…but
> I said I'd do it.

> BARRETT
> You're making a mistake, Kate.

(CONTINUED)

23 CONTINUED:

> KATE
> (slight chill)
> I've made others, David. I can
> understand Aaron's concern. If
> she is innocent, a weekend
> in jail can be an unpleasant
> experience.

Barrett turns away. He's furious. Aaron
looks at Claire, who bites her lip.

> AARON
> I'd better get a move on if I'm
> going to raise the bond money.

Claire rises. Barrett goes for their
coats.

> CLAIRE
> It was very nice meeting you,
> Judge Knight.

> KATE
> Next time we'll let the food
> settle.

> AARON
> I'm sorry, Judge. Thanks.

> KATE
> That's all right, Aaron. When
> Mr. Yoakum gets here I'll take
> care of the order.
> (MORE)

(CONTINUED)

23 CONTINUED:

                    KATE (CONT'D)
          (beat)
      And, Aaron…
          (beat)
      David worries about you.

Aaron smiles wanly. They go to Barrett,
standing by the door, holding their
coats. He gives Aaron his, and helps
Claire into hers.

                    BARRETT
      Please come again, Miss
      Zalazny.
          (to Aaron)
And next time, leave your weird friend at home.

                    AARON
      (rigid)
      Good night, sir. Thank you for
      dinner. Barrett doesn't answer.
      They go.

24 LONG SHOT — ACROSS LIVING ROOM

  as Barrett comes to Kate in f.g.

                    KATE
      Sometimes, David, there is no
      softness in you.

                    BARRETT
      Would you like some cognac?

                            (CONTINUED)

24 CONTINUED:

>   KATE
> If I didn't have to wait, I'd
> be on my way out.

>   BARRETT
> Kate, we're in the same
> business. You of all people
> should know my job isn't to be
> soft, or mellow, or charming,
> or muddle-headed!
>   (beat)
> He boils, that boy. He boils
> and he fumes and he has great
> integrity and all of those
> qualities are good…for a
> certain kind of lawyer. But
> that fire can burn and he
> has to know it. If he wants
> to take chances, that's his
> business, but what do we do
> when he takes chances with
> other people's lives?

>   KATE
> You can be wrong, David.

>   BARRETT
> I'm not.

She looks at him as he hands her the
cognac. He is dead certain. He's lost
the argument with Aaron, looked bad to
everyone in the room, but he's right…he
knows it, and Kate is suddenly afraid he
may be right.

                              DISSOLVE TO:

25 AARON'S APARTMENT — NIGHT

FULL SHOT on Aaron as he gathers up his stereo, his cassette recorder, his camera and his skis.

> CLAIRE
> I can loan you about twenty-five dollars.

> AARON
> Thanks. I think I can make it with what I've set aside for books, my savings account and these.

> CLAIRE
> Oh, Aaron, your skis, for god's sake!

> AARON
> Doesn't matter. The powder's been lousy the last two years.

He urges her toward the door, both of them laden down with negotiable merchandise.

> CLAIRE
> Where are we going to get rid of all this?

> AARON
> I'm a man with underworld connections.
> (MORE)

(CONTINUED)

25 CONTINUED:

                         AARON (CONT'D)
                    (beat)
               Besides, don't worry about my
               poverty. I'll become a gigolo
               and let your wealthy family
               support me.

                         CLAIRE
               Dynamite. Then see if you can
               get them to support me.

They exit, laden.

                                        CUT TO:

26 SERIES OF LAP DISSOLVES

    as Aaron and Claire hustle his goods.

    (We should make use of available standing
    sets for this sequence. The situations
    indicated here are merely to convey
    content.)

    Aaron in a pool room, selling his
    cassette recorder to a guy lounging over
    the soft drink counter.

    Aaron in what could be a dorm room, or a
    rooming house. Hustling the Head skis to
    a pair of dudes who are quite obviously
    trying to stiff him.

                                        (CONTINUED)

26 CONTINUED:

Aaron on a street corner with the stereo,
selling it to a dude in an Australian
bush hat and cutoffs. As a cop comes up
to them and starts questioning Aaron.

Aaron with Claire, selling books in a
late-night textbook shop.

Aaron showing his watch to a friend.

                              DISSOLVE THRU TO:

27 AARON'S APARTMENT — EARLY MORNING

Claire is asleep on the sofa, her coat
covering her legs. Aaron, looking wasted,
is asleep in a deep study armchair
beside the telephone.

27 CONTINUED:

CAMERA COMES IN on him. NO SOUND
THROUGHOUT THIS SCENE.

                              LAP DISSOLVE TO:

28 MEMORY SHOT — SOLARIZED AND SILENT

Aaron and Hallie touching. They are
learning each other's faces with their
fingers. Then they slowly come together
and kiss, as the PHONE RINGS.

The memory dream begins to dissolve,
like water colors washing down a
herringbone surface as we

SHARP CUT TO:

29 SAME AS 27

ON AARON as he jumps. It takes him a
moment to come to his senses and realize
where he is. He gropes for the phone. He
picks it up and mumbles unintelligibly.

                    YOAKUM
                (filter)
          Good morning.

                    AARON
          Mornin'…Bernie?

                    YOAKUM
                (filter)
          Yeah. Order's signed. I'm ready
          to go down to Charles Street
          Station. I thought you might
          like to meet me and lay some
          cash on me.

                    AARON
          Sure. Yeah. Okay. Meet you
          there in half an hour.

                    YOAKUM
                (filter)
          Okay. But hey, listen, Aaron…

                    AARON
          Yeah?

                                    (CONTINED)

29 CONTINUED:

                         YOAKUM
                    (filter)
          I'm not so sure this is a good
          idea. This chick is —

                         AARON
                    (cuts him off)
          Half an hour.

He hangs up rudely. Then he rises as
CAMERA PULLS BACK. He gets his coat and
starts for the door, quietly.

                         CLAIRE
          I want to go, Aaron.

He turns as CAMERA MOVES ANGLE and we
see that Claire has been awake since
the phone rang. She is sitting up,
looking very rumpled and sleepy, but
the expression on her face tells us her
attachment to Aaron is more than just
casual. He comes to her and sits on the
sofa.

                         AARON
          Maybe not, you think? Maybe I
          should go down alone.

                         CLAIRE
          I want to go with you.

She takes his face in her hands and
kisses him very tenderly.

                                   (CONTINUED)

29 CONTINUED:

                    CLAIRE
        I want to go with you.

He helps her to her feet and steadies
her as she gets into her shoes. As they
start for the door, together, we

                          DISSOLVE TO:

30 CHARLES STREET STATION — MORNING

There is an entranceway that can be
seen without having it connected to the
check-in desk area. There is a counter
and a divider wall up to waist level.
Cell doors and a corridor run off to
one side. A corridor down which Aaron
can look, and presumably down that way
are the lockups. An older man, perhaps
fiftyish, a DESK SERGEANT, is behind the
counter, talking over the divider to
Bernie Yoakum as Aaron and Claire come
in through the front door. Bernie excuses
himself, and carrying a black attaché
case that is cuffed to his wrist, he
comes to Aaron and leads him to a corner
out of earshot.

                    AARON
        Have any trouble?

                    YOAKUM
        No, Judge Knight was very
        cooperative. But, listen, man —

                          (CONTINUED)

30 CONTINUED:

> AARON
> (cuts him off)
> Don't start that stuff, Bernie.
> I want her <u>out</u>.

> YOAKUM
> Will you just, for cryin'
> out loud, take a look at the
> charge sheet? Will you? Can it
> hurt, it'll take a second!

Aaron shrugs okay. Bernie leads him back
to the counter whereon he can rest the
attaché case. He opens it with a key and
fumbles through papers in the pockets,
coming up at last with a Boston "rap
sheet." Aaron scans it, looks it over,
hands it back.

> AARON
> Where do I sign?

Yoakum looks heavenward. Then he fishes
in the case, brings out the bail bond
papers and gives Aaron a pen clipped
inside the case. He indicates where Aaron
should sign.

> YOAKUM
> You understand you're gonna be
> on the hook for fifteen hundred
> dollars if she doesn't show up
> for the arraignment on Monday
> morning?

(CONTINUED)

30 CONTNUED:

> AARON
> (ignores him)
> Do I sign here?

> YOAKUM
> (points)
> And here…and here. Both copies.
> Christ, you're stubborn.

Aaron signs. Claire stands behind him, watching, looking worried, but keeping it to herself. She knows nothing can dissuade Aaron. He's working on three-year-old memories, than which there is no deadlier drug.

31 ANGLE INCLUDING DESK SERGEANT, AARON AND YOAKUM — CORRIDOR TO CELLS IN B.G.

Yoakum looks over the papers, purses his lips in finality, tears off the proper forms, hands them to the Desk Sergeant and turns back to Aaron.

> YOAKUM
> You got a hundred and thirty
> bucks cash?

Aaron fishes it out, peels off the amount and hands it to Yoakum, who gives it to the cop. The Desk Sergeant does some paperwork as Yoakum and Aaron talk, then hands Aaron a receipt.

(CONTINUED)

31 CONTINUED:

               AARON
Thanks, Bernie. I appreciate
your losing the sleep.

               YOAKUM
It's my business. I don't mind
so much; it's when I get back
in the middle of the night and
go to bed, my wife makes bad
noises about my cold feet.

The Desk Sergeant laughs, then speaks
into a microphone on the counter.

           DESK SERGEANT
Ted, bring up the Benda girl.
We've got a release on her.

               YOAKUM
Aaron, listen, I've got to tell
you, babe, this girl isn't what
you think she is—

               AARON
           (angry)
Bernie, listen, I appreciate
your concern, man, but I've got
to tell you this is a sweet
innocent girl. I know her.
She's mixed up in all this by
mistake…

           DESK SERGEANT
Listen to your friend, fellah.
           (MORE)
                 (CONTINUED)

31 CONTINUED:

>   DESK SERGEANT (CONT'D)
>   This girl's a wrongo. She used
>   the card and tried to pin
>   it on her girlfriend. We're
>   holding the other one, too,
>   and it looks like she didn't
>   know a thing about it. It
>   was all this Benda kid's play.
>   She's a real—

32 CLOSE ON AARON

as he blows his top. He's had people
raining on his parade all night. He
hasn't slept much, he's hocked or sold
everything he owns, he's mad and he's
wild:

>   AARON
>   Shut up! What the hell do you
>   know about what people are
>   like? Everybody comes through
>   that door has to be salted
>   away, that's all you know…you
>   wouldn't know a saint if she
>   came in here in cuffs!

33 ON DESK SERGEANT

>   DESK SERGEANT
>   Are we talkin' about the same
>   girl?

34 BACK ON AARON, WITH CLAIRE PROMINENT IN F.G.

She's looking past him, down the corridor.

> AARON
> (still mad)
> Yeah, that's right. I know her, not you. She was something to put in the lockup to you, to me she's something else…

But even as Aaron is talking, CAMERA FOCUSES ON Claire and her expression of disbelief. HOLD on the expression for several beats as Aaron's tirade continues, but then we realize Claire is staring down the corridor as a girl is being led toward us by the MATRON.

Then Aaron stops short as he sees Claire's face. He turns and stares down the corridor.

35 SHOT PAST AARON TO HALLIE

as she comes closer and closer, and we

> INTERCUT WITH:

36 MEMORY SHOTS OF HALLIE

as she was—beautiful, young, vibrant, the very essence of hopeful, untainted womanhood…

(CONTINUED)

36 CONTINUED:

As she is—hair lank and dirty…skin
covered with sores…eyes dark and
haunted …the ankles thick with body
water…spastic movements, heavy breathing…
all the marks of a speed freak, a
righteous amphetamine user…(and please
makeup men, get it on! Show it the way
it really is!)

37 WITH AARON

as he turns back to the Desk Sergeant.

                    AARON
         Okay, where is she already?

                  DESK SERGEANT
                   (confused)
         That's her, buddy.

Aaron slowly turns back and we

                              FLASH INTERCUT:

38 MEMORY SHOT — HALLIE

                              CUT BACK TO:

39 PAST AARON — ON HALLIE

as the ruined thing that was Hallie
Benda comes through the unlocked door
of the corridor, and comes closer. Yes,
there is the shadow of the girl in the

                              (CONTINUED)

39 CONTINUED:

memory shots, but this is a caricature,
a hideous travesty of what Aaron
remembers.

40 AARON — EXTREME CLOSEUP

HOLD on his face. The sudden realization
of the death of dreams. The pain. The
disbelief. The terrible expression of
something ripping inside him, wrenching,
dying. HOLD HOLD HOLD on that expression
and

                                    FADE OUT.

              END ACT ONE

83: 6 NOVEMBER 70

"THE WHIMPER OF WHIPPED DOGS"

Part Two

ACT TWO

FADE IN:

41 INT. CHARLES ST. STATION — ON CLAIRE —
    MORNING

CLOSEUP on Aaron's date as she stares
at Hallie. In her expression we can see
stark disbelief that this fractured
creature from the lockup is the beautiful
girl Aaron has been raving about.

CAMERA PULLS BACK to include Yoakum, the
Desk Sergeant and Hallie and Aaron as he
helps her sign the release sheet.

> DESK SGT.
> Put down your home address,
> where you work, and the
> address of your next-of-kin.

> HALLIE
> (speaks for the first time on-
> camera)
> My sister's address?

(CONTINUED)

41 CONTINUED:

> DESK SGT.
> Is she your next-of-kin?

> HALLIE
> Yes.

The Desk Sergeant nods. Hallie writes.
Aaron copies the information on a piece
of paper, beside Hallie. She finishes. She
signs, Aaron signs.

> AARON
> Is that it?

> DESK SGT.
> She's free to go.

The four of them turn away from the desk
and walk forward toward the front door.
They stop.

> YOAKUM
> I'll be in court Monday morning
> for the arraignment.
> (to Aaron)
> Don't forget, that's 8:45 in
> session two.

> AARON
> She'll be there. Thanks,
> Bernie.

Yoakum squeezes Aaron's shoulder, then
he goes. The three of them are left
standing there.

(CONTINUED)

41 CONTINUED:

> CLAIRE
> Aaron, I've got a nine o'clock class. You probably have some talking to do. I'll get home okay.

> AARON
> Thank you, Claire.

> CLAIRE
> (to Hallie)
> I hope everything works out all right for you.

> HALLIE
> (wearily)
> Thank you. I'm sorry, I didn't even get your name.

> CLAIRE
> Claire Zelazny. Take care.

She smiles at Aaron — a smile tinged with concern — and she hurriedly leaves. Aaron turns to Hallie, who tries to look bright, but can't carry it off. She's too wasted.

> AARON
> Hungry?

Hallie nods.

(CONTINUED)

41 CONTINUED:

                AARON
              (continuing)
    Come on, I've got a few
    dollars. We'll go have some
    breakfast.

He starts to move, but she stops him.
She looks at him intensely.

                HALLIE
    I didn't have anyone else to
    turn to, Aaron. I waited a
    long time before I called…I
    didn't want you to think badly
    of me…

                AARON
    Let's go eat.

They go out the door as we:

                              DISSOLVE TO:

42 EXT. DINER — DAY

SHOT MOVES IN on a foggy window behind
which we can vaguely make out the forms
of Hallie and Aaron, sitting across from
one another in a booth. VOICES OVER as
we MOVE IN.

              AARON (v.o.)
    What happened to you after you
    dropped out of school?

                          (CONTINUED)

42 CONTINUED:

> HALLIE (v.o.)
> I went to work. A photocopying
> place. They stayed open all
> night to make up in volume
> what they lost charging 4¢ a
> page to reproduce.

> AARON (v.o.)
> I tried to find you a couple of
> times.

> HALLIE (v.o.)
> I moved around.

> AARON (v.o.)
> You moved around a lot.

CAMERA MOVES IN as we:

DISSOLVE THRU TO:

43 INT. DINER — DAY

A funky little eating place. Typical
diner. Hallie and Aaron in the booth,
eating. Coffee mugs steaming. CAMERA
MOVING IN on them with window behind
them.

> HALLIE
> I suppose. It wasn't easy.

> AARON
> Wouldn't your sister help?

(CONTINUED)

43 CONTINUED:

> HALLIE
> (sneering)
> Her? It's all she can do to
> stay out of the way of the
> vice squad. No help there.
> Ever since Mom died she hasn't
> wanted anything to do with me
> anyhow.

> AARON
> So you worked.

> HALLIE
> And I started dating.

> AARON
> You could've asked me, I'd've
> helped.

> HALLIE
> I couldn't, Aaron. I respected
> you too much. It would've been
> crummy you seeing me when it
> was so flakey.
> (beat)
> Anyhow...
> (beat)
> I met Dennis and we started
> hanging out together. Finally
> we got married and Dennis took
> a job as a proofreader for
> a publishing company. One of
> those vanity presses, you know,
> the kind where people who
> haven't any talent pay them to
> publish their book.

(CONTINUED)

43 CONTINUED:

> AARON
> I didn't even know you'd gotten married.

> HALLIE
> It wasn't much of a marriage. Mostly my fault, I suppose. I always wanted to go to the ballet or some concert — there wasn't any money. Then I had Vikki, and Dennis took off.
> (beat)
> Aaron...you won't let them take my baby away ...will you?

> AARON
> I don't know, Hallie. We'll see.

> HALLIE
> Things were just so hard, I didn't know what to do. My baby, that's all I care about, honest to god, Aaron.

> AARON
> Tell me about the credit card.

> HALLIE
> It belonged to my girlfriend's mother. She told me her mother gave it to her so we could rent a car. We were going to New York.

(CONTINUED)

43 CONTINUED:

               AARON
     New York? What about your
     baby?

               HALLIE
     We were going to take her with
     us. I figured if I made a new
     scene, in a new town, I could
     start over and bring Vikki up
     right. I had a job waiting.

Aaron is confused. Everything Hallie
says seems very logical, but he knows
the baby is in custody.

               AARON
     I thought they took the baby
     to the county home till the
     hearing?

               HALLIE
     What hearing?

               AARON
          (at sea)
     Weren't you arrested for
     desertion? The baby is with
     the authorities…or am I going
     crazy?

               HALLIE
     I don't know what you're
     talking about. My baby is with
     neighbors right now.
          (beat)
               (MORE)

                              (CONTINUED)

43 CONTINUED:

>   HALLIE (CON'D)
>   They're very nice people, next
>   door. They're watching her
>   while I work.

>   AARON
>   Don't they wonder what
>   happened to you…last night?

>   HALLIE
>   I called them.

>   AARON
>   I thought you only had one
>   call?

Hallie gets very upset. She addresses
herself to her plate, moving food with a
fork. She doesn't look up as she speaks.

>   HALLIE
>   I thought you wanted to help
>   me?

Aaron is confused by all this. It makes
no sense.

>   AARON
>   I do. My god, Hallie, I've
>   put up every penny I could
>   scrounge to get you out.

>   HALLIE
>   (coldly)
>   I appreciate that.

                                    (CONTINUED)

43 CONTINUED:

> AARON
>
> I'm only trying to find out what
> the circumstances are — I'm
> going to have to defend you.

> HALLIE
>
> You can always get someone
> else to do it.

> AARON
>
> Hallie! What's wrong with you?

> HALLIE
>
> Nothing's wrong with me, Aaron.
> What's wrong with you? Why are
> you third degreeing me like
> this?

> AARON
>   (suddenly)
> What are you using?

> HALLIE
>
> What?

> AARON
>   (intensely)
> Hallie, I sold or hocked
> everything I own for you. I'm
> on the hook for fifteen hundred
> dollars for your bail. You look
> like hell. I know you've been
> doing some kind of dope. I
> can't help you if you don't get
> upfront with me!

(CONTINUED)

43 CONTINUED:

Hallie looks at him with gentle sadness.

> HALLIE
> You've changed, Aaron. You
> aren't like I remember you.
> You're very cruel now.

> AARON
> (bewildered)
> Hallie, what are you doing to
> my head? I can <u>look</u> at you, I
> can <u>see</u> you…your skin is all
> rough and broken out, your hair
> is dead, your ankles are thick
> from body water…I have eyes to
> <u>see</u>, Hallie. I <u>know</u> what speed
> looks like. Why are you <u>lying</u>
> to me?

Hallie gets up from the table.

> HALLIE
> I think I'll walk home now.

> AARON
> (angry)
> I want to <u>talk</u> to you.

> HALLIE
> (as if in a dream)
> The cool morning air will
> be good for me. I must look
> really crummy after a night in
> that place.

(CONTINUED)

43 CONTINUED:

She starts toward the door. Aaron gets
up and follows her. She goes right to
the door. The WAITRESS behind the cash
register calls him.

> WAITRESS
> Sir! Your check!

Hallie is out the door. Aaron is hung up
between the two. He leans out the door
and yells.

> AARON
> Arraignment is at 8:45 Monday
> morning. I'll meet you outside
> session two at 8:00.
> (beat)
> Hallie? Eight o'clock!

But she is gone. He slowly lets the
door close, and comes back inside. The
Waitress waits. He comes to her, head
sunk, obviously still dwelling on Hallie.
The Waitress gives him the check, he
looks at it, not seeing, then digs all
the bills and change out of his pockets.
He counts it out and lays it on the
counter.

> AARON
> I'm eleven cents short.

The Waitress looks at him, sees what his
face says. She smiles.

                                    (CONTINUED)

43 CONTINUED:

> WAITRESS
> That's okay. Bring it next time.

> AARON
> I don't have anything for a
> tip.

> WAITRESS
> Next time.

He smiles thanks, turns to go, and stops.

> AARON
> It was very good pie.

HOLD for several beats. Then Aaron goes.
HOLD ON the Waitress as she looks after
him compassionately.

> DISSOLVE THRU:

44 INT. NLO — FOYER — DAY

as Aaron drags in, looking like hell. He
goes up the stairs.

> DISSOLVE THRU TO:

45 INT. AARON'S OFFICE

Nothing for a moment, then the door
opens and Aaron comes in. He throws his
coat on a chair and slumps down behind
his desk. For a moment, he just stares
at nothing, then begins shuffling papers
around. The door opens and David Barrett
enters.

> (CONTINUED)

45 CONTINUED:

Aaron looks up, and his face hardens. He
suspects Barrett may be right, and after
what he's just been through with Hallie,
he doesn't want any more static.

                    BARRETT
          Got a free minute?

                    AARON
          Sure. Just trying to get some
          of this off the desk.

                    BARRETT
          You look whipped.

                    AARON
          I'm okay.

                    BARRETT
          Last night wasn't the most
          pleasant evening I've ever
          spent.

                    AARON
          I'm sorry I loused up the
          party.

                    BARRETT
          It's probably me who owes <u>you</u>
          the apology. I went after you
          too loud.

                    AARON
          You thought you were right.

                              (CONTINUED)

45 CONTINUED:

> BARRETT
> That's beside the point. I <u>was</u>
> right, but it didn't give me
> the right to use a rubber hose
> on you. I apologize.

> AARON
> I got her out this morning.

> BARRETT
> How was it?

> AARON
> (in pain)
> She — she didn't look the same.
> I think she's been speeding.
> (1/2 beat)
> For a long time.

> BARRETT
> And the baby?

> AARON
> I...don't...know...

Barrett looks at him. Aaron is at a low
ebb.

> BARRETT
> You ought to be alone for a
> while.

He turns to go, stops.

(CONTINUED)

45 CONTINUED:

> BARRETT
> (continuing; softly)
> You know, it's been years since
> I've cried. The last time was
> when my father died. Isn't that
> a peculiar thing?

Then he goes. And closes the door
tightly. Aaron sits for a few beats, then
slumps a little more…then he lays his
head down on the desk, on his arms. Is
he crying? Perhaps.

DISSOLVE TO:

46 INT. COURTROOM — DAY

as Aaron comes through the door marked
SESSION TWO (plus whatever legend is
appropriate for a Boston courtroom).
The courtroom is staffed by only the
necessary people: JUDGE, PROSECUTING
ATTORNEY, BAILIFF, CLERK and COURT
RECORDER, plus half a dozen silent
players who will be defendants and
attorneys of cases also on the docket.

Aaron looks around. He looks at his
wrist and pushes up his sleeve to
check his watch. No watch. He sold it,
remember. A MAN comes through the door
just then and Aaron stops him.

(CONTINUED)

46 CONTINUED:

>   AARON
>   (whispers)
>   Excuse me, what time do you
>   have?

The Man extends his wrist, shows Aaron
the watch.

>   MAN
>   Nine-fifteen.

>   AARON
>   Thanks.

The Man goes and sits down next to a
woman.

>   CLERK
>   The Commonwealth vs. Hallie
>   Benda Peterson.

Aaron comes forward, through the
swinging gate.

>   JUDGE
>   Is Mrs. Peterson represented?

>   AARON
>   Yes, Your Honor. Aaron
>   Silverman of the Neighborhood
>   Law Office.

>   JUDGE
>   Where is your client, Mr.
>   Silverman?

>   (CONTINUED)

46 CONTINUED:

>   AARON
>   I'm afraid I don't know, Your
>   Honor.

>   JUDGE
>   That's rather a cavalier
>   attitude by counsel. Was your
>   client apprised of the time of
>   this arraignment?

>   AARON
>   Yes, Your Honor.

>   PROS. ATTORNEY
>   Your Honor, I've been looking
>   over the charge sheet on the
>   accused.

>   JUDGE
>   I'm familiar with it, Mr. Klegg.

>   PROS. ATTORNEY
>   With Your Honor's permission,
>   I'd like to make a motion
>   for the issuance of a bench
>   warrant.

>   JUDGE
>   Mr. Silverman, before we hold
>   your client in forfeit of bail,
>   can you suggest any reason
>   why such an order should not
>   be issued by the District
>   Attorney's office?

                              (CONTINUED)

46 CONTINUED:

                    AARON
        Your Honor, I suspect my client
        is ill. When last I saw her,
        she was not well. I ask the
        court's indulgence, to put this
        matter over for 24 hours. I'm
        sure I can produce Miss Benda.

The Judge glances down at the charge
sheet.

                    JUDGE
        I thought your client was Mrs.
        Peterson?

                    AARON
        I'm sorry, Your Honor. I meant
        Mrs. Peterson.

                    JUDGE
             (considers; then)
        All right, Mr. Silverman. I'll
        set this over till tomorrow at
        9:00, but be advised I'll call
        this matter first on the docket.

                    AARON
        Thank you, Your Honor.

                    JUDGE
        And Mr. Silverman...
             (beat)
        I suggest you learn the name
        of your client. It might serve
        to reassure the bench that you
        can locate her.

                              (CONTINUED)

46 CONTINUED:

Aaron looks woebegone, nods, and turns
to go. As he comes to the back of the
room, Bernie Yoakum is standing there.
They go out together.

47 HALLWAY

as Aaron and Yoakum emerge.

> YOAKUM
> She jumped bail.

> AARON
> Looks like it.

> YOAKUM
> Oh boy.

> AARON
> At least you didn't do an
> I-told-you-so.

> YOAKUM
> Can I help?

> AARON
> No, thanks, Bernie. I copied
> her home address off the police
> blotter. I'll find her.

> YOAKUM
> You'll <u>find</u> her?
> (MORE)

(CONTINUED)

47 CONTINUED:

                    YOAKUM (CONT'D)
          You poor dingdong, how the hell
          you gonna find someone in a
          city the size of Boston if they
          don't wanna be found?

47 CONTINUED:

                    AARON
          I've got to, Bernie.
                    (beat)
          I haven't got fifteen hundred
          dollars to pay you if I don't.

He smiles wanly and walks away as we
HOLD on Bernie Yoakum, looking sick
about it all.

                              FADE OUT.

          END OF ACT TWO

84: 13 NOVEMBER 70

"THE WHIMPER OF WHIPPED DOGS"

Part Three

<u>ACT THREE</u>

FADE IN:

48 INT. TENEMENT HALLWAY — ON AARON — DAY

as he opens the door of Apartment 6. The
door opens a crack and Aaron sees no one.
Then he HEARS a VOICE.

> DRUDGE
> Whaddaya want?

He looks down. There in the door crack
is a fat little head covered with hair
curlers.

> AARON
> Where will I find Apartment
> number fourteen?

> DRUDGE
> How the hell should I know?

(CONTINUED)

48 CONTINUED:

> AARON
> Here in the building, I mean.

> DRUDGE
> There ain't no fourteen…up to
> ten and that's all.

She starts to close the door. Aaron
holds it open.

> AARON
> Is there a Miss Benda living
> here…or a Mrs. Peterson?

> DRUDGE
> I don't like cops, but I'll
> call one, you don't get offa my
> door.

Aaron steps back, the door SLAMS. Hard.

> AARON
> (to CAMERA)
> Phony address. Yeah. Sure.

                                    DISSOLVE TO:

49 EXT. SUBURBAN NEIGHBORHOOD — DAY (STOCK)

as the NLO van pulls up in front of a
small, neat house. Aaron gets out and
walks up the walk.

50 EXT. HOUSE — ON AARON — DAY

as he RINGS the doorbell. A moment
passes, he RINGS again. Then the door
opens and a very plain, but clean,
HOUSEWIFE opens the door. She has on
slacks and a sweater and her hair pulled
back with a bandanna. She has a mixing
bowl in her hands.

> AARON
> Miss Benda?

> GRACE
> Mrs. Delany.

> AARON
> Uh, excuse me…are you Hallie
> Benda's sister?

> GRACE
> (a shadow on her face now)
> Yes…why?

> AARON
> I'm Aaron Silverman, from the
> Neighborhood Law Office. I was
> supposed to represent Hallie
> at an arraignment this morning…
> (beat)
> …but I'm afraid she's jumped
> bail.

GRACE DELANY stares at him a moment,
gauging him. Then she opens the door
farther.

(CONTINUED)

50 CONTINUED:

> GRACE
> This is just what I needed to
> make my day.
> (beat)
> But come on in, you can tell
> me the gory details while I
> make some banana bread.
> (beat)
> Do you like banana bread?

> AARON
> I don't think I've ever had it.

> GRACE
> Well, it's not bad for a start.
> Come on.

Aaron follows her as the door shuts and
we

CUT TO:

51 INT. DELANY'S KITCHEN — DAY

as Aaron and Grace enter. Aaron is
looking around, confused. Grace notices,
as she indicates a kitchen stool on
which he can sit, and she returns to the
mixing.

> GRACE
> You don't have to say a word. I
> can tell.
> (MORE)

(CONTINUED)

51 CONTINUED:

> GRACE (CONT'D)
> You're amazed that Hallie's
> slut sister, who runs down the
> street with a mattress on her
> back yelling "curb service,"
> lives in such a sweet little
> ivy-covered cottage.

> AARON
> (bumbles)
> I, er, uh —

> GRACE
> It's okay. That's what she tells
> everyone. Just to get the
> record straight, Mr. Silver — ?

> AARON
> Silverman.

> GRACE
> Mr. Silverman. I am not, nor
> have I ever been, a card-
> carrying streetwalker. Nor do
> I head up a suburban matron's
> call girl ring, nor do I even
> make nice on anyone but my
> husband, Dr. Philip Delany,
> your friendly neighborhood
> orthodontist.

> AARON
> (whipped)
> Can I have a glass of water,
> please?

(CONTINUED)

51 CONTINUED:

> GRACE
> I'll give you ginger ale. It
> helps settle the stomach.

She goes to the refrigerator, takes out
a bottle and pours him a glass of ginger
ale. He takes it, sips.

> AARON
> But I thought, Hallie said,
> that is, when her mother died —

Grace turns. There is no humor in her
voice or face now.

> GRACE
> Our mother lives three blocks
> from here. She has varicose
> veins, she plays a rotten hand
> of bridge, and the only joy
> she gets from her children are
> my two kids, whom she dotes
> on. God knows she never got
> anything but heartache from
> Hallie.

Grace comes over and slumps down on
another stool.

> GRACE
> (continuing; wearily)
> Why does she do it? Why does
> she lie to everyone?

(CONTINUED)

51 CONTINUED:

> AARON
>
> This time I'm afraid she's
> in serious trouble. With her
> husband gone and her baby in
> custody…

> GRACE
> (horrified)
> Vikki? Where is she?

> AARON
>
> The county home. You mean she
> never told you, never asked for
> help?

> GRACE
>
> Mr. Silverman, you'd better
> understand something. We're
> not talking about a rational
> human being here. Hallie is a
> pathological liar. Ask her if
> it's January and she'll tell
> you it's May.
> (beat)
> There is no husband. The baby
> is illegitimate.

> AARON
>
> Everything she said…everything
> she told me…she was lying…all
> of it.

> GRACE
>
> And that's why she didn't call
> us for help. We've helped too
> many times.
> (MORE)

(CONTINUED)

51 CONTINUED:

> GRACE (CONT'D)
> Phil won't give her another
> cent, and she's bled Mom dry.
> When she stole Mom's credit
> cards, that was the final straw.

> AARON
> She used one to try and rent
> a car. They caught her and
> she called me. I — I used to
> date Hallie. I went her bail.
> Arraignment was a few hours
> ago. She never showed.

> GRACE
> I thought you were something
> more than an attorney for her.

> AARON
> Do you have any idea where I
> could locate her?
>   (beat)
> Mrs. Delany, I think you
> should know: I'm almost dead
> certain Hallie is on drugs.
> Methedrine, some kind of speed.
> She looked bad on Saturday
> when I got her out of jail.

> GRACE
>   (head in hands)
> Oh god. Oh, dear god.

(CONTINUED)

51 CONTINUED:

> AARON
>
> Is there <u>anything</u> you can tell
> me to help me find her? I've
> gotten a twenty-four-hour stay
> from the court. If I can get
> her back, it'll be easier on
> her.

> GRACE
>
> No, nothing. We never knew
> where she lived. She never
> told us.

> AARON
>
> <u>Any</u>thing.

Grace thinks, ponders, considers, then
spreads her hands.

> GRACE
>
> I'm sorry.

Aaron rises, sets down the glass.

> AARON
>
> Well, thanks anyhow. I'll keep
> in touch with you. If she calls
> or anything, will you call me
> at the Neighborhood Law Office?

Grace nods agreement and walks Aaron
toward the kitchen door.

                                        CUT TO:

52 EXT. HOUSE — ON DOOR — DAY

As it opens and Aaron comes out. Grace stands there, looking devastated.

                    GRACE
        Where will you look?

                    AARON
              (shrugs)
        I don't know.
              (beat)
        Listen, you couldn't have
        helped, unless you'd known.
        She's like a lot of other
        people; I really think she
        doesn't mean any harm, but
        she has to keep scoring that
        dope, and when people like
        that run out of what they've
        got around to sell, they just
        start ripping-off their friends,
        relatives, mothers…

                    GRACE
        And finally they call people
        like you. She must have thought
        a lot of you, Mr. Silverman, to
        save you for last.

Aaron gets hit with that one. His stomach drops, his expression goes dead.

                    AARON
        Yeah.
              (beat)
        Goodbye.

                              (CONTINUED)

52 CONTINUED:

He turns to go, and the door closes.
CAMERA HOLDS ON Aaron as he comes toward
us and CAMERA PULLS BACK. He walks to
the bus and starts to get in, when the
door suddenly bursts open and Grace
Delany runs out.

                    GRACE
                 (shouts)
        Mr. Silverman! Mr. Silverman!

Aaron turns as Grace comes up to him.

                    GRACE
                 (continuing)
        She came once with a boy. To
        get money. She said it was for
        the baby. Phil wouldn't give it
        to her, we knew she was lying,
        but we didn't know what she
        wanted it for.
                 (beat)
        Phil and I both remembered
        the name of the boy. It was
        Joe Bob Holiday. He spoke with
        a very heavy Southern kind of
        accent. Tall boy, long hair,
        he got very nasty when Phil
        turned him down.
                 (beat)
        Does that help any?

                    AARON
        Maybe. I'll let you know.
        Thanks.
                                   (CONTINUED)

52 CONTINUED:

He gets in and drives away as Grace
stands there watching and we

DISSOLVE TO:

53 INT. NLO OFFICE — BARRETT'S OFFICE — DAY

PAT WALTERS, Aaron and Barrett.

> AARON
> And that's all of it.
> (beat)
> You were right, sir. I'm sorry
> I gave you such a hard time.

> BARRETT
> Mmm. Well, now you have to find
> her, and there's some help on
> that score.
> (beat)
> I had Hallie's girlfriend come
> in after we heard she hadn't
> showed up at the arraignment.
> (beat)
> Incidentally, you'll be
> interested to know the girl
> friend's attorney got the
> charges dismissed. It was
> obvious she'd been the dupe,
> not Hallie.

> AARON
> Did she have anything to say?

(CONTINUED)

53 CONTINUED:

               BARRETT
            (chiding him)
More than you deserve to know.

               AARON
Uncle! Don't hit me again.

               BARRETT
            (smiles)
Okay, just so you longhaired
young punks understand there
are a couple of good minutes
in even the old of us.

He slides a sheet of paper across to
Aaron, then another.

               BARRETT
A list of names and addresses
of all Hallie's friends the
girl could remember.

Aaron picks them up. Looks at them.

               AARON
How come the duplicate copy?

               BARRETT
I thought you might need
someone to help you check them
out. Two copies, _fer_ _shtay_?

               AARON
            (to Pat)
Hey, I hate to ask, with all
the cases you've got, but —

                    (CONTINUED)

53 CONTINUED:

Pat reaches over and takes a copy.

> PAT
> It's more than you deserve,
> treating this fine old
> gentleman the way you do.

Aaron gives a MOAN, clutches his head
and turns to go. Pat starts after him.
Barrett stops him.

> BARRETT
> Hey, Renfrew of the Royal
> Mounted!

Aaron stops and turns around. Barrett is
holding a wrist watch.

> BARRETT
> You'd better take this. So
> you'll know what time it is.

> AARON
> My watch! But I sold it Friday
> night.

> BARRETT
> I bought it from a student who
> came in today looking for you.
> (hands it to him)
> My gift.

Aaron takes it, slips it on, smiles his
thanks.

(CONTINUED)

53 CONTINUED:

> AARON
> Thanks.

> BARRETT
> You can pass on the thanks.
> You owe me twenty bucks.

Aaron grimaces, turns to go. Again,
Barrett stops him.

> BARRETT
> He was looking for you because
> you stiffed him. The watch
> doesn't run.

Aaron doesn't turn. But the shot catches
him in the space between the shoulder
blades. He cringes, and with Pat, he goes
as CAMERA HOLDS on Barrett, who lights a
cigar and settles back in his chair.

> DISSOLVE TO:

54 SERIES OF INTERCUTS — LAP-DISSOLVES —
SIMILAR TO SCENE 26

as Aaron and Pat, individually and
together, canvass the list of Hallie's
friends. In dorms, halls, shops, streets,
front stoops, pool halls, communes,
anywhere that is feasible to shoot,
using as much STOCK FOOTAGE as is
available and fits in with the season and
their garb.

> DISSOLVE THRU TO:

55   EXT. STREET CORNER — DAY

Aaron and Pat standing there, comparing
their lists, crossing off names. SILENT
BIT. Aaron points to a name, indicates
Pat should tackle that one, while he goes
55   CONTINUED:

after another. He consults his watch,
then makes a motion toward the coffee
shop on the corner, indicating he'll meet
her there at a certain time. Pat nods
and they go off in separate directions.

                                    DISSOLVE TO:

56   HALLWAY OF APARTMENT BUILDING — WITH PAT
     — DAY

as she comes down the hall, checking
apartment numbers. She finally stops in
front of Apartment 9 and KNOCKS. The
door opens and EUNICE JOHNSON stands
there. She is about Hallie's age, early
twenties, a little wasted-looking, but
pretty in an un-madeup way. Long hair
hanging loose, held in back by a macramé
barette that has long tassels hanging
down. She also wears a macramé belt
of exquisite design. (NOTE: Since this
SCENE will feature the new fashion of
Macramé, be advised the author can turn
the producers on to makers of same, and
in the mimeographing of this script, the
accent mark over the word macramé should
be tipped in, by hand if necessary.
After all, the actors have to know how
to pronounce it, don't they?)

                                    (CONTINUED)

56 CONTINUED:

Behind Eunice are three or four other
girls, all sitting around tables doing
the macramé crocheting. There are racks
of macramé goods everywhere.

This is obviously cottage industry. A
RADIO PLAYS in the b.g.

> EUNICE
> Hi. Can I help you?

> PAT
> I'm looking for Eunice Johnson.

> EUNICE
> You've got her. I'm it. Her.

They smile at one another. Pat indicates
the belt and goods.

> PAT
> Is that macramé?

> EUNICE
> Uh-huh. Did you come to buy or
> look? Either way makes us feel
> good.

> PAT
> I came to talk mostly, but that
> is beautiful work. May I come
> in?

(CONTINUED)

56 CONTINUED:

> EUNICE
> (guardedly)
> Uh, what did you want to talk
> about?

> PAT
> Hallie Benda.

> EUNICE
> (relieved)
> Wheew, you had me worried for
> a second. The landlord keeps
> saying if we're going to use
> the apartment as a factory
> we'll have to pay a commercial
> rate. Come on in.

She steps aside and Pat goes in.

57 INT. APARTMENT — DAY

The other GIRLS look up as Pat comes in.
Two of the girls at the tables are black,
one is white, one is oriental. They
continue looking.

> EUNICE
> (to girls)
> Friend of Hallie's.

She looks at Pat for her name.

> PAT
> Pat Walters. Hello.

(CONTINUED)

57 CONTINUED:

                    EUNICE
                (points to each girl)
            Sandy, Lucy, Vonda and O.E.,
            which stands for Octavia
            Estelle. Want some apple juice?

                    PAT
            Thanks, that'd be nice.

Eunice leads Pat over to an alcove with
a sink, fridge and stove, while the girls
go back to work.

58 TWO SHOT — PAT AND EUNICE

as Eunice opens refrigerator, takes out
a chilled bottle of apple juice, and
taking a cup from a mismatched batch of
cups on a shelf, pours Pat a drink.

                    EUNICE
            You know, you'd think someone
            who'd been through such
            awful stuff would be more
            compassionate.

                    PAT
            I beg your pardon?

                    EUNICE
            Our landlord. He was in a Nazi
            prison camp with his wife, you
            know.
                    (MORE)

                                    (CONTINUED)

58 CONTINUED:

> EUNICE (CONT'D)
> And he came through it and
> got out of Poland or Hungary
> or wherever it was, and he
> came here and made some money…
> so instead of understanding
> how people live, and trying
> to be nice, he gouges all of
> us living here. I just can't
> understand it. You'd think
> that kind of misery would make
> people kinder.

> PAT
> Did you ever see that film,
> "The Pawnbroker"?

> EUNICE
> Oh. Yeah. I see what you mean.

> PAT
> I suppose that kind of
> experience just kills people
> inside. Makes them hard; you
> know, their feelings are
> blunted. All they care about
> afterward is taking care
> of themselves. I guess it's
> just survival carried to the
> furthest extreme.

> EUNICE
> It's really sad.
>> (beat)
>>> (MORE)

(CONTINUED)

58 CONTINUED:

>   EUNICE (CONT'D)
> But all the same, I wish he
> wasn't such a creep.

>   PAT
> Did Hallie work here?

>   EUNICE
> Hallie? No, huh-uh. She just
> used to come over and sit
> sometimes. She's not very good
> with her hands and macramé
> takes a lot of skill.

>   PAT
> I'd love a belt like yours.

>   EUNICE
> Well, just take a look around.
> It's all for sale.

>   PAT
> Could we talk about Hallie
> first?

>   EUNICE
> What do you want to talk about
> her?

>   PAT
> She's about to get in some
> pretty big trouble.

>   EUNICE
> You aren't from the child
> welfare, are you?

>   (CONTINUED)

58 CONTINUED:

> PAT
>
> No, I'm from the Neighborhood
> Law Office. We were supposed
> to defend her on a bust for
> using a stolen credit card,
> but she never showed up at
> the arraignment. We're trying
> to find her so a warrant isn't
> issued. And that means before
> 9:00 tomorrow morning.

> EUNICE
>
> Oh, wow. Yeah, Ginjer Moore was
> making a lot of noise on the
> street about Hallie trying to
> pin it on her.

> PAT
>
> Well, Ginjer gave us a list of
> Hallie's friends who might know
> how we could find her, that's
> why I came to ask you.

> EUNICE
>
> No chance I'd know where Hallie
> is. We weren't very tight,
> y'know?

> PAT
>
> I gather you didn't like her
> much.

> EUNICE
>
> Not much. She messed over
> Ginjer.

(CONTINUED)

58 CONTINUED:

> PAT
> So you probably won't feel like
> a fink if you give me a way to
> find her.

> EUNICE
> I won't mind at all.

> PAT
> On the other hand, remember
> your landlord. A little
> compassion.

Eunice steps back, staring at Pat.

> EUNICE
> Wheew! Lady, you are trying to
> do a number on my head. First,
> it's knife Hallie, then it
> isn't, which way do you want me
> to move?

> PAT
> My way. I need to know where
> she is. But I don't want you
> to feel lousy about it.

> EUNICE
> So how can I do it without
> feeling like a fink?

> PAT
> By knowing she needs some help,
> and the only way she's going to
> get it is if we get to her in
> time.

(CONTINUED)

58 CONTINUED:

> EUNICE
> (holds up hands)
> No more! Hallie used to work
> with a little black guy named
> Obie Stover. She'd buy from
> him if he was holding, and
> he'd buy from her if she was
> dealing. She might lose a lot
> of contacts, but her dealer —
> never.

Pat raises the apple juice in a silent
toast as we

> LAP DISSOLVE TO:

59 INT. COFFEE SHOP — ON PAT — DAY

MATCH SHOP (with cup of apple juice from
Scene 58), as Pat lifts a coffee cup to
her mouth to drink.

> AARON'S VOICE (o.s.)
> Obie Stover.

CAMERA PULLS BACK as Aaron slips into
the booth across from Pat. She is
wearing a macramé belt now.

> PAT
> That's the name I got. And a
> general idea where he hangs
> out.

(CONTINUED)

59 CONTINUED:

> AARON
> Great. The kid I talked to
> didn't know where to find him.
> Give me the address and I'll
> take it from here.

> PAT
> Hold it. That's the inner city,
> Aaron.

> AARON
> I'll be all right down there.

> PAT
> Sure, maybe. But it's still
> "tell them nothing" for paddys.
> And you're a paddy to them.

> AARON
> You want to come with? I hate
> to ask you.

> PAT
> Come on, Aaron, stop that.

> AARON
> Okay. Finish your coffee and
> let's go.

Pat puts down the cup and stands.

> PAT
> I'd rather not. This was cup
> number three. But I'll go to
> the little girls' room and meet
> you out front.

                                    (CONTINUED)

59 CONTINUED:

She goes one way, Aaron goes the other
and we

DISSOLVE TO:

60 EXT. THE MATTAPAN BLACK GHETTO — DAY
(STOCK)

as Aaron and Pat walk through, together.

61 EXT. GHETTO STREET — DAY

as Pat talks to someone, who points back
in the opposite direction. Pat thanks
the MAN and they walk away.

62 EXT. GHETTO STREET — DAY

as Pat talks to a couple of LITTLE KIDS
on a front stoop. Very earnestly. They
talk to her, and one of them points
toward the corner. Pat smiles and
silently thanks them. They move off again.

63 EXT. EMPTY LOT — AARON — DAY

Through a broken link fence we can see
a young, very tall and thin black BOY of
perhaps seventeen, looping a basketball
into a rim made from an apple basket rim.
The lot is littered with filth and dead
beer cans, with the awful detritus of a
society choking itself with garbage.

(CONTINUED)

63 CONTINUED:

The boy, OBIE STOVER, is alone. Aaron
and Pat stop outside the fence and watch
him for a long moment.

> AARON
> I thought that girl said he was
> a little guy?

> PAT
> She must have meant years, not
> height. He has a good hook.

> AARON
> I didn't know you liked
> basketball?

> PAT
> I didn't know you had natural
> rhythm.

He grins at her, she grins back, and they
slip through the fence and CAMERA GOES
WITH THEM as they approach Obie, who
catches sight of them halfway across the
lot. He stops shooting, cocks over onto
one hip with the basketball under one
arm, and waits.

> PAT
> Obie?

> OBIE
> He just left. His momma call
> him.

(CONTINUED)

63 CONTINUED:

As they walk straight up to him.

                    PAT
          Oh, that's too bad. We got
          some small money here for an
          Obie Stover.

                    AARON
          Maybe you can tell us where he
          lives so we can deliver it.

                    OBIE
          What kinda money you got for
          Obie?

                    AARON
          Seventy-five dollars. We're from
          the Neighborhood Law Office.
          Some kid came in and said he'd
          burned this Obie for the money,
          so we're bringing it on over.

                    OBIE
          You shuckin' and jivin', mister.

                    PAT
          So you don't know this Obie?
          Right?

                    OBIE
          That's what I said.

                    PAT
          Let's go, Aaron.

                                   (CONTINUED)

63 CONTINUED:

They turn and start to walk away. Obie
watches, then calls:

                    OBIE
          Hey you. Wait up.

He lopes over to them.

                    PAT
          What you want...Mr. Helpful?

                    OBIE
          I'm Obie Stover.

                    AARON
          Sure you are. All of a sudden
          you hear we got seventy-five
          bucks and poof you become Obie
          Stover.

It should be understood that this is a
<u>seventeen</u>-year-old boy, and even though
he's black and hip as only ghetto street
kids can be hip, still he's seventeen
and he can be hyped. That's what Aaron
and Pat are doing. (It should also be
understood that the outdated idea of
pushers as <u>only</u> being insidious Fagins,
corrupting school children, is hincty
and old-fashioned. The nasty truth is
that <u>today</u> kids push to kids. Everyone
who isn't using is dealing. <u>They</u> don't
consider it criminal or evil; we do,
and we're probably right, but to attack
reality in this manner we must deal with
a typical dealer as <u>he</u> views it, for
counterpoint.)

                              (CONTINUED)

63 CONTINUED:

                    OBIE
          Hey, man, I tell you I'm Obie
          Stover an' you say I'm not. Who
          knows, you or me?

                    PAT
          If you were Obie Stover, you'd
          know where Hallie Benda is.

Obie draws back.

                    OBIE
          What kinda evil you whippin'
          on me? I thought you say you
          got seventy-five bucks for me?

                    AARON
          We're looking for Hallie. She's
          in big trouble. We're from the
          Neighborhood Law Office, we
          want to —

                    OBIE
          Get away from me.

                    PAT
          Obie, we want to <u>help</u> her!

                    OBIE
          I say get away from me or I'll
          do some bun-kickin', you hear?

At that moment, a tall, longhaired BOY
comes through the fence, starts toward
them. He calls out in a heavy Southern
accent.

                              (CONTINUED)

63 CONTINUED:

> JOE BOB
> Hey, you Obie!

Obie turns, panicking, sees Joe Bob, and
yells at the top of his lungs.

> OBIE
> (frantic)
> Get the hell outta here! Narks!

Joe Bob turns and bolts through the
fence. Obie takes off at a dead run in
the opposite direction after hurling the
basketball at Aaron. The wind is knocked
out of Aaron for a moment, but he gasps
at Pat…

> AARON
> Joe Bob Holiday!

He takes off after him, running full out,
as Pat follows and we

> FADE OUT.

END OF ACT THREE

85: 20 NOVEMBER 70

"THE WHIMPER OF WHIPPED DOGS"

Part Four

ACT FOUR

FADE IN:

64 EXT. GHETTO STREET — ARRIFLEX

with Aaron as he chases Joe Bob Holiday.
A twisting, turning, frantic run down
filthy streets and through alleys, at one
point Joe Bob banging into an ELDERLY
BLACK WOMAN carrying big shopping bags
that spill all over the street. Pat slows
to help her as Aaron goes after him.
Aaron gains. Joe Bob looks back…Aaron
is coming on. He cuts across a street
through traffic…Aaron does the same,
almost gets hit…keeps going. Finally,
Aaron gains enough and as Joe Bob turns
a corner he slips, skids, goes to one
knee, gets up and makes the move to run
but Aaron is on him. Aaron hurls him up
against the wall of the building. They
are both badly winded.

                    AARON
         Where's Hallie…?

                                    (CONTINUED)

64 CONTINUED:

Joe Bob can't — or won't — talk. He just
shakes his head and gasps for breath.
Aaron bangs him against the brick wall.

> AARON
> Where is she, man? I'm her
> attorney! Tell me!

Joe Bob still won't talk. Aaron isn't
crapping around any more. He's almost
frantic about finding her now. He looks
around, sees an alley, and drags Joe Bob
with him. They disappear into the alley.

65 ANOTHER ANGLE ON THE STREET

as Pat rushes up. She stops. Looks
around. No one in sight. She waits,
turning this way and that. In a short
while Aaron emerges from the alley with
a smudge of dirt under one eye, his
jacket and tie pulled askew and holding
his right fist the way a man would hold
it if he had a set of skinned knuckles.
Pat comes up to him, looking concerned.

> AARON
> He was meeting Obie to score
> some reds for himself and
> Hallie. I got the address.

> PAT
> Why'd he tell you?

(CONTINUED)

65 CONTINUED:

                    AARON
              (coolly)
         We talked.

                                    CUT TO:

66 EXT. COURT APARTMENTS — DAY

One of those lanai kind of places where
everybody can look in everybody else's
window. One or two stories high, but
all our action must take place on the
first floor. As Aaron and Pat come up to
Apartment "C" and Aaron knocks on the
door. No answer. He knocks again. Harder.
Nothing. Then he bangs on it. Nothing.
But the apartment door next to it opens
and a NEIGHBOR WOMAN sticks her head out.

               NEIGHBOR WOMAN
         She's in there.

Aaron and Pat look surprised.

               NEIGHBOR WOMAN
         She didn't answer last week
         when the police came, either.
         The way she treated that baby!
              (beat)
         She went out the bathroom
         window around back when they
         came last week.

Aaron and Pat exchange glances and Aaron
tears off.
                              (CONTINUED)

67 EXT. APARTMENT HOUSE — ARRIFLEX — DAY

with Aaron as he dashes around through
bushes, skinning his face on whipping
branches. He comes out in back and
CAMERA TILTS UP SHARPLY to show us
Hallie Benda, half out of the bathroom
window. She drops just as Aaron comes
around the corner. She takes one look,
and starts to run off.

                    AARON
                (chill)
            Don't make me chase you,
            Hallie.

She stops. Frightened. CAMERA IN FAST on
her face and the absolutely terrifying
expression of loss and hopelessness. This
is the end of it, whether she likes it
or not. She has done Aaron in, and she
knows he will have no mercy. CAMERA
HOLDS on her face.

                              DISSOLVE TO:

68 EXT. COURT APARTMENTS — DAY

as Aaron brings Hallie around the front
of the court. He's holding her by the
arm. Firmly, but not roughly.

69 THREE SHOT

as Aaron and Hallie come to Pat, with
the Neighbor Woman still behind her
screen door, watching. Pat and Hallie
examine each other.

                              (CONTINUED)

69 CONTINUED:

> HALLIE
> Why are you doing this to me,
> Aaron?

> PAT
> If he doesn't get you in to
> court by nine o'clock tomorrow
> morning there'll be a bench
> warrant issued for you—not to
> mention he'll be on the hook
> for fifteen hundred dollars.

> HALLIE
> (to Aaron)
> Aaron, I don't know her, why is
> she here? This is between you
> and me.

> AARON
> Why'd you jump bail? You knew
> what I had at stake, you knew
> I trusted you?

> HALLIE
> I was going to call you. The
> baby was sick, I had to watch
> her.

> AARON
> Stop it! What's the matter with
> you? The baby isn't here, the
> baby is with the county! You're
> lying.

> PAT
> Now what should we do?

(CONTINUED)

69 CONTINUED:

>   AARON
>   (exhausted)
> I didn't think it out any
> further than this. I don't <u>know</u>
> what to do.

>   PAT
> Let me call Mr. Barrett.

Aaron nods agreement. Hallie struggles
not too heavily to be free. Aaron keeps
a firm grip on her wrist. Pat turns to
the Neighbor Woman behind the screen
door, who — like most people today who
don't want to get involved — starts to
close the door. Pat catches her before
she can do it.

>   PAT
> Excuse me. Could I use your
> phone, please?

>   NEIGHBOR WOMAN
> Is it a local?

Pat grins and nods. The Woman holds the
screen door open and Pat goes in. CAMERA
COMES INTO CLOSER TWO SHOT with Aaron
and Hallie.

>   AARON
> It'll be all right.

>   HALLIE
> What are you going to do with
> me?

>   (CONTINUED)

69 CONTINUED:

> AARON
> I don't know. Mr. Barrett'll
> have some idea what's right to
> do.

> HALLIE
> This isn't a nice thing you're
> doing, Aaron.

> AARON
> Stop it.

> HALLIE
> How could you treat me like
> this, Aaron? We were in love.
> We went places together, you
> taught me so much.

> AARON
> I don't want to talk about it.

> HALLIE
> I don't love you any more.

> AARON
> Oh, god, just shut up, Hallie!

CUT TO:

70 INT. BARRETT'S OFFICE — DAY

Barrett on phone.

> BARRETT
> Yes, Pat.
> (MORE)

(CONTINUED)

70 CONTINUED:

> BARRETT (CONT'D)
> (beat)
> I'm surprised Aaron was able to
> locate her.
> (beat)
> Yes. Yes. Okay, call the police,
> and have Aaron make a citizen's
> arrest. Follow the police in,
> and have Aaron remand the girl
> back into custody.
> (beat)
> No, I don't think so. No. But
> tell Aaron whatever he does,
> he should <u>not</u> use force to
> restrain her. Just keep her
> there till the police arrive.
> (beat)
> Don't ask me how two of you
> can surround her…that's <u>your</u>
> problem.
> (beat)
> How's Aaron?
> (beat)
> Stay with him, Pat. This won't
> be easy for him.

                              CUT BACK TO:

71 SAME AS SCENE 69

as Pat comes out of the apartment. Aaron
is still hanging on to Hallie.

                                (CONTINUED)

71 CONTINUED:

> PAT
>
> Mr. Barrett says call the
> police, and hold her here till
> they come; make a citizen's
> arrest and remand her back
> into custody.

> AARON
>
> Watch her.

He releases Hallie's wrist, and
approaches the Neighbor Woman, who opens
the door again.

> AARON
> (continuing)
>
> Local.

He vanishes inside with the Neighbor
Woman and Hallie starts to make a move
to walk away, very casually.

> PAT
>
> I'm not as nice as Aaron. Don't
> try it.

> HALLIE
>
> I want to go call my lawyer.

> PAT
>
> Aaron's your lawyer.

> HALLIE
>
> I have another lawyer.

                              (CONTINUED)

71 CONTINUED:

> PAT
>
> Then why didn't he bring you
> in for the arraignment?

> HALLIE
>
> I just want to go to a pay
> phone and call.

> PAT
>
> Girl, I don't mind you <u>thinking</u>
> I'm dumb...just don't <u>talk</u> to me
> like I'm dumb.

> HALLIE
>
> You can't stop me from making a
> call.

> PAT
>
> You know, I think you're nuts.
> What do you think of that?

> HALLIE
>
> There's a pay phone down the
> street. I'll just walk down
> there and call.

> PAT
> (yells)
> <u>Aaron</u>!

> AARON'S VOICE (o.s.)
>
> A minute. I'm almost done.

Hallie starts to walk again. Pat grabs
her.

(CONTINUED)

71 CONTINUED:

Hallie and Pat struggle, with Pat
desperately trying not to be rough,
only to keep her from moving off. Aaron
emerges from the apartment and takes
Hallie by the shoulders, puts her back
in a corner.

> AARON
> Now we wait.

> HALLIE
> What are you going to do with
> me?

> AARON
> I'm going to put you back in
> jail.

> HALLIE
> (inflamed)
> You crummy bastard!

> AARON
> You want to call an attorney;
> use the phone inside.

Hallie makes no move to phone, she just
takes off after Aaron. Weaseling, working,
wheedling, whipping him.

> HALLIE
> You don't give a damn about
> me. All you care about is
> that bail bond. Big man! Big
> upholder of justice.
> (MORE)

(CONTINUED)

71 CONTINUED:

                    HALLIE (CONT'D)
        When it comes right down to it,
        you're like every other lousy
        fink in the world — you'll mess
        over people for a few dollars.

Aaron can't reply. CAMERA IN on his face.
Is she right? She's wounded him, no doubt
about it. He turns, looks at Pat. He
doesn't speak. Pat looks at him, there is
a long silence. Then Pat leaps in.

                    PAT
        Aaron! Are you kidding?! After
        what she's done, you're going
        to let her con you like that?

                    AARON
        Maybe she's right. Maybe it is
        the money…

                    PAT
        And your college career, and
        the rest of your life and
        everything you've worked for.
        Which is more important? This…
        this…liar or what you tried to
        do for her?

                    HALLIE
            (softly)
        Aaron, please…the cops are
        on the way…let me go…please,
        Aaron…I can't go back there.

                                    (CONTINUED)

71 CONTINUED:

                    AARON
        I…Hallie…stop…I <u>have</u> to —

                    PAT
        Aaron…stop it!

                    HALLIE
        Remember us, Aaron? Remember
        how we were together…how can
        you do this to me…

        CAMERA IN once more on Aaron's face as
        we

                            INTERCUT:

72 INTERCUT — MEMORY SHOT — SOLARIZED

        Aaron and Hallie together. Young love.
        Innocence. All very beautiful. The two
        of them laughing and running somewhere
        and Aaron whirling her around to hug her,
        lift her off the ground. Hallie's face in
        CLOSEUP and

                          CUT BACK TO:

73 MATCH-CUT SHOT ON HALLIE'S FACE

        Ravaged. Another girl entirely. Only the
        shadow of the un-speeding Hallie. Aaron
        grows cold.

                    AARON
        That was another girl.

                          (CONTINUED)

73 CONTINUED:

Hallie begins screaming at him, raging,
anything she cares to ad lib to build a
picture of the girl of today, rather than
the dream of yesterday, as we COME IN on
her faceand

DISSOLVE TO:

74 INT. CHARLES STREET STATION — DAY

as a PROWL CAR COP holds on to Hallie
at one side of the counter, Aaron talks
to the WATCH OFFICER in charge (not the
Desk Sergeant from earlier scenes). Pat
stands beside him.

                    AARON
          What do you mean, you can't
          accept her back into custody?

                    WATCH OFFICER
          We have no regulations for
          accepting someone who's out on
          bail, on the same charge. I've
          been here nine years and it's
          never been done.

                    AARON
          But she's jumped bail once
          already; the arraignment is
          tomorrow morning.

                    WATCH OFFICER
          Buddy, these are hard times
          and without authorization
                    (MORE)

                              (CONTINUED)

74 CONTINUED:

                     WATCH OFFICER (CONT'D)
      I am not, repeat NOT, taking
      any chances of a false
      imprisonment suit.

                     BARRETT'S VOICE (o.s.)
      Pat!

Pat Walters turns around and looks.

75 ENTRY HALL

(This written specifically so that Barrett
does not have to enter the scene in
which the Hallie character appears, thus
enabling his scenes to be shot apart
from hers on the schedule. Please note
this mechanical.)

Barrett stands there, with a file folder
under his arm. He beckons Pat to him.

76 WITH PAT

as she leaves her scene and walks to
Barrett, half-concealed by the entry
area.

                    PAT
      Mr. Barrett, they won't —

                 BARRETT
      I heard. I anticipated as much
      when you called. So I did some
      digging, and came up with this.
            (MORE)

                           (CONTINUED)

76 CONTINUED:

> BARRETT (CONT'D)
> (hands her file)
> Use it. I'll see you at the office.

Pat smiles, turns and goes back.

77 INT. CHARLES STREET STATION — DAY

as Pat returns. She spreads the file, within which are a few <u>very</u> <u>old</u>, yellowing mimeographed sheets.

> PAT
> Aaron…

He looks at the papers for a moment, while the Watch Officer grows steadily more uncomfortable.

> AARON
> Sergeant, I think this will provide all the authorization you need. It's a departmental procedural regulation covering contingencies such as this.
> (beat)
> As far as we can tell, it's never been modified, superseded or rescinded, so it's still in force.

He turns it around so the Watch Officer can read it. He does just that, looks perplexed, and shakes his head.

(CONTINUED)

77 CONTINUED:

> WATCH OFFICER
> This is a Suffolk County
> regulation dated 1922. I don't
> know —

> AARON
> (quick to leap on his
> indecision)
> Who issued the regulation?

> WATCH OFFICER
> (checks with finger)
> The Police Commissioner.

> AARON
> Well, then, you'd have to check
> with him, wouldn't you?

> WATCH OFFICER
> Or his clerk.

> AARON
> Fine.

> WATCH OFFICER
> (lamenting)
> But he's out of town. He won't
> be back for two days.

> AARON
> Then, obviously, cogito ergo
> sum, amicus curiae, deus ex
> machina, reductio ad absurdum
> — you have to hold her till you
> find out if this regulation is
> valid or not.

(CONTINUED)

77 CONTINUED:

The Watch Officer has listened to this
with growing disbelief. Now he throws up
his hands in defeat.

> WATCH OFFICER
> Okay, okay. Johnny...take her
> back while I check this out.

The cop holding Hallie starts walking
her back to the cells as the barred door
slides open. Aaron watches. Suddenly,
Hallie turns in the cop's grip and yells:

> HALLIE
> Damn you, Aaron! Damn you!
> Damn you!

She is still yelling as the barred gate
slides back with a SOLID CLANG.

78 CAMERA IN ON AARON'S FACE

wracked with torment. HOLD the
expression as we

> DISSOLVE TO:

79 INT. AARON'S APARTMENT — DAY

Aaron is stretched out on the sofa, arm
flung over his eyes. There is a KNOCK on
the door. Aaron gets up and answers it.
David Barrett stands there.

> BARRETT
> May I come in?

> (CONTINUED)

79 CONTINUED:

Aaron walks away, leaving the door open.
He goes back and lies down. Barrett
comes in, closes the door, and settles
into the easy chair facing Aaron. He
lights a cigar.

> BARRETT
> It's been three days since
> Hallie's arraignment. We
> haven't seen you at the office.
> We haven't seen the top of your
> desk, either.
>> (beat)
> Work is mounting up, Aaron.

> AARON
>> (wearily)
> Sorry. I've been a little tired.

> BARRETT
> Pat says you haven't been to
> class.

> AARON
> That's right.

> BARRETT
>> (angry)
> Stop it, Aaron!

> AARON
>> (won't fight)
> Seems like everybody's telling
> me to stop it these days. Okay,
> so I'm stopping it.

(CONTINUED)

79 CONTINUED:

> BARRETT
> No matter how hard I try,
> Aaron, I can't seem to work up
> a feeling of pity for you. You
> started this all wrong, you
> were running on three-year-old
> memories, and you got banged
> around, but when it came down
> to the bottom line, you did
> the right thing.

Aaron sits up, temper rising slightly.

> AARON
> Sure. I did just fine. I did
> what I despise in other guys:
> I copped-out on someone who
> trusted me.

> BARRETT
>   (hard)
> Benedict Arnold, right? You
> don't fit the part, Aaron. The
> girl you sent back to jail
> wasn't the girl you knew
> three years ago. People aren't
> statues, they change; they
> don't weather the seasons
> nearly as well as marble.
> Hallie Benda is gone. That
> girl in the Suffolk County jail
> is named Hallie Peterson…and
> she needs help…not an attorney
> feeling sorry for himself.

> AARON
> Go tell her that.

79 CONTINUED:

> BARRETT
> I'll tell <u>you</u>, wise guy!
> (beat)
> When will you stop letting
> your adolescent emotions cloud
> your lawyer's mind? You've got
> to think what's best for your
> client!

> AARON
> She isn't my client.

> BARRETT
> (meaningfully)
> Yes. Yes, she is.
> (beat)
> She needs help. If you didn't
> really know her three years
> ago, didn't know how weak she
> was, if you failed her three
> years ago...you'd better not do
> it today. She comes up for a
> trial next week, Aaron, and
> she's your client.
> (beat)
> She always was. Even three
> years ago.

Aaron looks at Barrett. We see the
reality of what Barrett has said dully
settling into Aaron's eyes. Finally, he
nods. Barrett has made his point.

FADE OUT.

<u>END OF ACT FOUR</u>

86: 27 NOVEMBER 70

"THE WHIMPER OF WHIPPED DOGS"

Part Five

<u>TAG</u>

FADE IN:

80 INT. COURTROOM — DAY

The Judge is Kate Knight. But it is the
same Prosecuting Attorney and Recorder
and Bailiff and Clerk from Scene 46.
Hallie sits in the place reserved for
the Accused, with a matron. Claire
Zelazny and Pat occupy the spectators'
area with a few N.S. EXTRAS. Aaron is
with them, but alone.

>   KATE
> Miss Benda, as you have
> indicated no counsel of choice,
> the court is prepared to
> appoint a public defender.

Aaron stands.

>   AARON
> With Your Honor's permission,
>   (MORE)

(CONTINUED)

80 CONTINUED:

> AARON (CONT'D)
> I will gladly serve as Miss
> Benda's attorney.

Hallie leaps up, screaming.

> HALLIE
> I'd rather die first!

Judge Knight bangs her gavel. The matron
urges Hallie to be seated.

> AARON
> Your honor, might I speak
> to you and the Prosecuting
> Attorney in chambers?

Kate considers it for a moment. Finally:

> KATE
> (gavel hits)
> We'll take a fifteen-minute
> recess. Mr. Silverman, Mr.
> Klegg, if you'll join me in
> chambers.

She leaves by the chamber door. The D.A.
and Aaron follow her.

CUT TO:

81 INT. JUDGE'S CHAMBERS — DAY

as Aaron comes in. Klegg is waved to a
seat by Judge Knight. Aaron stands.

(CONTINUED)

81 CONTINUED:

> KATE
> Well, Aaron. Apparently, David
> was right. I shouldn't have
> interfered.

> AARON
> If you hadn't, and if I hadn't,
> it would have been much worse
> for her. She's sick, your honor.

> KATE
> I read the report, Aaron. But
> we can't excuse criminal acts
> because we feel sorry for
> people. Or because we knew
> them once.

> AARON
> I'm not asking for Hallie to be
> forgiven, Judge.
> (beat)
> Her crimes were those
> of someone on speed. Not
> premeditated, just compulsive.
> She stole from her mother, her
> friends, anyone near her, to
> keep using. The lying, the
> amorality, the neglect of her
> child, they're all part of
> the habit-pattern of someone
> whose nervous system's been
> chewed up by drugs. If she's a
> criminal, Judge, then all the
> kids we've lied to about drugs
> are criminals.

(CONTINUED)

81 CONTINUED:

>   KATE
> Aaron, society isn't on trial.

>   AARON
> But it is! Every time a kid
> watches tv and sees a chemical
> answer to warts, or bad breath,
> or insomnia, every time a kid
> goes into a drug store and
> sees we have a pill to make
> her feel good or slow down
> or ease tension — we lie to
> her, and lead her to believe
> chemicals can solve all her
> problems.
>   (beat)
> We've been lying so long, now
> we're trying to stick kids like
> Hallie in jail for believing
> the lies.
>   (beat)
> She doesn't need jail, Judge.
> She needs medical help.

>   KATE
> Mr. Klegg? How do you feel
> about all this?

>   PROS. ATTORNEY
> Of all the cases I'm asked to
> prosecute, I despise these the
> most. Mr. Silverman may be
> right, your honor. If you want
> to recommend Miss Benda for
> medical rehabilitation, I won't
> fight it.

                                        (CONTINUED)

81 CONTINUED:

> KATE
> Thank you, gentlemen.

They rise, all clearly troubled, and they
leave the judge's chambers quickly.

CUT TO:

82 INT. COURTROOM — med. shot on int. door
— day

as Aaron and Klegg emerge. Aaron goes
back to the spectator section, as Pat
and Claire rise. They start toward the
back and Aaron stops, to look at Hallie.

83 ON HALLIE

She's turned around, staring with hatred
at Aaron.

84 WITH AARON & CLAIRE & PAT

as they go through the doors out of the
courtroom.

85 COURTHOUSE CORRIDOR — ON AARON AND
CLAIRE — DAY

> CLAIRE
> Will it be all right for her?

> AARON
> I don't know.
> (MORE)

(CONTINUED)

85 CONTINUED:

> AARON (CONT'D)
> The Judge is going to give
> her the chance, anyhow. But
> I'm starting to believe there
> aren't any happy endings this
> side of the movies.

> CLAIRE
> Can I buy you a cup of coffee?

> AARON
> Okay. Anybody likes me as
> much as you, I ought to treat
> better. Better than I have.

> CLAIRE
> And what makes you think I
> like you so much?

> AARON
> Don't you?

> CLAIRE
> Yes, but what makes you think
> so?

> AARON
> Because you lied to me.

> CLAIRE
> I did what?

> AARON
> When we got Hallie out of jail,
> you said you thought we'd like
> (MORE)

(CONTINUED)

85 CONTINUED:

>   AARON (CONT'D)
>   to be alone to talk, and you
>   had a class to go to.
>   (beat)
>   That was Saturday. You don't
>   have any classes on Saturday.

Aaron smiles at her. Pat chuckles and
walks away. Claire looks exasperated,
takes Aaron's hand and they walk away as
we

>   FADE OUT.

>   THE END

And there it is. All of it, just as it appeared in the first
draft. There has been a final draft, and as loudly as I decry the
rewrites that emerge from fear and ameliorative copping-out, I
must confess that the revisions requested by *The Young Lawyers'*
producer, Matthew Rapf, its story editor, Jim McAdams, its story
consultant, Jack Guss, and even those set forth by Miss Dorothy
Brown of ABC network continuity, were informed, constructive,
served only to tighten the story and its interior conflicts, and
on the whole made the script better and smoother than its first-
draft version. Note this day, friends: it may be the only time you
will ever hear me praise those who demand revisions.

(The only serious point of contention was the conversation
between Pat Walters and Eunice Johnson in act 3: the discussion
of the landlord who had been in a Nazi prison camp yet who
had so little humanity for his tenants. Jack Guss, Matt Rapf,
and Miss Brown all felt it was anti-Semitic and that it had to go.
As a Jew, my contention was—and is—that the brutalization
of people that kills their empathy for others transcends race or

religion, and while there was no intent to reflect "Jewishness" in the attitude of that unseen landlord—after all, Catholics, Freemasons, gypsies, trade unionists, and dissidents of all religious persuasions became inmates of Dachau, Bergen-Belsen, Auschwitz, Treblinka, and the other death camps, though history and casual memory choose only to deal with the horror statistic of six million Jews who met their terrible fates there—even so, the loss of caring in many Jews who went through that monstrousness is part of our heritage and to deny there are Jews who act as that landlord acts is to deny a truth all blacks know about Jewish slumlords. To pretend that a Jewish landlord cannot be calloused is as dishonest as allowing Italian-Americans to browbeat ABC into making all *The Untouchables* gangsters WASPs, when history and common knowledge tell us most of them were Sicilians. Not all, of course—Guzik and Schultz and Moe Dalitz and Bugsy Siegel and Mickey Cohen and Lou Rothkopf were Jews, sad to say—but unfortunately for all the decent Italian-Americans who have to contain the Cosa Nostra in *their* heritage, even as "Greasy Thumb" Guzik is part of mine, Capone and his contemporaries and their descendants are an immutable part of American history. All of which speaks to my insistence that the conversation about that landlord—who was not specifically intended to be Jewish—be retained.)

And now we come to the tears, mah fellow Ammurricans.

The script you have just read may never be produced.

Before you rant and scream at the egomania of a columnist who will take over four weeks to fill a newspaper with his commercial writings, let me assure you the bad news fell on my head this week as unexpectedly as I'm dumping it on yours.

Because everyone who has seen this script, everyone connected with the network or the show, not to mention my girlfriend and the actors on the show, has loved it. So why won't it be produced?

Well, would you believe Spiro Agnew killed it?

(Oh, *Jeezus!* There goes that paranoid asshole Ellison blaming the Veep again. How much longer must we put up with this irrational hectoring of a fine, good man who Loves His Country?!)

If you recall, five weeks ago when I introduced the script, my reasons for publishing it as segments of a column devoted to tv and its effects on our society were (a) for your simple enjoyment, (b) to see what a script looks like, in answer to many requests for same, (c) so you could compare the original with the filmed version, and (d) because I had to go to New York for several weeks on business and I wanted to make sure I had columns in advance with the *Freep*, ready to go.

And when I left, Paramount, ABC, and the staff of the show were very high on the script. It was to go into production late this month or early next, and air sometime in December or early January.

But while I was away, the networks got Agnewized.

Despite the drubbing Nixon and his toad Veep took in the elections—god bless the bulk of the American People for rejecting the terror tactics of Repression's Tots—the networks did not take note; they found that their hypocritical pandering to "relevance"and "commitment" ("The Glass Teat," 9/25/70) had backfired. Attempting to snare the demographic youth market, they slanted everything to the young rebels and the young doctors and the young lawyers and the young youth. And to hell with the older viewers, who were given Red Skelton as a sop.

But kids can't be hyped.

As I predicted (he said, humbly), the kids knew the same old cynics were behind these new "relevant" shows, and they stayed away in droves, reinforcing their disdain for tv and all it proffers. And the Middle American scuttlefish had their guts full of longhairs and militants jabbering "dig" and "like" and "that's where it's at" from every channel. So *they* rejected the shows, too.

Apparently, ABC (among others) didn't do such a hot job of *getting it all together*.

Precisely put, the bastards have no one to blame but themselves. For instance, when Nixon invited a horde of top producers and studio prexies to D.C. prior to the season's opening, and hipped them that there was a (shhh!) drug problem in the country, he asked or ordered that their first few shows deal with narcotics. And so, for weeks, every dramatic (and even comedy) series featured the wonders of rolling joints, kids o.d.'ing, college students running amuck on the ee-vil vapors of mary-joo-wanna, et cetera. Naturally everyone threw up hands and said fuck'it, and tuned in to Lawrence Welk. (We've got enough depressing stuff all around us, said Paul and Priscilla Patriot, we don't have to watch that crap on teevee, too. Turn on *Nancy*. And they did, too.)

So the terrified tremblers of teevee saw their ratings vanishing, and this is what it looked like, the week ending November 8, in the seventy-city Nielsen:

The Top 20

Flip Wilson	(NBC)
Mod Squad	(ABC)
Gunsmoke	(CBS)
Ironside	(NBC)
Men from Shiloh	(NBC)
Thursday Movie	(CBS)
Monday Movie	(NBC)
FBI	(ABC)
Lucy	(CBS)
Bonanza	(NBC)
Walt Disney	(NBC)
Hawaii Five-O	(CBS)
Sunday Movie	(ABC)
Room 222	(ABC)
Partridge Family	(ABC)
Kraft Music Hall	(NBC)
Nancy	(NBC)
Medical Center	(CBS)
Laugh-In	(NBC)
Newlywed Game	(CBS)

(It should be pointed out that the segment of Nancy wherein the Julie Nixon surrogate marries the David Eisenhower *Doppelgänger* is the one that made it into seventeenth place, but the ratings were so low—as was only fitting and proper for a series that awful—it didn't stop the NBC cancellation. Thank god.)

So I returned from New York to find that *The Young Lawyers* had only barely escaped cancellation in the purge that blissfully rid us of *The Immortal, Barefoot in the Park, The Most Deadly Game, The Silent Force, The Young Rebels, Tom Jones,* and *Matt Lincoln.*

But the price for being kept on the air is a high one. It is total Agnew-ization.

No scripts dealing with drugs. No scripts dealing with "youth." No socially conscious scripts. Lee J. Cobb comes into prominence, Zalman King fades back quite a lot, and a pure WASP attorney will be introduced to ease the identity crisis for the scuttlefish. (Steve Kandel, one of the more lunatic scriveners in Clown Town, when assigned the chore of writing the script that introduces the new characters, despising the idea, named him Christian White. It went through three drafts before anyone got hip to Steve's sword in the spleen.)

The show has been moved to ten o'clock on Wednesdays, and the really ugly part of the whole shake-up is that—needing, as they always do, a scapegoat—ABC has "kicked upstairs" the producer who very nearly lost his health trying to produce a good show while fending off the ABC brass and their nervous spasms. Matt Rapf is now executive producer. It's a bullshit title, and everyone knows it. They've brought in a new line producer (whose reputation has always been an enviable one, as a crusading liberal producer out of New York), and he's now faced with hurry-up scripts that were hurriedly put into work to meet the new guidelines.

So, "The Whimper of Whipped Dogs" probably won't get shot. Maybe, possibly, if the series lasts the season, they'll do it after January. But chances don't look too hot.

I haven't space this week to go into it, but next week I'll dwell a lot longer on what all this portends, because it is far from simply my script no longer being "suitable." It is the first genuine manifestation of Agnew's concerted attacks on television taking effect. And *that,* friends, heralds a return (after four weeks of artistic brilliance) to those fire-breathing columns of yore.

My anticipation is that after next week's verbiage my telephone line, which is now only tapped by the Los Angeles Police Department (you remember them, the people who brought you the death of Ruben Salazar), will have tie-lines into the Federal Building and very probably Spiro's bathroom:

Where, it is reported by a high government source, he masturbates with copies of the *Reader's Digest*.

Next week: death and transfiguration.

87: 4 DECEMBER 70

"Punk" is a fascinating word.

Out of the mouth of George Raft, James Cagney, or Humphrey Bogart it summed up the loathing of a man of guts for the yellow-spined cravens of the world.

As spoken by Paul Muni in *The Last Angry Man* it was an epithet comprising of equal parts bewilderment and compassion and angered frustration.

Combined with the words "longhaired," "dope crazed," "yellow," or "Commie pinko nigger fag kike greaser," it provides the basic tinkertoy slur in the hardhat vocabulary.

But like the words *pig, stoned, patriotic,* or *speed,* the meaning of "punk" has changed—if you will, radically.

A "punk" used to be an image cast in the mold of Marlon Brando or Lee Marvin or Jerry Paris in The Wild One. You know: leather-jacketed, essentially cowardly, tough only when backed by a horde, chains, or a busy broken beer bottle. It used to be the kind of young thug who beat up old ladies and stole their pension checks; it used to be chop&channel goons picking fights at the Big Boy for the amusement of the carhops; it used to represent a nadir of human behavior to which no self-respecting Jack Armstrong would sink.

But times change. And words change. And we now discover that Wheaties, the "breakfast of champions," rates twenty-ninth in nutritional value in a field of sixty dry cereals, losing first position to such sissy foods as Sugar Smacks, Froot Loops, and Apple Jacks. And so, in apparent defiance of Gertrude Stein, in a pardonable paraphrase, a "punk" is not always a "punk" is not always a "punk"...

When a "punk" grows up, he grows up to be Spiro T. Agnew.

Over the past three years, in this column, I have taken potshots at The Deadly White Spirochete, and for the most part they were bemused, offhand sideswipes. Until Dayton, Ohio, and what happened to me there (but that's all last year, and it's in the book, so I won't go over it again).

But this week, after the "shelving" of my script, and the abrupt, terrifying Agnewization of the television horror show, the time has come to admit that Spiro, Destiny's Tot, has had his way at last, that the coils of repression have settled around us, and now we can only hang here in boa-constrictored helplessness as the Orwellian nightmare synchs into focus. Grandiose terminology simply to say we have been royally, handsomely, thoroughly, expertly, and Kafkaesquely shafted, friends. Spitted. Roasted. Salted. And about to be savored.

One year ago, when Agnew began his campaign against the unruly media that persisted in laughing at his Willie Stark stance (poised like flamingo on one foot, the other jammed cleverly in the mouth), we all laughed, from our Ivory Towers of Intellectual Snobbery. He was another in the endless troll horde of demagogues and know-nothings with which the human race has been barnacled since the first Middle Pleistocene *Pithecanthropus* McCarthy harangued his pre-hominid companions with scarce rhetoric about the subversives endangering the tribe with that earlier red menace...fire.

Ignoring the warnings of history, we laughed. And the chuckling became ever more hollow as the attacks continued, as the media "fought back" with defensive arguments as to their impartiality and responsibility. Instead of attacking him front and center, they backpedaled.

The rulers of the greatest informational and propaganda medium in the history of the world, and they sank to their knees, touched their foreheads to the carpet, begged for indulgence, allowed this semiliterate troglodyte buffoon to lacerate them with the birch rod of scriptwriters' prepared canards. And emboldened by their supplications, he escalated. Upward and onward he spiraled, denouncing and declaiming, until he had concretized his reality to a degree where newspeak and changetalk were permissible.

(I. F. Stone, the brilliant observer of Administration skullduggery, in an article in the December 3 *New York Review of Books*, dealing with fabricated evidence in the Kent State killings, notes:

("To those who think murder is too strong a word one may recall that even Agnew three days after the Kent State shootings used the word in an interview on the David Frost show in Los Angeles. Agnew admitted in response to a question that what happened at Kent State was murder, 'but not first degree' since there was—as Agnew explained from his own training as a lawyer—'no premeditation but simply an over-response in the heat of anger that results in a killing: it's a murder. It's not premeditated and it certainly can't be condoned.'"

(Which is diametrically opposed to Agnew's later and frequent characterizations of the students as bums and dangerous degenerates heavily in need of thrashing. Or as Maxwell Anderson phrased it in *Lost in the Stars*, "There is only one course they understand—a strong hand and a firm policy.")

There are even those who contend that, due to Agnew's fiery denunciations of network analyses of Nixon's speeches, the FCC moved to express a degree of pinky-slapping in behalf of the Administration by enforcing a kind of "states' rights" return of one half-hour's primetime per night to local stations, in an effort to encourage "local analyses" of Dickie's dicta. I tend to think that's a bit of conspiracy paranoia. We all know that despite the F in FCC standing for "Federal," those boys can't be bought. Honest men, all.

And still we laughed. There might be some backpedaling, some soft- soaping, some ameliorating, even some compromise... but freedom of speech could not be killed. After all, it's been 236 years since John Peter Zenger's trial. What asses we were.

Agnew didn't slacken his pace. He kept it up...speeches, press interviews, rigged tv confrontations with militants, solo and massed attacks on the media and its front men, the commentators.

Culminating a month or so ago with a Sunday press interview show on which he seriously put forth the concept of television commentators going before a Joe McCarthy-style committee to state their political views and leanings. He assured viewers and interviewers (even as he had assured us before) that this was not intended as censorship, that these gentlemen of the video press would be "invited to volunteer to appear before such a committee" even as McCarthy's victims were "invited," and when asked to whom he was specifically referring, he demurred prettily. However, he *did* vouchsafe as how men such as, well, uh, er, like, say, Frank Reynolds of ABC might be required to state precisely where they stood.

I saw a film clip of that interview on the ABC *Evening News* the Monday following, and I saw the tiny smile Frank Reynolds allowed himself as he said, "And now, here's the other news."

Sock it toward them, Frank baby, I caroled. He isn't the most outspoken critic of the Monsters of Capitol Hill, but Reynolds has always tempered his sane and reasonable analyses of the news with a faintly radical air tinged by humanity. Thank god for Frank Reynolds, I thought. He offsets the Administration's rubber-stamping of his co-anchorman, Howard K. Smith, a man who patently loathes the young and outspoken troublemakers of this fair country.

Hallelujah for Frank Reynolds.

In January, Frank Reynolds vanishes from the ABC *Evening News*, to be replaced by Harry Reasoner, CBS's version of Howard K. Smith.

It may be that, as Cecil Smith of the *LA Times* says, working for the *Free Press* tends to make even moderate writers hysterical; and I'm falling prey to the paranoia of the conspiracy reaction-formation. But I cannot help seeing a direct correlation between Agnew's singling out of Reynolds as an Enemy of the People, and ABC's decision to boot the man off his nightly podium.

Which speaks to the recent comment by (I wish I could remember exactly who it was) who said freedom of speech is not served by an "equal time" proviso if one spokesman addresses

204,000,000 Americans on primetime and his opponent has a soapbox on the corner.

Similarly, I see a direct relationship between Agnew's scare rhetoric of the preelection days, and the networks' decision to quash all "relevant" drama addressing itself to contemporary problems. I see that relationship in the terrible polarization Agnewization has brought to the middle classes. Frightened, confused, sick to death of cries of revolution by longhairs and students and blacks, the scuttlefish have stayed away from "youth oriented" shows in droves. And—demographics be damned—the 18- to 36-year-old consumers recognized the shows as emerging from the same pit of cynicism and venality from which had emerged all those previous years of programming that turned them anti-tv. So ABC killed seven hours of primetime shows, most of which had the word *young* in the title, and silently cursed Nixon (who had ordained that the first shows of the new season would deal with drugs to combat the "dope problem"), and screwed many good men out of their jobs by refusing to accept the blame for its own hypocrisies, and, quite incidentally, as a by-product, shelved my script for *The Young Lawyers*.

Now, I am told by network mufti and various producers around town, they want nothing relevant, they want nothing youth-oriented, they want nothing controversial. They want shows that are familiar to the Middle Americans. Ideas tried and true. Spin-offs from accepted films: *Nanny and the Professor* is *Mary Poppins; Barefoot in the Park* and *The Odd Couple* and *The Interns* are based on popular films; debuting in January on ABC will be something called *Alias Smith and Jones* which, from its pilot script, is a sad-supposed-to-be-funny takeoff on *Butch Cassidy and the Sundance Kid*.

I could suggest that those who read "*The Whimper of Whipped Dogs*" for the last five weeks in this column write to the president of ABC, Elton Rule, and suggest they go ahead and shoot the script, since they laid out $4500 to have me write it, but to critics of me and this column (such as Laird Brooks Schmidt of 5485 Fernwood, and Bill Kerby of 908 S. Sycamore, the former who suggested I try writing something funny *intentionally*, and the latter who summed up his critique of my script by calling me a perfect asshole) that would obviously be self-serving...and they'd be right. So I won't bother making such an appeal.

I'll only point out that we can look forward to many years of timid, frightened, noncontroversial programming of *The Partridge Family* variety, and any attempts on our part to change matters will be met with blank stares and the instant descent of the thumb on our gnatlike selves.

Because, frankly, in a time and a place where the President says quite boldly he will not be moved by the appeals of people in the streets, what strength or purpose or courage or help can we expect from men who fear the loss of advertising revenues if they displease the Gorgon God of the Silent Majority?

A "punk" is a bully, and since this is not Middle Earth or Narnia or Erewhon or even a Charles Atlas ad in a comic book, wherein bullies get their comeuppance, since this is the most imperfect of imperfect worlds where bullies who are grown-up punks become Vice President of the United States, men like Elton Rule and his cohorts will continue to kick sand in the faces of men like Matthew Rapf, and will look for approbation from the Gorgon God. They know what happens to bad little networks who don't toss out the required ration of scapegoat meat.

Frank Reynolds is all too obvious an object lesson.

88: 11 DECEMBER 70

Among other things, this is a column in praise of Baxter Ward.

Ah! Baxter, twit thou never wert. Or bird thou never twit. Or something poetic.

In a city where one could boast of crusading, muckraking newscasters like Britt Reed of *The Green Hornet* or J. Jonah Jameson of *The Incredible Spider-Man* or Perry White of *The Daily Planet* or even Big Town's Steve Wilson of *The Illustrated Press*, Baxter Ward would be pretty small potatoes. But Los Angeles has George Putnam (transcendentally laughable), Tom

Reddin (Boob J. Boredom wearing the threadbare long johns of Captain Charisma), Ralph Storey (whose voice alone makes you long for the sound of fingernails on blackboards), Robert K. Dornan (microcephalic heir to the Joe Pyne mantle), and a gaggle of look-alike newsies named Marlow, Brokaw, Roberts, Sanders, Fishman, Bonds, Snyder, and Dunphy—all of whom report what's handed to them with no more concern for good or evil than an LAPD secretary typing up one of those "subversive reports" that find their way into CIA, U.S. Army, and Reagan Secret Police files.

With a field of winners like that, Baxter Ward stands out front like Simon Bolivar or Nat Turner. Or maybe even the Lone Ranger.

When he was running for mayor of our fair city, against Tom Bradley and Yorty the Berserk, he looked worse than the former but light-years better than the latter. That he didn't win says very little about Ward the man, I suspect, but provides us with some small reassurance that the day of selecting public officials by tv mien is not quite with us yet.

His recent stands on some topics of pressing interest, however, demand a closer scrutiny and a solid pat on the back: if for no other reason than to say well done thou good and faithful, and some of us are behind you. It makes it a little easier to be courageous, particularly when Agnew-assassinated examples like Frank Reynolds make it safer and saner to lie back as all but the obviously right-wing newscasters do these days. For a man standing out there all alone, it can be terribly chilly. So a vote of confidence is in order.

More, Baxter Ward seems to me a marvelously sane and rational human being. In these lunatic times that is very probably the highest accolade one can bestow on another human being. Where you or I would use a video perch of such preeminence to espouse our philosophies night in and night out, till whatever polarization we offended most had its way (as it did with Reynolds) and we were booted out on the street, Ward saves his shots till they count. That is the method of an honest man with gobs of common sense. He is scrupulously fair and remains uninvolved through most of the teapot tempests of day-to-day news reporting, holding back his fusillades for the meaningful encounters.

His personally offered positions, clearly labeled "comment," are uniformly interesting and informed. And the positions he defends in those comments are far and away the bravest of any newscaster working in the arena currently. Take for instance his November 4 statements about the election loss of Judge Alfred Gitelson, a man quite clearly defeated by racism for his decision in the Los Angeles School District integration matter.

Without going into the merits of Gitelson's decision in the affair—integrate at once, bus if necessary—Ward struck to the core of the matter with these words:

"One of the consequences of the Gitelson loss is bound to be a stirring within the Bar Association and the California judiciary. Both groups presumably will begin swift discussions on how to provide more security for judges—for their political protection."

And while a coven of insulated jurists, totally free of the checks and balances of public opinion or censure (as well as approbation), can be an unsettling concept—potentializing an elite cabal above recall or expulsion—as Ward points out, "Judges should judge as they see fit. They should not put self-preservation above duty. In fact, they should be prepared to sacrifice self-preservation for duty." And to this end, they should be protected from the racist or "neighborhood" pressures of the day.

This position, in a time when the uninformed lay audience feels courts are being too liberal, is heavily weighted by courage and conviction.

But it is only one of Ward's solid stances of recent memory.

Here are a few more.

July 14: "In the [state] legislature it is impossible to find one single legislator who says he is in favor of smog. But it is very easy to find a lot of legislators who vote for more smog, no matter what they might say. And just recently 14 from Los Angeles County alone voted to continue the smog created by lead in gasoline. We have been giving their names and their districts and towns each night, in case anyone wishes to write them, to suggest the legislator change his mind and his vote.

"Tonight we list the last five of the Los Angeles County Assemblymen who either voted to continue that kind of smog, or who failed to vote at all.

"Assemblyman   Wakefield...Assemblyman   Warren... Assemblyman Waxman...Assemblyman Unruh...Assemblyman Arklin..."

May 7: "...television has been receiving some blame for contributing to violence—it was charged that the presence of the cameras would encourage a crowd.

"And for us there was one final element this morning. Our newsroom received an invitation to be present at a campus difficulty. Violence was promised, and we were advised that our people would be safe from rocks if situated in a certain spot. We declined the invitation.

"We will continue to film assemblies, marches, speeches, or other public events up to the point of violence or ugliness. If the scene turns to destruction or tumult, we simply will stop our cameras and leave. And we will not show one frame of newsreel film of that kind of violence.

"And we realize that in this, we run some risks. We will be accused of deleting fact. To this, we reply—it will be only a visual deletion. We will report whatever damage information we have. But we will say it, only. We will not show it happening."

And though Ward's almost pathological drive to be fair leads him into occasional positional cul-de-sacs as embarrassing as Putnam's present-tense delivery leads him into syntactical foot-mouthings (such as Ward's comment of September 17 in which he expected the Chicano community to disavow the preceding night's riot, occurring as it did during the Salazar inquest, amid violent emotions charging the East Los Angeles barrio), his comments of September 10 and 11, and October 14 and 31, in re the Salazar matter, offer unarguable evidence that Baxter Ward is the only LA newscaster with the balls, heart, and integrity to offer what snipers and Walt Hickel call a "high profile."

September 10: "There were several opportunities for... impatience today. One came [during the Salazar inquest] when [the presiding officer: Norman] Pittluck failed to ask a deputy sheriff why he thought Salazar could be found at the Silver Dollar Bar when Salazar was said to be missing.

"Another came when Pittluck did not press a lieutenant for details on tear gas equipment, or did not ask a captain who authorized the projectile-type device....

"Pittluck's gentle questioning has followed mainly points apparently made available to him by the authorities. He was leading his witnesses through a path that had been carefully marked."

On September 11, Ward expressed further impatience that neither Salazar nor the death spot, the Silver Dollar Bar, was mentioned throughout a morning's testimony, and he expressed some astonishment that a witness who had previously granted tv interviews as well as full taped statements to the sheriff's department and the *LA Times* refused to be filmed, and later tried to disown the taped record of his statement with the plea that the hearing had put his life in jeopardy.

And on October 14, Ward summarized—with that Solomonesque fairness bristling—the community's dissatisfaction with the inquest and DA Younger's decision not to prosecute:

"The inquest disclosed that sheriff's officers receive no training in firing tear gas weapons. That failure cost Salazar his life, perhaps. A sheriff's department official explained it would cost the taxpayers $8000 a day to permit deputies to fire these weapons in practice sessions.

"For the sheriff to lay this lack of training on the dollar situation is an affront to the taxpayer. The taxpayer provides Sheriff Pitchess with a Fleetwood Cadillac car. And it costs $8000. No taxpayer has ever asked the sheriff to walk. And no taxpayer has ever asked the sheriff to hold back on gas gun training, either.

"Neither of the deputies who fired into the Silver Dollar Bar had any idea that the other deputy was in the area. The point is, both deputies thought it appropriate to fire into the doorway, without knowledge as to what they might hit.

"Both men were trained, apparently, to fire into a bar they felt was filled with people, regardless of the consequences.

Apparently, neither officer was trained to consider the possibility of just surrounding the place and waiting awhile to see what happened. Just because a place is considered to be barricaded is no reason to immediately blow it up or risk immediately killing someone who does not have a gun.

"'The inquest did not reveal why deputies did not respond decently and with humane concern to the insistence of those persons who told them Salazar had been hit. Because when the deputies were told he was hit, nobody was sure he was dead.

"The inquest did not reveal why the deputies who received that information never did act on it. They hung around for two and a half hours but never once permitted themselves to be concerned about the report of an injured or possibly dead man in the bar."

There was more, much more, to Ward's October 14 comment. Questions as to why the deputies hung around so long when it had been reported much earlier that the bar situation was clear, questions as to why the sheriff's department failed to respond to frequent and insistent calls to them from the manager of KMEX, inquiring about a possible accident to Salazar, questions as to obvious perjury by whole batches of witnesses.

And his October 31 comment went even further to cast doubt on the rationality of the sheriff's department ever having declared a "barricade situation" at the Silver Dollar.

All this, and much more in a time when Pitchess—a man despised in both the ghetto and barrio as the architect of destruction on the scene not only in East LA, but in Isla Vista as well—went unchallenged in the primaries and (as one newswoman put it) "will be our demigod for another four years, shooting every black, Mexican, and student he sees." It took some spine to speak out as Ward did.

It is appropriate this week's column should pay respects to Baxter Ward, for, even as I was writing it, he won his fourth Golden Mike award...for the October 14 comment.

It should mean more to him than even the tv Academy's Emmy as the Best Newscaster of 1967 in Los Angeles.

I have been able to discover very little about Baxter Ward personally. He is either terribly shy or terribly paranoid about publicity. Either way, if we are to judge a man by any yardstick, it should not be that he was born in Baltimore, or that he was responsible for creating Rona Barrett, or that he lost an election for mayor. It should be by his words and deeds. And on that scale, Baxter Ward clearly stands out as the best this terrified little hamlet has to offer.

KHJ deserves applause for giving Ward his head, and Ward deserves our support for having the head to use it.

With a half dozen more Baxter Wards, and one less George Putnam, licensed killers like Peter Pitchess might be forced to walk a trifle more carefully.

89: 18 DECEMBER 70

What with one thing and another, I've left all sorts of odds and ends unresolved in these columns for too many months, so with your indulgence I'll use this week as a shotgun session and take care of as many loose ends as I can before getting to some of the heavier items on the upcoming agenda.

•Several weeks ago the brilliant "Senator" portion of *The Bold Ones* on NBC aired a two-parter written by David Rintels (the mad dissident of the scriptwriting game), produced by David Levinson, directed by Robert Day and showcasing the consummate artistry of Hal Holbrook as the Senator. The name of the two-parter was "A Continual Roar of Musketry," and it purported to parallel the Kent State massacre and the hearings that followed therefrom.

It's a trifle late to suggest you watch it first run, but not too late to urge you to catch it in summer rerun. Aside from its expertise as fine drama, it is as close as we will come in the foreseeable future to a no-copout, sincere, honest representation of responsible High Art in the video medium. Yes, it was a trifle simplistic; yes, it managed (like *Patton*) to present the moderately far-left and far-right views, which may be a plus, I'm not sure;

and yes, it was far from as explicit an indictment of the National Guard and the Authorities as, say, I. F. Stone's report on police and Guard collusion in fabricating testimony…but it did not end with one of those "we are all at fault" numbers. It said: this one seems guilty, and this one seems guilty, and they must be brought to task for it.

Quite apart from its intrinsic merits as compelling viewing, as well-written and handsomely mounted theater, it is an object lesson for all of us when we castigate the juju box, as to what the outside limits (at the moment) seem to be when attempting to portray the *status quo* as the corrupt enterprise we've come to know so well. It was Universal being courageous, and we must give everyone connected with getting it on the air our thanks and respect. It may have served an inestimably worthwhile service.

I was part of a tv panel at USC last week, in company with 20th's Grant Tinker and Universal's Norman Glenn, and in the audience was a student who said her mother (who'd apparently been unsympathetic to the Movement before the show) sat there murmuring *right on* through the show. Now that may not be an indication of radicalization on the part of the Middle American per se, but it is the kind of acceptable agitprop material we need to see more of.

Mr. Glenn noted, however, that the ratings for the second half of the two-parter were considerably higher than for the first installment.

The second installment followed John Wayne's flag-waving special.

What that says to all of us is, I think, reaffirmation of our wildest fears, but maybe not. Either way, Rintels and the Universal cadre stuck their necks out, and as we said to Baxter Ward last week: *you are not alone.* And

Thank you.

•Some months ago I did a turn on those debased Winston commercials in which the anti-intellectuals had their ups. I noted, in particular, the commercial in which a prissy white-collar type advises his boss at the board table that Winston tastes good *as*, not *like*, and for his trouble is thrown out through the swinging

doors by the boss's yes-men. At the time I didn't know the name
of that actor, but since I've been informed his name is Damian
London, and I thought I'd pass it on to you and to any casting
directors who need a good character actor.

On the same subject, correspondent L. P. Desprez of Eau
Claire, Wisconsin, reports the following:

"As I was riding around on my bicycle this afternoon, I saw
some young boys, approximately age 11, playing an amusing
game that went like this:

"One boy was it and the other five or six would gather around
him, back him into a corner and hit him on the head, all the
while screaming, 'Whaat Doo Yoo Want? Good Grammer'r Good
Taste?!'

"I swear by whatever you would have me swear by that I did
not make this up."

We believe you, L.P. We believe you. Sob.

•Cowardice shows its colors in the action of NBC in promising
to kill *Bracken's World* in January. Or as pinafored Tricia Nixon
has advised us, "You can't underestimate the power of fear."
Which is to say, I had a 3000-word column all set to go (at long
last) on the Olympian awfulness of that series. Oh, you'd have
loved it, gang. Words like "debased" and "vomitous" and "evil"
garlanded the review. Simply marvy phrases like "stories that
make Jacqueline Susann look like Emily Brontë," "the aroma
of an Army co-op kitchen grease trap rises from this swill,"
and "never has so much psychotic behavior earned so many
no talents so much money" dotted the column like weevils in
pancake batter. But all that is pointless now. NBC is deserting
the ship before the rats turn on them, and I'd be the last guy in
the world to kick a wounded animal as it was trying to crawl
into the brush to lick its wounds.

•Miss Barbara Shoemaker of Long Beach dropped me a note
carping about having to wait forty-five minutes till a football
game ended before she could watch The Young Lawyers, and,
while she found it difficult to understand how some of us could
bear to watch a group of padded loons obviously suffering from
giantism push around another gaggle of plug-uglies, all for
possession of what she terms "a peculiar little pointed object,"

she opined the show was worth it. To her I pass along the information that, as of January, *The Young Lawyers* hangs onto primetime by its teeth by being moved to 10:00 Thursday nights and very shortly thereafter she won't have to worry about ABC's Monday night NFL broadcasts—because there won't be any. Incidentally, ABC has been getting alarmingly low ratings on the games and that, coupled with the many hours of new shows they've been forced to kill, all because the "youth audience" they expected to pull never materialized, should make all of you under thirty out there deliriously happy: by boycotting their hypocritical and exploitive programming, you've cost them millions of dollars, all by your little beautiful selves. Now don't that make you feel good?

Put gold stars up beside your names.

•A review of the *Don Knotts Show*, in brief, from notes, sans continuity, but with meaning clear:

Tuesday 7:30, NBC. The most forgettable hour in tv. Dull comedy skits...band blared so loud they overrode Smokey Robinson and the Miracles...Knotts is the ultimate morphodite nebbish...moronic, tawdry elevator skit, bloodless, improbable, awkward, tasteless...cheap Kiwanis stag humor. Lesley Warren singing with that phony white pseudo-country bullshit downhome pronunciation: goddamn you to the last tick of recorded time, Keely Smith, for ever introducing a singing style with bastardizations like "tahm," "goodbah," "ah," and "forgate" in it. Now every second-rater with aspirations of Caucasoid Soul substitutes it for feeling; I only wish on you that you should get hit by a falling Buddy Greco locked in an embrace with a downdropping Louis Prima from a fifty-storey office building, and the shrapnel should ricochet off Lesley Warren.

Big-time variety comedy shows are for wieners.

•Final note. The next time the Administration tells us how much freedom of speech and equal time there are in the good ole U.S.A., all together in unison leave us chant, "It ain't equal time if Nixon gets primetime to millions and the opposition gets a soapbox on the corner." Yeah, I know I said that a couple of weeks ago, but it bears repeating, especially when we note that NBC broadcast every loathsome moment of last January's Super

Bowl half-time ceremonies in which the War of 1812 was restaged, complete to bloody soldiers falling before booming cannons, extolling the grandeur and glory of mortal combat, but ABC refused to air the half-time festivities at the State University of Buffalo on October 31 because it was a peace demonstration. The swine bastards cut away for nine full minutes to give scores of incomplete games-in-progress rather than show the university's marching band forming the peace symbol.

Three days before the game ABC announced it wouldn't carry the "Give Peace a Chance" ceremonies because they were political in nature.

All the things that can be said about this disgraceful action leap to your minds as easily as they do to mine. So I won't belabor it, save to say I hope it makes enough of you so sick to your stomachs and ethics that you write the FCC and the necessary Congressmen to insist on a full hearing. If ever there was reason to have a network's license pulled...

Well, shit, they should've known better. The marching band, that is. They should have formed a hard hat, not a peace symbol. They should have planned a "John Wayne All-Amurican Celebration" instead. They should've known better. And so should we.

I'll believe there's "equal time" on the networks when I see TV Guide listings for specials like:

THE PLEASURES OF GRASS
DAVID FROST INTRODUCES THE WIT &
WISDOM OF ELDRIDGE CLEAVER
THE LENNON SISTERS SEX AND SADISM HOUR

and Punch Detergent solicits KKKers to show how the enzymes remove bloodstains from their sheets.

Frankly, folks, my karma feels threatened.

90: 25 DECEMBER 70

Turn off the bright lights, kindly remove the bamboo shoots from under my fingernails, and release my aged mother from the bingo parlors of Miami Beach, I'll confess.

This week I took payola.

My column on Baxter Ward sufficiently delighted the folk at Channel 9 for them to send me a promotional item I feel compelled to fess up I accepted. A Baxter Ward wristwatch. With only four numerals on the face, all of which are 9. And the hands blend in with the background so it's virtually impossible to tell what time it is. I suppose because the face of the item says WATCH BAXTER WARD, it is no more reprehensible to have accepted the gift than, say, keeping record albums sent for review or using movie passes sent to film critics, but since I keep getting letters from brain damage cases out there saying they trust me (apparently because I continue to insist I'm not to be trusted), latent guilt drives me to the point of confession.

I took the watch.

I also took the genuine simulated pressed cardboard watchband attached to it.

Anyone desiring to start a recall movement of this columnist for malfeasance in office had best know, additionally, that once before this I accepted payola. Which brings me to the deranged subject of this week's maunderings.

Last September I received a phone call from Jack Nesoff of the Hollywood Water Bed Company, advising me that because of the wonderfulness of myself, he was giving me a free water bed. *"Gloryosky, Zero!"* I caroled, leaping in the air in the elfin manner I adopt when confronted with loot, clapping my tiny pink paws in childlike glee. "Send it over," I said.

And it came over, and it was too big for inside the house, so

I put it out on the back porch and we slept on it all through the summer and it's just as lovely a sleeping experience as all those badly laid-out ads say it is; but then there's more to it than just sleeping, which I'll get into in a moment.

About a month later, I received a phone call from Dr. Michael Valentine Zamoro, who vouchsafed that my beautiful vibrations via this column were so surfeiting the community with happyjoy, that *he* was sending me a Shair Water Bed in what he termed the "oceanic" size. I will not here chronicle the chirrupings and guttural sounds that emerged from my face into the very air. "Send it over," is how it ended.

So over came this even *bigger* goddamn water bed, and I sold the first one cheap to Chris Bunch, who promptly put a spike heel through it. (At least that's how *he* tells it; you don't catch *me* asking that freak Bunch why he was wearing spike heels. It's all I can do to keep from commenting on his tacky dresses when he comes over for our Tupperware parties.) And then came winter, and while I suppose water beds indoors are the essence of heavenliness all year round, on a back porch during the monsoon season here in Elay, it is cold enough to freeze off your ass. And hers, too.

Nonetheless, I accepted payola, and went so far as to promise Mr. Nesoff I would do a column about his water thing, telling people how sweet can be the joys of watching television while fucking on a water bed. Now if *that* isn't rank selling of one's position for material remuneration, then The *$64,000 Question* was a charity telethon and the Teapot Dome scandal was a bookkeeping error.

Not to mention really stretching for a valid tv tie-in.

But since I've done it, and since I've used both Mr. Nesoff's Hollywood Water Bed and Dr. Zamoro's Shair Water Bed as launching pads for incredible carnal pleasures, not to mention ghastly video experiences, the least I can do is keep faith with them and describe to all of you throbbing little voyeurs how water beds, sex, and television meld for an evening's entertainment.

(For those in Kansas, reading this column some weeks after Los Angeles subscribers, let me describe what it is a water bed:

it's this big kinda triple-seamed rubber bag filled with water. Big
deal.

(I know there are all sorts of frames and lights and pads and
heaters and other jazz à la *Playboy* one can get to make the water
bed seem more sumptuous than a big balloon lying on a floor,
but neither of my benefactors apparently thought my vibes were
beautiful enough to slip me the full deal. And really, it matters
not, because all the benefits you'll derive from a water bed can be
derived without the accouterments. But keep the thing indoors,
know what I mean?)

Because there is a constant tidal effect when you move on
a water bed, sex is best enjoyed thereon while watching old
Western movies. I've found the rhythms are best established
with the aid of Audie Murphy, Randolph Scott, Rod Cameron
and Macdonald Carey shoot-'em-ups. Gary Cooper and Richard
Widmark oaters aren't so good: too much psychological stuff;
you break the beat too often while they go through agonizing
self-appraisal.

Indian attacks on wagon trains and fistfights on the edges of
cliffs are also pretty good. But cattle stampedes can be dangerous.
I know a guy who got hundreds of gallons of tap water (with a
dash of Clorox in it to keep it from getting funky) all over his
bedroom during a sex-cum-viewing trip with John Wayne in
Red River.

One feels disquietingly unclean performing some of the
more intricate sexual positions—such as "The Hong Kong Hod
Carryer" and "The Mesopotamian Mash"—while watching
family situation comedies. One gets the distinct impression Brian
Keith or Mary Tyler Moore is tsk-tsking at every stroke. This
same impression is conveyed by *Marcus Welby, M.D.* and Robert
Young. For this reason I strongly advise against fucking to reruns
of *Father Knows Best*. I would not even begin to evaluate the
trauma attendant on getting laid during *Lassie* reruns featuring
June Lockhart.

For serious viewing while engaged in a more cerebral breed
of sex, I highly commend to your attention the "Rocking Chair"
position for *First Tuesday* and *60 Minutes*. Not only is there a,
well, uplifting feeling pursuant to this coupling, but it is much

more comfortable for the extended length of *First Tuesday* airings. Groupies and gumchewers are not recommended for such sessions. I suggest magna cum laude graduates of Stanford currently engaged in eco research for one of the smaller corporations. Inexplicably, telex operators function well in this setting.

Never fuck on a water bed while watching *The Mod Squad*. There is the inescapable feeling that those three young finks are watching and that they will instantly dash into a phone booth to tell Tige Andrews you're out there doing something dirty. Visions of Clarence Williams III pulling the plug on your water bed leap unbidden to the mind. It is really hard keeping it erect with such horrors imminent.

Thank god *The Silent Force* has been canceled.

Red Skelton, Don Knotts, and Ed Sullivan, as well as Lawrence Welk, can best be watched while lying face to face on your side, moving slowly back and forth and allowing the tide to do all the work.

Only perverts watch *Laugh-In* while water-bedded.

Water bed masturbation is best served by George Putnam and the news as he sees it. Myopically.

For those engaged in mutually destructive sexual relationships, I recommend the water bed during speeches by Nixon. One has the overwhelming urge to clobber; and if you're involved with a fingernail digger/neck biter, Nixon is the one.

Rona Barrett's Hollywood report can make an erection fall faster than a spent Apollo missile.

A "cute" fuck can be obtained on your water bed during reruns of *Flipper*. Obvious, but cute.

For old marrieds, I reluctantly advise the *Tom Jones Show*. I realize it's forced and transparently phony, but realities are realities and for those who've been locked in connubial bliss to the point where the partnership has palled, a little cheap sensationalism never hurts. You'll hate yourselves afterward, of course, but remember, when two people love each other, anything is beautiful.

To date, the best shtup on record was obtained by a Van Nuys plumber's assistant and a casual Friday night pickup who works as a carhop at the Big Boy, on the following Saturday morning, atop a double water bed watching *The Bugaloos*. Windows were shattered for blocks around.

Thus, from Baxter Ward's punim on my watch, through KY sterile lubricant and Kama Sutra love oil, via Mayberry and Shiloh, we have examined the latest and most productive use to which can be employed the most potent form of education and communication the world has ever known.

Isn't it amazing how I can turn naked greed into an ennobling experience?

91: 1 JANUARY 71

As I sit down to write this week's installment—the ninety-first to see print—it is Christmas Eve day. Tomorrow is the day They decided— erroneously, historians tell us—He was born. By the time you get around to reading it, however, it will be into the New Year, 1971, and the decade will be rattling right along without pausing for more than a cursory glance back over its shoulder at peace on earth and et and cetera.

But that's all in the future as I sit here, and at the moment Christmas is hurtling down on me with the inexorable momentum of a cannonball whizzing across a battlefield. In case you haven't perceived from just these few words that I intensely abominate Christmas, let me dot the i and cross the t by saying I have always judged the only person in *A Christmas Carol* worth his salt to be Ebenezer Scrooge. Bob Cratchit is a weakling; Marley is a fink for the Hereafter, trying to save his ectoplasmic ass from Limbo; Belle was so marriage-slaphappy she couldn't muster up sufficient ego reinforcement to stand by her man till he overcame his personality problems; the Ghosts of Christmas Past, Present, *and* Future are not only buttinskies, but bullies as well; and Tiny Tim is a one-man diabetes plague:

"God bless us, every one!"

Terrific.

"God bless us, every one!"

Right, kid. Thanks

"God bless us, every one!"

All right, awreddy, you mongoloid, shut the fuck up!

"God bless us...awwwwkkkk..."

The only character in that whole damned offensive tract in praise of simpering goodness is Scrooge, a man who perceived the truth about Christmas with a degree of clearheadedness and cynicism I find laudable. It is the one cavil I have with Dickens—a man whose work I greatly admire—that he spewed forth such a treacly treatise and copped out as a storyteller by refusing to allow Scrooge to stand his moral ground.

In short, Christmas is to me humbug of a high order.

So omnipresent is the hypocritical hysteria surrounding 25 December that the closest thing to a Scrooge we have to admire on tv, Jack Klugman as Oscar in *The Odd Couple*, was shoehorned into a (really funny, dammit) takeoff on the Dickens "classic" in last week's segment. But refusing to defy convention, they had poor old irascible Klugman repent his perfectly logical attitude about not appearing in a holiday rendition of *A Christmas Carol* and off he went blathering tidings of good cheer, wassail, wassail.

I realize this admission of my loathing for such a sacred event will lose me hordes of readers, many of whom sat still all year as I pilloried Agnew, Nixon, Reagan, the Left, the Right, the Fervent Center, motherhood, apple pie, and the American Way. But if you'd spent a whole week watching re-reruns of *King of Kings* (in two parts), *The Robe, Demetrius and the Gladiators, The Story of Ruth, Miracle on 34th Street, Silent Night, Lonely Night, Miracle of Our Lady of Fatima, White Christmas*, and a horde of moronic specials among which only *How the Grinch Stole Christmas* (through which I cheered for the Grinch) stands out as palatable, you'd be cranky, too.

Christmas, it seems to me, sends everyone right off their chumps. They go berserk. My mail is clogged with hundreds of mass-produced Xmas cards all sporting prerecorded Muzak greetings, most of them hedging their best for Jews, Moslems, and Shintoists by proffering wishes for a "happy holiday," be it Hanukkah, Christmas, Whitsuntide, or whatever other pagan ritual you observe. In the supermarket check-out line, with nine hundred Valley consumers waiting to pay for the gallons of booze and eggnog they'll have to tipple up for their sodden guests, everything comes to a dead halt while the box boys and lady checkers rush over to one of their number clutching a walleyed puppy with a sprig of holly attached to his collar.

Everyone goes completely bonko.

(Yet in the parking lot, a stalled car nets its flustered driver a stream of obscenities from other motorists, delayed by ten seconds in their dash to the holiday parties and a little ineffectual groping of each other's wives under the mistletoe.)

Bah! Humbug! Bullshit!

If they spent *half* the money they waste on Xmas cards alone for meals for children, it would better serve the intent of the Prince of Peace. I'm sure there's a broken link in logic there somewhere, as my believing friends assure me, clucking their tongues and calling me a scrooge—not knowing they pay me the highest compliment. But even if my logic is spotty, you know what I mean. That is, you know if *your* minds haven't been brainwashed by a constant sound track of "Deck the Halls with Boughs of Whatever."

Moving right along in this warm and cheery evocation of the holiday spirit, I must now tell you that in a lifestyle I've pursued for many years, a life-style which does not allow for acceptance or bestowal of Christmas gifts, a blemish has appeared.

I received a Christmas gift that practically brought tears to my eyes.

The Young Lawyers is doing my script, "The Whimper of Whipped Dogs."

If you've been with us through the last few months of columns, you'll have read the script in its five installments, and you'll be aware that because of a network reluctance to dwell any further on youth, dope, involvement, or relevance, the script had been shelved indefinitely.

Well, last week, as I emerged from a screening of Joseph L. Mankiewicz's *There Was a Crooked Man*...(a Kirk Douglas starrer written by Benton and Newman of *Bonnie and Clyde* fame, which may not be as obstinately shitty a film as, say, George Seaton's *Airport*, but is nonetheless a shabbily direct steal in remake form of Mark Hellinger's 1947 masterpiece, *Brute Force*, almost scene by scene transposed into the Old West), I was stopped by Hank Coleman, head of business affairs for Paramount. "Hey, we're doing your script," he said, and seemed quite happy about it.

Just the week before I'd talked to the new producer on the series, Herb Hirschman, and he'd told me the chances didn't look good. When he'd replaced Matt Rapf as head honcho on the series, new scripts had been assigned that were less youth-oriented, and that had seemed to ring the death knell for "Whimper." Mr. Hirschman advised me, however, that he'd liked the script a great deal, and had tried to get ABC to okay its production by substituting the drug element with "black magic" and a kind of a Manson shtick. Having learned long since one must camouflage one's more fiery opinions, I died a lot inside, but said I wasn't sure that would work, since the drug element of the script, while not starkly in the foreground, was a major motivator for the heroine. He agreed, but said it was a matter of getting ABC to say yes or forgetting the script. I must confess at that point I was at my second-lowest ebb (rock bottom was when I learned the script was killed in the first place) and would have been just as happy to see the words laid to rest, rather than to twist and cripple them merely to ease the befuddlement of network programmers who had lost the pulse of the audience.

Mr. Hirschman was obviously concerned, and was very decent to me in confessing quite frankly that, because the script seemed richer to him than some of the new ones commissioned, he wanted to save it, and while we might not be as happy with a revised version in which black magic or a hippie cult leader served as analogue for a drug-oriented amorality, it was the only game in town and if we wanted to stand even a chance of winning, we might have to play it ABC's way.

I thanked him and he said he'd keep me informed on ABC's decision.

I heard nothing further till Jack Guss, the story editor of the series, saw me at that same screening. He said there was still hope, that ABC had rejected the idea of black magic, but had not yet given the go-ahead on the original version.

So when I emerged from the Academy Award Theater, and Hank Coleman buttonholed me to tell me ABC had said do it the way it was written originally, I must confess my heart gave a leap inside me and I damn near hugged him. (Those of you who (a) recall that Mr. Coleman was not terribly happy with the length of time it'd taken me to write the script in the first place, (b) understand the protocol of Hollywood in which heads of business affairs are the men who haggle out the terms of contract with one's agent, and (c) know Mr. Coleman, will realize how taken aback he was, and how motivated by pure joy I was.) (In fact, Mr. Coleman's son, standing beside him, looked momentarily panicked as this strange longhair tried to embrace his father.)

I sang all the way home.

The following Monday I called Paramount and spoke to Jim McAdams, the associate on the series, and he confirmed that, yes, they were going ahead with it. The script was being put "up on the boards" for a shooting schedule, and it was planned for in-front-of-the-cameras in two sessions: January 6, 7, and 8, and 18, 19, and 20. There were problems, of course, because the script had been laid aside while changes had been made in the series.

There might have to be cameo insertions of the new WASP attorney the network had insisted be added to the cast. Since we had lost the shooting days in Boston (where the series is laid), I might have to rewrite several scenes to take advantage of standing sets on the Paramount lot. Other minor fixes.

But they seemed so minuscule compared to the fate ordained earlier, I reaffirmed my desire to come in at their behest and do whatever changing was deemed necessary—consistent with my nasty insistence on maintaining the purity of the work.

And so, friends out there in Knobtwiddlesville, despite my blithely scroogelike attitude toward Christmas, this year I *do do DO* believe in Santy Claus. He gave me a surprise present I never thought I could get. And because of this amazing metamorphosis, I give *you all* a Christmas present (a bit belatedly; sometime in February if all goes well). The best present and the truest present

I could give, since it lies outside my power to give you peace and universal kindness. I give you the best part of me, my words. Thrown up on your screens for whatever joy and enlightenment they may contain, assuring you they were set down with love and attention and truth as I know it.

More than that I don't think you have the right to expect from *any* mere scribbler of sentences.

And if I may be pardoned for saying so, "god bless us, every one!"

92: 8 JANUARY 71

It is probably not premature to advise you that these next ten weeks of columns will be my last. After two and a half years of doing "The Glass Teat," I've begun to suspect my usefulness as a critic of television and the cultural scene surrounding it may be coming to an end. I don't want to go into it here...now. I'll use my final column to look back and assess whatever small good these words may have done. Suffice it to say, for the moment, there are no external pressures involved in my decision. Those who know me at all well will understand it is the call of my gypsy blood that compels me to close out "The Glass Teat" ten weeks from now. I've had my say, at considerable length, and having so done, I'd like to move on to something else. I haven't decided just what as yet, but as soon as I get it figured out, and providing the editors and publisher of the *Free Press* and I can get together on some new forum for this writer, you might even find me wandering around here muttering about something else every week. We'll see.

The reason I bring this up now, instead of springing it on you ten weeks from now, is twofold. First, I don't want you faithful fans should go into instant withdrawal, fat chance. The second part is that the lessons I've learned in doing these columns never seem to cease, and again this week I learned one, and I didn't want to pass up the mention of this blessed serendipity, something that might get forgotten by the time I bid adieu.

The lesson I learned this week was provided by Mr. Richard Cavett, a man whose late-night talkathons have provided me with an inordinate amount of meaty viewing these last two years. (By now the Lester Maddox-Jim Brown-Truman Capote contretemps has gone down as video history and we can look forward to seeing it rerun every year like those ghastly replays of *The Robe*, save with the Cavett show there is a certain joy to be derived from watching Georgia's gubernatorial pinhead crucify himself before our disbelieving eyes.)

Mr. Cavett sat as *amicus curiae* to the gladiatorial combat between film critic John Simon and a frenetic will-o'-the-wisp named Erich Segal, author of a book called *Love Story* and a film of the same name. And in the thrust of literary trident, the slash of Thracian invective, I learned an important lesson:

Without critics we are doomed to die a strangulating death of mediocrity.

Let's talk about it. First, Mr. Segal and his magnum opus.

Had I not seen *Love Story* only a few days before Mr. Segal appeared on the Cavett show, I might well have gone for his okeydoke and believed he had, indeed, written the great Mass American Novel. But unfortunately for Mr. Segal, I sat through every moronic moment of his great work and, for the first time, I adored the usually serpentine Mr. Simon.

In the event you are one of the six or seven people in the civilized world who have neither read the thin little novel that has sold millions of copies in hardcover and paperback while holding top spot for almost a year on the best-seller charts, or helped break box-office records in every major American city since the movie version opened, I'll quickly recap the plot. It will detain neither of us very long.

Oliver goes to Harvard. Oliver is Ryan O'Neal. His girlfriend is Jenny. She has a smart mouth on her. Ali McGraw is Jenny. They get married. She comes down with a serious—but unnamed—malady and has only a few months to live. Finally, with upper lip stiffer than one's credulity has to be to buy all this, she dies, leaving her young husband bereft. That's it. That's the *entire* plot, what with a few minor omissions about his wealthy family and their snobbishness, and her father who runs a bakery. You know, local color. That sorta stuff.

Now the thing about this totteringly ancient plot that seems to grab folks (mostly the ladies, from what I can gather) is the incredible depth of love Oliver and Jenny have for one another, and the tragedy of her early demise. And I grant you, summarizing a full novel in as brief a space as above, even a classic novel, makes it sound pretty silly. Which I guess is unfair. (*Moby-Dick* is about this coo-coo chasing a big fish. *Huckleberry Finn* is about this hippy orphan kid and a nigger, running around the river. *For Whom the Bell Tolls* is about a guy who decides getting laid is more fun than blowing up bridges. *War and Peace* is about...but you get the idea.)

Only trouble is, *Love Story* deals with the realities of love and death in the same way Dick Tracy deals with law and order. It is a schlock novel of the rankest form. It is cheap, treacly, mawkish, true-confession level sentimentality, played for every jerked tear in the ducts. It is what some critics once called a "three Kleenex movie." The night I saw it, at a screening for the Writers Guild, it was all one could do to make out the simplistic dialogue over the sounds of sobbing in the theater. Strong men and liberated women wept unashamedly. A veritable Niagara of empathy. It was all I could do to keep myself from laughing out loud. Cindy and I sat there, covering our mouths so we wouldn't do a bummer on the destroyed sympathizers all around us. A snicker *did* pass my lips, however, when at the end of the film, as Miss McGraw lay dying (rather prettily, not even a bedsore; apparently Mr. Segal picked a disease that smites yet does not wither), she implores Mr. O'Neal to hold her. Not satisfied with this clichéd denouement, Mr. Segal went one better into heart tug as she insists he not just put his arm around her, but actually crawl up onto the bed beside her.

That *really* collapsed the audience. Not a dry eye in the house. Except Cindy's and mine. I snickered.

"You're really fucked!" someone hissed at me in the dark.

No, you don't. Not on your pocket hanky, you don't. I won't cop to *that* one. I refuse to bite on a characterization of myself as a stonehearted sonofabitch who can't give in to a little simple humanity in the face of genuine tragedy. Because *Love Story* isn't tragedy, it's bullshit. Pure and simple lard. Maybe chicken fat. *Death of a Salesman* is tragedy. When Linda looks down at Willy Loman's grave and says she finally paid off the mortgage that day, and they're free, I go to pieces. *A Child Is Waiting* is a tragedy. When Burt Lancaster takes Judy Garland to the state home where overage mongoloids and retards scratch their beard stubble and mutter like infants, I weep unashamedly. Kent State is tragedy. Almost a year later, when I look at the face of that coed, kneeling beside her fallen classmate, I feel my gut move as if a snake were squeezing my heart. *Paths of Glory* is tragedy. When the scapegoat soldiers are taken out to be shot, I scream with pain and loss and emotion.

But not *Love Story*, thank you. That isn't tragedy. It is sinking to the lowest possible level of the human condition to wring a few bogus, ersatz tears from people who could watch Catherine Genovese get knifed to death right in front of them, and wouldn't make a move.

I'm not bought that cheaply. And neither are my tears.

It is this descent to crude bottoms that deprives *Love Story* of any claim to the big-A "Art." And I don't give a damn *how many* claims to nobility Erich Segal makes for his stupid book and movie.

Because—and here's the point—debasing emotions like love and recognition of one's own mortality are the cheap tricks of panhandlers, flack merchants, con men, hypocrites, tasteless and talentless charlatans.

John Simon apparently recognized all of the foregoing, because he came into Cavett's arena and—very politely, but very firmly—let Mr. Segal know he saw through him. Now Simon has never been one of my favorite people; he isn't the most lovable man in the universe, nor do I think he cares to be. But he is an honest critic, a man of taste and considerable wit, and his standards of cinematic excellence are at once rational and lofty. So, despite my reservations about Simon the Man, when Simon the Critic was pilloried by the Roman Circus crowd attending Cavett's show, I learned my lesson about the need for criticism.

Segal played to the mob like Pilate, or maybe like Willie Stark. He continually vindicated himself (to their applause and huzzahs) by saying he hadn't set out to write Art, but had somehow—magically, wonderfully, ain't I a cockeyed wonder?—struck a clear bell tone of human compassion that reached billions and billions around the world. Simon chose not to deal him the obvious blow. Simon is a gentleman. I am not. Neither am I one of the "effete litterateurs" Mr. Segal said was the only group who'd denigrated his effort.

What Mr. Segal and his book/movie represent is the mob taste for simple solutions and handy categorizations. Neither of these speak to Art in any way. Mr. Simon stated the case for the big A. He said the sentiment was false and cheap and forced, and when Mr. Segal demanded he give examples of *truth* in that area (though Simon was under no obligation to do so), Simon rattled off half a dozen better examples, from Thomas Mann to Schnitzler. It made Mr. Segal sit back in his chair.

The studio audience, of course, booed Simon roundly. He could have been no more hated had he said Jesus Christ was a closet queen or Kate Smith fucks aardvarks. He was quite literally (and literarily) attacking a sacred cow. And the mob will not tolerate such heresies.

Simon played on, unperturbed. He knew where he was. He was championing permanence, value, honesty, utter craftsmanship, ennoblement of the spirit, and good writing. He was not about to be bullied by a lynch throng.

It was one of the finest moments I've ever seen on television, and it ranks John Simon forevermore in my mind in the forefront of courageous critics.

Perhaps it's only a vainglorious attempt on my part to validate my own criticisms, to say that we need, desperately need men like John Simon, who will point out the optings for debased matter over the striving for ennoblement. Perhaps I have little faith in the massmind, the common taste. But when I see Jacqueline Susann and Erich Segal holding sway at the pinnacle of the best-seller list, when I see Jackie Gleason and Andy Griffith refurbished or reissued while East Side, West Side and Slattery's People vanish into cancellation, when I see Lester

Maddox and Ronald Reagan deified while Adlai Stevenson and Eugene McCarthy go off with broken hearts, I am forced to the conclusion that people don't always know what's best for them. And while I would take up arms to prevent rule by an elite cabal, even as I take up arms to try and end the rule of the yahoos, it seems right and good that we have men like Simon, critics of taste, with a perspective across the centuries, who can raise their voices to say Sturgeon's Law is true:

Ninety percent of everything is mediocre: people, puddings, plays, politicians, tv, books. I've said that before...often.

Without men like Simon to say there is something more golden if only we'd reach for it, we would sink into the quagmire of banality, sentimentality, mediocrity that the 90 percent live in eternally. For some of us, the hatred of the monkeymass is tolerable, if only we can touch that gold occasionally.

93: 15 JANUARY 71

THE RED MAN'S BURDEN

Part One

Years of close observation of people have led me to the conclusion that bigotry, racial prejudice, and hatred stem from a lack of personal acquaintance. I wish I had a dime for every time I've heard a white man bumrap blacks, only to amend the derogatory remarks with, "The only one I've ever met who was any good is that George Washington Carver Rastus White who repairs my car. He's really a good mechanic and honest as the day is long." I'd even take a nickel for every time I've heard an anti-Semite say, "Kikes are cheap and money-grubbing, except for my friend Israel Solomon Fishbein who is a sweet guy. Why aren't there more like him?"

Every time one of us (considered a "minority") leads, through no nobler activity than being our own decent selves, some locked-in soul to a realization that individuals are shitty but entire races or religions are not, we've helped straighten the world's head just a smidgen. Which, of course, behooves us to be as good and nice as we can, all the time. If it goes on long enough, upcoming generations will hear bigoted remarks so seldom they'll simply be phased out. Lack of acquaintance was at the bottom of my ignorance about Indians.

Thus, for a kid brought up on Western movies in which the Injun was always a slavering, brutal barbarian, the only good one of which was a dead one, biting the dust, it was a joy and a blessing for me to meet Russell Bates.

Russ is a thirty-year-old Kiowa. He was one of my students at the Clarion (Pa.) College Workshop in science fiction and fantasy. He's a fine—and improving daily—writer who also happens to be massively proud of, and enormously well-informed about, his Amerind heritage. Because we are friends, Russ has written me on several occasions (from Anadarko, Oklahoma) about the treatment of Amerinds on television. Many of the points he raised, and the observations he made, were fresh and startling. I'd like to share them with you, not merely because examination of every facet of tv's inability to portray history or reality in a truthful way is necessary to our understanding of the video *modus operandi*, but because the more acquaintanceship we have, the quicker decreases our prejudice.

While I'll be taking credit for these columns about tv and the Red Man, please be advised all I'm doing is paraphrasing Russ Bates, without whose comments and research these articles would never have come to be.

Thank you, Thay-nay-Tone. (Which is what Russ's maternal grandmother named him in the Bureau of Indian Affairs Kiowa Hospital. It means "Bluejay Tailfeathers.")

Conceptually, Russ points out: "When Man was civilized, he watched his fire flickering at the mouth of his cave and used his emerging imagination to conjure up horrors out of the darkness just beyond the light. It brought him a long way. But now his fire that he watches is programmed on the backside of a glass screen and makes little demand of his imagination at all. How much further can he go now?"

Probably not much further, but it's fascinating to note where tv is *now*, in terms of portrayal of the Amerind...and how it got there.

One core conclusion is obvious: tv merely *inherited* its sometimes blatantly horrendous misrepresentations of Amerinds from the movies. Thousands of Saturday-afternoon quickies (on which Russ and you and I grew up) drummed wrong ideas and cliché stock images into the heads of the average filmgoer but, more important, into the heads of destined-to-be writers, directors, actors, and producers.

And this, not merely in terms of the Indian always being the bad guy and butchering psychotics like Custer always being the good guy, but at a deeper level in portraying the Amerind as always stoic and devoid of any human feelings; printing them as complete primitives (the highest accolade Hollywood could offer was that they were "noble savages"); categorizing them as ludicrous, oddly funny people who worshiped impossible spirits. Thus dismissible because they had utterly alien senses of value. In short, the God Is On Our Side syndrome, carried out with Judeo-Christian missionary zeal that vindicates even genocide.

On this point, as a cultural aside, Russ notes, "Their eventual defeat was the product of tribal orientation: by the time there were any alliances at all, it was too late. Couple that with new diseases, an aversion to getting involved (some Indians fled ahead of the encroaching Whites like game flees before a party of hunters), misplaced trust, outright lying and chicanery on the part of the Authorities, and the clever stroke of wiping out the bison (destroy the food supply, destroy the Indian), and the genocide almost worked."

Ironically enough, speaking to the above, the whites brought their children's diseases and Indians dropped like mayflies, but the Indian gave the whites tobacco and syphilis, so maybe there *is* some justice in the world. Or maybe those Red Man gods weren't as silly as we thought.

We'll talk more a little later on about the present state of life of the Amerind, but getting back to the hub of the discussion—

tv's responsibility in the matter and its awesome burden of guilt, both by commission and omission—movies, and therefore, subsequently, tv have presented little of the more involved aspects of the Amerindian history or struggles for survival.

Most flagrant, and the part of the crime that infuriates Amerinds most, is that Indians rarely play Indians. Even taking into account that Anthony Quinn or Katharine Ross or Howard Keel or Dewey Martin might draw more white filmgoers than a nameless Indian in the roles these actors have created, except for an occasional Chief Dan George, Eddie Little Sky, Jay Silverheels, or Iron Eyes Cody,* the casts are invariably made up of Mexicans or whites.

I have it on good authority that Indians do have their favorite movie and tv actors, and they aren't Elvis Presley, Victor Jory, Ricardo Montalban, H. M. Wynant, or Gilbert Roland. Having very little druthers, Amerinds will settle for a Robert Loggia or a Charles Bronson, either one a pretty good choice.

Excuses for this condition are summed up in the complaint that there is a shortage of authentic Indian actors, though Jay Silverheels was supposed to have started a school for same.

Nonetheless, Amerind militants (who, because of the very real psychological block passed on and on by succeeding generations of Amerinds forced to live with the reality of having been defeated and subjugated by whites, are really out after economic or political blood, no shuck, no jive) find themselves—when they can amass the power—in positions like Buffy Sainte-Marie when Universal signed her to work in a segment of *The Virginian* last season. Miss Sainte-Marie insisted she be allowed to rewrite the script to make it conform to reality...and that Indians play Indians. Whether or not her demands were met, the show was rather innocuous, another of those Indians'-conflict-with-the-white-man's-world stories, with little new to add or say, and, thus, all for almost nothing. Squished down in the mulch of standard tv expediency and a universal (also Universal) policy of offending as few people as possible, even when dealing with "hot" topics.

...*Then Came Bronson*, last season, did a fairly accurate and in some ways very interesting episode about a Kiowa (played by Robert Loggia) who is unsure about his place in the white man's world, who takes his pregnant wife out in the desert to wait for a spirit message telling him what to do. Later in the season, they did another Indian story. It was considerably less successful than the episode noted above, despite the presence of Eddie Little Sky and Miss Sainte-Marie again. However, there was a dramatization of a holy peyote ceremony (Navajo? Hopi? Zuñi?) at which a real peyote song was sung. On the other hand, there were many technical errors—such as holding the ceremony in an open tent, which would *never* happen—and the plot was virtually pointless. However, these shows rated praise from Amerinds for at least the *attempt* to deal realistically and contemporaneously with the Amerinds' condition today.

On the other hand, there was a *Bracken's World* that reduced to low slapstick comedy an encounter between Century Studios and its staff with some ersatz Apaches hired as "local color" in a Western epic. Reaction to this show by our Mr. Bates, himself a Kiowa, remember, is best set forth in his own words:

"Oh, gawd! (Who is not an Indian spirit: one *never* takes the name of an Indian god in vain, on pain of losing one's place in the Over-The-Clouds place.) I have never sat through an hour when I more wanted to get my bow and put an arrow through the eye of the NBC peacock! As if it weren't bad enough on simply dramatic grounds, or ethnic grounds, I found *personal* affront when an actress, found objectionable to the Indians because she's 'Anglo,' is defended by her stage mother, who protests her daughter is part Indian, some tribe that starts with a 'K.' I cringed because I knew the next line. 'Kiowa?' someone asks. (I don't know who, 'cause I was trying to crawl under my couch, shouting, 'No! No! No!') A *flaming* arrow for the scriptwriter. I came as close to cursing as I'm capable. (I follow one of the old ways in this respect: there were no swear words in any Indian language; there are a few now, but they are all transliterations of English usages.)"

And on that note of impending warpath, I'll end for this week. But Bluejay Tailfeathers and I will return next week for part 2.

94: 29 JANUARY 71

THE RED MAN'S BURDEN

Part Two

For a long moment let's consider not the dream condition of the American Indian as television sees it, but the reality of life for the Red Man in this cataclysmic latter half of the twentieth century.

The Amerind today finds his lot painful and bewildering. It is on the one hand compounded by a patronizing and paternalistic bureaucracy, and on the other by himself. The Bureau of Indian Affairs administers Amerinds closely and loosely at one and the same time. The majority of the children are sent to government schools far away from their homes. There they are told that they are Indians and that's *why* they're there. But they are denied anything Indian: they may not speak the languages of their tribes, yet they are allowed to entertain with the songs, the art, and the dances of their tribes.

Yet they may not do these things for themselves.

Proficiency with English is very poor among Amerinds. Perhaps this is why they are not allowed to speak their native languages in school. However, that they *did* learn their native tongues first enforces the limitation on whether they can or even *want* to learn English with any degree of fluency.

English thus becomes second and secondary to most Indians, consequently hindering their education and their abilities to compete in most fields.

In the cities they fail miserably and consistently. They become clannish and withdrawn, falling into alcoholism and cringing poverty. Most of them are taken there by the bureau without much regard for their experience or employment history. If they failmost do—then they are abandoned and more brought in.

And when an Amerind manages to break through, to get on the upward path to fulfillment, the bureau appropriations always run short, because the major programs of the BIA are designed to help the mass of Indians—hospitals, schools, land administration, loans, food programs, jobs—and so help for *individuals* more often than not runs thin.

All of the above would seem to be noble enterprises, and in concept they are. Yet every one of them makes Indians more dependent than independent.

And there the machinery breaks down, for the dependency either can't or won't be served. The schools have a low quality of teachers, since the salaries are usually less than the state average... the hospitals are woefully understaffed and dangerously low on drugs and supplies, frequently decrepit...and the loans, apparently, are there for those who can prove they didn't need to borrow in the first place.

As Russell Bates (my Amerind connection for these columns) puts it, "The Amerind's state is partly his own fault. There is the language barrier, of course, but other cultural barriers stand in his way. He finds it close to impossible to unite to help himself because everything comes back to tribal differences, some ages old. There is an unwillingness or inability to learn simple things, such as adapting to the concept of time."

True. Indians had no clocks in their culture, so they refuse to honor appointments or even job reporting times in quite a few instances.

The workings of the law and courts totally escape them. In this respect—instant identification—they are not unlike many of us born with skins of other colors.

They are far from thrifty, having been raised to share completely all that is theirs. Obviously, this puts them at a decided conceptual disadvantage in a thoroughly materialistic society like ours.

Temperance seems to escape most of them. They are given to hopelessness and inarticulate frustration at the slightest setback or affront, so the retreat is into alcohol for most, drugs for a very few. The brightest and ablest Indians are in the very same bars with the dull and inept, drinking themselves into escape.

And the racial hatred for the white man that is passed on from generation to generation makes many Amerinds incapable of dealing with white society with any degree of trust. They seem unable to forget—down on a cellular level where it goes beyond mere slogans—where Indians were interred, food was withheld or they were forced to adapt to ways of life completely alien to them (hunters into farmers, for example). The highlight of it all—discounting the loveliness of the Sand Creek Massacre as shown in *Soldier Blue*—was the delivery of government issue blankets infected with smallpox to people weakened by hunger, despair, and lack of natural resistance.

Hold it. I'm dredging up the past. It is, of course, almost impossible not to fall into that trap when dealing with our treatment of the people who, bottom line, *lived here first* (one wonders how Good Amurricans who are outraged at destruction of "property" but seem unmoved by destruction of "lives" would justify patriotically, my country right or wrong, this flagrant usurpation of rightful ownership). Nonetheless, it is a trap I must resist here.

The sign NO INDIANS OR DOGS ALLOWED may be down, but prejudice against Amerinds is still very much with us. Or as Lenny Bruce used to say, people *in* Minnesota are quick to point out there is no Negro prejudice in the state (because there are so few Negroes in Minnesota...but they kick the shit out of their Indians).

So we return to tv and the Amerind, having learned—I sincerely hope—a few things about the *reality* as opposed to the fantasy promulgated by the tube.

Generally, Indians on tv are played as fools or bad types, without human consideration. *The High Chaparral* is a consistent exception to that cavil, however. Its portrayal of Indians tries to be authentic, and while it is far from great, it is at least eminently fair, even when dealing in comedic terms, which is saying a great deal.

(And in North Carolina, Indian children are refused entrance to schools at gunpoint.)

(Anywhere in the nation where there are Indians in large numbers, a quick review of police arrest records will reveal countless Indian names and almost no white *or* black names.)

There are, remember them, the WWII series in which Indians as soldiers were always played as feelingless killers, always the ones who crept into the Nazi camps and slit the sentries' throats.

Yet against these and the almost fifty years of erroneous images purveyed by motion pictures can be held up such sometimes productions of beauty and accuracy as NET's *Trail of Tears*, starring Johnny Cash (one-eighth Cherokee) as John Ross (also one-eighth Cherokee), leader of the Indian death march to Oklahoma in the dead of winter.

A dramatized documentary, the show was hailed by Amerinds as biting, straightforward, and dead on with historical accuracy. I don't know what kind of audience numbers that show drew, but those of us who saw it could not possibly have ignored the onus our race must bear for that singularly inhumane, bestial, and bloody episode in American history.

As a choice for the part of Ross, Cash was ideal. He has, at times, been very active in some of the Indian movements, most notably the Tribal Indian Land Rights Association, which is among the most vocal and well-known.

Historically, the show had more straight truth than ten years of tv and films. Andrew Jackson, for instance, was portrayed exactly as he was: a bitter, half-paralyzed, dying old man who still regarded Indians as he had when he invaded Florida. The forked tongues of politicians and other bureaucrats, as they mouthed over the "Indian problem" in Alabama, was laid painfully on the line.

And the show ended not as tv drama ends, with a happy upbeat about the enduring nobility of Man and a little laugh at human foibles, but on a note of unrelieved despair, pointing out that even when the Indians did settle Oklahoma, that, too, finally, was no longer theirs.

Is it any wonder, then, that a regular Indian holiday in this country is June 25, the date of Custer's Last Stand? It sounds funny, but the Indians are deadly serious about it. In 1966, one Indian I know threw a big blowout for the ninetieth anniversary.

He was not alone. In countless locations across the U.S.A. the same thing was done. As Bluejay Tailfeathers says, "Watch out! 1976 will mark the hundreth anniversary!"

(Tv-wise, the ninetieth celebrations were covered by network news and all reports were played for the laugh. Again, the Indians were played for clowns by *Gya-dah bonh*: the vision seen from afar.)

(NOTE: *Ah-kah-sohm zape* is "The Glass Teat" in Kiowa.)

And finally, here is a list of things Indians find offensive about portrayals of themselves on tv...quite apart from the outstanding gripe that Indians seldom play Indians, as mentioned at length last week.

One: Indians were not ruled by hereditary chiefs. The right of chief was won by contest, the most able and capable man becoming chief. Very few shows do this correctly; the only one that pops to mind immediately, god help us, was a segment of *Superman*.

Two: Indians *did* walk ten paces in front of their wives, but only because they carried the weapons and the wife was safer from attack if she walked behind her husband.

Three: Most tribes were not patriarchal, but rather were ruled by both a men's and a women's council. Some, in fact, could not make any decisions without the consent of the women. Female Liberationists please note.

Four: Indians had no qualms about attacking at night.

Five: One film depicted some very definitive Kiowa tortures which were exquisitely painful. Wrong. The Kiowas never tortured *at all*.

Six: Scalp-hunting was not native to the Amerinds. They learned it from, get ready, white bounty hunters, who were paid per scalp they produced.

Generally, tv and movies depict Indians anachronistically or completely incorrectly in language and dress, or hodgepodge it, using bits and pieces of entirely different tribes, many of whom never met one another save on reservations decades later. You see Sioux trappings on Kiowas, Comanches, Caddoes, Apaches, Utes, Wichitas, Navajos, etc. The same goes for languages. (One fink feature, *Garden of Evil*—starring Gary Cooper, Richard

Widmark, and Susan Hayward—had Yaquis all nicely Mohawked and done up in Eastern forest Indian costumes, though the locale of the story was supposed to have been Arizona and Mexico.)

None of this should surprise us too much. I've received letters from nurses and med students telling me how inaccurate most medical series tend to be; the column on hot lines last year conveyed the fears of real-life hot-line people about what the *Matt Lincoln* series would do to their image; why should the Indians be exempt from the hurried and inaccurate procedures of television production? Tv producers and network execs tend to dismiss this sort of complaint as simply beneath their notice.

After all, they say, we have x hours of primetime to fill. We can't be bothered with trivialities.

Even as most middle-class whites can't be bothered with the constant shrill complaints of blacks or Chicanos or Amerinds. It is just an enormous pain in the ass, and an imposition on their time.

On the other hand, which is more of an imposition: going to the trouble to tell it (forgive the phrase) as it was and is, or getting a tomahawk in the head or a coup stick in the front yard?

Or, as Russell Bates would put it:

Gya-poy-dah.

Which means *Peace.*

Yeah. Sure.

95: 12 FEBRUARY 71

HOW I CAME TO LOVE PEGGY LIPTON

Part One

It occurs to me belatedly, just seven weeks away from this column's demise, that though I have imparted in the past three years the most intimate details of my private life (and though I know I'll get at least half the specifics in this wrong, it reminds me of Alexander Woollcott's [or Wolcott Gibbs's or H. L. Mencken's] review of a book about snails [or ants or tortoises or something] in which he said, "The author told me almost more than I cared to know about snails."), I have somehow failed to mention Ms. Eusona Parker. The remarkable, magical Eusona Parker.

Ms. Parker and I have been together for going on eight years, maybe going on nine, who's counting? Eusona is my housekeeper. I never make the mistake of saying, "Eusona has been with me..." or of calling her my maid. A guest of dubious quality, at a party I threw a while back, made the error of taking Ms. Parker for a "maid," and of asking her for a glass of something or other, and was frozen solid in her tracks by Eusona's sweetly poisonous suggestion that she just go off and find the drink herself, honey, "I'm a guest here myself." Uh-uh, Eusona is *nobody's* maid. She is my partner and I'd damned well better not forget it.

At the risk of doing one of those nice Jewish lady numbers about how much a part of the family is the Negro nanny, and how much she loves the children, just as if they were her own, I must state flatly that I love, respect, and admire Eusona Parker more than all but one of the deadbeats to whom I am related by blood. She has saved my sanity more than once, and the only time she ever deserted me was during my 45-day marriage quite a few years ago to the carnivorous plant who was briefly but disastrously my third wife. Eusona refused to enter the same house with that creature, which should have been an instant tip-off to me. But then, as the world knows, I ain't terribly bright sometimes.

Quite apart from keeping the slovenliness of my nature from suffocating me in dust and dirty laundry, Ms. Parker is my gazette. She reads everything—including periodicals like *National Review* and the *Free Press*, for which I have neither the time nor the stomach—and clips pertinent data For My Eyes Only. She also listens to the radio a lot. (In point of fact, for the first three years of our relationship, I thought Eusona was hard of hearing, because she went about her work with an earplug jammed into her head. It was only when it slipped out one day, and I heard the tinny tones of a Dodgers' ball game, that I realized she was hooked into a transistor radio, nestling in her apron pocket.)

Thus, because of the incredible amount of information she has laid on me, I find it amazing that only now should I reveal her to you as a pivotal member of my "staff." But because of *The Thunderbolt* that oversight has been corrected, thereby providing the one and only justification for that racist newspaper's existence in my world.

You see, Eusona brought me a copy of *The Thunderbolt* a couple of weeks ago, and in it I found the meat for this week's column. That her act of information-dissemination would result in a column, I'm sure Eusona had no doubt; but that the column would preamble with comments about her, she could not have suspected. Thereby, for the first time in eight or nine years, putting me one up on Eusona Parker. It is a heady feeling, and one I expect to last only until she reads this column and rearranges every damned thing in the kitchen so I can't locate colander or cookware, once again effectively putting me in my place.

Ah, but till then! Till then, I will tell you about *The Thunderbolt* and the wonders contained therein.

You see, *The Thunderbolt* is a "White Man's Paper" out of Savannah, Georgia. Its masthead proclaims it as The White Man's Viewpoint and further states the paper contains: *The News Suppressed by the Daily Press*. Now, since we all know the daily press suppresses the left position on most news happenings, I was all aflutter to encounter this additional underground proof that it also suppresses the right position. (Thereby, naturally, leaving no position at all, if we are to give in to our multifarious paranoias.)

I'll avoid listing all the exposés of Zionist conspiracies *The Thunderbolt* has unearthed—from a subversive attempt on the part of the Synagogue Council of America to get Jewish kids exempt from the draft on religious grounds, to a senses-shattering study of Israel's secret espionage network—on the grounds that I feel slighted: what I mean is, I'm a Jew, see, and if the universe is *really* being run (as *The Thunderbolt* assures us) by an International Kike-Zionist Jew-Commie Money Conspiracy, they

must be playing favorites, because nobody's let *me* in on the deal,
and I'm pissed off. I want *my* share!

So we'll move right on to the other deadly menace *The
Thunderbolt* perceives so clearly.

The niggers.

(A philosophical aside, first, however. If one is a supporter
of the views of *The Thunderbolt*, I guess it is rational to think of
everything in terms of black/Jew takeovers, just as it would be
rational, if one were a maggot, to conceive of the limits of the
world being the inside of a rancid garbage bucket.)

On page 5 of the issue at hand (issue #131, November 1970),
there is a wonderful scientific article pillorying public schools
for not teaching racial differences, and the article is supported
with visual documentation of the differences between darkies
and The White Man. Such lovelies as diagrams of the facial
angle of skulls, from which we learn that the angle of a gorilla's
skull is 60 degrees, a Negro's is 70 degrees and a Whiteman's
[sic] is 82 degrees. And the legend under these diagrams reports,
"Intelligence can be guaged [sic] by the percentage angle of the
frontal brain [sic]. In the Negro, the fore brain is restricted."

Well, sir!

To the right of this inescapable evidence of Negro inferiority
is the (clearly retouched) photo of an African native—tribe
not mentioned—wearing a short-sleeved pima cotton shirt,
undistinguished slacks rolled to mid-shin, and nothing else
(though there is a black line around the left wrist that looks
suspiciously like a watchband, thereby giving the lie to the bold
inference that this is an aborigine). The retouching seems to be
in the area of the bare feet, which look like fishtails. The legend
under the badly printed picture reads:

> A rare photo of one of the two-toed tribesmen.
> They can run like the wind.
> (Note archaic facial features, clothing was loaned
> for photo, animal skins are regularly worn.)

And on the same page there is an illustrated item about "sacral spots" on newborn children, attempting to prove that Negro babies and monkeys have such spots in common.

As you can see, this is a *tasty* little newssheet.

Logically, at this point, those of you who know I do my utmost to tie these columns in with what comes over the tube must be asking, "Where does tv come into it?" Well, it does, and I'll get to that in a moment, in plenty of good time, friends, but let me set the milieu for you just a trifle more solidly:

Page 7 is a letters page, and smack in the center of the five-column sheet is a letter with the headline: Race Survival at Stake, and it goes like so:

"As time rapidly passes the situation grows increasingly worse. This situation of interracial mixture! Does no one give a damn about the young and the poor!

"Our White working class is falling into a plague of miscegenation!

"Our youth is also in the same situation!

"The mixing is not so much as with Negroes as with Mongolians.

"There are 1,000,000 Asians and almost 9,000,000 colored Mexicans, several thousand other, plus new colored immigrants pouring into the U.S.

"They marry our youth, our poorer, middle classes and spread to the rich masses and masses of little brown ones come into being, but no one cares!

"This is legalized Genocide, it is death of Whites. It's extermination of the Goyim: according to the Protocols of the learned elders of Zion!

"Do something! Do something! This is more important than anything that's ever happened, we are being murdered!

"These mixed marriages must be prevented, there must be inexpensive literature, which will break the ideas of 'Equal' Social 'Dances,' immorality, expose the enemy working which are destroying us. These Jews, U.N., sick Liberals are our enemies.

"Do something, we are dying.

"C.W., Savannah, Georgia."

Apart from the illiterate punctuation and syntax (which I trust the sick liberal typesetters of the *Freep* have not corrected as all such enemies of the Whiteman persist in so doing), this is the healthiest item in *The Thunderbolt*. It is merely moronic and uninformed and cataclysmically paranoid.

(You won't *believe* the letter on page 6 headlined: 15 Yr. Old Pasadena Girl Tells of School Terror, in which a tenth-grade Blair High School girl who signs herself "Miss K.S." tells how "last year my seventeen year old brother was beaten by a mob of wild Niggers, when he did not give them money," or this heroic child's struggle against having her precious bodily fluids polluted by the physical education department that insisted she swim in the school pool where—echh!—*niggruhs* had swum. "I would never go into a swimming pool where there has been or are Niggers in it. I refused to take swimming for that reason. My mother phoned the Board of Education and stated as such. They could not understand such a thing as they said no one had ever refused to take swimming for that purpose. My mother told them she was proud that I was the first one to refuse, but she prayed I wouldn't be the last...The next day I was told by the head physical education teacher that *'the Niggers are the same as the Whites, and the skin was the only difference!'* I told her maybe they were as good as her, but they sure were not as good as I am!" It goes on like that for a full column, and the strongest wish I had after reading it was not that this idiot child's playmates whip her as soundly as her brother got whipped, but that her dear old mother should need a transfusion that could only be supplied with a black man's blood. After which I'd make a hegira to Pasadena to offer the sweet woman a bucket of chitlins. But...I grow vicious. Onward.)

How all this plugs into the nipple of the great glass teat is in two featured articles dealing with miscegenation and the Jew Conspiracy on television.

I offer these items here in an attempt to give a fully rounded view of tv as seen by not merely *my* sick liberal Jew conspirator enemy eyeballs, but by the sane and rational world of the Whiteman that lies out there between Ellay and N'yawk.

96: 19 FEBRUARY 71

HOW I CAME TO LOVE PEGGY LIPTON

Part Two

SYNOPSIS OF THE THRILLING PART ONE: Mortally wounded by the henchmen of the murderous Baron Von Strycker, our noble hero, Harlan the Good, managed to introduce his readers to his housekeeper, an amazing woman named Eusona Parker. Ms. Parker, a power behind the throne, then gave Ellison the magic talisman *The Thunderbolt*, a white racist newspaper out of Savannah, Georgia. Ellison, bleeding profusely from the death-bolt attack of the Baron, segued from a character sketch of Ms. Parker into an analysis of *The Thunderbolt* dealing chiefly with that rag's world-view of everything wrong in this country being the result of a Jewish-Liberal Money Conspiracy or a Nigger Takeover. Still not having tied it all in to tv, Ellison cited extensively from the newspaper, quoting paranoid racist letters and articles. His last words, bubbled out through bloody lips, were:

"I offer these items here in an attempt to give a fully rounded view of tv as seen by not merely *my* sick liberal Jew conspirator enemy eyeballs, but by the sane and rational world of the Whiteman that lies out there between Ellay and N'Yawk."

All of this, amazingly, without *once* mentioning Peggy Lipton! The question burning on everyone's lips is: What the hell is that moron Ellison up to *now*?

For the stunning answer to this and other unasked questions, not the least of which might be *Whatever Happened to Baby Leroy? or How Many Cases of Shelled Walnuts Were in the Hull of the*

Andrea Doria When It Sank? go on to the SENSES-SHATTERING
SECOND INSTALLMENT (ohgodohgodohgodohgod)!

Two outstanding articles of unbiased reportage from *The
Thunderbolt* rivet our video attention and justify this column.

Article the first, on page 1 of *TT*, concerns itself with the
refusal of the Federal Communications Commission—heretofore
a singularly weak-willed operation—to renew licenses for far-
right racist clergymen Dr. Carl McIntire (you remember him, the
fathead who tried to bring Premier Ky over from Vietnam to
propagandize at a monster rally in New York, till Nixon told
him to stop making waves and, frankly, to fuck off) and Dr. Bob
Jones of "Bob Jones University."

(Note carefully, fellow readers, how bigots confuse the issue
by taking their racist stands in the name of Patriotism.)

McIntire's WXUR underwent a nine-month series of hearings
and the examiner approved the application for renewal, despite
outraged cries of dozens of different organizations on the Left
and Right, reporting he had found "only isolated infractions" of
biased programming of right-wing and racist opinions; but he
was reversed (as *The Thunderbolt* puts it, in a snit of pique) "almost
overnight by the FCC who found Dr. McIntire in violation of the
'*fairness doctrine*' [*The Thunderbolt*'s outraged italics, not mine]
in not broadcasting both sides of the political issues discussed."

After divesting ourselves of huzzahs for this finally meaningful
stance by the FCC, consider the quote by *The Thunderbolt*, and
file it under the heading impartial reportage, Savannah Division:
"Your editors do not know of any cases in which leftist owned
radio and tv stations have granted equal time to Patriots to
answer all the slanted news, editorial comments and slanted
views they continuously spew forth."

Earlier in the article *TT* bleats, "While there has been this
wholesale purging of Rightists from the air waves, the left wing
has become more blatant in their [*sic*] use of this media [*sic*] to
spread poison against [I think they mean *on, sic* again] American
traditions and heritages. Even openly pro-communist stations
such as the '*Pacifica Network*' has [*sic*] not been subjected to any
similar threats to their licenses."

It goes on and on, of course, pleading the hideous fates that have befallen such Men of God as McIntire and Jones, a pair of latter-day Elmer Gantrys whose mixture of redneck Oral Roberts harangue and sump water bigotry has netted them millions in dollar contributions from weak-minded little old ladies and Minutemen mired down in the Great American Swampland. To quote further would only serve to boggle the mind more and make the gorge become more buoyant when one realizes that poor, ineffectual, gagged, and handcuffed Carl McIntire is the same chinless purveyor of prejudice who *bought* Canaveral, Florida—lock, stock, and Hilton—for something between $23 and $40 million. Somehow I cannot work up *The Thunderbolt's* outrage that this slimy imbecile has been denied at least one outlet for his verbal hysterics.

As for Dr. Bob Jones, "the renown [*sic*] Christian minister," the loss of two licenses last May 7 of stations he owned makes me love the FCC just a little more. (Jones was scuttled, incidentally, by two "Black militants in Mississippi, Aaron Henry and Rev. Robert L. T. Smith," who got Jones's WLBT-TV license canceled on appeal to the Supreme Court. And get *this* comment by TT, fellow left-wing Commiesymp conspirators: "Nixon's phony '*conservative*' appointee, Chief Justice Warren Burger headed the three judge panel hearing the appeal. Burger actually reprimanded the lower board which approved the license for '*placing the burden of proof on the citizens who accused the station of promoting segregation.*'"

All of which...and the point for us...shows that we on the Left (wait a minute, lemme look and see, is that where I am... oh yeah, I guess it is) are equally paranoid as nits like *TT* and McIntire and Miss K.S. when we insist that Patriots on the Left are being squelched by tv and the Establishment-run media. Obviously, for how can we doubt the sane, logical, and literate comment of TT; we are *all* being badly used? There is *no* truth at *all* coming out of Cronkite's mouth. Forcing the conclusion that not only is there no war in Vietnam, nor has there *ever* been one, but we have (or do not have) racism in America, we have (or do not have) peace demonstrations, we do (or do not) have riots on campuses, and we do (or do not) have trouble right here in River City.

It is enough to make a man go gibbering into the night.

The only thing that stops me is that out there in the night, chances are good, lie in wait the staff members (all two of them) of *The Thunderbolt*, draped in percale.

Article the second, finally, is the one that gave me the biggest chuckle, and also brought to fruition one of the secret lust-dreams of my pixie heart.

It's a piece on page 4 of *TT* headed: TV—Race Mixing Saturation, and it is decorated with an ABC-TV promo photo of The Mod Squad's Clarence Williams III with "white co-star." Apparently *TT* doesn't read Life magazine, because "white co-star" is Peggy Lipton, an extremely attractive lady whose face and form and words adorned Life a few weeks ago and who has, for several years, resided in that special lockbox of my cranium wherein reside Marta Toren, the young Elizabeth Taylor, Brenda Vaccaro, the late Inger Stevens, and a nameless redhead who once worked as a Jackie Gleason billboard girl...all ladies for whom I have decidedly unclean thoughts.

So here I am, on this American Airlines 747 condominium, cruising along at 37,000 on my way to New York and then a lecture gig up in Bethel, Maine (40 degrees below zero, you could die from it), about three weeks ago, and I'm busily typing part 2 of my Amerind column, and the stewardess eases up and says, "I'm sorry, Mr. Ellison, but your typing is disturbing a gentleman in first class." I was sitting way up front in the lounge so I could work, you dig? My response was unruffled and gentlemanly, as is my wont. "Fuck him," I said, smiling cherubically.

She goes away, see. Then a minute later comes this big shadow falling across my typing paper. I look up, knowing it is the behemoth from first class, come to jam me out through a Lucite port, and I'm getting ready to deliver either a stinging retort or a savate kick in the crotch, whichever time and space permit, when the shadow guffaws and says, "Harlan Ellison, for god's sake!"

And it is Herb Schlosser, head of new projects for NBC, now president of NBC, a man to whom I have sold a series which ended disastrously (but we won't go into that here), and we spend some time amicably rapping. He lets me type, I feel warmth for him, and a little later, taking a break, I go back to his seat to rap some more, and find him sitting talking to (gasp, wheeze, pant) Peggy Lipton.

See, it is all tying together, ain't it?

So I insinuate myself into Ms. Lipton's ethereal company via Herb's introduction of me as "the brilliant genius tv critic of the *Free Press*." Humble lad that I am, I nudge a clod of cow manure with my toe and blush at his absolutely on-target appraisal of me. (The cow manure, incidentally, was a leftover from when the 747 was the flagship of Latvian National Airways. Their slogan: "Your Cattle Car in the Sky.")

He happens to have a copy of The Glass Teat right there with him, and he gives it to Ms. Lipton. Thereby convincing me that no tv exec worth his salt travels without a copy of the book in his luggage, close at hand for quick bon mots and factual analyses of the Industry. Also, I had given it to him when he'd come up to stop me typing.

So Peggy—by this time we were on a first-name basis—leafed through it and found my several references to The Mod Squad and Aaron Spelling, its executive producer.

After I had the stewardess put a piece of underdone steak on my eye, I went back and tried to reestablish friendly relations. I recanted all I had said, and swore I would praise outrageously the series from then on. (As steady readers of this column know, I am not above selling my integrity and/or body for someone who looks like Peggy Lipton.)

Thinking she might enjoy seeing herself in a really worthwhile publicity outlet, as differentiated from Leftist Communist Jew-Controlled Miscegenated Publications like Life, I showed Peggy The Thunderbolt.

After the stewardess put an uncooked frankfurter on the other eye, I went back and we chuckled intimately over the article which said, in part:

"The television networks blossomed forth this season from their vast waste land with new integration propaganda shows.

More than ever before, the Blacks have been elevated to stardom with routines portraying them as cute, amiable and brilliant."

(Remember, Eusona, you ain't cute, amiable, or brilliant. And you're not a Star, either, so find that goddamn colander!)

"Strangely enough, the detective or crime shows do not have any programs showing the Blacks in their true role in society, committing 85% of all crimes of violence, looting, burning, rioting and otherwise warring against White society. In fact, the Negro is always the good guy or the hero. The Whiteman in such shows is bigoted, prejudiced and always at fault."

(Which, Eusona, we know to be clearly not the case. Take the editor of TT, for instance. A pussycat if ever there lived one. And for god's sake, Eusona, don't mention last Sunday's Bonanza in which Lou Gossett played a black heavy. It might shatter TT's conception of The Conspiracy.)

"ABC-TV leads the networks with seven regular integrated programs. NBC has 4 and CBS 1.... CBS's *Glen Campbell Show* Oct. 25, featured him singing a romantic duet with Negress Dionne Warwick called 'Wives and Lovers' after which they hugged and actually kissed!"

(Now listen, Eusona, when you get here next Wednesday, I don't want none of that hanky-panky with huggin' and kissin' me. I don't give a damn if you *do* like me, I got my heritage as a Whiteman to pertect. Forget the colander.)

"All three tv networks are dominated by Jews." (I knew we'd make it in there somehow, Eusona; you dig, you blacks are just iggerent dupes for us!) "The Jew David Sarnoff heads the giant of the industry, NBC. The Jew William Paley heads CBS and Leonard Goldenson runs ABC." (Don't tell that to Elton Rule, he's the Token Goy at ABC.) "To see who directs and produces the majority of the shows all one need do is read the credit listings at either the beginning or the end of the program. Most of the time you will find them loaded with Jewish names.

"This is indeed a saturation campaign to brainwash the American people into accepting the African savage as an equal— in spite of all the evidence of their behavior we witness on the street.

"Television is a menace which has tremendous influence. Their specialty is the instilling of a guilt complex within White people designed to lower our racial pride, thus preparing the way for mongrelization of the White race."

And suddenly, after I'd read all that, my sense of humor went out for a smoke.

It is no surprise to any of us that deranged minds much like those behind *The Thunderbolt* exist. Nor is it any shock that even in Pasadena there are fifteen-year-old kids who've already been touched by the hand of death; lovingly stroked by the hairy claws of their bigoted parents. None of this is fresh, or new, or startling. But we need to have it dumped like shit on us from time to time, so we can stop and look around and say, "My god, maybe tv isn't as bad as we think it is. If it gives creeps like these some bad moments, then it's all worth it, even dumb series like *Barefoot in the Park* and *Julia*."

And in conclusion, after this long slide through the swill from Savannah, please note two things:

First, that I didn't give an address for you to subscribe to this sheet. One reading, even here, is more than enough to get their message. Through countless reminders in *The Thunderbolt* to "renew your subscription," I get the feeling that lack of funds will kill these animals quicker than a thousand columns.

Second, that the more we support *All in the Family*, the brilliant new CBS series that laughs at bigots and shows them for the crippled buffoons they truly are, the more we support sanity and the demise of garbage-can liner like *The Thunderbolt*.

97: 5 MARCH 71

APOLOGIA: Not only is it distressing to learn that the very editors who publish this column don't read the copy very closely (or that they are fuddled enough to trust me without question), but it is doubly distressing when that sloppiness of scrutinization results in a harmful act—no matter *how* innocently perpetrated the act may have been.

What I'm referring to, of course, is my column of two weeks ago. After spending installments 95 and 96 of this column laying bare the twisted gut of *The Thunderbolt*, a white racist newspaper whose only redeeming value is in the gallows entertainment we can painfully draw from laughing at its blind stupidity and moronic bigotry, I ended the evisceration by stating quite clearly I was *purposely* not including the address or subscription information for the filth sheet. My reason was quite simply that *The Thunderbolt* was in financial trouble—all through its pages it begs for subscription renewals—and while the idly curious might get some moments of amusement from their vicious attacks on blacks and Jews and members of the Left, sending five dollars for a sub would permit them that much more life. I added that one reading of this "newspaper" was sufficient to get its repetitious message, and if anyone was in accord with its policies and pronouncements, or was sufficiently curious about other editions, there were some obvious ways to get a subscription. But *I* wasn't going to aid and abet. It may be an arbitrary decision on my part, but it is my column, and I have the feeling there's enough anguish and madness in the world without sending five bucks to help the monsters at *The Thunderbolt* keep poisoning the minds of dullards.

In any case, I said it very clearly. No subscription or mailing information.

When the column appeared, the editor of the *Freep* included the masthead of *The Thunderbolt* with its sub rates, and an address. Apart from being dismayed that the staff didn't read what I'd written, just on the general principle if your name appears as responsible for what's in the paper, you should read it to make sure the columnist isn't running amuck...inserting that masthead is, to my mind, a harmful act.

I've said why I think so.

Further, I take full responsibility for what I lay down in these columns, but I choose not to take the rap for something someone else did. (On top of all this many of you—if I am to judge from the letters—thought I'd suffered brain damage, seeing the pronouncement and the contradictory act on the same page.) I've registered in the strongest possible terms my unhappiness with what went down with the editor of the *Freep*, Brian Kirby, who happens to be a very good man, as well as a close friend. Brian assures me he read the column, but adds he didn't think it was as serious as I've indicated. Apparently he didn't read the column closely enough, for on reexamination I cannot see any way that final paragraph could have been misinterpreted. Brian contends I'm making unnecessary waves: that running the info was not a bad thing...that you have a right to *all* the data. Well, I don't want to pillory Brian, but I conceive of that as obfuscation, and I urge those of you who may have been entertained by my columns *not* to help finance race prejudice and bigotry by subscribing out of curiosity to that detestable publication. But then, in the final analysis, only those morbid few who slow down and gawk at freeway slaughters would be interested in any larger doses of *The Thunderbolt's* vileness and paranoia. Perhaps I shouldn't have worried in the first place. This has been an unpaid apology and explanation.

NOTE: Remember that script that ran here in five parts? It airs over ABC next Wednesday, the eleventh of March, at 10:00 p.m. Watch *The Young Lawyers* and we'll talk about it here next week.

98: 12 MARCH 71

THE GREAT RAPE:

Part One

I am a bitter and vengeful man this week. Yesterday, as you read this, *The Young Lawyers* aired what was left after evisceration of my script, "The Whimper of Whipped Dogs." Those of you who read it here in five installments, who may have compared the written version to what was seen on screen last night, will understand my mood.

I am bitter and angry and vengeful and sick at heart, not merely because something over which I labored with love and dedication for three months was murdered, but also because, for two and half years of this column, I have been a fool. I have written a series of one hundred small articles (this is the 98th) which said, at core, this is the single-most-important medium for education and information and quality entertainment ever devised by the febrile mind of Man, and we must *not* desert it; we must not abandon it to the unmerciful hands of businessmen and Philistines and cynics who conceive of an audience as being boobs; we must try to maintain *some* standards of responsibility to our people and Our Times; we must resist the impulse to flee in horror and leave the spoils to the Visigoths. Or as Ray Bradbury has said, "The gargoyles have taken over the Cathedral."

I have spent many months of the past two and a half years writing of what I've seen on the tube and what it seems to mean to people sitting before *their* tubes all over this nation. I've reported back in as faithfully as I knew how, and always, at the back of my temper, was a tone of cynical optimism. I always felt something could be done, if only we kept at it, if only we deluged them with letters and threats of nonpurchase of rectal suppositories.

As recently as two weeks ago, sitting in a meeting of members of the Writers Guild dedicated to change and uplift of our guild, I listened to good writers who were disillusioned and weary, who said there was no hope, that one who cared about his craft and the truth of his writing was doomed to failure in television, that there was no way to break through and gain even the smallest trace of control of creativity once the script was written and handed in.

No! I shouted. No, that's not true. *I* did it! By going further than most tv writers choose to go, by rewriting for nothing, by insisting no one touch the words but me, by walking the sets with the production staff, by actually sitting on the set and making myself available for changes of lines...*I*, the great Harlan

Ellison, the wondrous and committed Artist, the seeker of truth and beauty, the Complete Writer...*I* have been able to carry my heart's blood and my mind's wonder to full fruition. My *Young Lawyers* script will show you it *can* be done.

They looked at me, and I was so sincere, because I had been through it (even as you readers went through it with me for many weeks), that they could not laugh. They were not convinced, because they had been bludgeoned so often, but they were willing to wait and see.

Now I come before them...and I come before you...to tell you I was a fool. A silly, vain, self-important, ego-surfeited asshole who actually thought he could take on a snake without a head and slay it.

I saw my show last night. It sucks.

Not only is it bad by any recognizable yardstick of dramatic criticism, it is a script that has been watered down and emasculated and raped and pounded till it became the worst of all possible end-products: merely another bland example of video porridge. It says nothing. It avoids and skirts and shies away from any positive statement or examination of character.

I want to take it apart, piece by piece, as I would the worst piece of amateur writing in a workshop, and lay it out so you can compare the show to the script, and see why it is that after three years of refusing to write television, and finally being seduced into believing I could sneak one past, I once more swear to you I will not expend my efforts on the box. Not that anyone will give much of a damn, but if you conceive of me as a writer with even the tiniest talent, you will be able to extrapolate and understand why it is that men with far greater talents refuse to write for tv, why they have deserted the medium out of frustration and terror, and have left it to the hacks. Even taking my work at the lowest level of craft expertise, you can project how much more hideous it must be for the Chayefskys, the Roses, the Mosels...who no longer care to throw their meat on that ghastly chopping block.

To effect such a dissection, however, I must castigate men I worked with, some of them friends. I must place blame for lack of responsibility, lack of strength, and lack of talent where it seems to me relevant. Perhaps some of what I will say is incorrect and cruel, but I am a bitter, angry, and vengeful man this week. And they have taken my child and ripped off its limbs and sent back the basket case with the admonition it was done out of expediency, and I should love the multiple amputee all the same. I am not that noble. If my friends and those who might care to hire me again are offended and conceive of me as an ingrate, as a sour-grapes troublemaker, I urge them to go fuck themselves. I subscribe to Cosimo de' Medici's remark, "Nowhere are we commanded to forgive our friends."

But understand at the outset that these men and women are not the true culprits. Through weakness of spirit or spine, they merely shovel the bodies into the furnaces; the *oberstleutnants* and *Gruppenführers* are the time demons at studios like Paramount, at networks like ABC, and in homes like yours—who insist *we have no time, the show airs in six weeks, hurry hurry hurry, we want our hours filled even if it's with shit, we don't care if it's good as long as it's Wednesday!*

There are, too, the Great Thieves, the saurian studios— archaic relics of a time long dead—who steal millions off the top to keep their inept and overpriced plants open, who take money away from what could be put on the screen to feed the voracious maws of the greedy unions. Studios like Paramount that forbid off-the-lot location shooting, even if it's a block away, because it might cost a few dollars; that steal and steal and steal just to keep their executive offices wall-lined with fine paintings but deny the most basic set decoration or research or shooting time to what they finally sell the public. Studios like Paramount that have learned no lessons from the deaths of MGM, 20th, and their like. They are a cancer in the tv industry, and by limping along year after year with parsimonious budgeting of series, they keep the level of video viewing at the swamp level.

These, and the System itself, are the great killers. They force a stultifying alienation between writer and director, between director and producer, between all the various creative levels that should pull together as a unit to produce work of at least *some* quality. But the doors are shut to the writer after the script comes in, and the doors shut on the director when his real and vital presence is needed after shooting and initial assemblage of footage. A first cut by a director is usually insufficient but *that* is where the director is excluded. And the film is turned over to businessmen.

It is the System, the entire structure of employee/employer relationships in television, that keeps the creators apart. The directors are compelled to believe the writers are merely sketch artists, setting down a diagram from which the director must urge sense and order; the writer is made paranoiacally aware of how useless he is after he's written the words; the actors feel contempt for the writers or an even unhealthier awe; the producers look on the entire pack as children who are unaware of the great stakes for which everyone is playing. And the trade unions bleed every dollar out of the budget and seldom proffer more than the same featherbedding ineptitude and by-rote techniques that have helped sink the industry to a new low of economic depression. And then they have the audacity to bleat about runaway production, the slimy parasites!

This is the System within which my script was produced. I was a fool to think it could turn out any way but badly. Given the System, and given the men and women who rationalize working within it—not criminals, just pawns—it was doomed from the words FADE IN. And I was imbecilic to think I had a chance.

And here is what they did to it:

•The solarization techniques asked for in the "memory shots" would have cost dollars for opticals, so they were filmed as straight camera work, and thus lost all effectiveness in establishing Zalman King's memories of the girl he once loved. They now flash so quickly and impotently they bear all the emotional load of a Delsey Tissue scrim-&-gauze commercial of Young Innocents loping in slow motion through a fog-bedewed forest.

•Judy Pace's lines were cut to the bone with such brutality that once again she looks like a talentless stick, which is far from the case. If Ms. Pace doesn't sue Paramount for systematically making her look useless and tongue-tied through an entire season, then she must cop to being a masochist.

•More about Lee J. Cobb later, but because of his refusal to say *anything* of importance on camera, he cut the heart out of every scene of which he was a part. I'll give you two f'rinstances. In a conversation about women's lib, using King Kong as a comedic symbol of male chauvinism, in which Cobb is supposed to say, "Next you'll be saying Fay Wray was representative of Women's Liberation because she didn't wear a bra," he chose to leave off the last six words, thereby rendering the sentence meaningless and less funny than it was to start with. A few speeches later on, he caps the lighthearted badinage with this speech: "In point of fact, I submit that poor simian is a symbol of man's never-ending search for a little true love, a good woman...and a thirty-foot banana." Naturally, Cobb left off the banana remark. An actor with the pompous self-importance of a martinet. More of this man in a bit.

•Zalman King is a good friend, and I hurt to have to put him down in any way because truly, in a show where bright moments were few and far between, he was the only really outstanding element. But he is as guilty of muddling lines as the worst amateur. He had difficulty pronouncing the name Hallie, and so everyone had to call her *Hay*-ley. A small matter, you say. Well, perhaps. But let's move on.

•All conflict between Cobb and King was watered down through every scene in which the older man should be angry with Zal for going out on a limb for an obvious wrongo. It was an attempt to humanize a character that Cobb had made sterile and officious throughout the series. He succeeded in blunting the attempt once more.

•The scene in which Pat and Zal gather together his goods to hock them was rewritten by myself to feature Phillip Clark as Chris Blake. I had serious misgivings about Clark when I went into the rewrite, because he was a character added late in the season to bring a "white middle class" image to a show dominated by a black and a Jew. But he was the *only* actor in the show who gave my words a chance without rewriting them out of his mouth. For which my thanks, Mr. Clark, and my apologies. It's a shame that scene couldn't have been shown as it was rewritten. It would have given you some decent footage to lay on another producer. But they cut you into a third of what you were there, Mr. Clark, and I'm sorry, baby, but you wound up being the token WASP on the series.

•The censors got to the scene where Phil, Judy, and Zal have been waiting at the police station overnight. I wrote it with Judy lying on a bench covered by her coat, her feet in Zal's lap. God forbid a black woman should have her feet in a white boy's lap. They were all sitting up asleep in separate chairs. Another small item? Sure. But are they beginning to add up?

•The sequence in which Zal tells the cop to shut up bumrapping Hallie? It went. Everyone knows you don't talk back to a cop.

•Same scene. Zal is supposed to be looking down the corridor of the jail release area, straight at Hallie as she comes out, and not recognize her because she's been on speed for three years. Lousy direction had him looking at the cop, so the impact of Zal's line, "Where is she?" and the cop's response, "That's her, buddy," become pointless. He just wasn't looking in the right direction. Which makes it dandy when you're trying to hit a point about what heavy speeding does to someone you've known and loved, someone you've remembered as sweet and innocent.

That's by no means all the corruptions, and I've only taken you through act 1. Care to go on a little further?

•Act 2. The entire lead-in scene in which Hallie gives a phony address and is apprised of arraignment date was cut, thereby making Zal's locating of her later weirdly implausible. All through the script vital information was omitted, making many of Zal's acts seem inspired by spirit messages or a mutant sixth sense.

•I wrote the part of Hallie Benda specifically for Susan Strasberg, because I respect her talent and I thought she was physically perfect for the part. But again lousy direction screwed me. Miss Strasberg tends to rant. She tears her hair and thrashes about. By not holding her in check, the director, Jud Taylor, permitted her to give one of the most overblown, hysterical, and phony performances I've ever witnessed. It also took twice as long to get through what was intended originally as a low-key, touching, and subtle portrait of a girl gone psychotic from speed and lousy living. It is obvious from the authentic makeup that Hallie/Susan is *heavy* behind drugs, yet Zal (who is supposed to be a hip, with-it, Now Generation attorney working among students and the underprivileged) keeps asking her if she's on drugs. *Jeeeeez*us! The fault in this scene lies not with Miss Strasberg, who saw an opportunity to *emote*, but with Jud, who couldn't handle her.

•The scene in the diner. As it ends, Zal finds himself without enough money to pay for the coffee and pie. He has hocked everything to get Susan out of the slammer. He's eleven cents and a tip short. The waitress sees he's beaten and unhappy, and she says okay, bring it in next time. Zal looks at her, for this simple touch of humanity, and trying to say thank you, says "It was very good pie." A little touch. A moment. A beat. The editing sliced it out. And that brings us to the heart of what fucked this show. The editing. And I can't even blame Fred Baratta, the editor at Paramount, because he's a *good* editor. He did the first assemblage of footage, but it was first cut by Jud and the producer, Herbert Hirschman. And after Herb left, and Jud was gone, Jim McAdams, the associate producer, had to complete the work. But by that time it was too late. It was in tatters.

I'll tell you all about that next week, when I finish this death rattle.

There are four more columns before I vanish forever from the juju box, and they're pretty good columns, but for posterity, troops, this is my final statement of the torture chamber tv has become. So come back next week for the dying words of a broken man.

Your friend and mine, Ellison the Fool.

99: 19 MARCH 71

THE GREAT RAPE

Part Two

Where was I? Oh, yeah, that's right. How I got raped when my script for *The Young Lawyers* came to thalidomide fruition. It's been a helluvan interesting week since the first half of this column appeared. I think my rape has left me with a dose of economic clap. Bad vibes from all over the Industry. I'm not playing the game, friends. I'm not being a good little boy and maintaining the gentleman's agreement which requires I possess a nobility none of my assailants seem to display. Jud Taylor, the director of "The Whimper of Whipped Dogs," says I've betrayed confidences by talking about what went on during the shooting of the segment. No, that's wrong. I have very carefully spoken of nothing that went on down at Paramount that I promised not to mention when it was possible I might be writing up the encounter for TV Guide. But first of all, I didn't do the article for that magazine, and I never promised not to speak my piece here in this column: they were two different ball games. But I haven't, in any case. I try very hard to keep my promises and act ethically. But why all the secrecy, Jud? Why can't I mention what it's like to work with Paramount and Lee J. Cobb and you? Why the fear that someone will break the code of silence and forget to be polite and finally, once and for all, attack those who've fucked-over the Work? Because in the final analysis it isn't my injured feelings, or your justifiable anger at me for lashing out: it's the Work, man. The piece of what-might-have-been-art but is now only bullshit. And the Work speaks for itself. It speaks in the voices of (for instance) students at San Fernando Valley State College, where I spoke last Friday.

I was asked to come in to a couple of media classes and rap about what happened to the show. The students were given the script to read and were required to watch the show. I took a hand vote on reactions to the segment, and in the first class thirty-eight out of forty who'd seen it thought it stank on ice. In the second class, nine out of forty liked it. (A subsequent hand vote of how many who'd liked it had also liked *Love Story* raised the hands of four of the nine.)

I had to stand there for the two hours and listen to intelligent and perceptive kids rake me over for a disastrous show, and man, did I look stupid saying it wasn't all my fault.

But Jud (and others) expect me to remain silent. They have told me I'm a badmouth. Jud said I betrayed him by (a) not being on the set for the last three days of shooting and (b) speaking out my anger when I'd promised to be silent. Well, (a) is sheer flummery because—as Jud well knows—the show's shooting schedule was revamped, lapping over onto days when I had a lecture gig in Maine, a gig that had been set up for six months prior to the shooting. And (b) I'm still handling here: I haven't revealed any confidences I picked up on the set, even those revealed by ABC in a press release dated 22 February 71 headlined "YOUNG LAWYERS" SCRIPTER FIGHTS FOR HIS WRITES. I've very carefully stepped around those privileged communications in these columns. Jud, you can believe that or not. What I'll say in this concluding installment will only be comment on what showed up on the screen, compared with the script. And *that* is open news.

But I've digressed, to answer Jud. Because I can't conceive of him—as I said last week—as a villain. Jud is a victim, just like me. And so is Herb Hirschman, the producer. And so is Fred Baratta, the editor. And Jim McAdams, the associate producer; and Jack Guss, the story editor; and Susan Strasberg and Lee J. Cobb and Zalman King, who performed in the play. Victims all. Sure they are. There are no villains, gang.

Which reminds me of a story.

A parallel experience I had about five years ago when Eye, the now-defunct Hearst magazine, asked me to do a piece on *Star Trek*.

In discussions with the producer of the show, Gene Roddenberry, he mentioned—almost as an aside—that, when they'd first shot the pilot for *Star Trek*, someone at NBC had decided Mr. Spock (Leonard Nimoy) shouldn't have pointed ears or Mefisto eyebrows and there had been a struggle to keep those physical differences between an Earthman and a Vulcanian. When I pursued the item, I ran into a brick wall. Everyone at NBC here on the Coast denied any such thing. According to them—and this was at all levels of executive responsibility— that was an outright lie. According to them, *every*one had adored Spock's alienness from the outset. So I passed over that bit of minutiae and carried on my research for the piece.

But someone slipped up, and in a batch of publicity material I was sent to aid me in preparing the article, I found a brochure on the series that had been prepared by NBC for its local affiliates, and in *every* photo, including the clear close-up head shots of Nimoy, the ears and eyebrows had been airbrushed into normal *homo sapien* format. So I had a piece of concrete evidence that had slipped past, and I took it back to New York and laid it on the desk of the head of programming and said, "Now what do you say?"

He immediately got on the phone and started calling around through NBC's great tower, and could find *no one*, not one single living soul who would cop to the responsibility. I found it difficult to understand how the man in charge could know nothing about it, but even more incomprehensible was that nowhere down through all the layers of honchos who dabble their fingers in every aspect of a show was there anybody who'd had a hand in it. But perhaps, like seasoned veterans, they knew enough to stay out of the line of fire.

Finally, they got their Lieutenant Calley. They found some poor schlep of an artist in the graphics department who remembered having actually done the physical airbrushing. He was offered to me as a scapegoat, and when I insisted he must have had instructions from *some*where, everyone turned

Little Orphan Annie eyeballs on me. I think they fired the poor bastard. I don't really know.

But what it proved to me was that the Industry is a snake without a head. It knows not what it does. And the Work gets masticated in the chippers. And there are no villains.

Get the parallel?

Jud is not a villain, and I'm not a villain, and Zalman isn't a villain, and good, sweet, easy-to-work-with Lee J. Cobb is not a villain. I'm just a troublemaker.

Well, the trouble has finally materialized for me. I was up for a job at Paramount last week, and the producer in question was hot to have me work for him. Until Thursday when the paper came out. On Friday he called my agent and said let's forget it with Ellison. That's one.

On Sunday I finally got through to Jud and we talked. He said I betrayed him. That's two.

Zalman is pissed off that a friend could fault his performance. That's three.

Monday morning I received another of the many anonymous phone calls that brighten my days. "You won't be working much, you little bastard," my caller said. "What the hell makes you think you can get away with calling the unions crooks?" He sounded angry. Maybe a grip or a gaffer or a propman. Who knows? That's four.

My mother in Miami Beach *loved* the show. That's five.

I'm waiting to hear from Miss Strasberg and Mr. Cobb.

But to pick up where I left off last week, enumerating the evils of that silly segment...

We were into act 2 when I left off. The diner scene in which Susan Strasberg chewed the scenery to indicate depth of emotion.

I've had an argument with a young actress about this phase of my complaint. She is willing to accept that the producer, director, and everyone else connected with the show are monsters, but she contends Miss Strasberg was well within her thespic rights in thrashing and bellowing, because "that's the way she interpreted the character."

I want to kill when I hear that from an actor or actress. It is a catchall excuse for not understanding the character *as written*. The script was highly specific about the tone of Hallie's sickness. It *never* indicated raving lunacy. It was a quiet, out-of-phase spaciness I was after. And it fit the context of the show, the interrelations with Zal and everyone else in the script. Interpreting is one thing, completely altering is quite another. Actors and actresses, it seems to me, have been so preconditioned by the blunt and oversimplified characterizations that pass for acting on tv, that they almost instinctively go for the on-the-button reading. When one sees a Hal Holbrook or a Geraldine Page reach for a subsurface beauty of truthful characterization, it is to stun one. We see it so seldom, I no longer feel charitable enough to allow an actor to say, "I can't read that line." Bullshit! You're an actor, *find* a way, godammit!

And though I understand Miss Strasberg did research to get the character of Hallie down, I contend she went to every source save the one that might have helped her: the author. For by selecting an incorrect psychological ambiance, she altered Hallie from a quiet psychotic to a raving psychopath with manic-depressive overtones. And *that*, friends, was not the character written for that script.

The entire scene in which Cobb persuades Zalman to cry was dropped.

In the scene with Phil Clark, where Zal says he's let her go and will pick her up later for the arraignment, someone confused downers with speed. Though I don't use, readers, I *do* know the differences between barbiturates and amphetamines. Apparently the change was made sometime early on, and I never caught it. That's *my* error, and it is a serious one, because anyone who is into dope in any way, hearing that dilettante-doper mistake, would switch off the set with a grunt of anger. Bullshit! he'd say.

And he'd be right.

The scene with the sister, Grace, was so truncated that at the point where Zal reveals for the first time that her sister Hallie is using, and Grace has a heart clutch of anguish, the nonvillains who did the cutting decided it wasn't important. And so we see a total stranger tell this woman her sister is on speed, as a matter of course, and the sister doesn't even pause a beat in the mixing of her banana bread. It was illogical, and crippling to the scene.

I was trying to say that, frequently, those closest to someone hurting from drugs are totally unaware of the addiction. I thought it an important and relevant point. Deleted, it makes the sister seem imbecilic and heartless.

For the record, I found that entire scene slow and badly acted. Awkward and stagy.

The watch. You recall Zalman hocked his watch—among other things—to get up the bail money. In the show, Cobb suddenly has the watch and gives it back to Zal. In the script Zal is amazed Cobb has it and asks him where he got it. Cobb says (or was supposed to say), the kid you sold it to came in this morning looking for you, I bought it back, you owe me twenty bucks. Zal starts to leave, and Cobb stops him saying, "He was looking for you because you stiffed him. The watch doesn't run."

Another small touch omitted, and not in itself important to the show, but just one more touch of characterization dropped in the rush to make the show fit and squeeze into time limits. Which would be valid if they hadn't run short and been too lazy to edit properly, filling in those deletions with footage that mattered instead of taking the easy way out and filling up about four minutes with drive-through stock footage of the NLO bus.

In the macramé scene they managed to cast a girl with no discernible talent, who butchered every line she spoke. They also managed to cut all references to the landlord. We talked about that some weeks ago. They thought it was anti-Semitic, and though I advised them that millions of Catholics, trade unionists, gypsies, and Freemasons were also victims of Hitler's death camps—and even rewrote the scene specifically to avoid *any* Jewish references—they still cut it all. Thereby making the relationship between the girl and the attorney (Pat in the original version, Chris Blake in the revised version) invalid. Additionally, they went to great (?ha!) expense to get macramé equipment and extras who knew how to do the knot-tying, and then managed to delete any explanation of what they were up to. The scene was weak and semipointless. Phil Clark as Chris struggled mightily with the scene—even as Zal struggled with most of his—but the casting was so inept and the script had been butchered so thoroughly, it was hopeless.

Whole scenes establishing rapport between Cobb and Zalman were dropped. In other scenes Cobb deluded himself (and everyone else) into believing a look or a line would suffice for a full speech. More the fools they.

When Judy Pace and Zalman finally find a link to Hallie, a black kid named Obie Stover, the logic of the scene is blown when Hallie's boyfriend, Joe Bob, comes on the scene. I specifically gave clues that Joe Bob had a heavy Southern accent so that when he calls out to Obie, and Obie yells, "Get outta here! Narks!" we will know it's Joe Bob. Instead, the casting was so sloppy they couldn't get anyone in the city of Los Angeles with a Southern accent, and Obie had to yell out, "Joe Bob, get outta here, narks!" Is there one among you who thinks it logical that a dealer would yell out the name of a client in front of two suspected cops?

Then the chase. I wrote it for about thirty seconds, just enough to lapse over an act break. But by ham-handed cutting, they wound up with the chase all in one act, and it looked like a rerun of *The Immortal* or *The Mod Squad*. Up one alley and down another, around and around, over lumber and up ladders. Bullshit! They wasted precious minutes that could have been spent in deepening character, instead of throwing that archaic chase into the story. It was a sop to the outmoded thinking of studios that believe their audiences won't sit still if you don't have ACTION!

Finally, Zalman finds Hallie. And here the show really crumbles to dust. She is supposed to try and get away through a back window. Paramount was too chintzy to use a second set, and they have Zal and Judy suddenly running up a stairway and catching Hallie as she dashes for a window. That's bad enough, but additionally some asshole inserted a shot of an apartment bell with the name HALLIE BENDA in it. Now you tell me, friends, if you were on the dodge, would you have your name on the door?

And then we have the payoff scene in which Zal has to make the decision to send Hallie back to the slammer, for her own good. The scene was written for bittersweet memory and the moment of growing up, and quiet madness. Instead, Miss Strasberg opted for more rug-chewing. She thrashed and flailed and screamed and it came out like a 1940 Warner Bros. gangster film..."Duke!

Don't send me back, Duke! Please, Duke, I love you, Duke! We can go away, Duke! I'll do anything you want, Duke! I'll be your slave, Duke! Please, please, PLEEEEEEZE, DUKE!"

Bullshit!

I won't even go into specifics about the tag after the final act. That was where I wanted to say something meaningful about dope, about how we lie to kids when we tell them via billboards and slick paper ads and tv that there is a chemical answer to any problem from athlete's foot to napalming Vietnamese babies. It was very probably a sententious and pompous series of speeches I'd written for Cobb and King, but it was the point of the show, the reason I wrote the fucking mess. But Mr. Cobb apparently couldn't bring himself to take a solid position. He couldn't even speak speeches rewritten for him five times (according to the ABC press release). He could not let those words come out of his mouth. He had to ameliorate by saying, "Judge Knight and I have discussed this, and she thinks kids today can't handle responsibility, so they use drugs."

I'm not allowed to talk about Mr. Cobb any further than that, at risk of Jud's thinking me a betrayer; all I'll say is that my dreams of working with the man who created Willy Loman were hideously dashed.

As were my dreams that something warm and human could be slipped past the chippers. I was a fool, as I've said many times in these two columns. I'm not playing martyr, and I really don't like self-flagellation. But it now becomes so clear that for two and a half years writing these columns I've been deluded and wholly foolish. I've lied to you consistently, and there is no possible way you can forgive me for it, so I won't ask.

I have three more columns to write after this one, but let's face it, gang, they're anticlimax. This is where it all ends.

For Zalman I feel sympathy. He worked as hard as he could to make the series and this show swing. For Jim McAdams I feel pity. He is like a man bound and gagged and forced to watch his family burned to death before his eyes. For Jud Taylor I feel sadness. He has talent, and he'll never be able to demonstrate it on television. For Matthew Rapf I feel charity. He was beaten and broken by the network, the studio, and by Mr. Cobb.

For the gentleman at Paramount who got me blacklisted off that job, for Mr. Cobb, for the actors and actresses in the show who were bad, for the men who are responsible for the wretched editing of my show, and for all the thieves who stole the money that might have made the time to do the show properly...to all of you I wish the worst. I wish nameless and terrible dreammonsters that will haunt you till you die.

And when that great Trendex in the sky finally hands down the ratings, I hope to god that god and all His high-level executives cancel you in midseason.

Bad cess to the lot of you. For my part, you can take your tv and roll it tightly and insert it forcibly.

I wish I were a drinking man.

100: 26 MARCH 71

I want to talk about the *Man Trap* show, a syndicated talk/panel series filmed in the studios of CHAN-TV, Vancouver, British Columbia. I spent a weekend up there recently, put in a guest appearance (one of my rare p.a.'s), and had a helluva good time on the show, and thought you might like to share another of my weird experiences out in The Quivering Universe.

But before I get to Vancouver, I have to start with the earthquake.

Jesus, by now you must know what a circumlocutious bastard I am.

February 9 at 5:59 a.m. I was asleep in my bed as were most of you in Los Angeles. At 5:59:31 the earth gave a burp and my bed filled up with house guests, naked ladies, and my dog Ahbhu. When I tell my friends I was not frightened, they get furious with me. Apparently there is something infuriating about a man who doesn't share the universal terror at being helpless atop the trembling earth. But that is the truth. Sorry.

(In point of fact, the only danger I was in came from Ahbhu.

The goddamn animal leaped onto the bed and wrapped all four paws around my neck. I might well have been the only earthquake victim to die by animal strangulation, had not one of the naked ladies pried him off me.)

That was 6:00 a.m. At 2:30 p.m. I attended a preview screening of *The Andromeda Strain*, what I thought was a very good translation of the Michael Crichton novel. It concerns itself with a planetary debacle.

Later that night men returned from the moon, and when it got dark we had a total eclipse of the lunar orb.

All in all, it was a cosmically heavy day for me.

Made no lighter in weight by the appearance at that screening of Jack Margolis.

Some of you may have heard of Jack.

In a lifetime of action, danger, adventure, and acquaintance with blatantly freaky people, I assure you I have met none freakier than Jack Margolis.

Describing Jack is akin to falling down a rabbit hole and trying to give a play-by-play of the Caucus Race featuring the Duck, the Dodo, the Lory, and the Eaglet. He is enormously tall. (Not as tall as Michael Crichton, who is something like seven feet and has to stoop to come through doorways, but *tall*, nonetheless. Of course, when one is 5'5", *every*one looks tall.) His hair looks like one of those mad experiments by Lugosi out of a 1930 horror flick, where a lab full of Van de Graaff generators and bus bars has managed to accomplish the growing of hair on a basketball. Jack is very hairy.

Very hairy. Very sorry.

(That was a line out of *Kismet*, and has nothing to do with anything, but since I'm in the last five weeks of this column I feel little in the way of restitution can be demanded of me if I get somewhat Joycean.)

Jack is one of those people, for true or not, whom one feels has "underground connections." If you want hash, a bail bondsman, an abortionist, a nude model, a hit man, a smuggler, a Chinese hunchback dwarf, a system of ripping off Bell Tel, a hot car, a kangaroo with a broken tail, a cure for rinderpest, a fast loan, a mail drop for Judge Crater, a long-out-of-print bit of pornography, or a Corvette from the mothball fleet...Jack Margolis is the first man one calls. He has written books extolling the merits of grass and orgies, he has long conducted a radio program of wry witticisms and bad rock, he is a dabbler in films, a writer for *Laugh-In,* and a man with the single-most- reprehensible attitude toward women of any living human being, save possibly Mort Sahl.

I find it difficult to call Jack "my friend." I'm not sure Jack *has* any friends, only allies. Suffice it to say, we are not at the moment actively engaged in cutting each other's throat. Though this column may sharply alter the *status quo.*

Anyhow, Jack and I sat together during *The Andromeda Strain* screening, and (as a man who loathsomely gibbers throughout a film) he asked me, "Have you been up to Vancouver to do the *Man Trap* show?"

I shook my head no, watching Kate Reid go into an epileptic trance on the screen.

"It's a syndicated show Al Hamel worked up with Dick Clark Productions. They fly you up to Vancouver and put you up at the Bay Shore Inn and treat you like a king and then you do this half-hour show where they take a male guest and throw him in with three chicks with sharp teeth who attack his position on various subjects."

Aside from his reference to women as "chicks," a vestigial chauvinist effrontery used by many lads in show biz (including Mr. Hamel), the recitation caught my fancy. After the film I told Jack it sounded sensational, and he very graciously offered to call the associate producer, Hank Saroyan, to suggest me as a possible guest. Thereby making me feel like a shit for denigrating this fine, decent, and uplifted human being in any way.

I mean, how can you put down a man who invites you to a 200-person orgy?

The next day, I received a call from Mr. Saroyan, who quizzed me on my positions re women. After naming the 174 basic positions I take on women (six of which are unnatural), he said I sounded just peachykeen and if I'd send him a bio and photo he'd put the machinery in motion to get me to Vancouver, adding the show paid minimum—which is two hundred bucks—and I had to take care of my own food.

That struck me as a trifle odd. How much, I wondered, can a person eat in Vancouver over a weekend? The more I thought about it, the more ominous it seemed. Not for a moment did I consider his remark to be grounded in chintziness; if one can't believe in the essential honesty and wonderfulness of Dick Clark, for god's sake, whom can one believe in?

I filed the food remark away in the back of my mind. But I vowed to take along a thermos of water and a packet of sunflower seeds. Perhaps Saroyan was trying to warn me away from all that foreign food and water. Dysentery in Vancouver? My mind reeled.

Saroyan (who is, quite incidentally, a nephew of William Saroyan, may his name be spoken with joy forever) also noted that the lady panelists I'd be facing included suchlike as Nina Foch, Meredith MacRae, Margot Kidder and/or Suzanne Somers. Nina I knew, from a *Burke's Law* I'd written some years ago, in which she played a murderess. Miss Foch's credentials as an intellectual heavyweight were solid with me, and I assumed if the balance of the panel was on her level it would be a dynamite encounter.

On Saturday, February 20, I flew up to Vancouver on Non-Skeddo Airlines in the company of Bob Einstein—another *Laugh-In* writer whom you may remember as Officer Judy from the *Smothers Brothers Comedy Hour*.

He is deranged. I will say no more about Einstein, save that he is *not* a nephew to Albert.

A moment's digression (as if this were the first) about Vancouver, however.

It is unbelievably lovely. The city itself is a city like all cities, but from the window of my room at the Bay Shore Inn, I looked out across water as blue as a sacred scarab from a Pharaoh's tomb. Fishing boats moored like old men taking the sun. Great swooping gulls that dove to fold in atop masts and rode the wind currents to my balcony where they observed me with detached bemusement. Great stands of virgin timber rising straight up to snowy mountaintops where the sun catches the ice crystals in

Omar Khayyám's "noose of light" and sends it back shattering against the eyes. Clear. So clear you can see all the way up Queen Charlotte Strait to the Pacific, or so it seems. One can turn *just so* and see the world the way it was before concrete and neon and Styrofoam; and a gladness jumps up in the heart. Perhaps for this reason Vancouver seems a happy city. Random people on street corners smile for no discernible reason. A movie marquee proclaims LITTLE BIG MAN starring CHIEF DAN GEORGE with DUSTIN HOFFMAN, and one understands small prides. The candy bars are nastier than American brands, but the wrappers are more polite. Dining is more leisurely than in Los Angeles. It might be possible to go to Vancouver for a long while and write good books there. The air, dear god, the sharp minty bright air!

A girl with her hair in braids and her body hidden inside a parka came down off one of those mountains, through the trees, and brought back the smell of the innocent earth, and she brought it into one of the rooms of the Bay Shore Inn, and smiled at me, and I gave her a glass of cola, and later that night we went to dinner.

Vancouver was a splendid place to be that weekend.

The next day I was taken out to the suburb of Burnaby to film *Man Trap*.

I am of a certain ambivalence about the concept of the show. It seems, at moments, to be merely a distaff-oriented *Joe Pyne Show* (may his name be spoken with distaste forever). The concept—pushed *hard* by the production personnel—is that a "good" show can only emerge from a vitriolic and bitchy confrontation between a male and females. To this end much of the a priori information fed the lady panelists is mock-up hype, misinterpreted by Mr. Saroyan and the show's producer, Bill Lee. I'll give you a f'rinstance:

Over the phone, and in an office interview, I made it abundantly clear that I *like* women, I like what they are and the way they think...most of the time. I am flat out in favor of Women's Liberation and what it's trying to do for *all* women, even those who choose to be galley slaves. A point of contention that might spark some discussion, I'd said, was my feeling that in the area of The War, women were hypocritical. That, apart from gold star mothers—those ghouls who send their sons out with the admonition to come back *with* their shields or dead *on* them—who then receive their children back in plastic bags and proudly hang that hideous gold star in their living-room windows, feeling perhaps they have struck an equitable trade—that aside from such Martha Mitchell monsters, women are the only group that has an effective weapon to stop The War...and *all* wars.

Lysistrata is the answer, of course.

For ten thousand years men have waged wars. Obviously we are either unwilling or incapable of putting an end to the filthy habit. We are helpless, and women are not. If they said, simply, "If you want to fight, you don't get to fuck," war would cease in fifteen minutes. Withholding their "favors" would be the most effective deterrent to war since the invention of gunpowder.

(Don't point out to me this is implausible. I know it. I am postulating a nobility on the part of *all* women that all *men* do not possess. Nonetheless, I am a Utopian and I like to let such wild schemes scamper through my head. I was expecting the ladies to point it out on the show, and thence would have begun the discussion.)

This mildly interesting conversational gambit was warped and brutalized into a cue card that said (I'm remembering, not quoting verbatim), "Mr. Ellison has some gripes against women. He thinks they're hypocrites and responsible for most of what's wrong with the world today, including the war in Southeast Asia."

Well, we got it straightened out rather quickly on camera, when Mr. Hamel—who emcees the show—laid that phrase on the audience and I said, "That isn't what I said, man; why are you making up all that nonsense?" And we were off to the races.

The ladies I faced were Meredith MacRae, Margot Kidder, and Suzanne Somers. Ms. MacRae you may remember from the later years of *Petticoat Junction* and an episode of *The Interns* about a week ago. She is married, bright, intelligent, amiable and has just that acceptable touch of show biziness that allows her to subscribe to the "good show" theory without allowing her ethics to be subverted. In short, she won't go for the show's okeydoke if she doesn't believe it.

Ms. Somers is an actress who has spent some years allowing her face and body to merchandise any number of products via paid commercials. This, in itself, is not enough to shove her into prison, though it has left its mark on her. Quite extraordinarily attractive, Ms. Somers has done many tv shows and has appeared in a slew of movies including *Daddy's Gone A-Hunting, Zabriskie Point, The Strawberry Statement,* and *Take the Money and Run.* But she will be best remembered as the motorcycle groupie in *Little Fauss and Big Halsy,* which oddly enough I'd seen the night before I went to Vancouver. In the film, virtually all one could remember of Ms. Somers was the magnificence of her bust, displayed to enormous (I think that's the proper term) advantage. Which is rather sad, because on reflection I realized she had brought a touching sensitivity to the part. When I met her in Vancouver, I could not remember what part she'd played in the film, for this reason, and Ms. Somers was a trifle cool in response to my bumbling but genuine attempts to place her in context. When I finally got past the memory of sexuality the screen image had proffered, and recognized her, she seemed to be willing to accept me into her world. I was enormously grateful for that, of course.

The third lady, Ms. Margot Kidder, is a Canadian actress of rare personal qualities. Twenty-two years old, driven to prepare herself as an actress since she was very young, Ms. Kidder had whizzed through a dozen schools all over Canada and has come out the other side as an exemplary human being. (You may remember her as the prostitute in *Gaily, Gaily.*) Her head is on very straight indeed; she seems content at passionately indulging a deep love affair with common sense and good taste; and her responses on the show were informed, committed, utterly rational, if just the slightest bit unnerving for their honesty. Her alternative suggestion to my *Lysistrata* theory was that committed women of beauty seduce David Eisenhower and his ilk, and once having hooked him, cut them off till they had promised to end the war.

(Ms. MacRae agreed that was a good idea, and I said I thought it was dynamite except that, if all the really beautiful and sharp women were busy screwing hawks and schleps, guys like me, already on the side of the angels, wouldn't get any. Ms. MacRae smiled and said, "We'd fuck you because we liked you." So I subscribed on the spot.)

The show went swimmingly, and the half hour was filmed without event. I think it was a provocative and funny show, but once more I'm brought back to my ambivalence, mentioned earlier.

Here is a show that is genuinely fascinating, yet it is based on what seems to me an essentially unhealthy premise. I was asked, on camera, what I thought of the show. That was a mistake. I told them.

And they naturally attacked my position: that I thought such shows gratuitously widened the artificial gulf between men and women, a situation already unconscionable in our society.

All of which brings me to some considerations of the morality and ethic that underlie the preponderance of shows devised for television. *Man Trap* is a successful show, albeit a new one (they've only been filming for three months as I write this); it runs on CTV, the largest Canadian network; it is syndicated in fifty-five American markets (and for reasons quite apart from ego I wish to god they'd get it in Los Angeles so you could see what I'm talking about here); it was devised by Al Hamel and Bill Lee and Dick Clark, who seem to be relatively decent human beings. (I say "relatively" because in a species that can produce Aquinas and Lieutenant Calley, *everything* is relative).

The show employs the services of literate, witty, and obviously intelligent women; it is produced with enormous expertise; and the format is attractively original.

Yet it is grounded in a basically ignoble premise.

Like so many other shows that dominate in popularity our screens these days. Consider:

Hee Haw glorifies rural chauvinism and bumpkinism; *Mission: Impossible* contends any sort of act may be condoned by "secret groups" in the name of law and order; *Hogan's Heroes* says Nazi prison camps are, at core, humorous places to spend a vacation; *The FBI*, particularly repellent in the light of current outcries for investigation of the department, promulgates a wholly romanticized image of government policing of the society; Bonanza continues to deal with the family unit in a time of that institution's decay and dissolution in terms of violence and unreality; *Mayberry RFD* lies to the Middle American by telling him 1901 Kansas City still exists, thereby making what he sees around him every day more confusing and terrifying; *The Mod Squad* says narks and snitching are essentially noble people and activities; *The Beverly Hillbillies* glorifies bad taste, stupidity, the merits of being *nouveau riche*, and adds that just plain folks have it all over them eggheads; *The Smith Family* takes the position that being a cop does nothing but make gentle the man involved daily with brutality and crime...

It is possible to go on and on, but the point seems made. And of course there are glowing exceptions: *The Senator, All in the Family* (about which a column to come), *The Great American Dream Machine, Sixty Minutes, First Tuesday, The Name of the Game* in recent months, *The Andy Williams Show* and a few others.

But these are observations one seldom makes when merely plonked down before the juju box. Caught up in the colorful images, the spark of noise and action, the utter banality of most series...one fails to grasp these underlying concepts that twist and wrench us away from an understanding of the world around us, that pervert our judgments and deaden our sensitivities.

Man Trap is another. It manages through the skill and expertise of Bill Lee and his staff, and the ladies of the panel, to surmount on occasion the smarmy bottom line of its *raison d'être*.

And one is compelled—even while enjoying oneself as thoroughly as I did on the show—to ask oneself why it is necessary to have a "good show" as Joe Pyne always did, at the expense of truth, forthrightness, honest evaluation, and sensitive discussion. Are we such a debased nation that we *must* have our bread and circuses and cannot sit still for honest human beings sensibly sifting through the problems of our times for answers?

To say these shows are merely "entertainment" is no answer at all. *Nothing* is merely entertainment, for if we accept as rationale for muddied ethics and morality that we are putting on a "good show" for the monkeys out there, then we must, by extension, subscribe to the idea that the thirty-eight people who watched Catherine Genovese get knifed to death in a New York street were fulfilling their roles merely by being "entertained."

And I shudder to think we have sunk to that level of spectator sportism.

101: 11 MAY 72

Lies I could tell, in profusion, pursuant to the demise (after two and a half years' weekly appearance in the Los Angeles *Free Press*) and rebirth of this column here, in *Rolling Stone*, with installment #101 would you believe. How I discovered from the lips of a dying Portuguese fisherman that Amelia Earhart is living in *ménage à trois* sin with Judge Crater and Algernon Blackwood in the Mato Grosso, and how I went chasing the exclusive. How I was beaten senseless by a pair of six-foot-and-taller professionals in Benedict Canyon and had to take a polygraph test at the West LA police station just to get the city attorney to file, and I'm well enough now, thank you. How I went down to Shreveport to deliver a college lecture and this incredibly carnal eighteen-year-old lady sorta kinda stuck to my coattail and I've been, er, uh, busy for a while. How I lead guided tours through the heart of Mount Vesuvius to earn enough bread to support my paperback book habit, rather than letting them slice off my balls with a cheese grater writing for television. But the simple truth is that I got tired of writing "The Glass Teat" for the *Freep* and spent the last six or eight months with the tube turned off, not to mention my brain. Yet *Rolling Stone* editors apparently know no fear, and Ms. Judy Sims (she of the maddening body and the nonexistent expense account) breached my defenses with lures of kinkiness and money, and here we all are again.

For an initial outing, try this:

Back in November my agent called and said, "ABC has given the go-ahead to Stan Shpetner on an ESP series he's producing at Universal. Cattle call at three o'clock today, screening room two." What it is, friends, a cattle call, is when they have maybe thirteen assignments for scriptwriting open on a series, and they invite 109 writers to come in and fight for them. It's illegal, according to the terms of the Writers Guild of America minimum basic agreement, but here we are in Year Five of the LBJ-Milhous Equal Opportunity Poverty Program, and even the Writers Guild averts its eyes.

So, in company with other stellar tv scenarists like John Bloch, George Kirgo, Larry Brody, and Bill Kozlenko, I hied me hence to Universal's red velvet ghetto viewing room, where I saw a film for tv shown on ABC last season, *Sweet, Sweet Rachel*, not the finest length of footage I've ever encountered, but at least an attempt to get ESP and psychic phenomena on the air.

After the screening, we hiked over to the Black Monolith in the Valley, the Universal Tower, to see the producer, Stan Shpetner. (Aside: in *2001*, Kubrick brought these apes to the monolith, see, and when they put their hands on it, why it upped their intelligence. I wonder if one brought a group of tv producers to the Universal monolith, and put their hands on it, if it would *lower* their intelligence. Just a thought.)

Mr. Shpetner proceeded to inform us that the proposed series, based on the film we'd seen, was to be called *The Sixth Sense*, and he introduced us to Tony Lawrence, who had created the series format. Mr. Lawrence, who had been working with Mr. Shpetner for some time, looked like a man who has been repeatedly stunned with ballpeen hammers. In the charade that followed, Mr. Lawrence turned out to be a charming and talented human being, the only one of that insidious network-toadying crowd (save for associate producer Bob O'Neill) entitled to wear a white ten-gallon.

The "briefing" by Shpetner was so inarticulate, and so demeaning, that half the writers walked out on it. There are some things even tv writers won't sit through for money. One of Mr. Shpetner's hooks to understanding the series (as he saw it) was that this was to be "Perry Mason with telepathy." The flesh did crawl.

I left the meeting utterly infuriated. Here was the first time anyone'd gotten even *this* close to doing ESP and allied subjects on television, and the honcho in charge didn't even understand what he was about! I went upstairs in the Tower to see a friend, and stomped around her office flailing my arms and trying to kick out the big smoke-glass window. (Aside: there is a legend around the Tower that Lew Wasserman, upon seeing The Windows, feared disconsolate writers forced to work on *McHale's Navy* or suchlike might try to hurl themselves to peaceful oblivion. So they called in Bruce Lee, the master of the Oriental martial arts—he played Kato on the *Green Hornet* series among other credits, and is known to the informed as the single deadliest man in the civilized world—and he took a run, and gave it a *savate* kick that shook the room, but the window didn't break, it just trembled like Jello-O. I mention this only to let you know that the impression of breathing open space one gets in a Universal office is mythical. In actuality, the offices are made up of removable walls that slide in and out on tracks, and it has come to pass that executives whose series haven't been renewed, have returned from lunch at the Universal commissary to find not merely the name changed on the door, but the door, the walls, and everything inside gone. It is 1984 come early. You can be erased at Universal, and every smallest evidence of your having been there, within moments. Also, the switchboard girls suddenly start saying, "There is no Mr. Whoever working on the lot at present.")

Finally, anyhow, I called Shpetner's office and said, "Listen, I have to talk to you. Now." He replied, "I'm having a meeting, I haven't time now." "Listen," I bellowed, "either you listen to sixty seconds of what I've got to say about what you don't know about your own goddam series, or I come down there and tell it doing an adagio on your desk."

So he listened. And when I got done, he said, "Hmmm. That's interesting. Why don't you come down and tell it to me again with these fellahs I'm talking to." So I went down, and there was Shpetner with his feet up on the desk, and he told these people, "Harlan had some very enlightening things to say about the series. Tell 'em what you said, Harlan, since they tie right in with what I was thinking."

And that was how I came to join the ranks of the Enemy for the first time in eleven years as a tv writer. I was hired on at a staggering sum of money weekly, to be "story editor" of that Saturday-night abomination in the eyes of God and/or Man, *The Sixth Sense*.

I spent seven weeks in a death cell at Universal, and if you are all good little boys and girls, and if the maggots don't get into the marmalade so the dog gets the flashes when he sneaks into the jar, Uncle Wiggily will tell you all about how horrendous a steady job in tv can be before one flees shrieking in terror from $1250 a week.

And more! In weeks to come, this column will bring you such tender morsels of criticism and comment as the inside story on how Preview House rips off the networks, the audience, the pollsters, and everyone else in sight ...an interview with lunatic Phil Mishkin, who writes *All in the Family*, and smokes dope so he can live in a world where the scuttlefish out in the Great American Heartland think Archie Bunker is a hero...my annual two-part review of the new season's mélange of brain-damaged offerings...idle chatter about what you're viewing *really* means and how it pollutes your precious bodily fluids...and just a lot of other good stuff. Be the first in your neighborhood.

All I can guarantee about "The Glass Teat" is what I guaranteed when it was a *Freep* feature: there will be no editorial censorship, my ethic and honesty will never be allowed to interfere with my getting a script assignment, some bitter pills will be offered along with a gallows chuckle or two. And I'm receptive to your desires about subject matter. More than that you don't deserve.

When you get pissed off, by all means write. When you're delighted, let the editor know.

Nice to see you again.

102: 25 MAY 72

Better the devil we know than the devil we don't know. That's what the Delphic doom-criers of the television Mad Caucus Race are saying. Around and around they scamper, the Dodos, Eaglets, Lories, and Mouses of ABC, CBS, and NBC—drenched by the downpour of Department of Justice antitrust suits threatening to shrink their corporate profits with the compassion of a Jívaro headhunter. It's all the talk this week in the Industry, and it's the springboard for us this installment, allowing us to bound into a review of network practices *passim* the financing, shooting, selecting, and programming of pilots, not to mention a review of the funniest half hour to flit across the little-screen in many a year, and why it'll never get on the air as a series. Oh, yes, gentle readers: death and destruction this week, as the specter of government intervention and retribution terrifies the grand old men on the network mountaintops.

The way the plot goes is like so:

On April 13 the antitrust division of the Department of Justice announced it would file suits against the three major networks and Viacom International, Inc. (a spin-off entertainment-supplying conduit of CBS), under sections 1 and 2 of the Sherman Antitrust Act alleging "that the companies have monopolized and restrained trade in primetime television entertainment programs." In effect, if successful, what a decision in the U.S. District Court in Los Angeles favoring the Justice Department would do would be to wrest control of network schedules from ABC, NBC, and CBS, and to take out of their muddy little paws decisions on what programs are put on the air, as well as *when* they go on the air. It would turn back control of these elements to advertising agencies and motion-picture producers, and would prevent the networks from producing any television entertainment or feature films. The suits exclude news programs and—as I read it, though I could be wrong—documentaries.

Now understand this: twenty years ago, advertising agencies pretty much controlled what shows were bought and aired. To a not inconsiderable degree, they still do. (General Mills, Post, Kellogg's, and Ralston-Purina to this day dominate what kind of programming is done for kids. *Bonanza*, sponsored in the main by Chevrolet, has never mentioned President Lincoln, though the series is set during the time of his Administration. A story outline proposed by writer Bob White for the *Cannon* series, dealing with the manner in which millions of dollars of legally overproduced amphetamines are skimmed off government-certified companies and find their way into the street dealerships, was killed on the grounds that "drug companies are heavy advertisers.")

So I'm not terribly overjoyed at the prospect of the Madison/Lexington Avenue gunslingers sliding back into the catbird seat, with all the attendant horrors of that kind of venality. (Stories are legend in the industry of shows being killed because the wife or paramour or grandma of some ad exec said she didn't like the pilot. I once had a script over which everyone at Universal was vastly enthused killed on the spot by an account executive because it dealt with a guy who lived with his mother in a Southern town, and this poor sot came from Decatur, Georgia, and still lived with his *maman*, and he was going through shit changes about it.)

Nonetheless, taken hour for hour, matching what went on the air twenty years ago and later, under the ad agency aegis, against the swill we *now* get, programming was much more liberal and a good deal more innovative. A few shows that pop to mind readily, whose like we don't see today, are *Playhouse 90, U.S. Steel Hour, Armstrong Circle Theater, The Bob Hope-Chrysler Show, Alcoa-Goodyear Award Theater, Alcoa Premiere, Du Pont Show of the Week, Kraft Suspense Theater,* and *Schlitz Playhouse of Stars*. Those are some undeniably heavyweight memories to throw up against *Me and the Chimp, Nanny and the Professor, The Mod Squad, Mannix, The FBI, Marcus Welby, M.D., Alias Smith and Jones, The Partridge Family,* and *The Brady Bunch*. Not to mention forthcoming horrors like The Rookies, Temperature's Rising, the reincarnation of *Dr. Kildare* and the return of *The Sixth Sense* in September.

Returning to the other hand once more, the whole thing scares me because we've seen what a keen job government has done in previous endeavors tampering with private enterprise. The concept of the Nixoid Philistines lobotomizing this close to the exposed tissue of the First Amendment causes my flesh to crawl. If the Justice Department successfully prosecutes and the creative reins are passed into the hands of independent producers, *truly* passed into their hands, with the government backing off and the advertisers being kept in their place, then this *could* be the answer we've variously lobbied for, individually and as a nation fucked over by the moguls to whom we entrusted *our* airwaves.

Naturally, the networks claim foul and on April 10, at a meeting with Justice officials, they refused to sign a consent decree on the charges. They are planning to make this a full-out fight; already they're massing their forces and their arguments. ABC, for instance, issued a statement that golly gee fellahs, we aren't monopolizing what goes on ABC...of five hours of daytime programming daily, Monday through Friday, only one half-hour series is produced by ABC...that's only 10 per cent of the total daytime schedule...of children's weekend programming, out of seven and a half hours, only one and a half hours is ABC-originated, representing 20 per cent of the total children's weekend schedule...and in evening primetime, only one regularly scheduled weekly series and seventeen out of forty-seven *Movies of the Week* are ABC product, making 10 per cent of the total from the network itself. In summary, ABC-produced product (according to ABC) makes up only 11.4 per cent of total programming. Now this would be dandy, if it were true; but it simply isn't. It's making statistics dance like heat lightning. Anyone who has worked even peripherally in the industry knows that while ABC may not *directly* produce all those endless hours of mindless bullshit, they control what and when, down to the last comma of every script. They accept or reject pilots, they make deals with stars, they censor scripts, they blackball directors, producers, writers, and actors (usually those who are "undependable," meaning those who buck network authority), they install in key positions on outside-produced series the toadies who are ABC-owned, and in general they ignore their responsibility to uplift the viewing taste of the scuttlefish, as opposed to doing everything in their power to debase it...as they have since they came to power.

But the pivot point around which the government case revolves is that to get a series sold, the producers must give up fifty per cent of their action to the network. The network takes half the profits and thus becomes a financial holder in even the series they don't *directly* finance. That's why we see endless re-runs of *The Lucy Show* and similar mindless claptrap that should, by all rights, have sunk of its own leaden stupidity: because the network bought out everyone else and they own the product lock, stock and henna. And since it's what they call an "in-house property," the network naturally gives it preferential airdate treatment over product they *don't* own outright. So if you want to get into the big time, you have to give away at least half your juice to the Big Cannibal. The government (justifiably) feels this is using the leasing rights to the public airwaves—granted to the networks and their outlets—to somewhat improper advantage. Blackmail and extortion are even easier words to juggle, and stripped of the bullshit they're probably more to the point.

This is going to be a tricky one, friends. There are solid arguments for and against either side of the battle. If government wins it could open up the hard-times industry to wider independent production, it could raise the level of quality merely by diversification of creators, it could create many more jobs simply because *everyone* would be trying to sell product. BUT: it could mean a reactionary eye and repressive thumb ready to be used against tv if it didn't support Administration actions, it could mean lowering of quality even further if the ad agencies pursue a policy of buying that which offends the least viewers, it could mean more fingers in each pie, more censors ready to boycott and kill, more steps between creator and viewer. If the networks win it could mean going on at this same troglodyte level of programming or dropping to even a *more* moronic level, if that's conceivable. BUT: it could mean the nets would gain strength from a court mandate and might experiment a bit more bravely. At this point no one can say which of these multifarious futures loom largest as probable. No matter which way we jump, however, it can be disastrous.

I would be inclined to stick with the devil we know— the networks—rather than the devil we don't know—the government—were it not for the track record of pilot production the networks have given us.

And as if some celestial network continuity deity wanted to give us a prime primetime example of the full spectrum of potentialities, on Friday night the fourteenth, the same day as the Justice Department announcement, CBS pre-empted its evening movie to present ninety minutes of unsold comedy pilots. And therein lies an argument that cannot be refuted, an argument that persuades me to go with the ham-hand of government.

Let me tell you about it:

Unsold pilots have to be "played off" if a network hopes to regain the money invested in developing and shooting such calling-card segments. But in displaying what *they* think is salable, networks give us a terrifying glimpse into their minds. The three unsold pilots composing CBS's *Comedy! Comedy! Comedy!* ninety-minuter are a glimpse I'm not sure I deserved. They covered the range from far right to mediocre center to hilarious left, the spectrum from unbelievably offensively bad to average run-of-the-schedule to sensational. And covering that range and spectrum, they let us know what we can expect from networks if they aren't whanged over the head by higher authority.

The first half hour was a horrorshow made two years ago and justifiably condemned to rejection. *Man in the Middle*, starring Van Johnson and Nancy Malone, was a classic example of why the hypocritical "relevance" the networks tried to pass off two years ago as honest concern for the upheavals in this country fell flat on its ethic. It was a turgid pudding of stock clichés about paranoid hippies, crazed Minutemen, rational middle-of-the-road Establishment complainers with neatly trimmed hair and a McGuffey's Reader bewilderment at "all the weird things happening in America." It reinforced with cartoon characterization and insipid situation and slanted arguments every fear and antediluvian prejudice of the middle class. It said kids are fucked and they only protest out of lack of understanding of the wonderful rational order and balance of the systems set in motion by their all-knowing parents. It said all conservatives are far-right lunatics setting up mortar emplacements on the rooftops. It said all old people are senile imbeciles. It said all young people dress like rejects from a freakshow casting call (and they all need a bath). It said women are simpering, silly geese who get their rationales for living from *Family Circle* articles on vest-pocket psychoanalysis. It said the world would be just fine and quiet and like it was in 1901 Kansas City if only all these assholes would pay attention to the tenets of living adhered to by the fat burghers, the Kiwanis, and the Rotarians. In short, it lied outrageously!

Johnson played his part with all the charm of an aging elf, mugging and grimacing as though time had not slipped by him, as though he were still squealing and winking in some vapid MGM puff pastry. In every scene he tried to dominate, the shadow of June Allyson lurked in the background, wincing in pain. Ruth McDevitt, who played Johnson's septuageneric mother-in-law, the bereft Bircher, played old age without a scintilla of dignity or poise, a ghoulish caricature of senior citizenry that went light-years beyond even the bizarre mode of a Marian Lorne, a distasteful affront to those who conceive of advanced years as a time of maturity, wisdom, kindness and gentility…and who receive from producers and directors who delineate character in this way a warped and senile image of their state of life in our times. The part of the hairy hippie was masticated and vomited back up by something named Elliot Street, an "actor" who clearly has no sense of morality in which parts he chooses to play. He is beneath contempt.

But more responsible than anyone else connected with this sewer of a pilot are its writer-producers, Harvey Bullock and Ray Allen, two men who would espouse the most evil, vilest party line if it meant they'd get inked in on a network schedule. They epitomize the no-talent, cliché-gorged, hypocritical, insensitive soul-selling of the Hollywood hacks. By pandering to the jingoistic, unrealistic prejudices of a nation gripped by confusion and fear, they serve a demon no self-respecting artist can stomach being in the same time zone with. No insult is too crass for them, no derangement of logic too far-fetched, no level of banality beyond their stoop, no punishment severe enough. Bottom line: *they* are the Enemy.

The second half hour, *Keep the Faith*, while by no means a sparkler of originality and inventiveness, looked like *A Midsummer Night's Dream* by comparison with the toilet flush of *Man in the Middle.*

An undistinguished but at least palatable lineal descendant of *All in the Family*, *Keep the Faith* was a Yiddish *Sanford and Son* dealing with a young, allegedly progressive rabbi (Bert Convy) and his older colleague (Howard Da Silva). It was a nice little half hour without any outstanding elements to recommend it, saved from total forgettability by a brilliant performance tendered by character actor Milton Selzer. Even Howard Da Silva—surely one of the dozen finest actors this country has ever produced—zombie-walked through his part, as though he knew it was a money gig and would never get serialized. A nod of approval should go to writer-producer Ed Simmons for at least a craftsmanlike job, but in the final analysis, it was just another of those half hours one spends while waiting for the apocalypse.

Bringing us to the final third of CBS's pilot peek into what it's all about the Justice Department is pissed at. And in one thirty-minute pilot segment it was demonstrated just how inventive, just how hilarious, just how pertinent, and just how wonderful networks can be when they hire the right people on the right project and turn them loose.

(CBS *produced* all three of these pilots, and the range from gawdawful to brilliant is mind-croggling.)

This Week in Nemtin was the best thing I've seen on the tube in a span of time my memory cannot compute. Purporting to be a news broadcast of the preceding week's events in the principality of Nemtin (140 miles long, all border, surrounded by "countries"), the show was outrageously funny from opening to closing. I suppose critics of the show could call it one extended

Polish joke, but I herewith confess (and will surely be damned for the admission) Polish jokes convulse me. (When Alan King, on the Oscarcast, said he stood in a queue for a movie that ran around two blocks, through a Polish tattoo parlor where he saw the word "Mom" misspelled, I broke up and fell out completely.)

Rather would I identify what *Nemtin* did as a video translation of Sholom Aleichem's Kasrilevka, the village of idiots, the village of "little people." (In Yiddish fiction, there is a great tradition used to explicate allegorical messages: the village from which the narrator comes is always the village of geniuses, good people, smart and quick and witty. The *other* village—Kasrilevka—is the village of the schmucks and schlemozls.)

What *Nemtin* did with outrageous style and clockwork timing was illuminate the foibles and ineptitudes of all of us, microcosmically, within the framework of a nation where the President (played deliciously by Edward Asner) appears on television to deliver the Independence Day message in his bowling shirt, with his wife decked out in her wedding gown and white gym socks. "Like you," he said soberly, "we will be celebrating this special day at home, enjoying the traditional meat loaf and cherry soda, singing catchy tunes." And then his wife gave the pledge of Nemtin allegiance: "Gimme an *N*, gimme an *E*, gimme an *M*..."

I don't know how you'd react, but for the people in my living room watching that show, there were universal bellyaches and uncontrollable tears from laughing so much. It just went on and on and on, without surcease. When one thought one had laughed as much as one could, a reporter would climb to the top of a mountain where Carl Reiner, as the "wise old Nemtik," sat pontificating on the universe (which he saw capsulized as an egg). And then he ate it. When one thought all the changes had been rung on the idea, out came the Nemtin All-Army Drill Team (two soldiers and a cadence caller) who did a routine choreographed so brilliantly I only saw half of it because I was lying twisted in a convulsive heap on the floor.

Remember the funniest thing you ever saw? *Nemtin* beats it by three points on the sphincter scale.

The day after the airing, everywhere I went, people were

talking about the show and still laughing. *Nemtin* satirized government, race relations, politics, life-styles of old, young, minorities; it lampooned sports, justice, family life, children's programs, war, public images. It went miles beyond *Laugh-In* or *The Smothers Brothers* or *That Was the Week That Was.* By using the analogue of Nemtin it said things about our uptight, super-serious attitudes as Americans that no network would permit were they unclothed and naked. With the brilliant Alex Dreier (a former newscaster turned actor) as the host-commentator, making even the most insane goings-on seem rational merely through the barrel-bottom timbre of his voice, the show was a holiday of style and class and wit breathtaking to sit through.

And coming back full circle to why it is the Justice Department is dissatisfied with network practices in what they make and put on the air, here is a little inside information about *why This Week in Nemtin* never got on the air, and probably won't, now that its time is past.

Coming up on summer replacement time last June, there were two CBS pilots vying for the 8:00 Thursday open slot. *Nemtin* was one of them. It was aced out by the other.

What brilliant series could have elbowed aside such an entry as *Nemtin?* What tour de force of artistry? What sure-fire audience-grabbing idea? Are you ready?

Me and the Chimp.

(Pause for shivers of disbelief.)

(Pause for tremors of terror.)

Me and the Chimp. A mindless moron concept about a typical Smith Family/Partridge Family/Brady Family family with a monkey for a house pet. *Me and the Chimp.* A witless farrago of clichés and creaking sitcom banalities that waste the talents of talented actor Ted Bessell and have him upstaged weekly by a simian. *Me and the Chimp.*

Steve Gentry, in charge of new projects and pilots for CBS, when queried about this unbelievable shunting aside of a fresh, new idea for the dreariest potboiler one could imagine, avers it was all because of Ted Bessell. The net was so hot for Bessell, so hot to make a long-term contract with an actor they think is a sure-fire audience-grabber, that they opted for a series everyone knew *in front* would croak.

Well, it's nice to be in Bessell's position, I suppose, but what about the network's responsibility to those of us who lend them the use of our airtime? They sacrificed hours of primetime to make a contract with an actor that might up their corporate profits later. This is cynical behavior of the rankest sort. And in rejecting the *Nemtin* wonder created by Saul Turteltaub, Ron Clark, Bernie Orenstein, and Sam Bobrick, magic elves all, in favor of a series going off at the end of this season, predictably, CBS demonstrated the callousness and self-interest that clearly prompted the Justice Department to take its action.

I cannot find it in my heart to feel sorry for crooks who themselves get taken. Or ladies who clearly and purposely give off come-on vibes and then get raped. Or soldiers who walk around with grenades ready and moan when they get their arms blown off. Or ghetto storeowners who fleece blacks and then scream when they're burned out. Or assholes who get caught in their own lies.

Similarly, I cannot lament too loudly what is happening to the networks. I can only despise them for misusing what we gave them, thus putting us in line for potentially even *more* disastrous events if the government acts as it usually does when it has a chance to grab a little more control.

I can only despise and revile them for not acting in good faith, with courage, with imagination, and at the peak of a form they can clearly demonstrate.

But fear and loathing are all that are left to us with time run out on the networks and the ominous shadow of Kleindienst overhanging television's future.

AFTERWORD

Revealed at Last!

What Killed the Dinosaurs!

And You Don't Look so Terrific Yourself.

It's all about drinking strange wine.

It seems disjointed and jumps around like water on a griddle, but it all comes together, so be patient.

At 9:38 a.m. on July 15th 1974, about eight minutes into Suncoast Digest, a variety show on WXLT-TV in Sarasota, Florida, anchorwoman Chris Chubbuck, 30, looked straight at the camera and said, "In keeping with Channel 40's policy of bringing you the latest in blood and guts in living color, you're going to see another firstattempt at suicide."

Whereupon she pulled a gun out of a shopping bag and blew her brains out, on camera.

Paragraph 3, preceding, was taken verbatim from an article written by Daniel Schorr for Rolling Stone. I'd heard about the Chubbuck incident, of course, and I admit to filching Mr. Schorr's sixty concise words because they are concise, and why should I try to improve on precision? As the artist Mark Rothko once put it: "Silence is so accurate."

Further, Mr. Schorr perceived in the bizarre death of Chris Chubbuck exactly what I got out of it when I heard the news broadcast the day it happened. She was making a statement about television...on television!

The art-imitating-life resemblance to Paddy Chayefsky's film Network should not escape us. I'm sure it wouldn't have escaped Chris Chubbuck's attention. Obvious cliché; onward.

I used to know Dan Blocker, who played Hoss Cartwright on Bonanza. He was a wise and a kind man, and there are tens of dozens of people I would much rather see dead than Dan. One time, around lunch-break at Paramount, when I was goofing off on writing a treatment for a Joe Levine film that never got made, and Dan was resting his ass from some dumb horsey number he'd been reshooting all morning, we sat on the steps of the weathered saloon that probably in no way resembled any saloon that had ever existed in Virginia City, Nevada, and we talked about reality versus fantasy. The reality of getting up at five in the morning to get to the studio in time for makeup call and the reality of how bloody much FICA tax they took out of our paychecks and the reality of one of his kids being down with something or other...and the fantasy of not being Dan Blocker, but of being Hoss Cartwright.

And he told me a scary story. He laughed about it, but it was the laugh of butchers in a slaughterhouse who have to swing the mauls that brain the beeves; who then go home to wash the stink out of their hair from the spattering.

He told me—and he said this happened all the time, not just in isolated cases—that he had been approached by a little old woman during one of his personal appearances at a rodeo, and the woman had said to him, dead seriously, "Now listen to me, Hoss: when you go home tonight, I want you to tell your daddy, Ben, to get rid of that Chinee fella who cooks for you all. What you need is to get yourself a good woman in there can cook up some decent food for you and your family."

So Dan said to her, very politely (because he was one of the most courteous people I've ever met), "Excuse me, ma'am, but my name is Dan Blocker. Hoss is just the character I play. When I go home I'll be going to my house in Los Angeles and my wife and children will be waiting."

And she went right on, just a bit affronted because she knew all that, what was the matter with him, did he think she was simple or something, "Yes, I know...but when you go back to the Ponderosa, you just tell your daddy Ben that I said..."

For her, fantasy and reality were one and the same.

There was a women who had the part of a home-wrecker on

a daytime soap opera. One day as she was coming out of Lord & Taylor in New York, a viewer began bashing her with an umbrella, calling her filthy names and insisting she should leave that nice man and his wife alone!

One time during a college lecture, I idly mentioned that I had actually thought up all the words Leonard Nimoy had spoken as Mr. Spock on the sole *Star Trek* segment I had written; and a young man leaped up in the audience, in tears, and began screaming that I was a liar. He actually thought the actors were living those roles as they came across the tube.

Why do I tell you all this; and what does it have to do with drinking strange wine?

Chris Chubbuck perceived at a gut level that for too many Americans the only reality is what's on the box. That Johnny Carson and Don Rickles and Mary Tyler Moore are more real, more substantial, more immediately important than the members of their own family, or the people in their community. She knew that her death wouldn't be real unless it happened on television, unless it took place where life is lived, there in phosphor-dot Never-Never Land. If she did it decently, in the privacy of her home, or in some late night bar, or in a deserted parking lot...it would never have happened. She would have been flensed from memory as casually as a popped pimple. Her suicide on camera was the supreme act of loathing and ridicule for the monkeymass that watched her.

When I was writing my television criticism for the Los Angeles *Free Press*, circa 1968–72, I used The Glass Teat columns to repeat my belief that those of us who cared, who had some ethics and some talent, dared not abandon to the Visigoths what was potentially the most powerful medium the world had ever known for the dissemination of education and knowledge. I truly believed that. And I said it again and again.

But it's been five years since I last wrote those words, and I've done so many college speaking engagements that Grand Forks, North Dakota, has blurred with Minneapolis, Minnesota, has blurred with Bethel, Maine, has blurred with Shreveport, Louisiana, and what I've come away with is a growing horror at what television has done to us.

I now believe that television itself, the medium of sitting in front of a magic box that pulses images at us endlessly, the act of watching tv, per se, is mind crushing. It is soul deadening, dehumanizing, soporific in a poisonous way, ultimately brutalizing. It is, simply put so you cannot mistake my meaning, a bad thing.

We need never fear Orwell's 1984, because it's here, with us now, nearly a decade ahead of schedule, and has been with us for quite a while already. Witness the power of television and the impact it has had on you.

Don't write me letters telling me how you've escaped the terror, how you're not a slave to the box, how you still read and listen to Brahms and carry on meaningful discussions with your equally liberated friends. Stop and really take stock of how many hours last week you sat stunned before the tube, relaxing, just unwinding, just passing a little time between the demanding and excoriating life-interests that really command your energies. You will be stunned again, if you are honest. Because I did it, and it scared me, genuinely put a fright into me. It was far more time than I'd have considered feasible, knowing how much I despise television and how little there is I care to watch.

I rise, usually, between five and seven in the morning, depending how late I've worked the night before. I work like a lunatic all day...I'm a workaholic...pity me...and by five or six in the evening I have to unwind. So I lie down and turn on the set. Where before I might have picked up a book of light fiction, or dozed, or just sighed and stared at the ceiling, now I turn on the carnivorous coaxial creature.

And I watch.

Here in Los Angeles between five and eight, when "Prime Time" begins (oh, how I love that semantically twisted phrase) we have the same drivel you have in your city. Time that was taken from the networks to program material of local interest and edification. Like reruns of Adam-12, The Price Is Right, The Joker's Wild, Name That Tune, I Dream of Jeannie, Bewitched, Concentration, and Match Game P.M.. I lie there like the quadruple amputee viewpoint character of Dalton Trumbo's Johnny Got His Gun, never speaking, breathing shallowly, seeing only what flashes before my eyes, reduced to a ganglial image receptor, a raw nerve-end taking in whatever banalities and incredible stupidities they care to throw at me in the name of "giving the audience what they want."

If functional illiterates failing such mind-challenging questions as "What was the name of the character Robert Stack played on The Untouchables?" is an accurate representation of "what the audience wants," then my point has been solidly made...

...and it goes directly to the answer to the question of what killed the dinosaurs and you don't look so terrific yourself!

But I wander. So. I lie there, until my low bullshit threshold is reached, either through the zombie mannerisms of the Adam-12 cops—dehumanized paragons of a virtue never known by L.A.'s former lunatic chief of police, Weirdo Ed Davis—or because of some yotz on The Price Is Right having an orgasm at winning a thirty-year supply of rectal suppositories. And then I curse, snap off the set, and realize I've been lying there for ninety minutes.

And when I take stock of how much time I'm spending in front of that set, either at the five-to-eight break or around eleven o'clock when I fall into bed for another break and turn on The CBS Late Movie, I become aware of five hours spent in mindless sucking at the glass teat.

If you're honest, you'll own up to that much time televiewing, too. Maybe more. Maybe a little less. But you spend from three to eight hours a day at it. And you're not alone. Nor am I. The college gigs I do have clearly demonstrated that to me. Clearly. I take show-of-hands polls in the audience; and after badgering them to cop to the truth, the vast bulk of the audience admits it, and I see the stunned looks of concern and dawning awareness.

They never realized it was that much; nor did I.

And the effect it has had on them, on you, young people and old alike; black and white and Hispanic and Oriental and Amerind; male and female; wealthy and impoverished; WASPs and Jews and Shintoists and Buddhists and Catholics and even Scientologists. All of us, all of you, swamped day after day by stereotypes and jingoism and "accepted" life-styles. So that after a while you come to believe doctors are all wise and noble and one with Marcus Welby and they could cure you of anything if only you'd stop being so cranky and irrational; that cops never abuse their power and are somehow Solomonic in their judgments; that, in the final extreme, violence—as represented by that eloquent vocabulary of a punch in the mouth—solves problems; that women are either cute and cuddly and need a strong hand to keep them in line or defeminize themselves if they have successful careers; and that eating McDonald's prefab food is actually better for you than foie de veau sauté aux fines herbes...and tastier, too.

I see this zombiatic response in college audiences. It manifests itself most prominently in the kinds of questions that are asked. Here I stand before them, perhaps neither Melville nor Twain, but nonetheless a man with a substantial body of work behind him, books that express the artist's view of the world (and after all, isn't that why they paid me two grand or better a night to come and speak? Surely it can't be my winsome manner!), and they persist in asking me what it was like to work on *Star Trek* or what Jimmy Caan is really like and why did Tom Snyder keep cutting me off on the Tomorrow show. I get angry with them. I make myself lots less antic and entertaining. I tell them what I'm telling you here. And they don't like me for it. As long as I'm running down the military-industrial complex or the fat money cats who play sneaky panther games with our lives, they give me many "Right on, brother!" ovations. But when I tell them how shallow and programmed television is making them, there is a clear lynch tenor in the mob. (It isn't just college kids, gentle reader. I was recently rewarded with sullen animosity when I spoke to a dinner gathering of Southern California Book Publicists, and instead of blowing smoke up their asses about what a wonderful thing book publicity through the Johnny Carson show is—because there isn't one of them who wouldn't sacrifice several quarts of blood to get a client on that detestable viewing ground for banal conversationalists—I quoted them the recent illiteracy figures released by HEW. I point out that only 8% of the 220,000,000 population of this country buy books, and of that 8% only 2% buy more than a single book a year. I pointed out that 6% of that measly 8% were no doubt buying, as their single enriching literary experience each year, Jaws or Oliver's Story or the latest Harold Robbins ghastliness, rather than, say, Remembrance of Things Past or the Durants' The Lessons of History or even the latest Nabokov or Lessing novel. So that meant they were hustling books to only 2% of the population of this country; while the other 98% sank deeper and deeper into illiteracy and functional illiteracy, their heads being shoved under by the pressure of television, to which they were slavishly making obeisance. They were, in effect, sharpening the blade for their executioner, assisting in their own extinction. They really didn't want to hear that. Nor do college audiences.)

A bad thing. Watching television. Not rationalizing it so that it comes out reading thus: "Television is potentially a good thing; it can educate and stimulate and inform us; we've just permitted it to be badly used; but if we could get some good stuff on the tube..." No, I'm afraid I've gone beyond that rationalization, to an extreme position. The act of watching television for protracted periods (and there's no way to insure the narcotic effects won't take you over) is deleterious to the human animal. The medium itself insists you sit there quietly and cease thinking.

The dinosaurs. How they died.

Television, quite the opposite of books or even old-time radio that presented drama and comedy and talk shows (unlike Top Forty radio programming today, which is merely tv without moving parts), is systematically oriented toward stunning the use of individual imagination. It puts everything out there, right there, so you don't have to dream even a little bit. When they would broadcast a segment of, say, Inner Sanctum in the Forties, and you heard the creaking door of a haunted house, the mind was forced to create the picture of that haunted house—a terrifying place so detailed and terrifying that if Universal Studios wanted to build such an edifice for a tv movie, it would cost them millions of dollars and it still wouldn't be one one-millionth as frightening as the one your own imagination had cobbled up.

A book is a participatory adventure. It involves a creative act at its inception and a creative act when its purpose is fulfilled. The writer dreams the dream and sets it down; the reader reinterprets the dream in personal terms, with personal vision, when he or she reads it. Each creates a world. The template is the book.

At risk of repeating myself, and of once again cribbing from another writer's perfection of expression (in this case, my friend Dr. Isaac Asimov), here is a bit I wrote on this subject for an essay on the "craft" of writing teleplays:

Unlike television, films, football games, the roller derby, wars in underdeveloped nations and Watergate hearings, which are spectator sports, a book requires the activation of its words by the eyes and the intellect of a reader. As Isaac Asimov said recently in an article postulating the perfect entertainment cassette, "A cassette as ordinarily viewed makes sound and casts light. That is its purpose, of course, but must sound and light obtrude on others who are not involved or interested? The ideal cassette would be visible and audible only to the person using it.... We could imagine a cassette that is always in perfect adjustment; that starts automatically when you look at it; that stops automatically when you cease to look at it; that can play forward or backward, quickly or slowly, by skips or with repetitions, entirely at your pleasure.... Surely, that's the ultimate dream device—a cassette that may deal with any of an infinite number of subjects, fictional or non-fictional, that is self-contained, portable, non-energy-consuming, perfectly private and largely under the control of the will.... Must this remain only a dream? Can we expect to have such a cassette some day?...We not only have it now, we have had it for many centuries. The ideal I have described is the printed word, the book, the object you now hold—light, private, and manipulable at will.... Does it seem to you that the book, unlike the cassette I have been describing, does not produce sound and images? It certainly does.... You cannot read without hearing the words in your mind and seeing the images to which they give rise. In fact, they are your sounds and images, not those invented for you by others, and are therefore better.... The printed word presents minimum information, however. Everything but that minimum must be provided by the reader— the intonation of words, the expressions on faces, the actions, the scenery, the background, must all be drawn out of that long line of black-on-white symbols."

Quite clearly, if one but looks around to assess the irrefutable evidence of reality, books strengthen the dreaming facility, and television numbs it. Atrophy soon follows.

Shelley Torgeson, who is the director of the spoken word records I've cut for Alternate World Recordings, is also a mass media teacher at Harrison High School in Westchester. She tells me some things that buttress my position.

1) A fifteen-year-old student summarily rejected the reading of books because it "wasn't real." Because it was your imagination, and your imagination isn't real. So Shelley asked her what was "real" and the student responded instantly, "Television." Because you could see it. Then, by pressing the conversation, Shelley discovered that though the student was in the tenth grade, when she read she didn't understand the words and was making up words and their meanings all through the text—far beyond the usual practice, in which we all indulge, of gleaning an approximate meaning of an unfamiliar word from its context. With television, she had no such problems. They didn't use words. It was real. Thus—and quite logically in a kind of Alice-down-the-rabbit-hole manner—the books weren't real, because she was making them up as she went along, not actually reading them. If you know what I mean.

2) An important school function was woefully underattended one night, and the next day Shelley (suspecting the reason) confirmed that the absence of so many students was due to their being at home watching part two the tv movie based on the Manson murder spree, Helter Skelter. Well, that was a bit of a special event in itself, and a terrifying program; but the interesting aspect of their watching the show emerged when a student responded to Shelley's comparison of watching something that "wasn't real" with a living event that "was real." The student contended it was real, he had seen it. No, Shelley insisted, it wasn't real, it was just a show. Hell no, the kid kept saying, it was real: he had seen it. Reasoning slowly and steadily, it took Shelley fifteen or twenty minutes to convince him (if she actually managed) that he had not seen a real thing, because he

had not been in Los Angeles in August of 1969 when the murders had happened. Though he was seventeen years old, the student was incapable of perceiving, unaided, the difference between a dramatization and real life.

3) In each classroom of another school at which Shelley taught, there was a tv set, mostly unused save for an occasional administrative announcement; the sets had been originally installed in conjunction with a Ford Foundation grant to be used for visual training. Now they're blank and silent. When Shelley had trouble controlling the class, getting them quiet, she would turn on the set and they would settle down. The screen contained nothing, just snow; but they grew as fascinated as cobras at a mongoose rally, and fell silent, watching nothing. Shelley says she could keep them that way for extended periods.

Interestingly, as a footnote, when Shelley mentioned this device at lunch, a chemistry professor said he used something similar. When his students were unruly he would place a beaker of water on a Bunsen burner. When the water began to boil, the students grew silent and mesmerized, watching the water bubbling.

And as a subfootnote, I'm reminded of a news story I read. A burglar broke into a suburban home in Detroit or some similar city (it's been a while since I read the item and unimportant details have blurred in my mind) and proceeded to terrorize and rob the housewife alone there with her seven-year-old son. As the attacker stripped the clothes off the woman at knife point, the child wandered into the room. The burglar told the child to go in the bedroom and watch television till he was told to come out. The child watched the tube for six straight hours, never once returning to the room where his mother had been raped repeatedly, tied and bound to a chair with tape over her mouth, and beaten mercilessly. The burglar had had free access to the entire home, had stripped it of all valuables, and had left unimpeded. The tape, incidentally, had been added when the burglar/rapist was done enjoying himself. All through the assault the woman had been calling for help. But the child had been watching the set and didn't come out to see what was happening. For six hours.

Roy Torgeson, Shelley's husband and producer of my records, reminded us of a classroom experiment reported by the novelist Jerzy Kosinski, in which a teacher was set to speaking at one side of the front of a classroom, and a television monitor was set up on the other side of the room, showing the teacher speaking. The students had unobstructed vision of both. They watched the monitor. They watched what was real.

Tom Snyder, of the NBC Tomorrow show, was telling me that he receives letters from people apologizing for their having gone away on vacation or visiting with their grandchildren, or otherwise not having been at home so he could do his show— but now that they're back, and the set is on, he can start doing his show again. Their delusion is a strange reversal of the ones I've noted previously. For them, Snyder (and by extension other newscasters and actors) aren't there, aren't happening, unless they are watching. They think the actors can see into their living rooms, and they dress as if for company, they always make sure the room is clean, and in one case there is a report of an elderly women who dresses for luncheon with "her friends" and sets up the table and prepares luncheon and then, at one o'clock, turns on the set for a soap opera. Those are her friends: she thinks they can see into her house, and she is one with them in their problems.

To those of us who conceive of ourselves as rational and grounded in reality (yes, friends, even though I write fantasy, I live in the real world, my feet sunk to the ankles in pragmatism), all of this may seem like isolated, delusionary behavior. I assure you it isn't. A study group that rates high school populations recently advised one large school district that the "good behavior" of the kids in its classes was very likely something more than just normal quiet and good manners. They were too quiet, too tranquilized, and the study group called it "dangerous." I submit that the endless watching of tv by kids produces this blank, dead, unimaginative manner.

It is widespread, and cannot possibly be countered by the minimal level of reading that currently exists in this country. Young people have been systematically bastardized in their ability to seek out quality material—books, films, food, lifestyles, life-goals, enriching relationships.

Books cannot combat the spiderwebbing effect of television because kids simply cannot read. It is on a par with their inability to hear music that isn't rock. Turn the car radio dial from one end to another when you're riding with young people (up to the age of fifty) and you will perceive that they whip past classical music as if it were "white noise," simply static to their ears. The same goes for books. The printed word has no value to them and carries no possibility of knowledge or message that relates to their real world.

If one chooses to say, as one idiot I faced on the 90 Minutes Live talk show over the Canadian Broadcasting Corporation said, that people don't need to read, that people don't like books, that they want to be "entertained" (as if reading were something hideous, something other than also entertainment), then we come to an impasse. But if, like me, you believe that books preserve the past, illuminate the present, and point the way to the future...then you can understand why I seem to be upset at the ramifications of this epiphany I've had.

Do not expect—as I once did because I saw Senator Joseph McCarthy of Wisconsin unmasked on television—that tv will reveal the culprits. Nixon lied without even the faintest sign of embarrassment or disingenuousness on tv, time after time, for years. He told lies, flat out and outrageously; monstrous lies that bore no relation to the truth. But well over half the population of this country, tuning him in, believed him. Not just that they wanted to believe him for political or personal reasons, or because it was easier than having waves made...they believed him because he stared right at them and spoke softly and they could tell he was telling the truth. tv did not unmask him. Television played no part in the revelations of Watergate. In point of fact, television prevented the unmasking, because Nixon used tv to keep public opinion tremblingly on his side. It was only when the real world, the irrefutable facts, were slammed home again and again, that the hold was loosened on public sentiment.

Nor did television show what a bumbler Gerald Ford was. He was as chummy and friendly and familiar as Andy

Griffith or Captain Kangaroo when he came before us on the
tube. Television does not show us the duplicitous smirk, the
dull mentality, the self-serving truth behind the noncommittal
statement of administration policy. It does not deal in reality, it
does not proffer honesty, it only serves up nonjudgmental images
and allows thugs like Nixon to make themselves as acceptable as
Reverend Ike.

And on the Johnny Carson show they have a seven-minute
"author's spot," gouged out of ninety minutes festooned with
Charo's quivering buttocks, Zsa Zsa Gabor's feeling about fiscal
responsibility, John Davidson on recombinant DNA, and Don
Rickles insulting Carson's tie. Then, in the last ten minutes they
invite on Carl Sagan or Buckminster Fuller or John Lilley to
explain the Ethical Structure of the Universe. And they contend
this is a rebirth of the art of conversation. Authors of books are
seldom invited on the show unless they have a new diet, a new
sex theory, or a nonfiction gimmick that will make an interesting
demonstration in which Johnny can take part—like wrestling a
puma, spinning a hula hoop, or baking lasagna with solar heat.

All this programs the death of reading.

And reading is the drinking of strange wine.

Like water on a hot griddle, I have bounced around, but the
unification of the thesis is at hand.

Drinking strange wine pours strength into the imagination.

The dinosaurs had no strange wine.

They had no imagination. They lived 130,000,000 years and
vanished. Why? Because they had no imagination. Unlike human
beings who have it and use it and build their future rather than
merely passing through their lives as if they were spectators.
Spectators watching television, one might say.

The saurians had no strange wine, no imagination, and they
became extinct. And you don't look so terrific yourself.

YOUR ATTENTION, PLEASE!

E-READS® & EDGEWORKS ABBEY®
ARE PROUD TO PRESENT 33 ASTOUNDING TITLES FROM

HARLAN ELLISON®

1. Again, Dangerous Visions
2. An Edge in My Voice
3. Approaching Oblivion
4. The Beast That Shouted Love At the Heart of the World
5. Children of the Streets
6. The City on the Edge of Forever
7. Dangerous Visions
8. The Deadly Streets
9. Deathbird Stories
10. Ellison Wonderland
11. From the Land of Fear
12. Gentleman Junkie
13. The Harlan Ellison Hornbook
14. Harlan Ellison's Movie
15. Harlan Ellison's Watching
16. I Have No Mouth & I Must Scream
17. Love Ain't Nothing But Sex Misspelled
18. Memos from Purgatory
19. No Doors, No Windows
20. Over the Edge
21. Paingod and Other Delusions
22. Partners in Wonder
23. Shatterday
24. Sleepless Nights in the Procrustean Bed
25. Spider Kiss
26. Stalking the Nightmare
27. Strange Wine
28. Troublemakers
29. Vic and Blood
30. Web of the City
31. The Glass Teat
32. The Other Glass Teat
33. Slippage

COLLECT THEM ALL!

CPSIA information can be obtained at www.ICGtesting.com
Printed in the USA
LVOW131603040613

336936LV00003B/384/P